Encounters at Indian Head

Encounters at Indian Head
The Betty & Barney Hill UFO Abduction Revisited

Edited and with contributions by

KARL PFLOCK *and* PETER BROOKESMITH

ANOMALIST BOOKS
San Antonio • New York

An Original Publication of ANOMALIST BOOKS

Encounters At Indian Head
Copyright © 2007 by Karl T. Pflock and Peter Brookesmith
ISBN: 978-1-933665-18-4
ISBN-10: 1-933665-18-1

Cover illustration by Thomas B. Allen, from *Look* magazine, Oct. 4, 1966, provided by The Mary Evans Picture Library (MEPL), maryevans.com

Book design by Ansen Seale

Karl T. Pflock and Peter Brookesmith have asserted their moral rights as editors of this book under the relevant laws of copyright

All rights reserved, including the right to reproduce this book or portions thereof in any form whatsoever.

For information, go to anomalistbooks.com or write to:

Anomalist Books
5150 Broadway #108
San Antonio, TX 78209

Anomalist Books
PO Box 577
Jefferson Valley, NY 10535

In memory of

Marcello Truzzi
friend, colleague, and *genuine* skeptic

Betty and Barney Hill
who at the very least left us with something fascinating to ponder

Karl T. Pflock
Great friend, colleague, and *rational* believer—
and without whom, this symposium would not have happened

Contents

Being There 9
    Karl Pflock and Peter Brookesmith

Images from Indian Head 19

Chapter One
    A Night and a Morning to Remember 28
    Dennis Stacy

Chapter Two
    Judging the Hill Case 70
    Marcello Truzzi

Chapter Three
    The Start of Something Rich and Strange 91
    Thomas E. Bullard

Chapter Four
    Beyond the UFO Horizon 127
    Hilary Evans

Chapter Five
    Of Time and the River 152
    Peter Brookesmith

Chapter Six
    There Were No Extraterrestrials 186
    Robert Sheaffer

Chapter Seven
    A Singular Visitation 209
    Karl Pflock

Chapter Eight
    Reflections on the Hill Case 239
    Walter N. Webb

Appendix
    "No One Should Know of This Experience" 272
    Martin S. Kottmeyer

Index 308

Being There

*How the Indian Head Symposium in 2000 came about,
what it was like to be there, and what we believe it achieved*

KARL PFLOCK AND PETER BROOKESMITH

The symposium held at the Indian Head Resort, New Hampshire, in September 2000 was a remarkable event in many ways. Not least of these was that it originated in an off-the-cuff but genuinely meant aside in an occasional correspondence we were having on aspects of the Hill case. On May 11, 1998, Peter suggested: "It would be pleasant to sit down over a long weekend with you, Ed [Bullard] and Martin [Kottmeyer] to thrash this case through, sometime in the next 12 months." The four of us had a persistent interest in the Betty and Barney Hill saga, and at some time all of us had corresponded with one another about it or about UFO abductions in general. We all more or less knew each other. Peter had in mind a lot of late nights, cheap tobacco and wine (with exotic ales for the others), piles of sandwiches and plenty of rambling discussion among four civilized people with sufficiently different takes on the Hill case to make even the digressions illuminating, or at least entertaining.

No Ship of Fools

Karl, ever one to seek an underwriter for his simple pleasures, suggested we turn this casual get-together into a paying proposition and make a book out of it – a publisher's advance would at least pay our fares to wherever we decided to meet. We even entertained a fantasy of having Tom Wolfe write a Technicolor Dreamflake account of our bizarre disquisitions and quaint divagations. In a typically unpredictable career move, he turned us down. Without a name like that to bandy about, literary agents began to look coolly on the idea.

Meanwhile, the group of potential participants had been shrinking, and growing again. Marty Kottmeyer couldn't afford the time away the farm, but he would write for us. Then, we felt that Walt Webb, the original investigator of the case, had to be included somehow. He had pressing commitments too, but would write for us. Ed Bullard was delighted to come and join us. We gathered up Hilary Evans, as the best authority we knew on the whole range of paranormal encounters, to put the case in a broader context. Dennis Stacy bravely agreed to trawl the literature and write a definitive brief chronology of the case and its aftermath. Peter's belief in its objective reality hovers around absolute zero, but he was more concerned to look at its "psychosocial" context than pulling its details apart (yet, he pulled some of them apart anyway). This led us instinctively to invite arch-debunker Robert Sheaffer, who gladly accepted the challenge.

But this line-up would have left Karl (and surreptitious sympathizer Eddie Bullard) outnumbered around the table – or the six-packs – by skeptics of varying degrees of intransigence. And we still wanted someone to give something like an outsider's impression of how the meeting went. We finally figured that we were after a professional journalist with some sympathy for abductions, and that made composer, music critic and occasional ufologist Greg Sandow a natural choice. We were confident he could exercise his wit impartially on the assembled wags, and balance the ufological politics to give Karl moral support, without confusing the two missions. Unfortunately, the sheer length of the papers and appendix from the original participants turned out to be such that Greg's contribution had to be omitted from this volume after all; as did another potential chapter, a memoir of Betty and Barney Hill by one who knew them intimately. We are hoping that Greg Sandow will have taken up our suggestion that he upload his contribution to his website (www.gregsandow.com).

Finally, we needed a genuinely impartial chairman – and one who was acknowledged far and wide for his lack of bias. Here again the natural choice was Marcello Truzzi, professor of sociology, founding member of (and early decamper from) CSICOP, publisher of the legendary *Zetetic Scholar*, tolerator of ambiguities, inexhaustible fund of jokes, and someone Peter had known for years. He was available. That gave us what we wanted: a representative sample of ufological expertise and approach, an absence of egotism and bellicosity (many were the eminent names we considered and discarded), and enough eclectic erudition to keep everyone well awake. On top of that, Betty Hill agreed to join us for dinner on our first night and to take us on a guided tour of the first encounter and putative abduction sites the following morning.

What we didn't yet have was a sponsor. Having planned to gather everyone together as near as possible to the Hills' encounter site in New Hampshire around the weekend of September 19, 1999 (one nice coincidence: the Moon would be performing exactly as it had 38 years previously), we had to put everyone on hold. Then, in the summer of 1999, Karl was invited to talk at ufological scandal-monger Jim Moseley's National UFO Conference – and speaking on the same platform in San Antonio, Texas, was Joe Firmage. He had recently retired – though not yet 30 years old – after making a comfortable fortune in Silicon Valley, and was now pursuing his interest in a range of matters paranormal. Karl and Joe met and talked, and the upshot was that at the end of the year we were exchanging memoranda of agreement. Our discussion and the book were going ahead. It was now a long way from beer and sandwiches, but a meeting of some of the best minds in ufology, with Peter modestly in attendance, could actually be realized.

All Due Thanks

It's only proper to thank one's sponsor. But, in witnessing such thanks being offered up in a variety of similar contexts, we've come to recognize a ritualistic tone in these acknowledgements that often has a smug sub-text: "Here was a rich man, and weren't we clever to pick his pocket? He won't even miss it." These are neither gracious nor dignified sentiments. Especially, they have no place in our own thoughts. For, despite his own well-publicized financial vicissitudes, Joe stuck by us. Without his combination of resources and firmness of purpose, this project most likely would have remained no more than a bright idea. So thank you, Joe Firmage.

While we're expressing gratitude, this is the place to thank our contributors, too. They produced their draft papers in good time for distribution to one another before the meeting, and in the months following they dealt patiently with lengthy and nit-picking queries, objections and suggestions from us, as they revised and expanded those papers in light of our discussions.

Of course we were delighted that Betty Hill could join us for an evening meal and a morning tour, and we want to thank her niece Kathy Marden, too, for chauffeuring Betty to Indian Head and sharing with us her childhood memories of the aftermath of her aunt and uncle's experience. We cannot go without thanking Mary Martinek, Karl's Spousal Associate, for her very professional and unobtrusive photographic recording of the proceedings, official and unofficial, and for recognizing immediately that the assembled savants were totally incapable of carrying out liaison with the hotel and stepping so capably into the breech. Final thanks go to Michelle Coulombe and her husband Don, our hosts at the Indian Head Resort, personal friends of Betty. Whether because of that connection or not, they certainly made a special effort to look after us: we had everything we needed, from audio-visual equipment to good food, to make the whole event run without a hitch.

This is also the place to register our sadness at the passing, since we all met at Indian Head, of both Betty Hill and, long before his time was due, Marcello Truzzi. We should so much have liked them both to see this book in print, quite apart from our personal sense of loss.

Off Stage and On

There are many vignettes we could paint of our few days at the Indian Head Resort in New Hampshire. One of the more piquant pleasures was listening to Budd Hopkins's friend and defender Greg Sandow deep in conversation about opera with Robert Sheaffer, a dedicated amateur tenor as well as near-choleric debunker of all things ufological. Another was observing that wherever Dennis Stacy went, a bottle of Tabasco sauce would shortly thereafter appear, even in the midst of a dissertation on electronics futures. Swapping jokes with Marcello Truzzi. Having Eddie Bullard announce that his pen was "dripping with venom" in readiness to disagree with Peter, while his face was wreathed in smiles. Wondering, from overheard snatches of conversation, just what Kathy Marden really thought of her aunt's story, as she fielded our varying and various questions and comments. Watching Betty herself, as if born to the profession, swing into tour-guide mode as she led us around her encounter sites. Seeing techno-experts Truzzi and Sheaffer entirely bemused by a simple cassette recorder's switches. Listening to Joe Firmage – looking for all the world like an extreme make-over of Steve Buscemi – quietly, seriously, and precisely explain why he thought it reasonable to take the Hills' story at face value, and why it was important. Leaning on the bar and hearing, from the ballroom in the distance, Don Coulombe doing a bizarre impersonation of Marlon Brando, telling endless jokes involving Viagra to an audience of sleepy, blue-rinsed geriatrics. And so it went on.

It came as a surprise to several of our participants that they weren't discussing their contributions in front of an audience. We thought we'd made it clear that this was a private meeting (by now elevated to the title "symposium"), but you can't catch everything, it seems. It's almost a core qualification for the title *ufologist* that one should take entrenched positions and defend them explosively, especially in public forums. But everyone agreed that the lack of an audience came as a blessed relief, and that the quiet, intimate setting had usefully deflated any incipient histrionic tendencies.

And just as we'd hoped, our discussions were always conducted in an amiable, collegiate, often witty fashion. Certainly there was strong disagreement, trenchantly expressed, but it was all done courteously and moderately. Perhaps even too moderately on occasion. From time to time, whole areas of severe disagreement surfaced unmistakably. But the opposed parties were no less obviously reluctant to elaborate on their positions, reasonable and defensible though they were. Perhaps this diffidence arose from an unwillingness to disrupt the even tenor of the meeting, or to risk generating disputes so acrimonious that they might spill beyond the meeting room to taint our socializing.

With hindsight, that would be our one reservation about setting up a closed session like the Indian Head Symposium. But our intent was to examine a single issue with all due care, in a field that is inherently divided over many matters, few of which can be conclusively resolved. We don't regret having weeded out notoriously confrontational characters, however expert they are alleged to be, from our list of potential participants. We were not looking for polemic but an impartial exchange of views. Despite the occasional failure to get some contentious issues out into the open, we believe we achieved far more with our closed sessions and our gentlemanly participants than we should have with a larger group or a public free-for-all. Given the opportunity and the funding, this seems a sensible way to go for a subject that, at one end of its various scales, has a tendency to merge with show business.

Going Back to Basics

If we discovered anything at Indian Head, it was that the facts of the case were anything but clearly established. Time and again, radically different assessments of the Hills' experiences and their meaning were diverted by unavoidable problems of detail. An exercise in diverse interpretations became a common quest to establish, as best we could, *what actually happened*. For example, whatever one makes of the Hills' alleged abduction story, their initial encounter has so far eluded definitive explanation. So much – like the location of the purported landing/abduction site on Mill Brook Road – has either to be taken on trust or left uncertain. We kept circling back to such crucial but unresolved issues as each episode of the story came up for illumination. In the process, it became apparent not only that the Hill case still bristles with unanswered questions but is perhaps even richer, stranger and more intractable than any of us – even those who'd been exposed to Betty before – had been altogether aware. The received history of the case turned out to be nothing like as straightforward as it has been made to seem through repetition, conflation of details and events, and dramatic honing by various parties over the years. And both the Hills and the case's earliest researchers omitted to note, query, or record things that now seem potentially significant, but that seemed genuinely trivial at the time.

The discovery of how much we *don't* know about the Hills' experience should serve as a warning to anyone who wants to consider, or reconsider, other "classic"' cases in ufology. It's especially true of those that seem less complex than the Hills' narrative, but that are ostensibly yet more probative, of anomalous or even extraterrestrially inspired events. Over the years, Betty Hill herself added and altered details to her tale – most notably shifting her reported reaction to the UFO's arrival from one of extreme terror to one of welcoming glee. In her later years she claimed she was waving and cheerily calling, "Hi, guys!" to her imminent captors. Among those present at Indian Head in 2000, only Karl had previously heard her claim that Delsey, the Hills' unfortunate dachshund, had broken out in sores and boils following their UFO encounter. This directly contradicts what Walt Webb reported in 1961.

In the months after the symposium, we (Karl and Peter) spent hours discussing the actual distance the Hills traveled, and almost as much time poring over large-scale maps. Finally we settled on common ground on which we could then base our different takes on the vexing matter of the Hills' "missing time." In this, as in other respects, John Fuller's more-or-less official history had proved an unreliable source.

And constantly re-emerging in our wide-ranging discussions was the difficulty of assessing the primary witnesses. In part this is a simple, if frustrating, problem well known to historians and biographers. At the time we met, the alleged events had taken place nearly 40 years previously. One of the participants was dead; the other was elderly and passed on before seeing this book in print. It's clear that Betty Hill, after the death of Barney, built her life around her abduction and her consequent UFO experiences. In the process, she not only changed key details of the original story, and added others, but put her perception of quotidian reality in doubt. Her claims to have witnessed years of mass UFO activity over New Hampshire – in which she was apparently "unable to tell a landed UFO from a street light" – did not help her cause. Nor did her claim to have organized a "Silent Network" of scientists and military men who gathered reams of data about these UFOs – but who are not, apparently, prepared to release their findings publicly. Like Robert Sheaffer, we "do not like the logic" of reasoning that Betty Hill's capacity for imaginative reconstruction must have been preceded by obdurate normality. Neither, however, do we like the logic of expecting her history to show signs of "significant loopiness," in Robert's phrase, before 1961 on the grounds of her later eccentricities. Some events, even imagined ones, can be life-changing for even the staidest of individuals. And there is here the added factor of Barney's premature death to consider.

The Hills as a Couple

Plainly the death of Barney affected Betty enormously, perhaps fundamentally. In one interpretation, that loss, rather than her abduction, would be the trigger for her later peculiarities. Our own suspicion is that her change in the 1970s from sober, and still unnerved, subject of an inexplicable event, to abduction proselytizer and all but crank is indeed a reaction to losing Barney – but less as a memorial to him than as an attempt to keep him alive in a metaphorical but emotionally imperative sense. As Scott Carr wrote in an item published in *Flying Saucer Gazette* (October 4, 2000):

> Betty Hill lives alone, but she is not alone. Though he died of a stroke in 1969, the presence of Barney Hill is as strong in her life as ever. She speaks of him often and with a smile, and with such a familiarity that it is as if he has merely stepped out for groceries. It is apparent to anyone who knows Ms. Hill, that she and her husband were, and are, soulmates, partners in life, and in the enigmatic adventure which brought them to fame.

In view of the problematic relationship between Betty Hill and reality over the final 30 years or so of her life, it would certainly be useful to know more than we were able to gather about her, and about Barney, as they were before 1961. However, significant potential informants such as teachers, work colleagues, and relatives are either dead or may no longer be reliable witnesses simply because of the distance in time and the Hills' modern notoriety. Nonetheless some attempt would, ideally, still be made to locate and interview anyone who knew the Hills well, and before their encounter. For instance, we know a fair amount about Betty and her family, but relatively little about Barney and his, beyond what Betty has told us. And, if it's possible, Barney's military records would be worth acquiring and reviewing. It might also be useful to know more about the Hills as a couple – to know what their specific, personal political views or ideals were, and how the community at large regarded them.

Marcello Truzzi had it right, it seems to us, when he commented that the most significant import of Hilary Evans's presentation was that it showed that "all of us can be nuts." (To which Hilary replied: "I hope I'd never put it quite like that!") More delicately put, then, that thought bears emphatic repetition when considering the characters of Betty and Barney Hill. They weren't "nuts" according to any measure we would employ today. But neither would they be considered exactly a run-of-the-mill couple, even today, and even without the legend of their abduction to weigh them down. The courage and commitment they displayed in their personal and political lives are notable by themselves.

We Haven't Heard the Last . . .

Despite these caveats, we also conclusively demonstrated a paradox – namely, that the Hill case remains capable of various interpretations: some complementary, some interlocking, some incompatible. But at the heart of all those analyses there remains a human enigma, in the Hills themselves. From whatever angle (and with whatever predisposition) one comes at the case, it probably will not be resolved in favor of any one approach without our knowing a great deal more than we do about the Hills (not to mention Zeta 1 and 2 Reticuli, adds Karl). It may prove impossible ever to know as much as we should like. Even had we undertaken our evaluations much, much closer in time to the events than we did, we should very probably have stumbled over much the same difficulties in this respect.

Some of us have long argued that knowledge – deep and broad – of the protagonist(s) in the great majority of UFO reports, and in *any* abduction account, is fundamental to making a fair evaluation. The Hill case stands both as a particular instance of this maxim and as a general lesson concerning the problems inherent in getting at the truth of any reportedly anomalous event. Not least among those problems, to our minds, is the unsettled and unsettling question of how one treats the delicate personal issues, discovered along the way, that may be pivotal in deciding how to assess a case like this. It may be quite painful for those involved, or in this case for their surviving relatives, to have such matters discussed openly or published. It is also uncomfortable for the researcher who has patiently won an experient's trust and who then appears to betray that trust by publishing negative or even damning conclusions. Researchers have often sidestepped this dilemma by smothering their subjects in pseudonyms, but that tactic merely makes their findings difficult, if not impossible, for others to verify.

Of course it can also be argued that when, in the 1960s, Betty and Barney Hill decided to make themselves public figures, they must have realized that they had also laid themselves wide open to public dissection. As editors and instigators of this project, we had both had long conversations and correspondence with Betty, and were personally fond of her, regardless of our radically different takes on her experience (as Karl understood it) or story (as Peter viewed it). On the other hand, we felt that our appreciation of Betty's co-operation should not stand in the way of stating the truth as one sees it, despite our unease at the possible consequences.

We knew from the start that we could never please everyone who's intrigued by the Hill case. But we do believe this book has been *fair* to the Hills and to their story, not only as a whole, but in each particular contribution. As a group, and as individuals, we set out in a spirit of disinterested enquiry and maintained it. We listened, and we learned. We did not entirely solve the mystery of the Hills' experiences, but we're satisfied we did something, at least, to peel away another layer or two of its onion-like wrapping.

And Speaking Personally

Peter Brookesmith writes: Karl and I prepared the foregoing in the winter of 2005/6. By then he had known for about a year that he had amyotrophic lateral sclerosis, a form of motor-neuron disease. The initial prognosis suggested he could expect to live at least another three years, perhaps six, and maybe much longer. But toward the end of April 2006 the disease struck his respiratory system. A little over a month later, he was dead.

From first to last, he faced his sentence (for that was what it was) with astonishing aplomb, courage, and wry humor – like the Marine he was so proud to have been. ("There is," he once told me, "no such thing as a former Marine.") Despite constantly failing stamina, he worked on this book almost to the end – indeed until the day before he died. What he could not complete was taken over and finished, with admirable skill, by his wife Mary Martinek. To her I owe a vast debt of gratitude. In turn, Mary and I would like to thank Ian Ridpath in England and Brett Holman in Australia for checking technical details in the account of Marjorie Fish's Star Model for us.

Karl and I had many disagreements in ufology, one of which is recorded in this book. But our disagreements never clouded our friendship, and he was a truly great friend. We also agreed about much: the dubiousness of pretty much all abduction research and "evidence," for instance. And our shared tastes for libertarian politics, political history, and a species of surreal humor, hardly put a brake on our sense of rapport. I still miss the curmudgeonly old toad, his irreverence, his erudition, his integrity, and his conversation. And no doubt I will for years to come. May he rest in peace.

Images from Indian Head

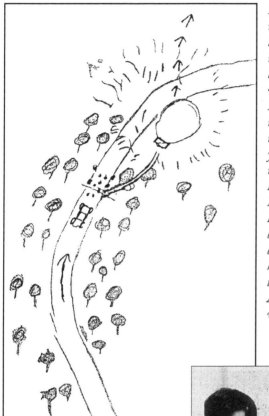

Barney's sketch map (left) of the roadblock and clearing where the Hills' abductors' craft landed is almost a mirror image of the location that Betty believed was the UFO's landing site. As Karl Pflock discovered, there is indeed a clearing at the point indicated by Barney a few yards off Mill Brook Road (a minor dead-end spur off New Hampshire State Route 175). It's been suggested that the Hills' car was turned – either by Barney, in his confusion, or by the aliens themselves, causing him to mistake which side of the road the encounter site lay. Arrows show the direction in which the UFO soared away.

Betty and Barney Hill with their copy of John G. Fuller's The Interrupted Journey. The Hills felt that Fuller would give a more accurate account of their experiences than had Robert Luttrell in a series of articles printed in the Boston Traveler. However, Fuller introduced his own errors and omissions into the story, largely to enhance its dramatic effect. In comparison, Luttrell's mistakes are fairly minor, and exactly why the Hills found his series offensive remains something of a mystery. (MEPL)

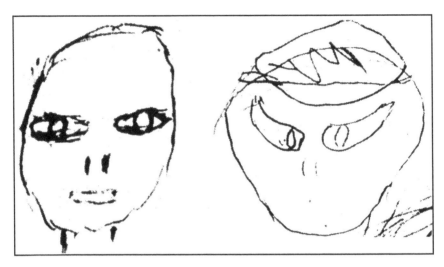

Barney's sketches of the face of the aliens who abducted him (top; MEPL): the "leader" is on the right; and the alien from Bifrost as seen on TV, in The Outer Limits *episode "The Bellero Shield" (below; United Artists). The wraparound nature of the Bifrost alien's eye socket appears to be echoed in Barney's drawing of the leader, and their full-on appearance in the left-hand image. Barney drew pupils where, in close-up on TV, a pair of human eyes can clearly be seen behind the actor's mask. In this still, the actor's eyes are hidden in shadow.*

Above: In 1964, Barney Hill and investigator Walter N. Webb reconstructed the first close encounter the Hills had with the UFO, on US Route 3 just south of what is now the Indian Head Resort. Here, Barney re-enacts staring at the UFO through binoculars as it came within 100 feet of the road, looking "as big as a four-motor plane". The car is a later model of the Chevrolet Bel-Air the Hills were driving in 1961. (Walter N. Webb)

Left: In Webb's 1964 reconstruction, Barney follows the UFO as it crosses from the west to the east side of US Route 3. Barney then approached the UFO, only to be terrified by the eyes of one of the figures on board, whom he could see clearly through the windows of the craft. (Walter N. Webb)

The first encounter site as it looks today. A few hundred yards to the south, Interstate 93 crosses the road, and street lighting has been installed since what was bare countryside in 1961 has become a scattered village. (Dennis Stacy)

IMAGES FROM INDIAN HEAD 21

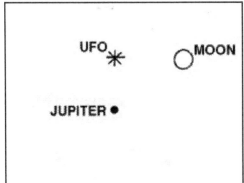

The Hills' first close encounter with a UFO on September 19/20 1961 was immediately preceded by Betty Hill noticing a bright star near the Moon and, a short time later, another much brighter star-like object higher up — "like a star, a bigger star, up over this one." This diagram shows the Moon, the planet Jupiter (the most likely candidate for the "star" near the Moon) and the apparent UFO, as they appeared to her.

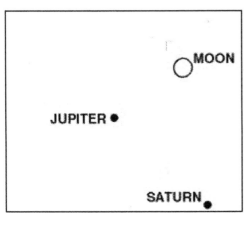

Skeptics, notably Philip Klass and Robert Sheaffer, have suggested that Betty's "bigger star" was the planet Jupiter, and that Saturn was what she had described as "a bright star near the Moon." This diagram shows the relative positions of the Moon and the two planets on the night of the Hills' abduction.

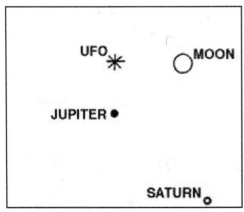

Defenders of Betty Hill's original account point out that Saturn was 12 times fainter than Jupiter on the night of September 19/20 and Betty was therefore unlikely to have mistaken one planet for the other. Further, Jupiter was not directly "up over" Saturn, but above and well to the left of it. This diagram shows the known positions of the planets and the Moon at the time of the sighting, and the position of the UFO as Betty reported it.

22 ENCOUNTERS AT INDIAN HEAD

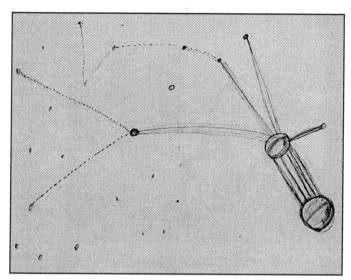

Betty Hill's sketch, made under hypnosis, of the "star map" shown to her during her abduction. It supposedly charts the alien's home planet and interstellar trade routes used by the aliens. Betty dotted most of the minor stars randomly, simply to indicate the galactic background. (MEPL)

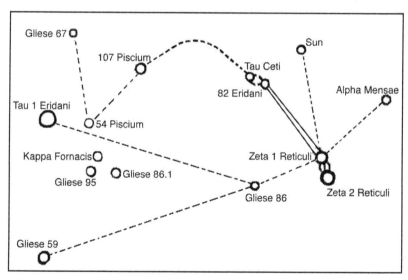

In 1974 Marjorie Fish, using beads on strings, created an elaborate model of stars within 10 parsecs of the Sun, whose planets (if any) would be able to support life. By inspecting the model from all angles, she believed she was able to identify the viewpoint of Betty's alien star map and so name the stars themselves – as labeled in this diagram. While Fish's work remains valid in terms of mid-1970s' astronomy, doubts remain about both the reality and accuracy of Betty Hill's recall under hypnosis. (Mendoza)

The Indian Head rock seen from US Route 3 in 2000. The simulacrum collapsed in 2004 and no longer resembles a human profile. The outcrop is part of Cannon Mountain, behind which a UFO passed while apparently tracking the Hills on their journey south from Colebrook, NH. (Dennis Stacy)

Creators of the 2000 Indian Head Symposium Peter Brookesmith (left) and Karl Pflock demonstrate shared tastes in hats and boots at the "UFO landing site" in the midst of the New Hampshire forest. (Mary Martinek)

Below: Participants in the 2000 Indian Head Symposium. Left to right: Marcello Truzzi, Peter Brookesmith, Greg Sandow, Dennis Stacy, Karl Pflock, Thomas "Ed" Bullard, Robert Sheaffer, and Hilary Evans. (Mary Martinek)

Symposium sponsor Joe Firmage (center) discusses some finer points of ufology with Ed Bullard and Betty Hill during the tour of the Hills' encounter sites. (Mary Martinek)

Members of the Indian Head Symposium in conference. Discussions were held in private and were marked by consistent cordiality and a collegiate atmosphere – in striking, and fruitful, contrast to many public debates on ufology. (Mary Martinek)

Betty Hill at the Indian Head Symposium with a sculpture of one of the aliens as she knew them. Her description of the creatures she met during her abduction varied over time: for instance, originally they had huge noses, although Barney reported them as having mere slits for nostrils (as shown in his sketches). But with eyes with distinct pupils, hair, stocky bodies and clothing, these "original" aliens were quite distinct from the blank-eyed, pencil-thin "Grays" reported by later abductees. Betty considered most of these reports to be artifacts of incompetent hypnosis. (Mary Martinek)

Betty Hill entertains Ed Bullard and Hilary Evans at the Indian Head Resort. At extreme left is Kathy Marden, Betty's niece, who gave participants an intriguing sketch of Barney's personality before and after the UFO encounter. (Mary Martinek)

Like a latter-day Snow White and her entourage, Betty Hill prepares to lead Symposium participants into the forest to view the clearing where, she believed, she and Barney were taken aboard a landed UFO. Later, as members of the group emerged from the woods clutching cameras and other impediments, a passing pickup came to a squealing halt. "Did ya see a moose?" called a passenger. "Nope. Looking for UFOs." Faces fell, the engine roared, and the truck sped away. (Mary Martinek)

A long view of the site where the UFO landed, with Symposium members in the distance. There is no suggestion that the space among the trees was formed by the craft – such clearings are a common, natural feature of the New Hampshire forest. (Mary Martinek)

1. Betty and Barney Hill leave restaurant at Colebrook at 10:05 p.m. on 19 September 1961.

2. First sighting of UFO near Lancaster.

3. UFO passes behind Cannon Mountain.

4. First encounter: UFO hovers low and crosses the road, and Barney leaves the car to view it through binoculars; Barney drives off in a panic, and within a distance of "five or six blocks" the couple hear mysterious beeping noises.

5. Two points at which Barney may inadvertently have turned off Route 3 onto NH State Route 175.

6. On Mill Brook Road, the Hills meet a roadblock and are taken to the UFO, which has landed in a nearby clearing among the trees.

7. "Somewhere near Ashland" the beeps return briefly.

8. The Hills see a sign reading "Concord 17 miles" and full consciousness returns.

9. Betty and Barney Hill arrive home at State Street, Portsmouth, shortly after 5:00 a.m. on 20 September 1961.

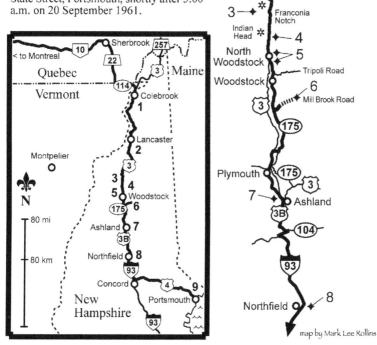

map by Mark Lee Rollins

IMAGES FROM INDIAN HEAD   27

CHAPTER ONE

A Night and a Morning to Remember

A freshly researched, succinct history of the Hill abduction case reveals what was missing or suppressed in the standard account

DENNIS STACY

The night of September 19, 1961, found a mixed-race couple, Eunice (Betty) and Barney Hill, driving south on U.S. Highway 3 from the Canadian border toward their home in Portsmouth, New Hampshire. They were returning from a much-needed vacation that had taken them first to Niagara Falls, which Betty had never seen, and Montreal, Quebec.

Although the marriage was working well, both were under some job stress. Barney Hill, aged 39, was suffering from a recurring ulcer, which he had recently had X-rayed and for which he was taking medicine. And while he liked his job as an assistant night dispatcher at the Boston post office, the long hours and daily 120-mile, round-trip commute were taking their toll. Betty Hill, aged 41, was overtaxed, too. Employed by New Hampshire as a child welfare worker, she was creaking under her current caseload, which included 120 assignments. But Betty had a weeklong vacation coming up, and as Barney drove home on the morning of the 15th, the idea of a quick getaway vacation crystallized.

Betty readily agreed over breakfast, and the next morning the Hills rose early and completed packing their 1957 Chevrolet Bel Air for the trip. To save on expenses, they carried their own food so as to avoid the expensive tourist traps along the route. When they finally pulled out of their driveway in the pre-dawn darkness, there was a third occupant in the car – Delsey, the family dachshund. Behind the wheel, Barney began booming out a popular song, "Oh, What a Beautiful Morning!"

The vacation was uneventful – that is, everything went largely as planned – until the last leg of the return trip. South of Lancaster, in the Pilot Range of the White Mountains, Betty, surveying the scenery through the rolled up windows, noticed a second bright star or planet near the nearly full Moon. The last time the luminous Moon had caught her attention, this second companion hadn't been there.

Conscious Recall

Something else attracted Betty's attention. Unlike the earlier light source, this one appeared to be moving. She mentioned it to Barney, who also looked at it, and they agreed that it was probably one of those newfangled satellites the U.S. and Soviet Union had begun sending up only four years earlier.

Underneath her feet in the front passenger seat, Delsey turned restless. Betty suggested they pull over to the side of the road and kill two birds with one stone. They could walk the dog and watch the light at the same time. Now that they were stopped themselves, they could see that this second "star" or satellite was definitely moving on its own. Betty handed Barney the dog's leash and returned to the car, retrieving the 7 x 50 Crescent binoculars they had brought along for sightseeing. They weren't much help at this juncture, still resolving only a single light source.

As they continued south, the satellite explanation seemed less and less likely. The light appeared to change speed and direction, to grow brighter and closer, almost as if it were deliberately stalking them, or at the very least remaining in their immediate vicinity. Barney slowed the car and kept a wary eye on the light, several times coming to a complete rest for a better look. During one of these stops, Barney exited the car to retrieve a 22-calibre pistol hidden in the trunk. Near Cannon Mountain the light executed an abrupt series of maneuvers, and Barney braked sharply into a picnic turnout. Outside the car, he vocalized an escalating series of alternative explanations. It might be a commercial airliner on its way to Canada, he said, failing that, a Piper Cub full of lost hunters, or perhaps even a helicopter. Betty voiced the obvious objection to each one: all those things made noise, this made none.

They took turns looking through the binoculars. Barney could now make out a shape as opposed to a nebulous light source. Whatever it was looked like the wingless fuselage of an airplane, with blinking lights along the side. Delsey whined. Betty handed her husband the binoculars and got in the car with the dog. Barney now believed the object to be circling them and drawing closer. For the first time, he got the unnerving feeling that they were being *observed*.

He restarted the motor and continued home, driving at a snail's pace now as he warily eyed the approaching object, clearly visible through the windshield. At the base of Cannon Mountain he came to a momentary stop in the road. A darkened aerial tramway ran up the side of the mountain, culminating at a single very bright light on the top. As the object passed out of view behind the peak, this beacon inexplicably blinked out. Betty remembered thinking: anyone up there now would have a helluva view of the object. But would there be anyone in the restaurant at this late hour? She looked at her wristwatch, but there wasn't enough ambient light in the car to ascertain an accurate reading.

Barney engaged the clutch and drove on. The light-bearing object re-emerged from behind Cannon Mountain and passed to the west of the car, where it continued to parallel them. But they had entered forest terrain now, and it became increasingly difficult to keep the object in continuous sight. The Hills briefly stopped again near The Flume, another local tourist attraction. Unable to get a clear view, they drove on, passing a small motel in the process. Betty saw a light behind a window and a man in an open doorway, and the fleeting thought flashed through her mind: we could end this now. But the object had roused her curiosity, so she kept silent.

The motel retreated in the rear-view mirror, lost in the enveloping night. As the Chevrolet rounded a curve, the object suddenly loomed much lower and closer ahead. Up to this point – perhaps because the lights attached to the object were blinking on and off – Betty had viewed the object as spinning on a central axis. Now it was suffusing a steady, white glow, or streak, on its visible side. Betty again put the binoculars to her eyes – and just as promptly exuded an audible breath. The thing was clearly structured and huge into the bargain, although exactly how huge, or how far away, was virtually impossible to determine, given the dark, featureless background. Other details were now visible, too. The single streak of white light resolved into a double row of lighted windows running almost the entire length of the object, and a single red light was now visible at both ends.

"Barney, you've got to *stop*," Betty said. "You've never seen anything like this in your life."

The first close encounter

Barney stopped for at least the fourth known time that night, in this instance in the middle of the road near a closed summer tourist attraction known as Natureland, its two faux-Indian teepees visible in the headlight beams. (This site is now occupied by a small entertainment center, The Whale's Tale Water Park.) They were just south of Indian Head, a mountain so-named because of a rocky outcrop resembling a human face in profile. Leaving the motor running, Barney slipped the .22 into a coat pocket and tried balancing the binoculars on the top of the open, vibrating door. This proved unsatisfactory, so he moved a few feet away into a roadside field.

Simultaneously, the object traced a silent west-to-east arc across the road, arriving at a point over an open field to the left front of the car. Barney now estimated it to be no more than 100 feet away, perhaps 50 to 80 feet up in the air, with a width variously described as the distance between three telephone poles or the length of a four-engine passenger plane. The double row of windows was now decidedly discernible, even without the benefit of binoculars.

As fearful as he was by now of being captured, Barney also found himself strangely attracted toward the object hovering nearby. Consequently, he moved further away from the comforting confines of the car – where Betty was repeatedly entreating his return – and eastward into the field, closer to the huge, hovering object.

Through the double row of windows Barney could see several figures, as many as eight to eleven, who appeared to be returning his gaze. They looked human in form and were dressed in shiny, black leather uniforms with black caps. The ship tilted toward Barney, as if permitting a better view of him for those onboard, and, as if on command, all of the figures at the windows but one stepped back toward a perceived control panel, where they busied themselves. The solitary commanding figure continued to stare in Barney's direction as the object lowered itself even closer. At this point, the red lights on either side of the ship slowly slid out and appeared to be attached to the pointed ends of two fin-shaped objects.

Barney's fear of capture intensified. At the same time, he couldn't tear his gaze from the binoculars. Fine-focusing on the leader, he found himself staring into the most unusual pair of eyes he had ever seen. The sight was so startling that Barney was now able to break out of the fixation in which he had found himself. He hurtled across the field toward Betty and the parked car, vocalizing his fear of imminent capture. Throwing the car into gear, he sped off down the deserted road, ordering Betty to keep a look out for the object. But it was now nowhere to be seen.

From the rear of the car came an unusual, irregular beeping noise, apparently electronic in nature. Neither Betty nor Barney could identify its precise location, but the car itself seemed to lightly shudder or shake in sympathy with it. Adding to their confusion, both Hills now experienced a tingling drowsiness. They drove on in sleepy silence – odd in light of what had just happened – remembering little more of this stretch of the journey than a road sign indicating they were near Ashland, approximately 35 miles south of Indian Head. The strange sound was repeated a little while later, but in their haze of drowsiness neither had a clear idea of how many minutes had elapsed between the two beeping episodes. Betty finally broke the silence by asking Barney whether he believed in flying saucers now. "Don't be ridiculous," Barney answered. "Of course not."

Their consciousness was slowly clearing, in the way a light fog dissipates before the rising Sun. Connected with this clearing was their seeing another highway sign informing them they were only 17 miles from Concord. In and around Concord they looked for any place where they might be able to stop and get a cup of coffee, but none of the local diners or other alternatives were open at that hour.

Dawn began to break while they were still on Route 4, just west of Portsmouth. Once home Barney looked at his watch, but it had ceased running. When Betty checked her own watch a short time later, it, too, had stopped sometime during the evening or early morning hours of September 19-20. "It looks like we've arrived home a little later than expected," Barney said.

Barney began unpacking the Bel Air. For reasons unclear even to herself, Betty asked that the luggage be stored in a rear hallway rather than brought directly inside the white frame house, and that the leftover food be thrown out. While Betty walked Delsey, Barney finished unloading the automobile, in the process of which he came across the binoculars and noticed for the first time that their leather holding strap was cleanly and freshly broken.

While coffee brewed, Barney went into the bathroom and, using a small mirror, conducted an examination of his groin area. Two years later, he still couldn't explain why he felt compelled to conduct this spontaneous search. "I don't know, I didn't know why at the time," Barney told journalist John Fuller, who eventually wrote a book-length account of their experiences, "but I felt unclean. With a grime different from what usually accumulates on a trip."

At around the same time Betty noticed a powdery pink substance on her dress, which she threw away. Having second thoughts, she retrieved it and hung it on a clothesline, where the powder evaporated or blew away, leaving behind a visible stain. Later in the day she stashed the dress and the shoes she had worn that night in the rearmost recess of her closet and never wore either again.

Over coffee, the couple tried to reconstruct and render sensible the night's events. Barney was particularly puzzled by the object's silence. Noise, any sort of noise, would permit him to cling to his mundane aircraft explanation – despite its admittedly most odd behavior. But there had been no sounds associated with the unusual object, unless one counted the beeping noises that followed its seeming departure. Neither could fill in events between the two beeping episodes, nor could either complete memories of the elapsed time traveled between Indian Head and Ashland. One thing they could agree upon, however: the night's sequence of events was so outlandish and inherently unbelievable that they would discuss it with no one.

Aftermath

A caveat arose that very same day, though. Mid-afternoon, after a restorative sleep, the Hills again tried to put two and two together, with similar incomplete results. Barney, known as a meticulous dresser, had become perplexed when he woke and went to put his clothes away. Burrs and other scraps of vegetable matter clung to his socks and the bottoms of his trousers, bringing back memories of the time when he left Betty and the dachshund Delsey in the car and crossed the field toward the hovering craft, binoculars in hand. More personally perturbing, perhaps, he found the normally polished and shiny tops of his best pair of shoes scraped and scuffed. How and when did *that* happen, he wondered.

Betty thought it best at this point at least to share their experience with her sister, Janet Miller, who had had her own UFO encounter several years previously. She had been driving on Route 125, between her home in Kingston, New Hampshire, and Haverhill, in neighboring Massachusetts. Near Plaistow, N.H., she saw in the sky what appeared to be a huge glowing object, surrounded by several smaller objects. She had the presence of mind to stop at a house and induce the occupants to come outside. Then they all watched in surprise while the smaller objects entered the larger one, which then flew away.

Barney grudgingly agreed to Betty's request. In the course of the sisters' conversation, the question of possible radioactive contamination arose, given the Hills' close proximity to the unidentified craft (and given the public's fear of "radioactivity," which was writ large at the time, and which Betty and her sister both clearly assumed to be a possible side-effect associated with "flying saucers"). Janet informed or reminded Betty that one of her neighbors was a physicist; she would check with him and get back to Betty. "In a few moments," according to Fuller, "Janet was back on the phone to tell Betty that the physicist said any ordinary compass might show evidence of radiation if the needle became seriously disturbed on contact with the car's surface."

This is spurious science, though, as Barney recognized at the time. While a compass will readily react to a local magnetic field, it would remain unaffected by any residual radioactivity. For that, a Geiger counter would be required. Regardless of who got their science wrong in this instance – Betty, her sister, Fuller, or the neighboring physicist – Betty began asking Barney after the whereabouts of the cheap compass they had carried on their trip.

Barney, still skeptical, was at first uncooperative with this latest development but soon surrendered the compass. Betty rushed out to the driveway, to find a light rain falling. She began sweeping the compass over various parts of the wet car. It behaved normally, until she reached the trunk area. To her surprise, the trunk lid was randomly spotted with about a dozen small, polished circles the size of silver dollars. When placed over one after another of these burnished spots, the compass needle promptly reacted. In Fuller's phrase, it "went out of control." Immediately, Betty associated the strange circles with the beeping sounds heard earlier, as they, too, had originated from the car's trunk area.

Hurrying inside, Betty implored Barney to come see the circles and the compass reaction for himself, but he begged off, ostensibly because of the rain. At that moment, the couple renting an upstairs apartment from the Hills dropped by. Seeing Betty's agitated state, they inquired as to its cause, and she blurted out a hurried account of the UFO encounter, concluding with the discovery of the circles on the car. Reluctantly, Barney went outside with the couple while Betty again phoned her sister. Janet, too, had been busy in the interval since their last contact, having spoken with the former Newton, New Hampshire, Chief of Police, who said that the Hills should inform Portsmouth's Pease Air Force Base of their sighting.

Emboldened by these developments, and still fearful of radiation exposure, Betty was eager to comply, while Barney remained wary and reluctant. When he eventually relented – "But if you do call the Air Force Base, leave me out of it," he told her – Betty placed a call to Pease AFB in Portsmouth, a Strategic Air Command (SAC) facility. Ultimately, she was connected to an AF police officer, who less than eagerly received her report. For her part, Betty omitted some of the details, such as the row of double windows they had seen, details she thought might be perceived as too way out, or potentially embarrassing and/or discrediting. For his part, the officer on the other end of the phone grew noticeably more interested when Betty referenced the extending wing tips, or fins, and their red lights. Informed that Barney, by proximity, had been more privy to this part of the experience than her, he asked to talk to her husband directly.

Barney Hill hedged his bets, too, purposefully deleting any mention of the figures he had seen aboard the craft. Yet his conversation with Air Force personnel also softened his initial skepticism. After all, if they were willing to take the subject seriously, why shouldn't he? This feeling was reinforced the following day when a Major Paul W. Henderson of the 100th Bomb Wing, Pease AFB, called, requesting further information. Eventually, Henderson filed Air Intelligence Information Report No. 100-1-61, which duly wended its way to Project Blue Book at Wright-Patterson AFB, Dayton, Ohio, the Air Force agency then in charge of investigating reports of unidentified flying objects. Researchers would later learn that at 2:14 a.m., September 20, 1961, radar at Pease AFB picked up an anomalous return. Betty Hill is convinced that this was "their" UFO, leaving the scene of their second encounter. Most ufologists who have examined the evidence are inclined to accept the explanation that the "weak target" recorded was the result of a temperature inversion, and that the timing was merely coincidental.

Word starts to spread

The Hills' mutual vow of silence had disintegrated almost upon its inception. In a matter of hours, not only did the neighbors upstairs know about their experience, but so did Betty's sister and her family, along with their physicist friend and a former Newton, New Hampshire, Chief of Police. And now the Air Force knew. Others would soon be apprised as well.

Two days after Major Henderson's interview, Betty went to the Portsmouth library and checked out one of the few books locally available on the subject, *The Flying Saucer Conspiracy*, published in 1955 by retired Marine Major Donald E. Keyhoe. Betty raced through it in a single sitting, but Barney refused to read it at all. On September 26, 1961, she typed out the following letter and mailed it off to Keyhoe, then the head of the National Investigations Committee on Aerial Phenomena (NICAP), based in Washington, D. C. For reasons not completely clear, the version published in Fuller's *The Interrupted Journey* is lightly edited and altered, the most glaring example of which is the omission of the sentence in which the Hills say they are seeking the services of a psychiatrist, specifically one practiced in hypnosis. It is reproduced here, unedited for spelling or grammar.

> The purpose of this letter is twofold. We wish to inquire if you have written any more books about unidentified flying objects since *The Flying Saucer Conspiracy* was published. If so, it would certainly be appreciated if you would send us the name of the publisher, as we have been unsuccessful in finding any information more upto date than this book. A stamped self-addressed envelope is being included for your convenience.
>
> My husband and I have become immensely interested in this topic, as we recently had quite a frightening experience, which does seem to differ from others of which we are aware. About midnight on September 20th, we were driving in a National Forest Area in the White Mountains, in N.H. This is a desolate, uninhabited area. At first we noticed a bright object in the sky which seemed to be moving rapidly. We stopped our car and got out to observe it more closely with our binoculars. Suddenly it reversed its flight from the north to the southwest and appeared to be flying in a very erratic pattern. As we continued driving and then stopping to watch it, we observed the following flight pattern.
>
> The object was spinning and appeared to be lighted only on one side which gave it a twinkling effect.
>
> As it approached our car, we stopped again. As it hovered in the air in front of us, it appeared to be pancake in shape, ringed with windows in the front through which we could see bright blue-white lights. Suddenly, two red lights appeared on each side. By this time my husband was standing in the road, watching closely. He saw wings protrude on each side and the red lights were on the wing tips.
>
> As it glided closer he was able to see inside this object, but not too closely. He did see many figures scurrying about as though they were making some hurried type of preparation. One figure was observing us from the windows. From the distance, this was seen, the figures appeared to be about the size of a pencil, and seemed to be dressed in some type of shiny black uniform.
>
> At this point, my husband became shocked and got back in the car, in a hysterical condition, laughing and repeating that they were going to capture us. He started driving the car – the motor had been left running. As we started to move, we heard several buzzing or beeping sounds which seemed to be striking the trunk of our car.
>
> We did not observe this object leaving, but we did not see it again, although about thirty miles further south we were again bombarded by those same beeping sounds.

The next day we did make a report to an Air Force officer, who seemed to be very interested in the wings and red lights. We did not report my husband's observation of the interior as it seems too fantastic to be true.

At this time we are searching for any clue that might be helpful to my husband, in recalling whatever it was he saw that caused him to panic. His mind has completely blacked out at this point. Every attempt to recall, leaves him very frightened. We are considering the possibility of a competent psychiatrist who uses hypnotism.

This flying object was at least as large as a four motor plane, its flight was noiseless and the lighting from the interior did not reflect on the ground. There does not appear to be any damage to our car from the beeping sounds.

We both have been quite frightened by this experience, but fascinated. We feel a compelling urge to return to the spot where this occurred in the hope that we may again come in contact with this object. We realize this possibility is slight and we should, however, have more recent information regarding developments in the last six years.

Any suggested reading would be greatly appreciated. Your book has been of great help to us and a reassurance that we are not the only ones to have undergone an interesting and informative experience.

Betty Dreams

A week and a half later, over the course of five successive nights, Betty experienced a series of vivid, nightmarish dreams like nothing she had had before. (Another account has the nightmarish dreams lasting six nights.) Coincidentally, the nights of the nightmares coincided with Barney's workweek, so he was not aware of them until Betty brought them up later. While sympathetic, he didn't display any significant interest in their content, so Betty let the matter drop between the two of them, although she did discuss the matter with her sister and a few other friends.

At the suggestion of one of her co-workers at the New Hampshire Department of Public Welfare, Betty pecked out a description of her dreams, using the same typewriter she had used to write Keyhoe. "Two events happened of which we were consciously aware; these are also incorporated in my dreams," she wrote. "First, we sighted a huge object, glowing with a bright orange light, which appeared to be sitting on the ground. Our reaction was to say, 'No, not again,' and then we consoled ourselves with the self-assurance it was the setting Moon." The second consciously remembered bookend, as it were, was Betty asking Barney if he believed in flying saucers now, and Barney responding, "Don't be ridiculous. Of course not."

Betty edited her dreams to give them a chronology they initially lacked. "In fact the first dream told was the last one dreamed," she noted. "My emotional feelings during this part was of terror, greater than I had ever believed possible."

In her dreams, then, almost simultaneous with seeing the lighted saucer, a roadblock suddenly loomed ahead, manned by eight to eleven men in similar uniform. Barney slowed the car for them to disperse, but they didn't. Instead, the car's motor died and they surrounded the Bel Air. "We sat there motionless and speechless, and I was terrified," Betty wrote in her dream diary. Then "they opened the car doors on each side, reached in and took us by the arm."

Still in her dream, Betty lost consciousness at this point, but struggled to wake up. The feeling was one of swimming upstream, or struggling up from the bottom of a deep well, she wrote. When she regained dream "consciousness," she and Barney were being marched along a path in the woods, each escorted by the mysterious men. Barney, who appeared to be in a somnambulistic state, was supported by a man on either side, with others following behind. Betty called out his name, but Barney didn't respond. Then the man on her left addressed Betty directly, speaking English, but with a foreign inflection. He assured her that they wouldn't be harmed. "All they want to do is make some tests; when these are completed in a very brief time," according to Betty's typed notes, "they will take us back to the car and we will go safely on our way home. We have nothing to fear."

While walking through the woods, Betty had time to observe her captors. They were all shorter than her husband; she estimated their height at somewhere between 5 feet and 5 feet 4 inches tall, similar to her own, as measured without and with high-heeled shoes. "Their chests are larger than ours," she noted. And so were their proboscs, she added, "although I've seen people with noses like theirs – like Jimmy Durante's." (The late Jimmy "Schnozzle" Durante was an American comedian noted for his prominent proboscis.)

In complexion, their dream captors or escorters were of a tint "like a gray paint with a black base." Betty further described their lips as having a bluish tinge, and their hair and eyes as very dark, verging on black. All were dressed alike, in short jackets and trousers "of a light blue navy color" tinged in gray. "Shoes were a low, slip-on style, resembling a boot." She couldn't remember any jewelry or insignias, but recalled that "they were all wearing military caps, similar to Air Force, but not so broad on the top."

Overall, "they were very human in their appearance, not frightening. They seemed to be very relaxed, friendly in a professional way (businesslike). There was no haste, no waste of time." (Shortly after, however, they would become more insistent on a timely agenda, reminding Betty on at least two occasions that the sooner she complied with their requests, the sooner she and Barney would be returned to their car.)

Boarding, examination, conference

Reaching a clearing in the woods, Betty's dream-self confronted a disc-shaped object perceived as "almost twice as wide as my house is long." It was dark from this angle of approach, which she assumed to be its rear. She and Barney were led up a short step or two onto a sloping ramp that led into the interior of the craft-like object. Once inside they were separated, Barney being led away along a curved corridor to another room, where he was to be examined separately. Betty was approached by an "examiner," a different figure than the one perceived earlier as the "leader." He also spoke English, but not as clearly as the leader. He proceeded to ask Betty several questions, such as how old she was, and what she ate. When she tried to explain, he seemed not to understand the meaning of words like meat, milk, and vegetables.

Betty was then physically examined, in both gross and fine manner. Samples of her hair, skin, and nails were taken. Then an electronic instrument was wheeled over, its many wires ending in needles. Betty compared it to an EEG machine without a print-out, or tracing, device. The needles were applied to different areas of her body, temples, neck, armpits, hips, legs and so on. A four-to-six-inch needle was then attached to one of the wires, which Betty was told would be used as a pregnancy test. Although assured that the test would be painless, Betty began writhing in pain when the needle was inserted in her navel.

"They decided to end the testing," Betty typed in her notes. "The examiner left the room, the leader gathered up all the test samples and put them together in a drawer, and I put on my dress and shoes." Abruptly, several of the crew re-entered the small, colorless room and engaged the leader in excited conversation, employing "words [and] tones with which I was [not] acquainted." The leader left, only to return almost immediately. He opened Betty's mouth and pulled at her teeth. Why do his teeth come out and not yours, he wanted to know. Betty tried to explain that humans lost their teeth over time, and that Barney had dentures, whereas she didn't yet.

"Proof" offered – and withdrawn

The leader failed to grasp either concept readily, but the conversation expanded to encompass her own incredulity. How was anyone going to believe *her* experience without physical proof of it? Maybe he could give her something to take with her? He agreed and asked her what she would like as evidence. She pointed to a large book, filled with incomprehensible "symbols written in long, narrow columns."

She asked where he's from, and he asked if she knew anything about the Universe. "I said no, but I would like to learn," Betty replied. He went to a wall and pulled down a map. "It was a map of the heavens, with numerous size stars and planets, some large, some only pinpoints. Between many of these, lines were drawn, some broken lines, some light solid lines, some heavy black lines. They were not straight, but curved." The leader indicated that the lines represented expeditions. He then asked Betty if she knew where the Earth was on the map, and she admitted she had no idea. Sarcastically, he said that if she didn't know that, it would be impossible for him to explain his place of origin; he then snapped the map back in place.

But others knew more about these matters than she did, Betty protested. Not sure how it could be arranged, she nonetheless suggested "a quiet meeting with scientists, or top people in the world." When he asked why, Betty said because you "would have a chance to meet us and study us openly." At this, the leader smiled, but said nothing. "I was in the middle of trying to sell him this idea," Betty recalled, "when several men appeared with Barney, who was still in a daze."

As they were about to exit the craft, an animated argument erupted between the leader and crew. The former approached Betty and retrieved the previously proffered book. To her protests, the leader responded that "it had been decided that no one should know of this experience, and that even I would not remember [it]." An angered Betty told him that she *would* remember, that nothing could make her forget. The leader laughed, saying he would do his best to see that she didn't, but that if she did, no one would believe her. In any event, he added, Barney would remember nothing, "would think of things contrary to the way [she] knew them to be. This would lead to confusion, doubt, disagreement."

They were then led through the woods back to their car, Barney slowly surfacing from his daze, but evidencing no emotion, as if "this was an everyday occurrence." The leader advised them to wait until they had departed. From their vantage point, the Hills watched as, in Betty's words, "suddenly the ship became a bright glowing object, and it appeared to roll like a ball turning over about 3-4 times and then sailing into the sky. In a moment it was gone, as though they had turned out the lights."

An exuberant Betty then told Barney that that "was the most marvelous, most unbelievable experience of my whole life." She patted Delsey and said, "There they go. And we are none the worse for the wear."

Betty and Barney entered into their car and drove away. "Do you believe in flying saucers now," she asked Barney, who had said nothing to this point. "Don't be ridiculous," he answered. The beeping noises were heard again. "Good luck and good bye," Betty dreamed. "I am going to forget about you. If you want me to forget, I will."

A few weeks after their onset, remnants of Betty's nightmares reportedly resurfaced in real life. They were again driving in the New Hampshire countryside one day, when a stalled car, surrounded by several people, suddenly loomed ahead, partially blocking the road. Barney slowed their car accordingly. As he did, Betty experienced an almost uncontrollable urge to throw open her door and run. "Barney – keep going," she commanded. "Please don't slow down. Keep going, keep going!" Barney avoided the "road block" as expeditiously as he could, and the couple, both shaken by Betty's uncharacteristic emotional outburst, returned home.

Coming Out of the Closet

At NICAP headquarters in the nation's capital, Betty's letter was passed along to then secretary and later Assistant Director Richard Hall. Hall in turn sent a copy of it to astronomer Walter Webb, a lecturer at the Hayden Planetarium in Boston. Webb had become interested in UFOs following his own sighting in 1951. More to the point, though, he had investigated several important cases in New England for NICAP, his case reports of which were widely regarded as scientific models. Now Hall wanted to know if he would like to look into the Hill encounter.

Webb's initial response was one of reluctance and skepticism, feelings shared by most serious NICAP members and other UFO researchers and organizations of the day. Many within the field felt that it had been badly tarred by the association in the public's mind of the UFO subject with so-called "contactees" – people claiming not only to have been aboard the "flying saucers" but to have held extended conversations with their occupants – who invariably turned out to be from nearby known planets like Venus and Mars. Accordingly, reports of beings seen in connection with UFOs were customarily viewed with suspicion and given short shrift.

Webb weighed his options. On the one hand, the notion that these strange objects *could* be occupied had a certain logic to it, even if most of the extant claims to that effect to date hadn't. On the other hand, the Hills never claimed to have conversed with the reported beings, nor to have had some cosmic wisdom imparted to them as a consequence – only to have briefly glimpsed them at close range. One would never know how reliable the case was without further investigation. In the end, Webb picked up the phone and arranged for a meeting on October 21, 1961.

The interview with Betty and Barney Hill lasted from just past noon until about 6:00 p.m. that night. If Webb had originally thought the case would unravel upon the most cursory examination, he began to think otherwise as the interview wore on by the hour. He questioned the Hills both together and separately, suspecting that one would eventually contradict or trip the other up on some aspect of their shared experience. Then he questioned them again, prying for any apparent misstep. Ultimately, Webb came away convinced that the Hills were a credible couple relating an incredible encounter to the best of their memory and ability. (To his eternal regret, Webb failed to examine the spots on the car on this occasion.)

Webb returned to Boston and began compiling ancillary data. These included the weather conditions for the night in question, notated maps and compass readings, and the locations of various astronomical bodies during the duration of the sighting. Five days after the interview, he composed a cover letter and submitted his six-page report to NICAP, along with sketches of the object the Hills had given him.

A second early investigation of the Hill case came about by a more circuitous route. In the first week of October 1961, the XIIth International Astronomical Congress convened in Washington, D. C. Two of those in attendance were IBM employees C. D. Jackson and Robert E. Hohmann. Jackson was a senior engineer, Hohmann a staff writer. Both were also NICAP members, and so arranged to have lunch with Major Keyhoe during the course of the conference. When Hohmann wondered aloud why he hadn't heard of any good UFO reports of late, Keyhoe raised the Hill case.

Their collective reaction was similar to Webb's: skeptical, but intrigued. They mulled over whether they should become more deeply involved or not; then receipt of a copy of the initial Webb report tipped the scales. Hohmann subsequently wrote the Hills, requesting a meeting, which took place toward the end of November. When Jackson and Hohmann arrived in Portsmouth, the Hills were also entertaining a longtime friend, Major James McDonald, a recently retired Air Force intelligence officer who had at least a passing personal interest in UFO reports.

Time goes missing

The five engaged in a question-and-answer session that consumed the better part of five hours. After one recounting of chronological events, either Jackson or Hohmann – exactly who is not clear from Fuller's account – asked the Hills why it took them so long to complete their asserted itinerary. Shouldn't they have arrived home at least a couple of hours earlier than they did? How did they account for the apparent period of missing time?

Neither Hill had a ready answer. In fact, the implication of the question seems to have left both of them disturbed and unsettled. In his own words, Barney was "flabbergasted," Fuller reported, while Betty crossed her arms and dropped her head. When the conversation resumed, Major McDonald suggested the use of hypnosis as a possible recovery method applicable to periods of amnesia. Neither he, nor Jackson or Hohmann, however, knew a psychiatrist to recommend to the Hills.

Instead, beginning on November 11, 1961, Betty and Barney began retracing their steps, revisiting Indian Head and its environs in hope that some physical impression might jog their "blocked" memories. (Later, once they became aware under hypnosis of a second encounter site, they added the search for that location to their weekend jaunts, too, although it would not be until September of 1965 that they came across a mutually agreeable candidate, and then only by sheer serendipity.)

In March, Betty lunched one day with Gail Peabody, a co-worker and close friend to whom she had already confided the contents of her disturbing dreams. She told Gail that she and Barney were considering hypnosis. Gail promptly recommended Patrick Quirke, a psychiatrist and the medical director of Baldpate Sanitarium in nearby Georgetown, Massachusetts. In a letter to Dr. Quirke dated March 12, 1962, Betty summarized their situation:

> We are seeking the services of a psychiatrist who uses hypnotism, and are wondering if it would be possible to make an appointment to see you on a Saturday morning? My husband and I are both employed, but our working hours are such that this would be convenient for us. If this is not possible we could make an appointment at your convenience.
>
> We have a unique reason for requesting this interview. The enclosed bulletin of the National Investigations Committee on Aerial Phenomena, briefly describes an experience that occurred to us last September 19-20, 1961. We have been interviewed by Mr. C. D. Jackson and Robert Hohmann of IBM.
>
> Many puzzling aspects remain, so it is believed that hypnotism could clarify these. We have handled this experience confidentially with the exception of NICAP and a few close friends.
>
> We do have a complete story of the report written by Mr. Walter Webb, of the Hayden Planetarium, which we would be willing to send to you, for your review. If you do not have time available to see us, or would

prefer not to do this, would you be willing to suggest another psychiatrist willing to undertake this.

Quirke met with the couple two weeks later. He heard them out sympathetically, as would any professional, but also as an individual with a personal interest in UFOs. It was his considered opinion that they hadn't experienced a collective hallucination (something that the Hills had considered). He also advised against hypnosis at this time, warning that it might prove traumatic. Better, he said, to let the memories gradually surface over time.

Earlier in the year – probably January – Barney discovered a nearly perfect ring of warts around his groin. More troubling, though, were the other problems that soon beset him. Stress associated with his work schedule increased, causing his ulcer to flare up again. His blood pressure levels rose, as did his intake of alcohol, with which he had had problems in the past. Physical separation from his sons, living in Philadelphia with their mother, added further aggravation. Eventually, one of his doctors suggested he seek psychological counsel and steered him to Dr. Duncan Stephens, in Exeter, New Hampshire. Barney began regular therapy with him in the summer of 1962, which would continue for a year. In the course of recounting his life experiences with Dr. Stephens, Barney inevitably raised the incident at Indian Head, but both he and the psychiatrist treated it as peripheral, rather than intrinsic, to his psychological stress.

Meanwhile, a series of isolated small events was underway that would ultimately culminate in the Hills becoming full-fledged UFO celebrities. On August 21, 1962, astronomer Webb appeared as a UFO guest on Boston's WBZ radio talk show, *Program PM*. By prior agreement, Webb had arranged for Barney Hill to call in anonymously to relate his sighting. But at Webb's urging, Barney omitted any mention of the entities seen through binoculars. This would appear to be the first public airing of the Hill case, apart from the summary NICAP had published in *The UFO Investigator* (January/February, 1962), which also treated the Hills anonymously.

On November 23, 1962, the Hills were invited to the home of their minister to meet with a small discussion group. Betty and Barney spoke of their experiences and stayed after the meeting ended to answer questions. Captain Ben Swett of Pease AFB, well known locally for his own active involvement with the use and study of hypnosis, was present on this occasion. On March 3, 1963, at the invitation of the Hills, Webb led a discussion on life in the Universe before their church's Couples Club, during which the Hills again related their UFO experiences. Webb cannot recall whether Swett was present at the meeting or not. Finally, on November 3, 1963, the Hills described their Indian Head experience (with Betty reading her account of her nightmares verbatim) to a meeting of the Two-State [Massachusetts/Rhode Island] UFO Study Group held in Quincy, Massachusetts. At the time, several New England states, New Hampshire and Vermont foremost, were reporting elevated numbers of UFO sightings, resulting in increased public interest in the subject.

After one of these semi-public presentations, probably the first or second church-related meeting, the Hills chatted with Swett, who unambiguously recommended they pursue hypnosis. Barney related the suggestion at his next session with Dr. Stephens, who sent him up the therapeutic ladder to Dr. Benjamin Simon in Boston, a highly regarded psychiatrist and neurologist practiced in the art of hypnosis.

Barney Hill Under Hypnosis

The Hills had their initial consultation with Dr. Simon on December 14, 1963, now more than two years after their original experience. A weekly schedule was agreed upon, with the Hills arriving at Simon's office at 8:00 a.m. on Saturdays. The first of these meetings took place on January 4, 1964, the last on June 27 of the same year. During the first three sessions, no attempt was made to regress the Hills to the night in question. Instead, Simon used this time to familiarize the Hills with the hypnotic process and to determine whether they would make good trance subjects. Both Hills proved to be excellent subjects, that is, capable of falling into what Simon referred to as the third, or somnambulistic, stage of hypnosis, the deepest of the three. In this stage, Simon said, "positive or negative hallucinations can be induced, and [any] post-hypnotic suggestions given…will be very effective." Simon also used these early sessions to establish and reinforce certain cue words that would facilitate the induction of the hypnotic trance in the future.

A probably over-theatrical sense of Simon's techniques can be gleaned from a brief scene filmed for the 1968 BBC-TV documentary *Flying Saucers and the People Who See Them*. The psychiatrist is shown on camera facing the Hills. In an onrushing staccato delivery, Simon says: "Now, Mr. and Mrs. Hill, fix your eyes on mine, fix them on mine, now clasp your hands in front of you, tight, tight, tight, tight, tight, tighter! As they get tighter, you're going to sleep, you're going into a deep, deep sleep. Your eyes are getting heavy, they're closing, they're closing tight. Now, your hands are relaxed. You will relax fully, relax fully, your head falls forward, now you're in a very deep sleep. We're going back, we're going back to September

19, 1961, when you were returning from your vacation, we're going back to September 19, 1961…" The next scene shows both Hills with heads drooped and eyes closed.

In his sessions with the Hills in 1964, however, Simon hypnotized them separately so as to avoid contamination. While one was in the inner sanctum of his office, the other would wait outside in the waiting room. In addition, at the end of each session, Betty or Barney would be given a post-hypnotic suggestion to forget what had just transpired. Because Barney was deemed most in need of therapy at this juncture, he was the first to be regressed to the night in question. As was his custom, Simon tape-recorded the session, which took place the morning of February 22, 1964. An edited transcript of this session constitutes Chapter Five of Fuller's *The Interrupted Journey*.

Simon had Barney begin his recall in Montreal, before they left for Portsmouth. In general, Barney's testimony under hypnosis matched what he had told Webb and other investigators under conscious recall. Different details inevitably arose, of course, as Simon was questioning from the viewpoint of a psychiatrist, not a UFO investigator. At one point, for example, Simon elicited some apprehension from Barney as to whether they would be allowed to rent a motel room in Canada because Barney was a Negro. He admitted it was of some concern.

In Colebrook, New Hampshire, they had to park and walk to a restaurant. "And everybody on the street passing us by is looking," Barney remembered. Inside the restaurant, "all eyes are upon us. And I see what I call the stereotype of the 'hoodlum.' And I immediately go on guard against any hostility." But the Hills were served without incident and continued south on Route 3. (They had also had no problem renting a room outside Montreal earlier in the trip.)

As consciously recalled, Barney remembered Betty drawing his attention to a light in the sky, which he believed to be an airplane, possibly a Piper Cub. He was somewhat put out by her insistence that it wasn't a plane. Simon asked if Betty believed in UFOs, and Barney replied, "Yes, Betty did believe in flying saucers." He then recounted that Betty's sister "said she had seen an object flying, long and cigar-shaped, and smaller objects coming to it and flying away from it" in 1957.

Stopping in the highway at Indian Head, Barney expressed being startled. "I want to wake up!" he demanded. Simon relaxed him and told him to continue. Barney told Simon that he was scared but trying not to show it for Betty's benefit. Then, sobbing, Barney screamed, "I gotta get a weapon!" Simon calmed Barney again, then asked if he thought he was about to be harmed. "Yes, I open the trunk of my car," Barney confided. "I get the tire wrench…part of the jack. And I get back in the car." In reality, Barney had fetched Betty's .22 pistol from the trunk. Taking the gun across the border had been a violation of Canadian law; consequently, the Hills and Fuller no doubt thought better about mentioning it in print.

Still, the episode raises troubling issues about relying on Fuller's *The Interrupted Journey* as some sort of *ur*-text, free of mistakes both of omission and commission. We have already seen, for example, how, for reasons unknown, he left out an entire sentence in his reproduction of the letter Betty Hill originally wrote Major Keyhoe. This is not an attempt to disparage Fuller as a person or journalist, so much as to warn the reader that no written or recorded account of *anything* should be mistaken for the events themselves.

Reliving the first encounter

As recalled consciously, Barney remembered approaching the object on foot, binoculars in hand. Up close, he told Simon, the object looked like a big pancake with a huge row of windows, "only divided by struts – or structures that prevented it from being one solid window." Behind the windows, figures were staring back at Barney.

These figures are described almost exclusively in human terms by Barney, both consciously and while hypnotized. One, who looked friendly, had a "round face," Barney told Simon. "I think of…a red-headed Irishman. I don't know why." Yet the one who would become perceived as the leader, Barney said, had an "evil face…He looks like a German Nazi. He's a Nazi…" Barney described him as wearing a uniform with a "black, shiny jacket" and having a black scarf draped across one shoulder.

Barney also heard the leader telling him not to be afraid, without moving his lips. "Stay there," he instructed Barney, "and keep looking. Just keep *looking* – and stay there. And just keep looking. Just keep looking." Simon asked how he knew this, did he hear it, feel it? "I *know*," Barney said, adding agitatedly, "It's pounding in my head!" Then he literally screamed, "I gotta get away! I gotta get away from here!"

Simon calmed him down and asked, "How can you be sure he was telling you this?" Barney answered, "His *eyes*! His *eyes*. I've never seen eyes like that before." Earlier, Barney had told Simon that leader's eyes were slanted, but not like those of a Chinese person. He tried to describe their appearance in more detail, then asked if he could draw them. Simon assented and the sketch of the leader Barney subsequently produced, along with several others, appeared in Fuller's *The Interrupted Journey*.

In his testimony, Barney had now returned to the car and was driving away from Indian Head on Route 3, but the leader's eyes wouldn't leave him. "Oh, those eyes!" Barney cried again. "They're in my *brain!*" He pleaded, "*Please* can't I wake up?" But Simon soothed his growing anxiety and asked him to continue. Although some of the particular details mentioned above had emerged only under hypnosis, Barney's general outline of events to this point in time was consistent with what he had consciously remembered. Now he was to enter totally into *terra incognita* – the so-called "missing time" portion of their trip. This is all new country, not previously recollected by either Betty or Barney.

The eye motif, or experience, continued to predominate in Barney's account. As the car rounded a curve, red/orange lights were seen, along with a line of men blocking the road. Barney feared they were going to be robbed. "Oh – oh, the eyes are there," he told Simon. "Always the eyes are there. And they're telling me I don't have to be afraid." Simon asked about the men in the road. "They won't talk to me," Barney said. "Only the eyes are talking to me. I – I – I – I don't understand that. Oh – the eyes don't have a body. They're just eyes." He talked to himself, as if trying to make sense of the scene he was seeing, and eventually explained, "*I* know what it is. It's a wildcat. A wildcat up a tree. No. No. I know what it is. It's the Cheshire cat in *Alice in Wonderland*. Ah, I don't have to be afraid of that. It disappeared, too, and only the eyes remained. That's all right. I'm not afraid."

Simon asked if the eyes belonged to the leader, and Barney answered, "I don't even see the leader…All I see are these eyes…They're just *there*. They're just up close to me, pressing against my eyes…" Asked a series of questions about where the men and the vehicle were now, where he is – in or out of the car? – Barney could only respond that he's floating somewhere, neither here nor there…just floating.

"You wish you had gone with them?" Simon asked.

Barney replied pensively, pausing between sentences. "Yes. Oh, what an experience to go to some distant planet. Maybe this will prove the existence of God. Isn't that funny? To look for the existence of God on another planet?" He seemed to address Betty for a moment, then said, "Well – it looks as if we're getting into Portsmouth a little later than I expected…" Barney's voice trailed off at this point and Simon opted to bring him out of the trance, telling him that he will feel fine and will remember nothing of what has just transpired. Barney's first impulse was to reach for a cigarette.

First reactions

After the Hills left, Simon returned to his recorder and dictated the following remarks to himself:

> During the explosive part of the patient's discussion, he showed very emotional discharges. Tears rolled down his cheeks, he would clutch his face, his head, and writhe in considerable agony. When he first described the eyes, he drew circles in the air which were in the shape of the eye that he ultimately drew. He actually drew a curve representing the left side of the face, and drew the left eye on it, without any other detail. When asked which eye this was, he showed some confusion. Then he drew the rest of the shape of the head, and also drew in the other eye and the cap and the visor. And then, as an afterthought, he drew in the scarf. Mrs. Hill was induced by post-hypnotic suggestion in anticipation of the time when she will be interviewed. She was in the waiting room for the entire period.

It's worth noting here that only 12 days prior to Barney's first hypnosis session, an alien being had been portrayed on the TV program, *The Outer Limits*. As first noted by skeptic Martin Kottmeyer, the episode in question, "The Bellero Shield" – itself a retelling of Shakespeare's *Macbeth* in modern garb – featured a glowing entity with strangely slanted eyes from the planet Bifrost. One of the characters asked the alien if it could read her mind, to which it responded that it could not: "I cannot even understand your language. I analyse your eyes. In all the universes, in all the unities beyond all the universes, all who have eyes, have eyes that speak." While Betty Hill has maintained on several occasions that she and Barney didn't watch *The Outer Limits*, this does not absolutely preclude the possibility that Barney may have seen it, or the relevant part of it.

When they returned to Dr. Simon's office the following Saturday (February 29), Barney assumed that it would be Betty's turn to undergo hypnosis. Simon began, however, by asking Barney how he'd been, what he remembered from the previous session. "I remembered 'eyes,'" Barney replied. "And I thought these 'eyes' were telling me something. And I became alarmed because I thought my very sanity was in jeopardy."

Simon made small talk before returning to an issue that clearly interested him. "But tell me – what do you think about this 'eye' business," he inquired. "What do you think of? Does it connect up with anything? Does it suggest any thoughts to you?"

Barney: "No, it doesn't. Well, yes – I might say the only connection it does have is a foreboding type of effect. Of betraying. Of having been given a warning. This is the only kind of effect it has on me."

Simon, a question or two later: "Do you recall the eyes as part of the session we had? Or was it something that just hung over with you?"

Barney: "The eyes just seemed to hang over from that."

Simon now hypnotized Barney again. "You will go back a bit, *before* you had the experience with the eyes," he intoned. Barney picked up at the point, also consciously recalled, at which they had stopped to walk the dog and bring the binoculars to bear on the distant object. His testimony under hypnosis here closely paralleled what he had previously told Webb and other investigators. Eventually, he went into more detail about what had happened at the second encounter site, where they were allegedly taken aboard the object they had seen earlier.

For reasons unknown to him, Barney had turned left (east) off Route 3, and soon found himself lost on a small road deeply bordered on both sides by woods. As he rounded a curve, a group of men signaled him to stop. (He described a cluster of six.) He thought there might have been an accident (the scene was brightly lit), but nonetheless reassured himself by reaching out to touch the pistol on the seat beside him. He had the feeling, though, that if he didn't use it, he wouldn't be harmed.

Three of the men came up to his side of the car and assisted him out. It's difficult to determine what state of consciousness Barney believed himself to be in at this point. In the earlier session of hypnosis, he spoke of "floating." Now, he told Simon that his eyes were tightly closed and that he felt "disassociated…I am there – and I am not there." He also was unaware of what was happening to Betty at this time. He had the vague sensation of being dragged through the woods – he could feel the tops of his shoes scraping along the ground – then up a ramp. When he did finally open his eyes, he was lying on his back on a table inside what looked to be "a hospital operating room. It was pale blue. Sky blue." And then he closed his eyes again. Shortly, he felt a cold sensation around his groin, as if someone were putting a cup around it. Next, he was walking, being guided through the woods to the car. Its lights were off, as was the motor. Delsey the dog was underneath the front seat. Betty came down the road to the car and they grinned at each other. "We both seem so elated and we are really happy," Barney remembered. "And I'm thinking it isn't too bad. How funny. I had no reason to fear."

Sitting in the car, they watched the object – looking like the Moon – depart. "It was a bright, huge ball," Barney said. "Orange. It was a beautiful, bright ball. And it was going. And it was gone."

Given Betty's loquacious description of events inside the object to follow, Barney's account can be viewed as almost vague in comparison. Even so, it transpired that quite a bit more allegedly happened to Barney in the examination room than Fuller reported in *The Interrupted Journey*. Barney no doubt felt that it was too personal to appear in such a public format, and so Fuller apparently agreed to omit the material, just as he had earlier turned the pistol into a tire tool. To find out what else Barney said transpired in the ship, we have to turn to the following brief paragraph, taken from Walter Webb's second, 1965 NICAP report:

"He felt a cup-like device placed around his genitals and believed a sperm specimen was somehow withdrawn. His left arm was scraped for skin cells, and his ears and throat were checked. He was rolled over on his stomach. A cylindrical object was inserted up the rectum, and once again the witness believed something was extracted."

All of this, it goes without saying, was remembered only under hypnosis. But because Fuller omitted Barney's recounting of it, we can safely assume that, out of comity, he omitted any thoughts regarding these extraordinary events that Dr. Simon may have dictated to himself as well.

It's also worth noting that, during his hypnosis sessions with Dr. Simon, the circle of warts around Barney's groin became inflamed and he had them removed by electrolysis. Neither Simon nor the skin specialist Barney consulted seemed particularly concerned about the warts, though they nagged Barney as a possible confirmation of events as recalled under hypnosis.

Betty Hill Under Hypnosis

According to Fuller, Dr. Simon first placed Betty Hill under hypnosis on March 7, 1962, although we know this date to be wrong. Earlier in *The Interrupted Journey* he had the Hills arriving at Simon's office, and Barney subsequently being hypnotized, on February 22, 1962. The correct year for both of these events was 1964.

As he had done with Barney, Simon regressed Betty to a time prior to their alleged encounter with the first UFO. She, too, recalled their search for a motel outside Montreal. She also recalled a waitress at a small drive-in restaurant speaking to her in French, Betty responding that she didn't understand French, but the waitress nonetheless telling her "she was sure I was French."

They were now south of Lancaster. Betty told Simon that the Moon is not quite full, "but very bright and large…There was a star down below the Moon, on the lower left-hand side…[and then] a bigger star up over this one. And it hadn't been there."

For the most part, Betty's recall up to this point paralleled what she and Barney remembered consciously. They pulled over to the side of the road, to exercise the dog and examine this second "star" through binoculars. Now a new element emerged. "It was moving fast," Betty says, "but it went in front of the Moon, and I saw it. I saw it travel across the whole face of the Moon, and it was odd shaped. And it was flashing all different colored lights." (This Moon-transiting aspect of the sighting was not consciously recalled, or at least not previously mentioned.)

Betty was asked by Simon to elaborate on the object's shape. Was it anything like a plane's?

"No," Betty answered. "Not like a plane. All I could think of, like a cigar…It was long, and there weren't any wings…It was just like holding a cigar up in front of the Moon, with all these lights flashing around it."

Barney looked through the binoculars, too, re-entered the car, and told Betty, "They've seen us, and they're coming this way." She laughed and asked him if he had "watched *Twilight Zone* on TV," but Barney didn't say anything.

Simon: "Why did you mention *Twilight Zone*?"

Betty: "Because the idea was fantastic."

Simon: "Had there been anything like this on *Twilight Zone*?"

Betty: "I don't know. I never see *Twilight Zone*. But I had heard people talk about this program, and I was always under the impression that it was a way-out type of thing. And so when he said that they had seen us, and that they were swinging around and coming in our direction, I thought his imagination was being overactive."

Simon asked Betty to describe the motion of the cigar-shaped object, and she verbally recreated the diagram portrayed in her original letter to Major Keyhoe. "It would go along straight, and then it would suddenly go up straight," she said. "And then it would flatten horizontally. And it would it would drop straight down. This seemed to be the overall pattern. It wasn't done in an exactly precise way. It would jerk out. It would flatten out." Meanwhile, Betty added, "it gave the appearance of spinning all the time."

Betty described much stop-and-go driving, with references to local landmarks like Cannon Mountain, the Old Man of the Mountain, The Flume, and Indian Head. She felt that "something is going to happen" – she wasn't aware of what – and hoped she wouldn't "be too afraid when it does." As consciously related, she reported a small motel on one side of the road and the belief that it could all end here and now: "All we have to do is drive in here, and this object will go away."

But she said nothing, and Barney drove on.

Instead, just south of Indian Head, they stopped in the middle of the highway at Betty's urging. They took turns looking at the object through binoculars, Barney opining that it was a plane or something, Betty asking if he'd ever seen a plane with two red lights before. Finally, he exited the car, binoculars in hand, and moved away, walking toward the object.

As he moved further away, Betty began screaming. "Barney! You damn fool, get back here!" She called for him to return several times and was just about to leave the car in pursuit, when he came running back in a panic. "He was saying they were going to capture us," Betty said. "We had to get the hell out of there." He re-entered the car and sped away. "Look out! Look out!" he shouted. "You can see them. They're right overhead." Betty rolled down her window and stuck her head out, but could see nothing above them. "I couldn't see the light. I couldn't even see the sky. I couldn't see anything."

Now she heard the repeating beeping sounds, described as "some kind of electrical signal," and felt the car subtly vibrating. An anticipated electrical shock never materialized.

Simon asked her what happened next. As with Barney, Betty seemed to have a difficult time moving beyond the beeping noise to the next sequence of events. Her breathing deepened and Simon had to coax her to continue. At this point she began sobbing.

Betty told Simon that they've been driving along – exactly where or how long she doesn't remember – when she suddenly saw the men in the road, and cried: "I've never been so afraid in my life before!"

Simon continued to soothe her. "It's all right now...You're safe here. Tell me about the men in the road."

The abduction remembered

Betty recalled Barney making a "sharp left-hand turn off the highway," another sharp curve, and then "men standing in the highway." Barney stopped the car and the motor died. He tried restarting it, but it wouldn't fire up. Through sobs, Betty said the men split into two groups and approached the car, one group coming to her side, the other group to Barney's side. They appeared to be dressed in uniforms, but not of a kind she could readily identify. She thought of fleeing into the woods but then found herself in some sort of somnambulistic state, struggling to wake up.

When she finally forced her eyes open, the men were escorting her and Barney through the woods. Barney, who was behind her, appeared to be walking in his sleep. Several times she called to him to wake up but received no response. One of the men walking beside her asked her if Barney was his name. He was the only one who spoke to her at this point, in accented English, and would appear to be the same figure she referred to in her dreams as the "leader." "Don't be afraid," he assured her. "You don't have any reason to be afraid. We're not going to harm you, but we just want to do some tests. When the tests are over with, we'll take you and Barney back and put you in your car. You'll be on your way back home in no time."

The Hills were led into a clearing, where what Betty believed was the object they'd seen earlier was now sitting on the ground in darkness. They were taken up a ramp and into it. Barney was led away to another room. When Betty protested, she was told that they only have enough equipment in one room to examine one person at a time. "If we took you both in the same room, it would take too long," the leader said.

Another man she hadn't seen before, whom she referred to alternately as the "doctor," or "examiner," came into the room. She sat on a stool in a corner. They pushed up the sleeve of her blue dress and examined her arm. Then they brought some sort of machine over – "something like a microscope...with a big lens" – that gave her the impression that they "were taking a picture of my skin."

Using something resembling a letter opener, the two took a skin scraping from her arm. The one who had led her through the woods placed the sample on a piece of cellophane or plastic, and then put it in a drawer. While these procedures unfolded, the two sometimes spoke in English, at other times in a language Betty could not understand. The examination continued. The doctor looked in her eyes with a light, then opened her mouth and examined her throat and teeth. Using something like a Q-tip, he took a sample out of her left ear, and, as before, the leader prepared it and placed it in the top drawer. A hair cutting was taken and treated in the same fashion. The doctor felt her neck, behind her ears, then down her back and shoulders. "They look my hands all over," Betty said. Then a scraping was taken underneath a fingernail, and the nail itself clipped. These samples joined the others in the drawer. Her feet were next examined by hand. "And then the doctor," she added, "the examiner says he wants to do some tests, he wants to check my nervous system."

The doctor unzipped her dress and she slipped out of it. Betty lay down on a nearby table on her back, and the doctor approached with another instrument, one she could only describe as "a whole cluster of needles, and each needle has a wire going from it..." The needles were applied to different points on her body, just touching and not causing any pain. She was rolled over on her stomach and the procedure repeated. When she was turned on her back again, the doctor was holding a long needle, "bigger than any needle I've ever seen." Betty asked what he intended to do with it, and he explained that it was a simple test, he just wanted to put it in her navel.

Unlike the previous needles, this one caused considerable pain, and Betty began screaming for the examiner to take it out. The leader approached, ran his hand in front of Betty's eyes, and told her that she wouldn't feel it. And indeed, the pain disappeared. Betty still wanted to know why they put the needle in her navel. The leader informed her that it was a pregnancy test. Simon asked Betty point-blank if they made any sexual advances to her at this stage, but Betty answered that they didn't. Simon, no doubt feeling he had gone far enough for the first session, brought Betty out of hypnosis, assuring her that she would feel fine and would remember nothing of what she had just said.

After the Hills left for the day, Simon again dictated notes to himself:

> This interview went on rather smoothly until the areas of fear in the latter part of the sighting of the flying object, when she began to show marked disturbances. Tears were running down her cheeks; she squirmed in her chair. The same occurred with very marked agitation during the procedure that seemed to be taking place in the strange object. During the apparent medical examination, tears were running down Mrs. Hill's cheeks, her nose was running. Although she accepted a Kleenex quite readily, it was felt best to stop at this point, even though she was still in the 'operating room,' because of the degree of agitation which ensued. Both were given appointments to return a week from today.

At their next session, prior to inducing hypnosis, Simon chatted casually with Betty, who said she'd had two nightmares since their last meeting. She couldn't remember anything more about the first one other than it involved "water, a lake, I think, and a shoreline." The second involved a small light that bounced toward her and then away, and which she was fearful was about to touch her. She couldn't remember if she actually screamed or not, but she did tell Simon that she woke up and then woke Barney up.

"You deliberately woke him up," Simon asked, to which Betty answered yes.

Misunderstanding and confusion

Simon now hypnotized Betty and took up the questioning where he broke it off previously. Again, she described the pain of the needle in her navel and the leader making it go away. Simon inquired if there was a light in the room, and Betty said it was "brightly lighted," that there was something like a spotlight or desk light behind her left shoulder, maybe six inches in diameter.

The examination table she was lying on was white, or metal, but in any event, hard, "it wasn't soft in any way." The examiner handed Betty her shoes. She put them on and stepped down from the table. She slipped her dress on, and the examiner zipped it up in the back. Betty asked if she could return to the car now, but was told that Barney isn't ready yet. The examiner departed, leaving Betty alone in the room with the leader. As in her dreams, she asked him for proof; he in turn asked what she would like, and she pointed to a large book, which he handed her.

Under hypnosis, Betty described the book as in a language she couldn't understand, adding that the writing went up and down instead of across. Speaking of the writing, she said it "had sharp lines...some were very thin and some were medium and some were very heavy. It had some dots. It had straight lines and curved lines."

Again, as in her dreams, Betty asked the leader where he was from and he eventually responded by approaching a wall of the room. In her dream, the leader pulled down the map in a way that make one think of an old roll-up window shade or slide screen. In her hypnotic narrative, there is an opening in the metal of the wall from which he retrieved the map. The latter looked much as Betty had dreamed – different-sized dots connected by various kinds of lines, and so on. Before, however, only "expedition" lines were mentioned; now the leader talked of trade routes (indicated by heavy lines), places only occasionally visited (solid lines), and expeditions (broken lines).

The leader asked if she knew where she was on the map, and when Betty answered no, he said, well, then, I can't tell you where I'm from! As dreamed, this was said somewhat sarcastically, and then the leader snapped the map back into place. As recounted by Betty under hypnosis, the leader was a somewhat more congenial figure. He allowed the map to roll itself up before replacing it in its wall opening. Betty asked to see it again, but the leader merely laughed.

She continued to look through the book, but suddenly there was a commotion in the hall. A group of men, the examiner included, entered the room, and the examiner asked Betty to open her mouth. He tugged at her teeth, wondering why they didn't come out as Barney's did. It was Betty's turn to laugh. Barney had dentures, she explained, but then found herself trying to explain how humans lost their teeth over time. She was asked what "age" and "year" meant, and attempted to demonstrate time by showing the leader her wristwatch, but was unsuccessful.

A similar loop of misunderstanding arose when she tried to explain what humans eat. Vegetables…what were vegetables? Squash…what as squash? Yellow…what was yellow? In an attempt to point to an example of the latter, Betty looked around the room, but found it singularly colorless, and she wasn't wearing anything yellow herself.

Betty's frustration grew. She explained that she was "a very limited person," but that there were others who could answer the leader's questions and who would be happy to talk with him. She expressed concern that if he did come back, though, she wouldn't know where to meet him. The leader laughed. "Don't worry," he said, "if we decide to come back, we will be able to find you all right. We always find those we want to." Asked what he meant by that last remark, the leader only laughed again.

At that moment, Barney was brought back along the hallway, a man on either side, his eyes still shut tight. "He missed an awful lot," Betty laughed to Simon. Here Betty's testimony closely followed her dream account. The men had a huddled conversation, and the leader eventually retrieved the book he had given Betty, an act that made her furious. "I won't forget about it!" she protested. She's told it will be better if she does forget, and that "Barney won't remember a single thing." In any event, should she remember anything, Barney was "going to remember it differently from you…all you are going to do is get each other so confused you will not know what to do."

They are led back along the path in the woods to their Chevrolet. "Why don't you stand by the side of the car," the leader suggested, "and watch us leave?" Barney and Delsey are already in the Bel Air when Betty arrived on her own. "Barney is still in a fog, but his eyes are open, and he is acting more normally now," Betty said.

Going home

As they watched, "it starts glowing…getting brighter and brighter," according to Betty. It was "a big orange ball, and it is glowing, glowing, rolling just like a ball." Then it shot quickly out of sight. As they drove away, Betty challenged Barney: "Now, try to tell me that you don't believe in flying saucers."

"Oh, don't be ridiculous!" he answered.

Betty thought he was joking, but then the beeping noise was heard again. "Well," she said, "I guess that is their farewell."

Simon was curious as to whether Betty and Barney discussed events aboard the object between the two of them. "Your memory is sharp now," he asserted. "Did you at some time tell Barney about your experience. About being in the vehicle?" No, she answered. "And he didn't speak to you about being in the vehicle?" Simon continued. "I can't remember any time he mentioned being inside of it," she replied. Betty explained her own reluctance to raise the issue by saying she "wanted to please the leader, because he told me to forget about it." And Barney? "They had done something that made him keep his eyes shut...Maybe it was the fear of remembering it, too."

Simon continued to question Betty about events up to and after their return home, but the details are largely lost in Fuller's summary gloss. Simon dismissed Betty, and Barney was brought in to crosscheck some of her testimony. Following the roadblock capture, he spoke of being told to keep his eyes shut but was uncertain of how he was so told. "That was what I couldn't understand," he said on at least two occasions. He did believe, though, that the same voice speaking to him now was the one (that of the "leader") first heard near Indian Head.

Inside the object, Barney was led along a corridor to a room with an examining table, which his feet overlapped. His shoes were removed. "They looked at my back," he said, "and I could feel them touching my skin right down my back. As if they were counting my spinal column." Turned over, his mouth was examined (although he says nothing about his dentures being extracted), and he felt something scratch "very lightly, like a stick, against my left arm."

Barney was soon reunited with Betty at the car, where they watched the object leave. Asked if either discussed with the other their experiences aboard the object, Barney maintained that they did not. "Why not?" asked Simon. "I didn't remember it," responded Barney.

Simon: "I see. This memory had just been wiped out? Do you think that she had seen the vehicle?"

Barney: "I didn't know."

Simon: "And you don't know it today?"

Barney: "No."

Simon: "All right, then. We'll stop there."

Simon Seeks Explanations

In subsequent meetings at his office, Simon would continue to induce hypnosis in the Hills, but with a shift in emphasis and his own interests. The abbreviated transcripts contained in *The Interrupted Journey* indicate that he is no longer so concerned in detailing events during the so-called period of "missing time" (a phrase that would go on to become the title of Budd Hopkins's first book on the abduction phenomenon, published in 1981). Simon was now in search of possible causes, issues of contamination (i.e., Betty's dreams), internal inconsistencies in a narrative he could not accept as literal reality, and, of course, the mental welfare of his patients.

In his own writings on the case and in interviews with Walter Webb, Simon conceded that the original encounter with a UFO probably occurred more or less as the Hills described, although he attributed the UFO to some sort of terrestrial craft, possibly of a classified military nature. At the same time, he could not bring himself to sign off on the reported abduction aspect of their experience. According to Webb, he "proved to be so skeptical of the spaceship hypothesis that he refused to read the literature and sightings reports I made available to him on the subject." In one conversation with Webb, Simon even referred to alien abduction as a "supernatural" hypothesis. But, in any event, Simon was a therapist from the beginning, not an investigator of UFO incidents.

He asked Barney, under hypnosis, if Betty talked in her sleep, to which he answered no. Did she tell him the content of her dreams directly? Barney said yes, but then corrected himself, explaining that she would usually be talking to someone else, such as when they were interviewed by Walter Webb. (We have also seen that Betty discussed her dreams publicly in Barney's presence at least once, possibly more often, before undergoing hypnosis.)

Simon: "Now all this dream about being taken aboard – and all the details about it, this was all told to you by Betty, wasn't it?"

Barney: "No. Betty never told me. Only about my teeth."

Simon asked him how he knew what had happened aboard the craft. "I was hypnotized by Dr. Simon," Barney responded. "He made me go back to September 19, 1961, when I left Montreal, and I told him what was happening to me each time he asked…"

Continuing to probe, Simon again asked how much information he might have absorbed from Betty's dreams, but Barney was adamant. "I never believed her dreams," anyway, he explained.

"If you don't believe her dreams," Simon wanted to know, "why do you believe yours?" Barney says that he "never dreamed about UFOs until last Sunday…I had them on Sunday night and on Tuesday night and on Wednesday night. And this is the first time I have ever dreamed of UFOs."

Earlier, Barney had told Simon of feeling disassociated when he saw the UFO, and Simon now asked him to elaborate. It was as if "I had my body moving, and yet my thinking was separate from it," Barney explained, "I had never felt like this before in my life." And he never felt that way again, he added, until he was hypnotized in Simon's office and the psychiatrist made a "doggie" appear in the room (as a way of testing the depth of Barney's trance).

"This was an hallucination then, was it?" wondered Simon. Barney agreed. "Then how about this story of being kidnapped. Couldn't that have been an hallucination, too?" To which Barney answered: "I wish I could think it was an hallucination."

What about the communication with the leader, Simon asked, what language did he use? "He did not speak by word," Barney said, "I was told what to do by his thoughts making my thoughts understand." When Barney was asked if it was like mental telepathy, he had to have the term explained to him. He again spoke of having "these eyes" in his head. Simon brought him out of hypnosis here, telling him that he will begin to consciously remember more and more of what he has been recalling under hypnosis. (Simon was even more explicit at the end of his next session with Barney, saying, "Well, we'll hope that you will open up more and more about that as to what you were doing as those things begin coming back, as there comes a point where there's no gain in constantly repeating a thing in the hypnosis until we can bring it into consciousness. We want to get it into consciousness to the extent that you can tolerate it, without any anxiety, and this will come." This had been Simon's therapy plan all along, of course, not the investigation of a UFO sighting.

Dreaming and not dreaming

Betty was hypnotized again, and again Simon homed in on her dreams, whom she told them to, when, and whether Barney was present. It emerged that Betty told her dreams to her sister, Janet, and her supervisor at work. It was the latter who suggested that the dream events must have actually happened to Betty, "because if [they] had not happened, then you wouldn't be acting this way."

"Didn't all these things that you feel happened – didn't they happen in your dreams? Couldn't this *all* have been in your dreams?" Simon persisted. Betty answered with an adamant "No," and, when Simon asked why she was so sure, she said "because of the discrepancies." In her dreams, she noted, she walked up steps into the craft, "here [under hypnosis], I didn't walk up steps. I walked up a ramp." In the same context, Betty raised the issue of the map, saying, "If I could draw, I could draw the map." She seemed uncomfortable attempting it this very moment, though, so Simon suggested she do it at her leisure; which she eventually did.

Simon asked Betty how she could account for the fact that the men could speak to her in English and yet not know about such things as dentures and aging. "Maybe they've been studying us," she suggested. "But in a dream," Simon insisted, "this could all happen. Things don't have to be explained in a dream. Did you feel that they could communicate with you in any other way than words? Were they able to transfer thoughts?" Obviously, Simon's interest here was why Barney seemed to report one mode of communication with the men, and Betty another. "I don't know about thoughts," Betty admitted.

As was his custom, after the Hills left, Simon dictated a few brief notes to himself:

> There seem to be indications that a great deal of the experience was absorbed by Barney Hill from Betty, in spite of his insistence that this was his own. And there are definite indications that her dreams had been suggested as a reality by her supervisor. The implications are self-evident, and it is planned now to continue these interviews at a more conscious level. Both of them appear to have been remembering more now after the sessions.

Simon now interviewed the Hills without the use of hypnosis, replaying portions of testimony recovered under same in their presence. From his own dictated notes:

> The first interview with Mr. Hill was now played back to Mr. and Mrs. Hill together and carried to the point of the sighting and the outburst of extreme anxiety that Mr. Hill had. He showed considerable distress at this, but seemed to manage it quite well. And as it proceeded, he took out a piece of paper and began to draw. In this drawing, he sketched out again a head, with some very staring eyes, of almond shape, but not slanted. At the end of this, he seemed to very well composed and wished to be assured of its fantasy nature. Both wish to continue in this fashion, and a date was set a week from today to continue the playback of the hypnotic sessions. It is of interest when the playback was begun and the cue word was used, Mrs. Hill went into a trance. Both were then intentionally put into another trance and were told that they would not respond to the cue word when they heard it on the playback, but only when it came directly from me.

In other words, both Betty and Barney Hill were excellent, deep-trance hypnotic subjects. When asked point-blank if such were the case in a BBC-TV documentary aired in 1969, Simon responded, "They are, they hypnotize very easily, they show spontaneous amnesia, and could be taken back in time."

"Regarding the second encounter (the abduction story), he [Simon] believes it happened only in Betty Hill's dreams," Webb wrote in his NICAP report, "and that Barney, upon hearing his wife tell about her dreams repeatedly, finally felt he must have been abducted, too. A kidnapping by space beings, in the psychiatrist's opinion, has all the earmarks of a nightmare – its bizarre nature, inconsistencies, etc. And a detailed dream can occur in a flash."

Since Fuller failed to provide complete transcripts of the Simon-Hills sessions, we have to look elsewhere for a candid assessment of Simon's feelings as to what other psychological and interpersonal factors may have been at play here. For example, we have no way of knowing whether Fuller's summary of Simon's dictated notes represent the whole of the latter's thoughts on the subject, or whether they have been condensed and edited to better accommodate Fuller's own view of the phenomenon and the story at hand. Regardless of where they originally manifested, though, we have the following comments as related by Webb, based on his own interviews with Simon.

Labeled "Confidential," they appear in his second NICAP report as follows: "To understand why Dr. Simon selected this hypothesis, one must see into the personalities of Betty and Barney Hill. In some respects, they are completely contrasting types. Betty is dominating and possessive. Barney is passive, highly suggestible, and full of repressed anxieties and fears. She is white and he is Negro. Both are the products of previous marriages…"

Another previously confidential Webb paragraph is also worth repeating:

> Dr. Simon found examples of sexual symbolism in the witnesses' stories under hypnosis. The obsession with the eyes of the figures and the needle penetrating the navel were such symbols. Barney's description of a genital-rectal examination and his inspection of the area after the UFO sighting indicated to Dr. Simon latent homosexual feelings, a fear of attack on the genitals. Dr. Simon emphasized that dreams are expressions of unconscious conflicts and wish fulfillments.

Webb himself was more accepting of the possibility that, if the first encounter had to be taken seriously, so did the second one. Moreover, "regarding the Hills' hypnoanalysis," he wrote in the same report, "I am not particularly impressed by sexual symbols as employed in modern psychiatry. Almost anything can be described as a sex symbol, as Vance Packard has pointed out, and, in my view, such symbols are frequently used to excess in psychoanalysis."

By the summer of 1964, Simon's treatment of the Hills was drawing to a close. Since early April, when he first began replaying the Hills' hypnotic sessions back to them, Simon rarely resorted to hypnosis. Instead, the meetings centered on listening to the tapes and discussing the issues and contradictions they raised. Initially, Betty and Barney's anxieties increased as they heard what they had said, then subsided over time.

As Fuller put it, "By June everyone recognized that there would be no full conclusion, either to the therapy or the incident which played so big a part in it. Both the doctor and the Hills regretted that it would be impractical to continue into deeper therapy over the long period of time that would be necessary." Simon left himself open to further consultations, if the Hills felt in need of them, but thought they had reached "a good stopping place, at least for the time. More important was the Hills' awareness that they were feeling much better – and less disturbed, even though everything had not been completely resolved."

Epilogue

And there the matter might have rested – a largely private affair between patients and doctor – but for events again beyond the Hills' control.

Although the Hills disagreed with Dr. Simon's conclusions, they were of a similar opinion – that the hypnosis sessions had successfully eased their discomfort and reduced internal tensions in both of them. At the same time, a transfer to the Portsmouth post office greatly relieved some of Barney's job-related stress. As work ended on October 25, 1965, however, someone approached Barney in the post office and handed him a copy of that day's *Boston Traveler*, with its front-page headline: "A UFO Chiller: Did THEY Seize Couple?"

An enterprising reporter by the name of John H. Luttrell had attended the November 1963 meeting of the Two-State UFO Study Group in Quincy, at which the Hills had discussed their experiences. Luttrell subsequently acquired an audiotape of the Hills' talk and later learned that they had been in therapy with Dr. Simon. Through an inside source – possibly Simon's secretary – Luttrell gained access to some of the tapes or transcripts of Simon's sessions with the Hills. Neither source could be considered in any sense a formal interview (indeed the Hills refused to speak to him), but Luttrell used them to put together his five-part series of *Traveler* articles. United Press International (UPI) also picked up the story the same day, turning the Hills into instant, if reluctant, "celebrities." They considered suing the reporter and his paper for violation of privacy but dropped the idea on legal advice.

Simon was in Washington attending professional meetings when the story came out, and his office called to tell him that "all hell had broken lose." The callers gave Simon a good impression of how the general public interpreted the articles. He described them as falling into four categories: The Despairing, The Mystics, The "Fellow Travelers," and The Sympathizers.

The Despairing were those people, Simon wrote, "who were apparently emotionally or mentally ill and who saw in hypnosis, as it was presented by the reporter, the magical solution to their problems." The Mystics were those interested in ESP, astrology, and so on, who saw their beliefs confirmed by hypnosis and the Hills' experiences, while Fellow Travelers were those who "knew the answers to the mysteries of life," which they also believed were confirmed by what the Hills had undergone. Sympathizers were those who called to support Simon for the way he had been dealt with in the articles, which had left the impression that some of the more "fantastic statements" in the articles came in some way from him.

As it turned out, another writer was also in the area, researching a series of summer UFO sightings centered around Exeter, New Hampshire. Eventually, *Saturday Review* columnist John G. Fuller wrote a long article about the sightings for *Look*, which he later expanded into the book *Incident at Exeter*. One of the people Fuller contacted in his travels was Conrad Quimby, publisher and editor of the Derry, New Hampshire, *News*. Quimby first told him of the Hills, whom Fuller subsequently sought to interview. Shortly after, the Boston paper made the Hills' story public.

Fuller wrote in the Foreword to his own book on the encounter that with their privacy destroyed, "the Hills felt that as long as the story had been released, the facts of the case should be carefully presented. [They] had sat on this story for nearly five years; they were not seeking publicity… The Hills asked me if I were interested in documenting the story with their co-operation."

Fuller agreed, and also secured the participation of Dr. Simon, who contributed an Introduction to the book. All three parties were to share in the profits, with 50 percent of the proceeds and of any sub-rights sales going to the Hills, 25 percent to Fuller, and 25 percent to Simon. *The Interrupted Journey: Two Lost Hours "Aboard a Flying Saucer,"* was published by Dial Press of New York in October of 1966. Bolstered by two excerpts that appeared in the popular *Look* magazine that month, the book became a national bestseller.

In 1975, the NBC network turned *Interrupted Journey* into a made-for-TV movie, titled *The UFO Incident*. James Earl Jones portrayed Barney Hill, and Estelle Parsons played Betty. In the United States it can still be seen as an occasional late night or early morning re-run.

No End to the UFOs

Within days of the publication of Luttrell's articles, in late October 1965, the Hills saw their second UFO. As recounted in Betty's *A Common Sense Approach to UFOs*, she and Barney were returning from her parents' home and had halted at a stop sign. "Directly in front of us, just above tree top level, there was a ufo using all red lights. It was flying back and forth as though it was trying to attract our attention. Then it looked as if it landed in a tree area."

It would not be the last UFO Betty Hill would report. On the evening of June 10, 1967, computer scientist and ufologist Jacques Vallée and his wife, Janine, found themselves standing around a chalk circle in an isolated field somewhere in New Hampshire. With them were John Fuller, Robert Hohmann, C.D. Jackson, Dr. Simon, and Betty and Barney Hill, among others. Hohmann, one of the early interviewers of the Hills, had convinced himself that Betty had become, in his words, a "transducer" while she was aboard the saucer – that is, that she was somehow able to communicate with the "humanoids." For her part, Betty believed that the alien leader could find her again, if and when he wanted to – in other words, that he knew where she lived. (This intimation seems to have gone back to at least November of 1961, when she and Barney made their first trip back to Indian Head in search of the capture site. Upon their fruitless return home, Betty wrote in *Common Sense*, they found a pile of dried leaves on the kitchen table. Clearing them away, she discovered the missing blue earrings she'd been wearing the night of their encounter.)

Not long before this gathering, Vallée noted, Betty had said something to the effect that "The Aliens ought to pay a little visit to Mrs. So-and-so," and a few weeks later, sure enough, a strange light was seen over her house. Everybody became convinced that the extraterrestrials were picking up on Betty's thoughts and acting on them. She claims to have seen a saucer at treetop level again, just the other day."

For the 10 days preceding the gathering at the chalk circle Betty had been directing mental messages at the aliens, asking them to return to the spot, so that those humans assembled might demonstrate their goodwill toward the aliens. In the event this exercise was successful, Hohmann wanted Betty to request a third visit, this time showing "their craft to millions of people." But no landing or other contact took place that hot, humid night. In a diary entry, Vallée noted that "artificial satellites crossed the sky, then a meteor and lots of lightning bugs: at every such incident Betty jumped up excitedly." On the other hand, he added, "if I had met a group of little aliens on a lonely road, and they had dragged me inside their craft, perhaps I would be as inclined as she was to see flying saucers everywhere."

Such meetings were an indirect consequence of the publicity surrounding their original experience. Following the appearance of Luttrell's articles, and again after Fuller's book was published, the Hills were bombarded with phone calls and letters from people reporting their own sightings and encounters. Not a few of these contained complaints about how their reports were treated by the handful of civilian UFO groups then in existence. Gradually, Betty used these contacts to establish what she referred to in her book as the "silent network," described thus: "We discuss our findings only with each other. We have no membership lists, no dues, no publications. We are unknown to the media, ufo organizations and the general public."

But Barney Hill would not long be a participant. On February 25, 1969, at the age of 46, he suffered a cerebral hemorrhage and died seven hours later. Vallée was not alone in noting that Barney was the more conservative of the two in his attitude to UFOs in general, and that Betty was clearly the couple's dominant partner. With his passing, Betty became ever more immersed in the phenomenon and her silent network. One of the latter's first objectives, she noted, was "to isolate areas where ufos come to in large numbers and on a fairly regular basis." Parked near such an area one night, Betty said that, "to my amazement, I counted 26 ufos come in and land in the field." On another occasion, "in all, thirteen came in, landed and pointed a white beam skyward. Then, all the beams went out." Moreover, according to Betty, "in a three year period of time, I filmed more than 200 different kinds of ufos. In my lectures, I showed 80 slides, not just ufos, but ufos doing different kinds of things. One slide shows 30 ufos ready to protect a craft that landed when a person tries to walk up to it."

Betty Hill was, indeed, now seeing flying saucers everywhere.

Betty Hill continued to be actively involved with the UFO subject for more than four decades following her original encounter. In 1995, she published *A Common Sense Approach to UFOs*, in part a retelling of the 1961 Indian Head experience and in part a catalogue of the hundreds of UFO sightings she subsequently reported. Although the book provided hardly any scientific or statistical evidence to support its claims, its author was anything but bashful about making sweeping assertions. For example: "UFOs do not fly around alone. They fly in squadrons of 100 or more. Most of them do not use any lights. They do not materialize or dematerialize. They turn their lights off and on. Most of them fly under 500 feet. When they leave, they travel at tremendous speeds. In this way they protect themselves. They are not offensive, but will protect themselves if forced to do so. No one walks up and knocks on the door."

She was also adamant about what constituted an actual abduction, even when such pronouncements clearly clashed with the accounts of other abductees. Claims of being taken aboard a UFO and physically examined against one's will were virtually unheard-of prior to Indian Head; in its highly publicized wake, however, thousands of such reports would eventually surface and seemingly continue to this day. The foremost proponents of UFO abductions over the years were New York abstract artist Budd Hopkins (*Missing Time, Intruders*), then Temple University historian David Jacobs (*Secret Life, The Threat*) and Pulitzer Prize-winning Harvard Medical School psychiatrist John Mack (*Abduction, Passport to the Cosmos*), all of whom relied heavily on regressive hypnosis in the absence of conclusive physical evidence.

But Betty Hill would buy none of it. "If the abduction is a real one," she wrote in *Common Sense*, "the person does not need hypnosis; for he will recall over a period of time his own experience. All he needs is patience.

"Real abductions do not result in therapy, as the person has very little stress or fears and views his abduction experience as a positive one. No one has ever been abducted more than once.

"When a person tells me he learned of his abduction through hypnosis, I suggest he go back to the one who gave him his problems in the beginning, and preferably, 'do not mention my name'."

Meanwhile, time marched on. Dr. Simon died on January 7, 1981. John Fuller passed away on November 7, 1990. "In September 1991, the thirtieth anniversary of my experience," Betty wrote in *Common Sense*, "I retired from public life. I did a flurry of TV programs, news, radio and interviews to announce my retirement." Betty Hill passed away at her Portsmouth, New Hampshire, home on Sunday October 17, 2004, after a years-long battle with cancer.

A Note On Sources

In order to achieve a free-flowing narrative, the editors and I agreed to forego footnotes in the above account. The thinking was to bring the reader up to speed, so that he or she could better assimilate the information and arguments contained in the other essays presented here. While scholarly citation certainly has its appropriate uses, our collective feeling was that citing every statement and quote in this particular presentation would distract readers from readily absorbing the story itself. Where feasible, then, general references have been woven directly into the account. As far as possible, I have tried to avoid any editorial commentary of my own.

Still, the reader is justified in wondering just where the above information originated, so a short note on sources seems in order. It goes without saying that the present author relied a great deal on journalist John G. Fuller's full-length account of the Hill case, *The Interrupted Journey: Two Lost Hours "Aboard a Flying Saucer,"* with an Introduction by Benjamin Simon, M.D. The book was a bestseller when it was published in 1966 by The Dial Press, N.Y. Over the years, however, it became known among the UFO community at large and others that Fuller was hardly an absolutely reliable narrator. Some alterations in actual events were made in agreement with the Hills themselves. During an early stage of the encounter, for example, Fuller has Barney pulling a tire tool out of the trunk; in reality, it was Betty's .22-caliber pistol that he fetched. In another instance, Fuller edited the letter Betty originally wrote Major Donald Keyhoe, omitting a key sentence about the Hills considering psychiatric assistance, presumably under the all-forgiving umbrella of "artistic license."

Astronomer Walter N. Webb's two published accounts of his early investigation of the case, conducted for the National Investigations Committee on Aerial Phenomena, also proved invaluable, as they are some of the earliest source material we have. These include a typed, six-page, single-spaced report submitted to NICAP on October 26, 1961 (*A Dramatic UFO Encounter in the White Mountains, N.H., September 19-20, 1961*), and a much longer follow-up (*A Dramatic UFO Encounter in the White Mountains, New Hampshire, The Hill Case – Sept. 19-20, 1961*) dated August 30, 1965. The latter included many original documents, including copies of the Hill-Keyhoe letter, the Air Force's report of their investigation of the Hills' sighting, sketches by Barney and Betty Hill (including the "star map" seen by Betty), and Betty's typed notes of her post-sighting dreams.

A succinct summary of the case and its surrounding controversy, along with a wealth of bibliographical references, can also be found in Jerome Clark's *The UFO Encyclopedia*, 2nd Edition, The Phenomenon from the Beginning, Volume 1: A-K ("Hill Abduction Case," pp. 489-504), Omnigraphics, Inc., Detroit, Michigan, 1998. Also consulted was Clark's own interview with Betty Hill, "Betty Hill: The Closest Encounter," published in *UFO Report* for January 1978. An intimate impression of the Hills can be found in the diaries of computer scientist and ufologist Jacques Vallée, published as *Forbidden Science: Journals 1957-1969*, North Atlantic Books, Berkeley, California, 1992, pp. 272-8.

Audio/visual material consulted include *Flying Saucers and the People Who See Them*, a 1968 BBC TV documentary, which included interviews with both the Hills and Dr. Simon, and "The Bellero Shield," a 1964 episode of *The Outer Limits*.

Betty Hill herself was interviewed at Indian Head, New Hampshire, during the course of the September 19-21, 2000, Symposium that resulted in this book. Some additional background material, or maybe the appropriate word is atmosphere, was provided by Betty Hill's self-published *A Common Sense Approach to UFOs* (Greenland, New Hampshire: 1995), although the latter is almost maddening in its glaring lack of reference to specific names and dates. The author also had access to an unpublished manuscript by Betty Hill's niece, Kathy Marden, "Memories of Betty and Barney Hill."

Any lapses in representation and interpretation of the above partial list of sources consulted and cited should be attributed to this author alone.

**Dennis Stacy** was editor of the MUFON *UFO Journal* for 12 years. Since 1994 he has co-edited and published the print edition of *The Anomalist*, an annual journal of mysterious phenomena. He was the co-editor (with Hilary Evans) of *UFOs 1947-1997: Fifty Years of Flying Saucers*, and co-author (with Patrick Huyghe) of the *Field Guide to UFOs*. He has contributed articles to such popular magazines and journals as *Omni, New Scientist, Smithsonian Air & Space, Fortean Times*, and *New Age Journal*. In 1995 he won the Donald E. Keyhoe Journalism Award for his six-part *Omni* series on UFOs and the U.S. government. Dennis Stacy lives and works in San Antonio, Texas.

CHAPTER TWO

Judging the Hill Case

Assessing anomalous phenomena always presents researchers with special difficulties. The Hill abduction case is no exception

MARCELLO TRUZZI

The year 1961 was an eventful one. It was perhaps most visibly marked by the unsuccessful U.S. invasion of Cuba's Bay of Pigs and the Soviets' construction of the Berlin Wall, but it was also a year with significant news about space flight. The newly inaugurated President John F. Kennedy promised to land humans on the Moon within a decade. On April 12, Yuri Gagarin became the first human to orbit the earth with a 1-hour 48-minute flight in the *Vostok 1*. He was soon followed with suborbital flights by U.S. astronauts Alan Shepard in *Freedom* 7 on May 5 and Virgil (Gus) Grissom on the *Liberty Bell* 7 on July 21. Soon thereafter, on August 6, Soviet cosmonaut Gherman Stepanovich Titov circled the Earth 17 times. And this was the year that the National Aeronautics and Space Administration Manned Spacecraft Center was established as NASA's mission control for space flights. These events, along with movie and television science fiction (in 1961 most notably, perhaps, the series *The Twilight Zone*) made outer space a salient subject for many Americans.

And Then There Were UFOs

In addition to the events of that year, the media steadily described many reports of what were initially called "flying saucers" in 1947, but which later became termed "unidentified flying objects" (UFOs). So by 1961, the general public had been exposed to 14 years of many mass media accounts of sightings and landings of reputedly extraterrestrial craft and even glimpses of and alleged encounters with their occupants.

The account of the alleged UFO abduction of Betty and Barney Hill on September 19-20 developed in this context, and much of the controversy around the case has been concerned with its possible cultural influences – especially from earlier science fiction films like 1953's *Invaders from Mars* and 1954's *Killers from Space*, which contained some motifs similar to those in the Hills' tale.

The Hills' story underwent numerous tellings and elaborations, and this adds to our problems in reconstruction. The first year saw the Hills interviewed (on September 21) by Major Paul W. Henderson, Betty's writing (on September 26) a letter to NICAP's Donald E. Keyhoe, their extensive interview (on October 21) by the National Investigations Committee on Aerial Phenomena (NICAP)'s Walter Webb, and then by C.D. Jackson and Robert E. Hohmann (on November 25). This was followed by about a year and a half of public silence until the Hills' gave further descriptions to a church discussion group on March 3, 1963, and to a Quincy UFO group on November 3, 1963. The tale broke into general public view in a five-part series by John H. Luttrell, Sr., published in the *Boston Traveler* (October 25-29, 1965). But its widespread distribution came from journalist John G. Fuller's 1966 book, *The Interrupted Journey: Two Lost Hours "Aboard a Flying Saucer,"* its excerption as a two-part article in *Look* magazine, and in the made-for-television movie adaptation, *The UFO Incident*, starring James Earl Jones and Estelle Parson and broadcast on October 20, 1975.

From the very beginning, advocates for the validity of UFOs considered the Hills' case particularly controversial, and there were strong differences of opinion about it between the main national UFO groups at that time. Since the Aerial Phenomena Research Organization (APRO) had previously accepted some "occupant" tales, this made the Hills' case seem feasible. However, NICAP was far more conservative and had generally rejected past (and largely discredited) "contactee" stories, which they feared the Hills' story resembled. Even the then nonconservative ufologist James Moseley said he feared that the Hill case "will discredit the whole UFO movement" (Moseley quoted in Klass, 1968: 227). As David M. Jacobs has noted: "The Hill case came to represent a line over which many researchers would not step. After years of struggle to build the scientific legitimacy of the UFO phenomenon, this extreme case threatened to bring down what little UFO researchers had accomplished. In effect, the Hill case became the test to show how tough-minded investigators could be. In order to move into the mainstream, they were keen to demonstrate that they would not automatically accept any claim no matter how credible the witnesses"

(Jacobs, 2000: 195). As Jerome Clark pungently notes, it became a battle between "ufologists" (those who sought a scientific approach to UFOs) and the less rigorous but more imaginative "saucerians," and: "Ufologists saw the contactee movement as consisting of little more than fraud and social pathology; its participants were, in ufologists' estimation, either crooked or crazy" (Clark, in Jacobs, 2000: 136).

The controversy continued, fueled by further alleged alien-abduction episodes, most notably the 1973 Charles Hickson-Calvin Parker case in Mississippi and the 1975 Travis Walton case in Arizona. And the 1980s saw a dramatic escalation following the publications in 1981 of *Missing Time* by artist Budd Hopkins and in 1994 of *Abduction: Human Encounters with Aliens* by Harvard psychiatrist John E. Mack. Historian David Jacobs, himself a major researcher and advocate for the abduction phenomenon, even felt confident enough, at least in retrospect, to write that "a new era had opened" and that "UFO research had turned away from object studies toward abduction analysis" (Jacobs, 2000: 204). In light of this changing climate within the UFO research community, the Hills' story, to many investigators, now no longer seemed either so unique or so incredible, and many have felt their case history warranted re-examination.

So, more than four decades after the original incident, the essays in this volume constitute a retrospective unpacking and re-evaluation of key events both during and surrounding (before and after) the Hills' remarkable narrative. Their tale has special significance for ufology, the would-be science of unidentified flying objects, for it not only involved a UFO sighting but introduced what would later become recurrent themes of alien abduction, physical examinations, "missing time," hypnotic recollection, and secondary evidence (in the Hills' case, a purported star map).

Although Barney Hill died of a cerebral hemorrhage on February 2, 1969, Betty Hill continued to be a vigorous, popular figure and frequent guest at ufology gatherings, working with other "abductees," and even self-published a book, *A Common Sense Approach to UFOs*, in 1995. She added further controversy to the case by reporting numerous other sightings, but after 1972 no further face-to-face encounters at what she described as a "landing area" in a rural spot near the small town of Kingston, about 20 miles southwest of Portsmouth, New Hampshire.

Evaluating the Hills' Story

The Hill case, like any new claim, may come into bolder relief if we first consider some pertinent background issues. These include such fundamental conceptual questions as:

(1) How important is it to avoid error?
(2) What sort of validation is to be sought?
(3) What is the role of parsimony?
(4) How do we judge the extraordinariness or "unreasonableness" of a claim?
(5) What constitutes legitimate evidence for the claim? And
(6) How demanding should we make the burden of proof?

Let us briefly consider each of these issues and how they relate to the Hills' case.

On the importance of avoiding of error
There are two fundamental types of human error that we need to avoid. Statisticians refer to them as a Type I versus a Type II error. A Type I error consists of thinking something special is happening when it is not. A Type II error consists of thinking nothing special is happening when it actually is. Usually, the more effort we make to avoid one type of error, the more open we may be to making the other type.

Conventional scientists predominantly want to avoid a Type I error. That is, they don't wish to accept the Hills' claims if they are invalid. On the other hand, many proponents of their story don't want to dismiss their claims if they happen to be true. Usually, we especially want to avoid a Type II error if the reality of the claim (though about a rare or infrequent phenomenon) is viewed as important. And that importance may come from quite nonscientific issues. For example, the fact that the CIA and the military showed interest in UFOs in the 1950s may have been quite unconnected with any supposed covert belief by them in aliens. The fact that anomalies were showing up on radar posed the threat that such strange blips might be mistaken for incoming enemy Soviet missiles that could erroneously start World War III. Thus, they were important in relation to issues of national security that had nothing to do with extraterrestrials. Many who are proponents of UFO claims may similarly view the reality of UFOs as philosophically or even theologically important, quite aside from their scientific relevance. John G. Fuller's reflection upon the Hills' episode exemplifies such a position when he concluded: "There are no final answers. Where one question existed before, several others have come up to take its place. But if it can even momentarily be speculated that the event is true, the far-reaching implications concerning the history of the world are obvious" (Fuller, 1966: 340).

To a large degree, I would suggest, the critics of and the advocates for the Hills' testimony are oppositely concerned about avoiding a Type I versus a Type II error. Critics most fear making a Type I error while proponents most fear making Type II. And for both groups, the desire to avoid one over the other form of error may be related to a wide variety of disciplinary and even personal reasons. Thus, an astronomer (such as the late Carl Sagan) seeking funding for trying to make radio contact with distant planets (SETI) might view as obstructive, if not competitive, some ufologists' argument that we don't need to go looking for alien intelligence "out there" if the aliens are already here.

Critics of the Hills' story view it as highly improbable (if not impossible), but I suspect many proponents may be less impressed by its improbability than by its significance should it still happen to be true. And such importance is largely related to the sort of prior theoretical and cultural outlook or cognitive schema the analyst brings with him or her when first entering the discussion. That in turn acts as a filter and searchlight for data that will be congruent with that schema. So, for example, if you are inclined to accept their story, you may notice something like the Hills' early mention of "missing time" when they were interviewed by Webb (which he ignored), and if you are inclined to be dismissive you will be more likely to notice that Barney's earliest comments suggest there was no "missing time." Proponents and critics of what is fundamentally an incomplete and thus ambiguous account of the events will quite expectedly (given the ways of human cognition) end up with rather different mental mosaics as they reconstruct what seems to them the most reasonable and parsimonious picture of what really happened.

Type I and II errors are directly reflected by what Leonard Zusne and Warren H. Jones (1988: 4) described as two polar principles, which scientists need when dealing with extraordinary claims. These they termed the Principle of LaPlace (that "extraordinary proof be produced for extraordinary claims") and the Principle of Hamlet (that "all is possible"). In the final analysis, scientific analysis must balance those two perspectives.

On the significance and varieties of validity

For most analysts of the Hill case, the central issue is its validity. What really happened to them? The incomplete data in the case force us to recognize that our judgment of them must rely on a great many inferences and usually involves the background information we bring with us. It also highlights the critical point that we distinguish our beliefs (which usually rest on probabilities) from knowledge (which, as justified belief, results in certainties).

The matter is compounded by a distinction that can be made between objective versus subjective validation. That is, one might not be able to demonstrate the objective truth of the Hills' story as science demands, but one can become psychologically convinced the story is true because of a wide variety of personal or existential experiences with which the Hill claims are congruent. Though most critics emphasize the need for objective (intersubjective) justifications, many people do not demand such strict scientific criteria for validity. As Dr. John E. Mack acknowledged: "The information about alien abductions is predominantly experiential (i.e., reports from the experiencers themselves... and cannot be verified by the methods of the physical sciences" (Mack in Jacobs, 2001: 246). If one has directly experienced UFO encounters or even abduction, or is involved with many that make such claims, it becomes easy (perhaps largely as a result of interpersonal trust) to validate subjectively similar claims of others. With those like Dr. Mack, this propensity can become extreme. David M. Jacobs, who considers himself a mere "Realist" believer in the abduction phenomenon, notes that some proponents like Mack, whom Jacobs terms the "Positives" (for they believe the abductions are benign) have even argued "that occult and metaphysical interpretations represented the best hope of understanding the phenomenon" (Jacobs, 2001: 206).

Once we enter into the realm of metaphysical validation, we may be entering realms far afield from science and may be opening the door to theological and other forms of alleged validation, including revelation. On such religious and cultic directions, see James R. Lewis's *The Gods Have Landed* (Lewis 1995).

Finally, it must be noted that even objective validation involves many controversies among methodologists, especially when we are concerned with the degree to which the social sciences (including psychology) can properly emulate the physical sciences. Further, recent controversies initiated by postmodernists and social constructivists about scientific method and its validation process have further eroded confidence in the positivism and materialism that is characteristic of most UFO critics. In opposition to the older paradigm for validation, Mack contends that "the way we construct reality is politically as well as scientifically determined" and that "The worldview of scientific materialism... has functioned as a kind of guiding secular religion for many of us in the West, but it is gradually being eroded by the increasing number of anomalies that challenge its primacy, the abduction phenomenon being one of the clearest examples" (Mack in Jacobs, 2001: 246 and 247).

On the use and abuse of parsimony

Precisely because of the ambiguities present in the Hill case, both proponents and critics are inclined to bring up the principle of parsimony. Parsimony (sometimes also referred to as "Occam's Razor" or the "Economy Principle") is the general philosophical guide that one "should not multiply entities unnecessarily"; that one should accept the simplest adequate theory. For example, in this volume, Sheaffer's essay specifically invokes this rule as key grounds for rejecting the Hills' abduction story. Advocates for the Hills, however, can argue that what looks and quacks like a duck should more readily be taken to be a duck. Thus, for some proponents, taking the Hills' claims at face value (as we likely would do with merely ordinary claims) seems the more simple process.

Unfortunately, aside from the possibility that the Universe's construction ignored this principle, the principle of parsimony contains two major problems. The first is that, as physicist and philosopher Mario Bunge has demonstrated, simplicity is largely a myth, for we don't have clear criteria for determining when a theory is simpler; and in science: "Progress in every domain works through an increase in complexity" (Bunge 1963: 98). In regard to the Hill case, Keith Thompson pointed out this problem in determining what explanation is truly simpler when he observed that "One of the most interesting aspects of this case is the way certain debunkers have attempted to diminish the Hill's extraordinary narrative by making counterclaims, which, although intended to settle the case in mundane terms, required leaps of logic exceeding those of Betty and Barney" (Thompson, 1991: 60-61).

The second major problem with parsimony is that even where we might have consensus that one theory is simpler than another, the real debate is usually over which theory is properly adequate for covering all the relevant facts. Most of the time, alternative theories are not truly equivalent in their scope and their coverage of all the elements (especially background variables) that they seek to explain. Critics of parsimony have even suggested that too often there is little justification for adopting it other than laziness (Lacy, 1993: 399; relevant to these issues, see Thorburn, 1918, and Sober 1990). Einstein has often been aptly quoted for saying: "Everything should be made as simple as possible, but not simpler."

On the question of what is extraordinary

Certainly, the Hills' tale of UFO abduction constitutes an extraordinary claim. And, as skeptics often remind us, within science "extraordinary claims require extraordinary proof" (Truzzi, 1976: 4). Unfortunately, this maxim often obscures rather than clarifies the issues involved, for it leaves unsettled the question of just how and why the claim is dubbed "extraordinary," and it neglects to define what would constitute "extraordinary proof." Let us then first examine what may be questionable or "unreasonable" in the Hills' claims and then go on to consider the issues of what constitutes acceptable evidence and what level of proof might be reasonably demanded.

As I have explained elsewhere (Truzzi, 1978), when considering the reasonableness of a claim, we normally are concerned with three sometimes separate facets. First, we can consider the claimed event, and we can speak of that falling somewhere on a continuum from most ordinary to the most extraordinary. This facet or dimension concerns the content of the claim. Second, we can examine the witness(es) to or narrator(s) of the claim, and they can fall on a continuum from most credible to most noncredible. Credibility includes both the issues of authority (expertise) and authenticity (honesty). And, third, we can consider the narrative account for the claim, which can range from the most plausible to the most implausible. This facet concerns the form rather than the content of the claim. Claims that appear unreasonable can vary in each of these three areas, producing nine different general combinations. Thus, for example, a non-credible witness (someone drunk) might claim he saw an extraordinary event (a unicorn) but tells his story in way that otherwise seems plausible; or perhaps a credible witness might claim an ordinary event with an implausible narrative (as when an honest person relates seeing some common thing but tells the tale in a way which seems fanciful).

The problem with extraordinariness

In the case of the Hills' story, the major claimed event is their abduction by aliens in a UFO. The degree to which that is labeled "extraordinary" is directly related to the preconceived probabilities and viewpoint on UFOs and extraterrestrial contacts that the labeler brings to hearing the story. Obviously, if one believes other stories of alien abduction, the Hills's tale will be judged in relation to that background. As cognitive psychologists have stressed, we interpret new information in terms of the mental schema we bring to it. And we selectively perceive and process new information in congruity with those schemas. Extraordinariness is always relative to what one sees as "ordinary."

For some advocates of the Hills' story, it is just one of many such tales, and consistency with those others makes it seem even more "ordinary." On the other hand, if one is already inclined to dismiss such a tale of extraterrestrial contact as physically impossible (as, notably, was the Hills' own psychiatrist Dr. Benjamin Simon), one will interpret the evidence in a direction that makes it congruent with a merely psychological scenario (so Simon saw their memories as dream contaminated).

As regards the final analysis of the extraordinariness of this case, matters may be as Jerome Clark concluded: "The resolution of the Hills case awaits the resolution of the UFO question itself. If UFOs do not exist, then Barney and Betty did not meet with aliens. If UFOs do exist, they probably did...." (Clark, 1966: 251). Though we might not fully concur with Clark on the likelihood in the latter case (since UFOs might be real but not of extraterrestrial origin), his statement exemplifies my point that the Hill's tale would be judged less extraordinary if framed in a context that accepted the existence of extraterrestrial UFOs.

In addition to the central claimed event of extraterrestrial abduction, the Hills' story involves controversial sub-events or topics that have also been characterized as more or less extraordinary. These include such elements as hypnosis and the problems of memory, the allegation of missing time, the aliens communicating via telepathy, and the star map. As with the central claim, each of these elements has its defenders and critics, and that seems to be largely a function of the schemas of the analysts. For example, as Benjamin Simon noted, "The charisma of hypnosis has tended to foster the belief that hypnosis is the magical and royal road to TRUTH" (Simon in Fuller, 1967: 9). This view may have led to some over-reliance on hypnosis in abduction research. Budd Hopkins, perhaps the leading defender of hypnotically elicited abduction memories, goes so far as to say that the Hills' case now can function as "a control in weighing the validity of subsequent hypotheses regarding the etiology of abduction accounts" (Hopkins, in Jacobs, 2000: 217-218). In contrast, critics have warned, "Those who claim that hypnosis adds to the credibility of the abduction accounts are misrepresenting the situation" (Randle, Estes and Cone, 1999: 339). Hopkins cites the conclusion of psychologists Steven Lynn and Irving Kirsch that "hypnosis does not reliably produce more false memories than are produced in a variety of nonhypnotic situations in which misleading information is conveyed to participants" (Lynn and Kirsch, 1996: 151). This misses the point that neither does it produce fewer false memories, and more recent experiments by Joseph Green and Steven Jay Lynn indicate that hypnosis can give false confidence in the case of inaccurate memories (Grabmeier, 2001).

The issue of credibility

Consideration of the Hills' credibility seems more straightforward. A claimant can, of course, be quite sincere or authentic while the claim itself may be false or invalid. It is important to separate authenticity from validity since various combinations are possible, including an inauthentic witness to an actually valid event. In general, most analysts have concluded that Betty and Barney Hill were authentic in that they fully believed what they claimed. The results of their hypnosis support the conclusion that they were fully sincere if, as their skeptical hypnotherapist noted: "... hypnosis is a pathway to the truth as it is felt and understood by the patient. The truth is what he believes to be the truth, and this may or may not be consonant with the ultimate nonpersonal truth" (Simon in Fuller, 1967: 9). On the other hand, it must be noted that Betty told psychiatrist Dr. Berthold Schwartz that in addition to a personal and family history of psychic experiences, "all my close family members have witnessed UFO sightings, my parents, my sisters and brothers, my nieces and nephews" (Quoted in Evans, 1994: 158-159). As Hilary Evans observed, such a background "could imply a readiness to look for a paranormal explanation when something unusual occurs" (Evans, 1994: 59).

A major point repeatedly made by the Hills' supporters to emphasize their credibility has been to point out that the Hills shunned any publicity and agreed not to tell anyone about the episode except their relatives and a few close friends. However, Terry Matheson raised some doubts about this when he wrote: "[I]f they were so reticent to discuss their experience, how did all these newspaper people get wind of it, and in the case of the reporter from Boston, how was he able to acquire enough information about their abduction experience to write a series of articles on it without interviewing them? For all their supposed preoccupation with privacy, the Hills must have passed on accounts of their experiences to more than just a small circle of relatives and acquaintances – in short, they must already have spoken in public." Further, Matheson notes: "How did the UFO study group learn of their experience to begin with, and why did the supposedly publicity-shy Hills agree to give a public lecture?" (Matheson, 1998: 53). In his paper in this volume, Karl Pflock raises similar questions about their supposed shyness.

Unfortunately, issues of credibility exist around later, significant versions of the story. Thus, the version of the events presented to us in John G. Fuller's book, in what is probably the best known account of the tale, has been questioned by some who suspect Fuller (who later went on to write a number of highly sensationalistic books about various even more controversial topics like psychic surgery and ghosts) may have been less interested in getting at the facts than in telling a good story. Mark Rodeghier made an interesting distinction between what he termed "an author who happens to be writing a UFO book and a UFO investigator who happens to be writing a book" (Rodeghier, 1994: 23). He suggested Fuller was in the former and largely exploitative role and noted that Fuller removed a critical sentence (indicating she was already considering the use of hypnosis) when he quoted Betty's letter to Donald Keyhoe. This flatly contradicts Fuller's writing that she had first considered hypnosis only months later when it was suggested to her by Major James MacDonald. Rodeghier contends that this distortion was quite intentionally introduced by Fuller to make his narrative more dramatic (Rodeghier, 1994: 6). Because of its widespread impact, it seems likely that Fuller's general retelling of Betty's story may even have influenced her own later recollections of the episode.

To complicate matters further, after 1970 Betty Hill claimed to have had many UFO sightings and made the assertion (which perhaps stems more from investigator Robert Hohmann than directly from Betty) that she had become a "transducer" – i.e. she was able to contact the aliens and get them to land. These claims are generally dismissed even by ufologists who accept her original tale and have certainly had a negative impact on her earlier down-to-earth image. As Jerome Clark noted: "Her critics believed that her status as a UFO celebrity had affected not her honesty but her judgment. Ufologists feared that her recent claims would adversely affect the credibility of her earlier experience" (Clark, 1996: 244-245). Archcritic of ufology Philip J. Klass sarcastically observed: "Until the night of September 19, 1961, Barney and Betty Hill were in most respects a typical middle-class couple, largely unknown outside a modest circle of friends and business associates. Today they are world-famous celebrities" (Klass, 1968: 248). In addition, Klass suggested their story might in part have been fueled by greed. As Jim Schnabel, discussing Klass's views, pointed out: "The Hills' 40 per cent share of the [*Look*] magazine, book and film rights had eventually amounted to more than a quarter of a million dollars" (Schnabel, 1994: 97).

Although I think such elements suggest a motive for the Hills' embellishments and are reasons to question their credibility, such charges most strongly extend only to Betty's later elaborations. Though some, like Sheaffer in his essay in this volume, view her later "tendency to tell fanciful tales" as "fatal" to her credibility about her initial story, we probably need to distinguish the original Betty Hill narrative from her later accounts. Jacques Vallée noted that Betty's later interactions with her sister Janet (who had seen a UFO in 1956 and told Betty about it) and other "believers," particularly Robert Hohmann, probably did much to produce the later elaborations. As Vallée put it: "Even when we recognize that Betty had been influenced by the believers and that Janet and the others now see a UFO in every starry light, the original 1961 sighting does remain unexplained" (Vallée, 1996: 282).

The issue of plausibility
The third facet of "reasonableness" we might consider is the narrative's plausibility. That is best derived by examining the story's internal coherence and comparing it with similar descriptions whose form of argument and evidence is generally considered to be convincing. In the case of the Hills' narrative, we certainly must recognize that it is far from a systematic set of observations presented with rigor and precision – such as we might expect, say, in an anthropologist's field report. By scientific standards the evidence is almost entirely anecdotal, so must be judged as "not proven." Even under the less stringent and broader standards for arguments and evidence found in the courtroom, the testimony presented by the Hills and their supporters would unlikely survive competent cross-examination and critical examination before a jury. Such an essentially agnostic conclusion about the Hills' narrative seems shared by most writers. Jerome Clark, who is largely sympathetic to their account, echoed a common view when he concluded: "The notion that the Hills encountered extraterrestrials and interacted with them aboard a spacecraft is unprovable, of course" (Clark, 1996: 250). The "of course" strikes me as the key operative phrase.

Perhaps the most intensive examination of the narrative itself has been that by Terry Matheson, a professor of literature. Matheson recognizes the virtues of Fuller's account of the story, which "presented the abduction material itself in a sober and restrained manner" and "contained few, if any of those lurid and sensational elements... associated with some of the more outlandish UFO-related studies"; and he states the book "proved a standard against which future books on the subject would be evaluated" (Matheson, 1998: 49). But Matheson views much of this as Fuller's rhetorical strategy to gain credibility and goes on to examine what Matheson argues (I think mostly successfully) are many and serious contradictions in the narrative. Though the Hills' own reports may withstand much of Matheson's attack upon Fuller's account, Matheson raises a great many questions neglected by other analysts, and, in my view, seriously undermines the plausibility of the total narrative, at least as we have it from Fuller. (On some of the limitations in Matheson's approach, see Bullard, 2000: 86-94.)

On the nature of evidence

Though all scientists agree that evidence can vary in strength, there are some that deem some evidence too lightweight to be admitted. That is, they set a threshold for what they are willing to call "scientific evidence." Many hard-line critics simply consider anecdotal evidence as "unscientific" and inadmissible. In the Hill episode, this becomes very important. As Hilary Evans noted of their case, "there is not a scrap of supporting evidence" and the Hills' "testimony is our only reason to suppose that anything occurred at all" (Evans, 1987: 158).

Of course, such extreme dismissal of mere human testimony from science is draconian and ignores the routine use of such admittedly fragile evidence in the social sciences and clinical medicine. Many of life's most important decisions, even in our courtrooms, are based on mere anecdotal evidence. (An anonymous cynical humorist has even asserted that "'data' is defined as the plural of 'anecdote.'") Nonetheless, eyewitness testimony is recognized as highly unreliable even in the law courts. So we certainly need to be cautious and critical in weighing its merits, and we need to seek any corroborative evidence that may be available.

In the Hill case, the alien's star map drawn by Betty under a post-hypnotic suggestion led to its analysis by Marjorie E. Fish, who concluded the alien craft's origin (based on the brightest two stars on the map) corresponded to Zeta 1 and 2 of Reticuli. Her analysis was seized upon as corroborative evidence by advocates for the Hills and was debated in *Astronomy* magazine in 1974-75, but most astronomers involved today probably accept the analysis by Carl Sagan and Steven Soter that concluded the map's seeming pattern was really a chance result.

Even if we accept a detail as evidence, we may disagree as to what the evidence supports. Evidence often can be cognitively framed either to support or deny a hypothesis. That is, in many cases positive evidence can be creatively reframed to become negative evidence. In an old joke, Dr. X concludes dogs are smarter than cats because you cannot teach a cat to pull a cart, but Dr. Y argues that cats are smarter than dogs precisely because you can not teach a cat to pull a cart. The same sort of reframing process has been applied to some of the evidence in the Hill case. Whereas for some supporters the reports produced under hypnosis seem more likely to be valid, for many critics the use of hypnosis implies a greater probability of fantasy. Similarly, some proponents have made much ado over the Hills' reporting "missing time," a gap they see as confirming the abduction story. In sharp contrast, Jacques Vallée tells us that Dr. Simon said he placed "no value whatsoever on the time-loss experience. 'When you travel you don't pay attention to what time it is,' he told us. 'Also, remember, these people were lost.'" (Vallée, 1996: 281)

On the standard for proof

A major problem with reaching a conclusion about the Hill case is lack of agreement as to what burden for proof should be demanded (on this general issue, see Truzzi, 1998: 152). In everyday decision-making, and in normal science, the standard for acceptance is merely a preponderance of evidence, and this criterion also applies in most civil litigation. Some advocates for the Hills' claim seem to want us to accept this level for the burden of proof. Many, if not most critics, contend that since extraordinary claims require an increase in proof, so demand the standard expected in criminal court proceedings, proof beyond a reasonable doubt. Unfortunately, the latter burden may beg the question: since we are then confronted with the fact that there is no agreed upon or clear criterion for when a doubt stops being reasonable. I have elsewhere argued (Truzzi, 1998a: 150-151; and 1998b: 152) that demanding so heavy a burden of proof may actually make a hard-line skeptic's position quite unfalsifiable and so itself pseudoscientific.

In any case, the criterion of proof beyond a reasonable doubt seems to me to make little sense for science. In our criminal law, we assume the suspect is innocent until proven guilty and the reason for this heavy burden of proof is to protect the small citizen from the giant state. But in science, the burden of proof is on the claimant. So, those who make claims like the Hills' are considered to be "guilty" of error and must then prove "innocence." And, of course, it is quite one thing to protect the individual against the state and quite the opposite here, where we seem to want to protect the scientific community from what may be the revolutionary ideas of the individual claimant. Does science really have so much to fear from the claims of a Betty and Barney Hill, that we must not only place the burden of proof on them but also demand that they offer proof beyond a reasonable doubt?

Yet, skeptics do seem to be correct that extraordinary claims require stronger proof than ordinary ones. And the rule of mere preponderance of evidence may simply be too generous to extend it to every idea no matter how farfetched. Perhaps the best criterion we might use is in the midway position we find in many statutory laws, in which the demand is for what a judge or jury finds to be clear and convincing evidence. This might be a standard best used for extraordinary claims such as that of the Hills.

In any event, evidence does not necessarily produce the basis for us a reach a decisive conclusion. Nor need our conclusions be limited to a simple dichotomy. In science, as I have noted elsewhere, consideration of evidence may lead us to conclude that a claim "is either merely suggestive (interesting), compelling (appears significant and likely), or convincing (appears to be valid)" (Truzzi, 2000: xxv). On this scale of proof, I think it would be fair to say that most of even the staunch advocates for the Hills (a noteworthy exception is Stanton Friedman) have contended the evidence for their story is merely compelling rather than convincing.

What Is the Value of the Hill Case?

So, where does all this leave us?

As I have argued, the significance of cases is largely a function of what frame of reference we bring to them, and a major feature seems to be the way we view the whole matter of the likelihood of extraterrestrial life and the probability of visitations from alien species. The debate about life on other worlds is far from new and was debated by philosophers and scientists long before our space age (for excellent surveys see Dick, 1982 and Crowe, 1986). These early disputes were often based on deductive or logical arguments without need for empirical considerations. For example, in a 4th century B.C.E. "Letter to Herodotus," the philosopher Epicurus wrote that "there are infinite worlds both like and unlike this world of ours. For the atoms being infinite in number... are borne on far out into space. For those atoms... have not been used up either on one world or on a limited number of worlds, nor on all the worlds which are alike, or on those which are different from these. So that there nowhere exists an obstacle to the infinite number of worlds" (Quoted in Crowe, 1986: 3).

If we accept such an argument for infinite worlds being inevitable if we have an infinite Universe, it certainly would make extraterrestrial life and intelligence more plausible. But today we are less likely to see such thought experiments being used and are more likely to seek empirical evidence. That too, goes back further than is usually appreciated. Even before the infamous debate of the 1890s over Giovanni Schiaparelli's and Percival Lowell's claims about canals on Mars, we have the "Copy from the Memorandum Book of Fred Wm. Birmingham, the Engineer to the Council of Parramatta. A machine to go through the air. A.D. 1873," perhaps the first credible report of a Close Encounter of the Third Kind, which allegedly took place in 1868 (cf. Chalker, 1982). It is our degree of familiarity with background factors such as these that affects our interest in, and often our openness to, contemporary claims of extraterrestrial contact. As Jerome Clark has noted in his examination of the prehistory of the

UFO abduction phenomenon, although UFO reports did not really begin until the 19th century, reports of many earlier anomalous phenomena, such as alleged encounters with merfolk, have probably influenced our views (Clark, 2000: 17).

For many if not most scientists, the whole matter seems largely irrelevant and uninteresting. When Albert Einstein was asked his opinion on UFO reports in 1952, he reportedly said, "These people have seen something. What they have seen I do not know and care less" (Einstein quoted in Plank, 1968: 76). The reality of the situation is that people seriously interested in episodes like those of the Hills are mainly ufologists, most of whom are only amateur scientists or journalists. I would suggest that this limited audience of participants in the debate is immensely important for our understanding of UFO controversies. We need to remember that ufology is a small subculture, and its perspectives and priorities are not necessarily representative of the larger scientific community.

In terms of the considerations I have raised in the previous section of this introduction, the fact seems rather clear that the scientific case for the Hills' reported experiences being objectively valid is a weak one; as the essays in this volume demonstrate. Nonetheless, I would contend that we might still learn much from it.

It may be that our approach to the case has been somewhat inverted. Most of the debate has been over whether or not their tale supports the extraordinary (that aliens have visited our planet and abducted them). I would suggest rather the opposite might be the case. Imagine, hypothetically, that we all accept that aliens visit our planet, so that this was an ordinary rather than extraordinary claim. If this were the case, we might imagine the Hills taking their claim that they were kidnapped to a prosecuting attorney. Were all this the case, he might use the mere preponderance of evidence criterion to assess whether or not the evidence for what would here be an ordinary abduction was strong enough to bring a case. Given the lack of any corroborative evidence, the contradictions in the narrative accounts (for example, Betty described the abductors recalled from her dreams as having very big noses, while Barney said they merely had little slits for breathing), and that the main memories seem to have come from dreams, it seems unlikely that any normal lawyer would think they had a case worth pursuing. And yet ufologists pursue this case even though the claimed events are actually extraordinary and require stronger proof rather than the lower standard we would expect if the events were ordinary. This, it seems to me, suggests that it is the very *extraordinariness* of the claim that makes ufologists take the case seriously at all. Thus, its extraordinariness (if we accept that such events as alien contact can really happen) makes the rather mundane evidence seem interesting and worthy of our attention. In short, I am suggesting that the Hill episode may tell us more about the state of ufology than it tells us about any actual abduction event.

The Most Promising Approaches

Jerome Clark has observed that after the 1960s, consensus in ufology had largely broken down and that there are now three major schools of thought: materialists, advocates for the extraterrestrial hypothesis; occultists (followers of conspiratorial and metaphysical explanations); and culture commentators, advocates for psychosocial theories (Clark in Jacobs, 2000: 139). And, as we noted earlier, David M. Jacobs points out that those in the abduction research community seem divided between these first two camps, into what he termed the "Realists and the Positives" (Jacobs, 2000: 205). I would suggest that the emergence of the abduction phenomenon and the increased interest in the "occultist" perspective as found among the "Positives" may be a major social contributor to the renewed interest and our reconsideration here of the Hill case.

Perhaps the developing psychosocial approach has the most promise. For one thing, it can progress whether or not the Hills' account has objective validity. As John Saliba has noted: "The meaning of the flying saucer phenomenon might lie more in its social and psychological dimensions than in whether extraterrestrials exist or not, or in what the aliens themselves are supposedly saying and doing. In other words, belief in flying saucers and alleged encounters with their occupants might reveal something important about human nature" (Saliba in Lewis, 1995: 241).

I think these potential revelations might be both sociological and psychological. As I suggested above, the changing structural and ideological character of the UFO research movement, perhaps even as influenced by growing ideas of postmodernism that question scientific methodology, may tell us a great deal about why our focus has shifted back to such cases as that of the Hills. Jerome Clark's look at pre-Hill cases that he termed "paleo-abduction" reports seems particularly relevant here (Clark 2000: 20-25). In many ways, sociologically, UFO research may have moved from its earlier concern with seeking acceptance as a science (ufology) and has sought legitimacy and significance as a contributor to other, more humanistic, perspectives. While some in the more materialist approach who condemn this trend argue that "the abduction tail is wagging the ufology dog," some, even such as the "Realist" Jacobs, continue to search for a new methodology that might avoid the escape into what some critics of the new abduction interest characterize as bordering on demonology.

Meanwhile, the psychosocial approach may best move us forward in terms of new psychological understanding. Although critics of alien abductions, UFOs, and other reports of anomalies dismissively suggest that many if not most such reports may be due to hallucinations and distorted memories, we must not forget that these "explanations" are themselves invoking largely mysterious areas. The fact is that we still have a great deal to learn about the psychology of human error. Even if the Hills were hallucinating and/or producing false memories, we need to know more about such processes.

This is especially true for a case like the Hills', since they shared what their critics might call a collective hallucination. Looking at another well-known episode of such a shared delusion, Terry Castle asked: "Are we to conclude that hallucinations can be shared? Or that spectral delusions, like the germs of a virus, can somehow be transmitted from the brain of one person to another?" (Castle, 1994: 11). Is the Hill case just one example of the exotic but fascinating clinical phenomenon, a "psychosis of two" that psychiatrists call *folie à deux*? Kottmeyer (2001) has argued against that explanation, apparently based on Richard Noll's (1990) depiction of that esoteric syndrome as requiring extreme dominance and subordination.

However, a broader definition, demanding only "shared psychotic symptoms brought about by a close relationship between the percipients" (Appelle, Lynn and Newman, 2000: 168), seems more typical of the literature where many varieties of the disorder have been noted (cf. Gralnick, 1942; and Sacks, 1988). It has been noted that in these cases "dominance and submission are not always manifest" (Gralnick, 1942: 237), and there have been cases that involved more than two people. At least one case has been described that involved a dozen family members (Waltzer, 1963). In any case, the dynamics that produce *folie à deux* remain mostly mysterious, and Kottmeyer's conclusions are premature at best. Looking in a very different psychological direction for explanation, new brain research may prove a fruitful direction. If Philip J. Klass was correct in his early conjecture that what the Hill encountered might actually have been a "glowing plasma" (Klass, 1986: 227), the neurophysiological approach of Michael Persinger (Persinger in Jacobs, 2000), which has examined electrical effects upon the brain to produce such subjective experiences, might be a promising direction for our understanding of the Hill case.

Whether the future confirms or denies the Hills' claims, research into such cases seems likely to contribute to our overall knowledge. And that alone should make further examination worth our while.

References

Appelle, Stuart, Steven Jay Lynn and Leonard Newmanm. "Alien Abduction Experiences." In Etzel Cardeña, Steven Jay Lynn and Stanley Krippner, editors, *Varieties of Anomalous Experience: Examining the Scientific Evidence*. Washington, DC: American Psychological Association, 2000: 253-282.

Bullard, Thomas E. "Abductions Under Fire: A Review of Recent Abduction Literature," *Journal of UFO Studies*, ns 7 (2000), 81-106.

Bunge, Mario. *The Myth of Simplicity: Problems of Scientific Philosophy*. Englewood Cliffs, NJ: Prentice-Hall, 1963.

Castle, Terry. "Contagious Folly: An Adventure and Its Skeptics." In James Chandler, *et al.*, editors, *Questions of Evidence: Proof, Practice, and Persuasion across the Disciplines*. Chicago: University of Chicago Press, 1994: 11-42.

Chalker, Bill. "The Mystery of 'A Machine to Go Through the Air' 1873, Parramatta, New South Wales, Australia," *UFO Research Australia Newsletter*, 3, 1 (Jan.-Feb. 1982).

Clark, Jerome. "The Extraterrestrial Hypothesis in the Earl UFO Age." In Jacobs, 2000: 122-140.

Clark, Jerome. "From Mermaids to Little Green Men: The Prehistory of the UFO Abduction Phenomenon," *The Anomalist*, No. 8 (Spring 2000): 11-31.

Clark, Jerome. "Hill Abduction Case." In his *The UFO Encyclopedia, Volume 3: High Strangeness: UFOs from 1960 through 1979*. Detroit, MI: Omnigraphics, 1996: 235-253.

Crowe, Michael J. *The Extraterrestrial Life Debate 1750-1900: The Idea of a Plurality of Worlds from Kant to Lowell*. Cambridge, England: Cambridge University Press, 1986.

Dick, Steven J. *Plurality of Worlds: The Origins of the Extraterrestrial Life Debate from Democritus to Kant*. Cambridge, England: Cambridge University Press, 1982.

Evans, Hilary. *Gods • Spirits • Cosmic Guardians: A Comparative Study of the Encounter Experience*. Wellingborough, Northamptonshire, England: The Aquarian Press, 1987.

Fuller, John G. *The Interrupted Journey: Two Lost Hours "Aboard a Flying Saucer."* New York: Dell, 1966.

Grabmeier, Jeff. "Hypnosis May Give False Confidence in Inaccurate Memories." *Ohio State University Research News*, August 26, 2001. (http://www.osu.edu/researchnews/archive/hypnomem.htm)

Gralnick, Alexander. "*Folie à Deux* – The Psychosis of Association: A Review of 103 Cases and the Entire English Literature: With Case Presentations," *Psychiatric Quarterly*, 16 (1942), 230-520.

Hopkins, Budd. "Hypnosis and the Investigation of UFO Abduction Accounts." In Jacobs, 2000: 215-240.

Jacobs, David M., editor. *UFOs and Abductions: Challenging the Borders of Knowledge*. Lawrence, KS: University Press of Kansas, 2000.

Jacobs, David M. "The UFO Abduction Controversy in the United States." In Jacobs, 2000: 192-214.

Klass, Philip J. *UFO Abductions: A Dangerous Game*. Updated Edition. Buffalo, NY: Prometheus Books, 1989.

Kottmeyer, Martin S. "Folie à D'Oh," unpublished paper, 2001.

Lacy, A.R. "Parsimony, Principle of." In Jennifer Bothamley, editor, *Dictionary of Theories*. London, Detroit and Washington, D.C.: Gale Research International, 1993: 399.

Lewis, James R., editor. *The Gods Have Landed: New Religions from Other Worlds*. Albany, NY: State University of New York Press, 1995.

Lynn, Steven and Irving Kirsch. "Alleged Alien Abductions: False Memories, Hypnosis, and Fantasy Proneness." *Psychological Inquiry*, 7 (1996).

Mack, John E. "How the Alien Abduction Phenomenon Challenges the Boundaries of Science." In Jacobs, 2002: 241-261;

Matheson, Terry. *Alien Abductions: Creating a Modern Phenomenon*. Amherst, NY: Prometheus Books, 1998.

Noll, Richard. *Bizarre Diseases of the Mind*. New York: Berkley Books, 1990: 127-136.

Persinger, Michael. "The UFO Experience: A Normal Correlate of Human Brain Function," in Jacobs, 2000: 262-302.

Plank, Robert. *The Emotional Significance of Imaginary Beings: A Study of the Interaction Between Psychopathology, Literature, and Reality in the Modern World*. Springfield, IL: Charles C. Thomas, 1968.

Randle, Kevin D., Russ Estes, and William P. Cone. *The Abduction Enigma*. New York: Forge/Tom Doherty Associates, 1999.

Rodeghier, Mark. "Hypnosis and the Hill Abduction Case." *International UFO Reporter*, 19, 2 (March/April 1994): 4-6 & 23-24.

Sacks, Michael H. "*Folie à Deux*," *Comprehensive Psychiatry*, 29, 3 (May/June 1962), 270-277.

Saliba, John A. "UFO Contactee Phenomena from a Sociopsychological Perspective: A Review." In Lewis, 1995: 207-250.

Schnabel, Jim. *Dark White: Aliens, Abductions, and the UFO Obsession*. London: Hamish Hamilton, 1994.

Sober, E., "Let's Razor Ockham's Razor." In D. Knowles, editor, *Explanation and Its Limits*. Royal Institute of Philosophy supplement vol. 27. Cambridge: Cambridge University Press, 1990: 73-94.

Story, Ronald D. "Hill Abduction." In his *The Encyclopedia of UFOS*. Garden City, NY: Dolphin Books/Doubleday & Co., 1980: 172-176.

Thompson, Keith. *Angels and Aliens: UFOS and the Mythic Imagination*. Reading, MA: William Patrick/Addison Wesley Publishing Co., 1991.

Thorburn, W.M. "The Myth of Occam's Razor." *Mind*, 27 (1918): 345-353.

Truzzi, Marcello. "Editorials." *The Zetetic* (now *The Skeptical Inquirer*), 1, 1 (Fall-Winter, 1976): 4.

Truzzi, Marcello. "On the Extraordinary: An Attempt at Clarification." *Zetetic Scholar*, 1, 1 (1978): 11-19.

Truzzi, Marcello. "The Skeptic/Proponent Debate in Parapsychology: Perspectives from the Social Sciences. Some Reflections." In Nancy L. Zingrone, *et al.*, editors, *Research in Parapsychology* 1993. Lanham, MD, and London: Scarecrow, 1998a: 147-151.

Truzzi, Marcello. "Unfairness and the Unknown." In Edward Binkowski, editor, *Oxymoron: The Arts and Sciences Annual*, Volume 2: The Fringe. New York: Oxymoron Media, 1998b: 147-152.

Truzzi, Marcello. "The Perspective of Anomalistics." In William F. Williams, editor, *Encyclopedia of Pseudoscience*. New York: Facts On File, 2000: xxiii-xxvi.

Vallée, Jacques. *Forbidden Science: Journals 1957-1969*. New York: Marlowe and Co., 1996.

Waltzer, Herbert. "A Psychotic Family - *Folie à Douze*." *Journal of Nervous and Mental Disease*, 137 (1963), 67-75.

Zusne, Leonard, and Warren H. Jones. *Anomalistic Psychology A Study of Magical Thinking*, Second Edition. Lawrence Erlbaum Associates, 1989.

Marcello Truzzi acted as moderator of the Encounters at Indian Head Symposium in September 2000. He received his doctorate in sociology from Cornell University in 1970 and was a professor of sociology at Eastern Michigan University in Ypsilanti, where he was department chairman from 1974 through 1986. He was also director of the Center for Scientific Anomalies Research and editor of the center's journal, the *Zetetic Scholar*. He published a dozen books and many articles in a wide range of journals over several fields, including psychology, folklore, anthropology, and the history of science, as well as sociology. His professional associations included the American Sociological Association, the American Folklore Society, the Parapsychological Association, and the Society for Scientific Exploration, of which he was a councilor for a period. At various times he was involved with both proponent and critical or skeptical organizations concerned with scientific anomalies, from the J. Allen Hynek Center for UFO Studies to the Committee for the Scientific Investigation of Claims of the Paranormal. His sociological work ranged from the ethnography of occult organizations to the study of the reception and rejection of deviant research efforts in science. Professor Truzzi died in February 2003.

CHAPTER THREE

The Start of Something Rich and Strange

The Hills' account of their abduction is in a league of its own. So why should we take it as something more than just a story?

THOMAS E. BULLARD

Ufologists had seen nothing like the Hill abduction before. They wasted little time on George Adamski and other 1950s contactees, dismissing the usual yarns of angelic Space Brothers who were here to save earth from atomic fallout and nuclear war as naïve, not very imaginative mixtures of wishful thinking and con-artistry. They held most occupant reports in little better regard. Frank Scully had no sooner described little men and crashed saucers in his book, *Behind the Flying Saucers* (1950), than the whole story evaporated as a hoax. Most entity accounts came from Europe or South America where U.S. investigators had no chance for a face-to-face interview, while multiple-witness cases close to home, like the Flatwoods Monster of September 1952 and the siege of a Kentucky farmhouse in August 1955, smacked of mass hysteria and sensationalism. A rare example with persuasive credentials came from New Guinea in 1959, when missionary Rev. William Gill and more than 40 of his parishioners watched human-like figures wave from the upper deck of a UFO.

If occupants kept a precarious toehold in the canons of serious ufology, alien kidnap in any form belonged on the trash heap of hoaxes and silly rumors. The idea had a pedigree as old as Charles Fort (1959, 264), who said, "I think that we're fished for," and speculated that we were property of otherworldly beings. Writers H. T. Wilkins and M. K. Jessup elaborated this theme into a sort of UFO gothic literature in the 1950s as they interpreted vanishing ships and airplanes as evidence of UFO hostility, though in most of their examples the link with UFOs was tenuous or nonexistent (Wilkins 1954: 139-140, 250-254; Jessup 1955: 119-144, 162-167). *Fate*, a magazine widely available at newsstands, published a story in January 1960, that creatures like flying jelly bags tried to drag two Swedes into a landed UFO, then described the kidnap of a Brazilian man, Rivalino Mafra da Silva, in the June 1963 issue. Short beings invaded da Silva's home and threatened to kill him, then the next morning, with his 12-year old son the only witness, two smoking spheres whisked the man away and he was never seen again.

Before the Beginning

Accounts of capture and return were exceptionally rare prior to the Hills. Investigators heard Brazilian farmer Antonio Villas Boas describe his October 1957 abduction soon after the event, but only brief references lacking in detail appeared in the literature (by Riley Crabb and James Moseley in 1960, and by Max Miller in 1962). In fact the sensational sexual character of the claim prompted most ufologists aware of the case (and they were few) to keep it under wraps until the Hill testimony was already a matter of record. Another antecedent appeared in the Prince George (B.C.) *Citizen* of December 11, 1957. According to this story, a short being in a space suit, with a cylindrical head and compound, insect-like eyes, paralyzed the witness and pulled him into a UFO, then flew him to Mars and back in an hour. An even more promising tale, published in the May 1953 issue of *Action*, a short-lived men's magazine, claimed that a UFO collided with an airplane piloted by Fred Reagan. Drawn into the ship by aliens that resembled three-foot tall stalks of metallic asparagus, Reagan received a medical examination in a room with faint lighting. He was then found unconscious in a field, and died a year later from brain deterioration caused by intense radiation. Investigations undertaken in later years confirmed that this yarn was a hoax (Gross 1989: 57-58).

An intriguing class of precursor might be called the cryptic abduction, a UFO report without overt abduction activity yet suffused with oddities and witness reactions that made no sense at the time but acquire significance in retrospect as suggestive of abduction phenomenology (Clark 2000: 20-28). A striking example is the case of Pvt. Gerry Irwin, a young soldier driving through the Utah desert on the night of February 28, 1959, when he spotted a flaming object and left his car to investigate a possible plane crash. The local sheriff found Irwin unconscious several hours later. He remained unconscious for nearly 24 hours – due to hysteria, according to a doctor's diagnosis – and later went AWOL while under a compulsion to return to the site in Utah. Army doctors found him psychologically normal but revealed nothing of what he said when given sodium amytal. Formerly a reliable soldier, Irwin deserted in July and was never seen again (Lorenzen 1962). Scattered through the literature of the 1950s are close encounters accompanied by the missing time, odd silences, and panic reactions that now spell abduction.

The prospects are gossamer thin that the Hills ever ran across these accounts. In her newfound interest in UFOs, Betty might have chanced upon the writings of contactees Reinhold Schmidt, who described paralysis and flotation (Schmidt 1958), or Orfeo Angelucci, who claimed a tingling sensation, a room with glowing walls, a souvenir he took home, and amnesia while in the company of aliens (Angelucci 1955: 20-36, 83-96). We know for certain that she read the third UFO book of Donald Keyhoe, *The Flying Saucer Conspiracy* (1955), within days of her sighting in 1961. Keyhoe headed the National Investigations Committee on Aerial Phenomena (NICAP) and was the leading UFO proponent of the 1950s. While he maintained a cautious stance toward occupant reports, on pp.238-246 he recited several South American reports in which hairy dwarfs attack people, and another rumor of a jet pilot who spotted his counterpart when a saucer flew close. In the same book he related two instances of vanishing aircraft to UFOs (pp.13-14, 288-299) – the disappearance of Flight 17 off Florida in 1945, later to become a cornerstone of Bermuda Triangle speculations, and the case of an F-89 jet sent to investigate a large radar blip over Lake Superior in 1953. Radar operators watched the blip of the interceptor merge with the larger mystery blip, which then disappeared from the screen. Search and rescue found no trace of the missing plane.

An inventory of plot and imagery the Hills might have borrowed from UFO lore finds the cupboard rather bare. The closest approximations to their eventual story were obscure or inaccessible, while the readily available literature introduced the fewest and least distinctive ideas. From Keyhoe Betty learned the possibility of kidnap and the short humanoid entity; scientific purposes and a technological interior belong to the realm of reasonable inference – but add all these hints together and the Hill story still requires a strenuous creative leap. The richer imagery of 1950s science fiction movies might suggest large-headed aliens (*Invaders from Mars*); a rounded interior within the UFO (*Earth Versus the Flying Saucers*);

reproductive interests (*I Married a Monster from Outer Space*); and telepathy, mind control, and examination (*Killers from Space*). Casting a wider net to encompass folklore could take in fairy legends of kidnap and supernatural lapse of time. Even so, neither well-known folklore nor familiar science fiction foretells the abduction story very persuasively in its details or sequence of events. Bits and pieces of the story stick out like nuggets for a trained eye to spot, but a collection of loose elements still does not an abduction story make, and the fact remains that no fully assembled model sat on the cultural shelves waiting for the Hills to pick it up.

The First of its Kind

The Hill case belongs in a league of its own. The story inaugurates a new genre of UFO literature, and a distinctive type of encounter becomes possible where no plot lines quite like it existed before. If the story is an invention or fantasy and nothing more, the Hills deserve applause for transcending pale derivation to achieve a robust and individualized creation. Whatever they borrowed, they contributed a great deal more even as they selected and synthesized an abundance of ideas from culture in their process of innovation. The Hills created a fruitful and evocative masterpiece – if, of course, the story is just a story.

The alien kidnap idea struck a responsive chord and became a plausible horror story for modern ears. Abduction is a legend in the technical sense that extranormal danger befalls a victim from out of the blue, unexpected, undeserved, and unjust, with a power to strike anyone at any time (Luthi 1981: 24). If this category of experience is age-old, the particular guise is up-to-date as extraterrestrials replace fairies or demons and magical technology supplants supernatural power. Some 300 abduction reports appeared in the literature by 1985 and another 450 accumulated by 1992 (Bullard 1994: 45). A survey of 13 abduction investigators found that their files included a total of about 1700 cases (Bullard 1995: 13). The total number of real or imagined experiences out there and still unreported or unrecorded must be truly breathtaking. The subject began its career in high-profile mass entertainment on October 20, 1975, when NBC-TV aired *The UFO Incident*, a dramatization of the Hill encounter, and reached a vast audience through Steven Spielberg's *Close Encounters of the Third Kind*, released in December 1977. Abduction has since become a staple theme in movies, television, advertising, cartoons, tabloid journalism, and best-selling books by Whitley Strieber and others. The subject has acquired the prominence of a cultural icon and now enjoys almost universal familiarity. The idea has seeped into the groundwaters of current thinking to acquire useful intellectual and psychological functions, so acceptable that some people now interpret the unsettling and unfamiliar experience of sleep paralysis as an instance of abduction and, according to one explanation, hide the reality of childhood sexual abuse behind a screen memory of abuse by aliens as a more tolerable substitute.

This popularity arrived by slow degrees. Ufologists should have welcomed the Hill report as a dream case. It had just about everything they wanted – two witnesses of high repute, a close encounter of long duration, detailed observation with the naked eye and optical assistance, investigations by a distinguished psychiatrist and a noted journalist, and of course, the ultimate inside story on UFOs and their occupants. Instead ufologists did not know quite what to make of this remarkable case. Left in isolation, its implications largely ignored, the Hill report scarcely figured into ufological thinking for years to come. The public reacted with awe and amazement on release of John G. Fuller's book and *Look* magazine articles in October 1966, but also kept a distance. No explosion of copycat reports followed, and only 25 cases entered the literature between 1966 and 1971. Just five of these count as detailed and reasonably reliable, while the sole domestic example was the encounter of Nebraska patrolman Herbert Schirmer in December 1967. A cluster of nine abductions arose out of the October 1973 UFO wave, when the encounter of Charles Hickson and Calvin Parker made national headlines, but despite this publicity the phenomenon still kept to the shadows.

Only in 1975 did abduction begin a move to the forefront. Some 25 reports surfaced in that year alone, and 11 of them represent quality cases. The most celebrated was the five-day disappearance of Travis Walton in early November, an incident that again drew national attention to abduction. Skeptics saw more than coincidence in the timing of the Walton claim – it arrived two weeks after broadcast of *The UFO Incident*, while another notable abduction from Tripp Pond, Maine, also followed close on the heels of the TV movie. Any rush to conclude that the TV depiction suggested abduction to some receptive imaginations must reckon with the fact that abductions increased throughout the year. Sgt Charles Moody reported an encounter in the summer, and ufologists quietly investigated cases like the 1973 experience of Patty Roach and incidents Sara Shaw remembered from 1953 (Randle 1988: 17-19, Druffel and Rogo 1980: 6-11). Betty Andreasson first contacted J. Allen Hynek in August to report conscious memories of her 1967 visitation (Fowler 1979: 14). If the Hill movie and Walton furor failed as causes, they succeeded as catalysts to jog the memory of witnesses and channel them toward ufologists. Sandra

Larson joined the growing ranks of people from late 1975 onwards who gained insight into a puzzling experience through TV coverage or popular magazine treatment, then contacted investigators with UFO and missing time experiences that would evolve under hypnosis into abduction scenarios (Clark 1998: 573-576). By the end of 1975 the abduction bandwagon had started to roll. It has not slowed down in 25 years.

A Curious Consistency

The history of abduction divides into three convenient eras separated by influential social events: an early gestational period covers 1966 to 1977, from release of the Hill story until *Close Encounters of the Third Kind* appeared in theaters; a middle consolidation period lasts from 1978 until 1987, when two books, *Intruders* by Budd Hopkins and *Communion* by Whitley Strieber, spotlighted the phenomenon and introduced striking new abduction ideas; and a subsequent period from 1987 till the present when abduction becomes a mainstream idea, familiar to everyone and widespread in the media. A collection of 437 reports from the literature serves as a basis for generalizations about what has changed and what has remained the same in abduction reports since the Hill case made its debut. These reports provide enough descriptive detail for meaningful comparison and meet a minimal standard for witness reliability. They number 52 reports for the period through 1977, 131 for 1978-1986, and 254 from 1987 onward.

Constants in the Abduction Story

Table 1 reveals at a glance the surprising consistency of the story, as many content elements recur in similar percentages over the three periods. The left column shows that striking motifs like paralysis and missing time, humanoid occupants and large eyes, examination rooms and conferences persist as mainstays of the story from the Hill report till today. If these elements seem likely to thrive on account of their familiarity, other less-common story contents also reappear at a steady rate – sudden entry, tall humanoids mingling with the short, Nordic or human occupants, nightmares and scars. No one of these ideas may count as surprising in itself, certainly not beyond the reach of imaginative invention, but persistence of so many elements in stable proportions over the years deserves notice.

If the Hill story serves as progenitor for subsequent abductions, the descendents maintain a family resemblance from earliest offspring to the latest. For over 30 years the narrative core of abduction accounts has included a surrealistic capture sequence in which short humanoid beings

Table 1
Percentage of Elements Present in UFO Abduction Reports
Across Three Time Periods (1957-1977, 1978-1986, 1987-1998)
(adapted from Bullard 1999)

	1957-77 %	1978-86 %	1987-98 %
Beam of light	38	35	31
Drone, hum	24	21	13
Highway capture	49	35	17
Beings present	59	55	60
Outdoor capture	33	31	24
Paralysis	35	30	33
Bedroom capture	18	34	59
Missing time	75	71	74
UFO present	73	58	41
Flotation	47	41	42
Sudden entry	40	31	40
Occupants			
Humanoids	84	83	84
Staring eyes	14	15	24
Dark eyes	17	48	71
Std. humanoids	65	64	71
Hairlessness	82	84	94
Vestigial ears	74	85	95
Short hmnoids	63	59	62
Tall humanoids	24	24	23
Nordic/Human	22	23	19
Large eyes	86	90	94
Slit mouth	96	95	96
Vestigial nose	92	90	96
Large cranium	88	96	95
Gray skin	87	81	86
Leader	27	23	23
Onboard			
Exam room	89	85	92
Disk craft	71	75	65
Implants	19	23	29
Cool temp.	88	93	92
Round room	83	81	94
Reprodctv exam	25	26	41
Indirect lighting	63	69	63
Scan	44	32	37
Task assignment	21	25	45
Examining table	89	93	95
Otherworld	23	24	16
Telepathy	73	68	91
Exam occurs	71	71	76
Cataclysm	21	21	27
Instrumntl exam	41	35	39
Forget	48	48	55
Conference	35	36	31
Aftermath			
Aftereffects	81	73	80
Skin/eye irritatn	26	17	9
Nightmares	33	31	33
More ESP	33	17	9
Scars	19	20	21
Repeat encounters	48	59	76

take mental control over their captives and transport them into a UFO, where they receive a standardized examination in a typical room and later communications and messages, then return home with full or partial blockage of memory that later breaks down to account for strange dreams, anxieties, and sensations. Most narrators retell the original story with little modification or embellishment – a fact that impresses the reader with numbing clarity after examining a few hundred reports. Some critics argue that the story has evolved over the years and varies a great deal, but these arguments depend on a selection of exceptional accounts rather than a representative sample. Judging from a large collection of reports, a complex but monotonous basic plot survives intact, despite the creative potential inherent in the abduction theme, and impervious to most of the suggestions that have proliferated in mass and popular culture.

We might ask: what would we hear if abductees described a genuine experience? Even if the aliens did everything the same way every time, the observer would still be an important variable. No two would ever describe the same events in exactly the same way. Observers are fallible, memory is prone to distortion, and descriptions are unstandardized. Comparing witnesses' verbal descriptions of aliens with the pictures they draw shows how misleading the words can be. These variables sum to an inevitable latitude in the descriptions. Add the likelihood that these aliens are not complete automatons but adapt to circumstances, treat some individuals one way and some another, and treat the same individual in different ways at different times. Throw in the possibility of deception and thought control. Haze it all over with the emotional state of the captive – amazement, fear, surprise, induced stupor – and it comes as no surprise that the various portrayals should present a somewhat chaotic picture. That's what we would reasonably expect from people recalling real events.

At the same time we would expect some unity of alien purpose, some commonality of technique, if the events have a basis in reality. In fact we do see a body of consistencies. The reports include the recurrent elements tabulated in Table 1, and a number of lesser motifs as well. The recurrence of aspects of the reproductive procedures (see Table 2, p. 100) shows the historical depth of some story elements and indicates that they were around before publicity highlighted them. Here again are characteristics of a reality remembered and not a fiction imagined. True, some abductees elaborate their stories in idiosyncratic ways – Betty Andreasson comes first to mind – but the common core persists with notable consistency. John Mack and others take an interest in spiritual aspects at the expense of the physical, but even as they downplay the physical side to emphasize their interests, the old constants still riddle the abductees' stories. They may be hard to find amid the love and philosophy, but they are there. Not every claim of abduction is genuine. There are hoaxes and honest errors to cloud the picture. Then too, a genuine experiencer could add imaginative elements or be led astray by suggestions, whether from investigators or aliens. Despite all the noise, there is still a signal. It is that persistent, stable core of motifs, and whatever their origin or meaning may be, those motifs are there as a descriptive fact. "Stability" does not mean carbon copies. It means – if the reality interpretation is correct – that witnesses of similar experiences describe similar events within the range of variability that the experience and the shortcomings of human observers allows.

Changes in the Story

More interesting to explore than the similarities are the differences. The middle column of Table 1 shows mild alterations while several distinct trends appear on the right. An unmistakable variation shifts the capture setting from outside to indoors. The highway hijack of the Hills characterized many early reports, and the approach of a UFO left a memorable clue to abduction on those fateful drives, but as the highway scenario has diminished, so have observations of a UFO present at the time of capture.

A theory flourishes that abduction results from sleep paralysis as the number of bedroom locations increases. Distinctive and recurrent properties accompany sleep paralysis, such as a sense of flotation, monotonous droning sounds, missing time, ambient luminosity, and inability to move. If sleep paralysis really explains abductions, or at least bedroom abductions, the corollary applies that more sleep-related reports should mean more reports of experiential phenomena related to sleep paralysis. The highway or the out-of-doors provided the abduction site of choice in the early years following the Hill abduction. Only about 15 percent of abductions were then bedroom visitations, but this pattern made a dramatic and undeniable reversal over the years. Bedroom abductions have multiplied at the expense of other sites until the easiest way to see aliens is now simply to stay at home. Two thirds of abductions now occur there and often in conjunction with sleep, but the expected increase in sleep-related phenomena as a proportion of all effects has failed to materialize. Far from gaining ground in parallel with the growth in bedroom intrusions, the proportion of reports that mention key sleep-related effects has remained constant over time, while the proportion of cases mentioning auditory effects like droning sounds during the capture process has actually decreased slightly. The outcome we see is the opposite of what we should expect if more and more

Table 2
Reports Over Time of Elements Related to Reproduction

	To 1977	'78—'86	1987+
Total reports containing reproductive elements	33%	31%	41%
Reproductive examination, needle in abdomen	10	17	27
Sexual activity	6	4	3
Rejection as reproductively unsuitable	4	1	1
Missing fetus	2	2	4
Hybrid, clone	6	6	9
See or hold baby, beings indicate desire for baby	6	1	2
Nursery, presence of children, presentation scene	4	2	5
Incubatorium, tanks, bodies or body parts	4	2	5
Message about reproduction, interbreeding	2	2	2

people mistake sleep paralysis for an abduction experience (see Table 3).

In the pre-1978 group there were only eight bedroom cases, so those percentages swing more wildly than where samples are larger. Even so, there is no clustering of sleep paralysis traits toward the bedroom category. Paralysis, the most characteristic trait, is no more common among bedroom cases than in outdoor or highway encounters. No pattern connects floating sensations with the bedroom or sleep. Beam or UFO appearances favor outdoor locations over indoor ones, and that comes as no surprise. Oz effects also favor out-of-door localities, where presumably silence or

Table 3
Sleep-paralysis phenomena in relation to location of capture

The categories checked were Beam or UFO Visible, Oz Effects, Drone or similar sound effect, Paralysis, Missing Time, Sudden Entry, and Flotation. These are the surrealistic elements or elements closest to classic sleep paralysis phenomena. The three time groups are for pre-1978, 1978-1986, 1987+ (actually through circa 1995-96). The three location categories are Bedroom/Household (B), Outdoor (O), and Highway (H). Numbers represent percentages.

	pre-1978			1978-1986			1987+		
	B	O	H	B	O	H	B	O	H
BM/UFO	50	94	96	50	70	93	48	78	91
OZ	25	0	25	5	12	23	6	13	17
Drone	13	28	33	18	30	18	16	9	17
Paralysis	25	50	25	28	30	28	37	16	37
MT	75	61	83	65	60	78	65	74	91
Sudden Entry	38	50	42	30	33	25	42	41	37
Float	88	61	38	35	42	55	48	33	57

---

absence of activity would be more noteworthy. All in all this breakdown into categories only confirms what the aggregate shows – as bedroom cases have increased over the years, potential sleep-related phenomena have not. Their description seems unconnected with sleep paralysis and calls into question its explanatory value.

Another undeniable trend is the growing prevalence of multiple encounters. Once was enough for the Hills, but a whole lifetime of abduction has become the norm. Certain details of the Hill story have proven rare in the literature or, from a skeptical viewpoint, never caught on and consequently diminished or died out. These elements include the wedge-shaped room, the souvenir book, the star map, and caps and scarves as part of alien attire. Dwindling claims of eye and skin irritation or increases in ESP and paranormal experiences may owe more to irregular attention from investigators than to a genuine tendency.

David Jacobs (1998: 55-57) warns that descriptions of entities, alien messages, and notions of intent partake of more volatility than other parts of the story. In this sample, intentions, interpretations, attitudes, and feelings certainly vary among abductees and investigators with a mercurial fluidity that befits a subjective nature. Messages continue to predict an impending cataclysm, but its cause has shifted with cultural fashion from nuclear war to ecological threats. A growing emphasis on apocalypse, instructions to forget until the time is right, and assignments of some unconscious task to help prevent world destruction or ameliorate its consequences perhaps reflect the spiritual meanings that have crystallized around abduction over the years. More telepathy as the communications mode of choice, and more implants and reproductive elements in the examination may spring from the widening familiarity of abduction.

The description of entities holds mostly constant in the present sample. They begin as short humanoids and so they remain, with a steady minority of Nordic beings and little room for monsters, despite the diligent advocacy of Hollywood. One area of apparent change centers on the structure of humanoid eyes. The Hills describe distinct pupils, so do Herbert Schirmer, Sgt Moody, Betty Andreasson and other early abductees. By 1981 the influential first book of Budd Hopkins, *Missing Time*, shows these pupils enlarged until they fill the entire eye, and in 1987 Whitley Strieber's *Communion* enshrined the vast shiny dark eye as the norm. A cursory look at the recent literature seems to confirm that abductees have fallen into step behind these cultural influences. The ambiguity of verbal descriptions handicaps any search for change, but abductees provide enough pictorial illustrations of humanoid entities to open a more reliable avenue of comparison. With 17 examples from the early period, 28 from the middle, and 71 from the late, the darkening trend turns out to be little trend at all in the latter two periods, where entirely dark eyes make up 61% and 69% of the total, respectively. The early period is more problematic. Only one illustration shows an unmistakable instance of full darkness, while six present pupils of more or less average size. In five cases the eyes have pupils, but so large they nearly fill the visible surface, while another five illustrations are ambiguous – no pupils, but whether the blank eyes are dark remains uncertain. Counting both large and ambiguous pupils as dark gives a total of 65% and brings the early sample into line with its successors, suggesting that the overall history of the eye motif shows more resistance than responsiveness to the beguilements of cultural images, though critics could question this conclusion as special pleading.

Cultural source hypotheses derive little sustenance from the timing of changes. An established truism among skeptics asserts that the standard humanoid originated with Spielberg's *Close Encounters* (e.g., Peebles 1994: 234), but 26 illustrations on record prior to release of the movie tell a different story – 13 show standard or near-standard humanoids and five others show deviant humanoids. Another eight illustrations depict non-humanoid or very deviant entities. This evidence demonstrates beyond a doubt that typical humanoids preceded *Close Encounters*, but a better case for influence can be built around *The UFO Incident*. Of nine illustrations on record prior to October 1975, only three approximate the standard form and two others show deviant humanoids, while the remaining four veer off from the norm. Nearly half of the occupants represent unusual types at this early stage, and either the small sample of illustrations is unrepresentative or cultural sources, familiarity, and expectation have helped to create a stereotypical image. Whitley Strieber's *Communion* introduced squat blue entities and its graphic description of a rectal probe enhanced reporting of this rare incident, though both motifs remain scarce.

The hybrid scenario, reptile and insect entities, military abductions, and abductees identifying themselves as aliens join the story as novel additions – or the perception of them – over the past dozen or so years. Most striking among these is the hybridization project. With its stolen fetuses, embryos floating in jars, and nurturing sessions when humans meet their hybrid children, the hybrid scenario seems far removed from the Hill encounter or any other early report. Critics charge that multiplication of these claims in the wake of books by Budd Hopkins (1987) and David Jacobs (1992) proves the influences of investigators and culture explain the abduction phenomenon. Table 2 indicates a knottier problem. The total proportion of reports with aspects of the hybrid scenario stayed about the same during the first two periods, then rose after publication of Hopkins's best-selling *Intruders*. This growth is not very dramatic in overall numbers, but the density of elements increases and a new, well-formed episode takes shape from parts of the story formerly scattered and obscure. While the promotion of investigators has highlighted the hybrid scenario, whether they have created or only called attention to it remains a question still. What a comparison of reports also says is that the development of the episode is new, but its origins are not. The basic elements have roots deep in abduction history, some as far back as the Hills and Antonio Villas Boas.

In his research for this symposium Karl Pflock uncovered a remarkable and revealing document – Walter Webb's 1965 report to NICAP on the Hill case. Webb was the initial investigator and interviewed the Hills a few weeks after their encounter in 1961. He participated in the subsequent investigations and was privy to results of the hypnotic sessions, some of which, to save Barney's embarrassment, John Fuller omitted from his book. On p.11 of the report, Webb summarizes some of these hidden details of Barney's examination as they emerged under hypnosis: "He felt a cup-like device placed around his genitals and believed a sperm specimen was somehow withdrawn. His left arm was scraped for skin cells, and his ears and throat were checked. He was rolled over on his stomach. A cylindrical object was inserted up the rectum, and once again the witness believed something was extracted."

Here at the beginning of abduction awareness we read of examination events that could belong to the most recent case on the books. The skin scrapings and the ear-and-throat checkup may simply echo Betty's dreams, but the sperm extraction and rectal probe originate with Barney. If he created a fantasy, he contributed as an active rather than a passive partner.

Despite its exemplary quality, Webb's report apparently dropped out of sight with the publication of *The Interrupted Journey* and went unseen except by a few NICAP insiders. David Jacobs rediscovered the sperm extraction incident in early 1976 when he questioned Betty about it, but the idea circulated thereafter with the substance of a rumor rather than a fact, something everyone had heard but no one could trace to a source. A special status enshrines this motif. It soared to prominence after Budd Hopkins described reproductive procedures as a standard routine, and it now holds a central position in speculations that a program to breed hybrids explains the entire abduction phenomenon. An anal probe of cylindrical shape figured in a memorable incident of Whitley Strieber's *Communion*. Even to well-versed students of abduction this probe seemed unprecedented, but in reporting this motif as well as the sperm extraction, we now know that Barney Hill got there first.

Reading Barney's hidden testimony after 35 years of obscurity raises goosebumps with the thought that here is a kind of independent evidence, a proof of sorts that abduction reports are all alike from the earliest to the latest. Of course the reality is less clear-cut. People did read Webb's report and its contents possibly influenced some key investigators. Hopkins started his investigative career with Ted Bloecher, who may have learned of the report through his contacts with NICAP, while Hopkins may have passed along hints of the anal probe while investigating Whitley Strieber's abductions. Any critic who wishes to search for possible vectors will have no trouble finding them. Any history of sperm-taking during the interim between the Hill case and the early investigations of Hopkins in the late 1970s, or anal probes prior to the publication of *Communion* in 1987, holds interest for what the evidence might tell us about investigator influences on shaping the abduction story.

A review of early reports shows that neither motif is very common, though both put in appearances. Among the abduction cluster of 1973 is the case of Leah Proctor, a college student who went missing for several days then walked into a sheriff's office on October 24, recalling from conscious memory an abduction that included a rectal exam along with other familiar procedures (Randle 1988: 45-52). A Spanish case supposed to have happened in 1978 came from one Julio F. Under hypnosis he reported an examination that included wires attached to his anus and other parts of his body, and extraction of bodily materials by means of these wires. His captors extracted semen as well, but since this story appeared in the early 1980s, the ideas may result from contamination; or alternately, since the beings tapped him for every sort of body fluid, their recourse to his anus and penis may represent thoroughness rather than a significant motif. Reproductive interest was common from the start, but for males the usual form was sex of the old-fashioned kind while most descriptions of mechanical or high-tech procedures came from female captives. Few aliens took an interest in the genitals of male abductees, according to accounts published before about 1980. An early exception is Gilberto G. Ciccioli, an Argentinean man who reported an abduction near Buenos Aires on October 4, 1972, and claimed that the aliens took both blood and a sperm sample. Brief mention in *Flying Saucer Review* (Vol 19/6, 1973: 16-17) gives no hint about the means of extraction and leaves the reliability of the report in doubt. Again from South America, Antonio Villas Boas discussed his case once more in 1978 and added that the female occupant collected a sperm sample in a container (Webb 1994: 289, note 31). A young Brazilian man, Jocelino de Mattos, reported that entities used a tubular device to take a sperm sample and placed the sample in a cellophane package during his abduction on April 13, 1979 (Gevaerd 1984). This incident received extensive investigation in late 1980 and early 1981, before any of Hopkins' cases entered wide circulation.

For both motifs the pedigree runs thin. Domestic accounts of sperm extraction do not turn up in the abduction literature between the Hill case and the findings of Hopkins – for one early example, see the case of J. E. (Hopkins 1981b: 54-55). At least no one can blame Webb's report for spreading an epidemic of tales about semen-robbing aliens prior to Hopkins. Perhaps chance can account for the few cases on record, though in all fairness most early investigations, or at least the printed reports, were often sketchy, and the possible sensitivities of abductees or investigators could leave blank spots for the datum in question. We can only say that these extractions as well as anal probes did occur in the literature, and they offer some shreds of evidence for continuity in the examination procedures throughout the history of abductions.

The Hills captured the core abduction story better, we know now, than we ever imagined, but they did not exhaust its full range of events. There is no surprise here – it would be unreasonable to expect the first report to encompass all that could happen, either because only a partial phenomenology unfolded during a single encounter or because investigators grasped only a portion of the witnesses' experience. The Hills' immediate successors rounded out the story with the rest of its episodes and incidents in short order. Most motifs were present at least in rudimentary form by the mid 1970s, and by 1980 the literature contained, if not fully developed episodes or descriptions, precursors recognizable in retrospect for all the core content. Abduction quickly gave up its secrets, and narrators have added little since. Perceptions, interpretations, and emphases change – for instance, staring eyes became important only when David Jacobs recognized them as a theme, but a review of the record confirms that staring incidents happened before anyone noticed them.

In terms of actual content, most pieces of the puzzle were laid on the table in the 10 years following publication of Fuller's book in 1966, and herein lies a genuine surprise. A more extravagant claim than alien abduction is hard to imagine. If imagination was unencumbered with reality in these accounts, even the prodding of a modest imaginative talent might be expected to have driven the Hills' story off toward space opera, romance, adventure, and much else, and surely enough people have shared this claim to provide the necessary talent. Both the proliferation of abduction ideas in culture and the typical creative dynamics of narratives argue that abduction, like the Roswell story, should have burst from its frame to scatter plots in all directions and to elaborate contents in astounding abundance. The opposite has happened, as abductees manifest a surprising conservatism. That so much opportunity should beget so little real difference in so many years is surely a mystery – if the story is just a story.

Abduction Memories or False Memories?

An effort to understand abduction turns sooner or later to the human players – what sort of people are abductees, how important is the investigator's part? A story with a surreal, dreamlike atmosphere and so many sexual preoccupations sounds tailor-made for a psychological solution. Early in the game critics took a confident stand that such strange accounts must originate with strange people. In one evaluation the Hills underwent a *folie à deux* and UFO experiences in general traced to various modes of psychopathology (Grinspoon and Persky 1972: 238-239), in another Betty Andreasson's abduction issued from a fantasy brought on by personal stress (Taves 1979-1980). Philip J. Klass (1988: 32, 187-188) dismisses many abductees as hoaxers seeking recognition and profit, while various explanations invoke fantasy proneness or a boundary-deficit condition as personality traits that leave some people unable to distinguish truth from fiction (Kottmeyer 1988; Bartholomew, Basterfield, and Howard 1991). Another theory championed by psychologist Michael Persinger (1990) locates abduction and other paranormal phenomena in the temporal lobe of the brain, where abnormal activity provokes strange sensations and hallucinatory experiences.

The critics misplaced their confidence in the abnormality of abductees. Repeated application of standard psychological tests such as the Minnesota Multiphasic Personality Inventory (MMPI) have failed to find any trace of psychopathology among abductees as a group (Bloecher, Clamar, and Hopkins 1985: 33; Parnell and Sprinkle 1990: 55; Rodeghier, Goodpaster, and Blatterbauer 1991: 72; Stone-Carmen 1994: 313). In fact subjects claiming entrance into a UFO scored slightly lower – that is, nearer the mid-line of normalcy – than subjects claiming nothing more than the observation of a distant light, according to one study (Parnell 1986: 47). Individual abductees may deviate considerably from the norm, but the proportion of extreme scores approximates the parallel ratio within the general population (Rodeghier *et al.* 1991: 73). The fantasy-prone hypothesis has stumbled in every test (Rodeghier *et al.* 1991: 70; Ring and Rosing 1990: 70), while one study, notable because it originated with skeptics, cleared abductees from charges of fantasy proneness, psychopathology, and temporal lobe activity (Spanos *et al.* 1993: 628-629).

In general abductees fail to light up with any distinctive psychological traits, and conform to the personality profile of a typical cross-section of society. The few differences are themselves intriguing. The abductees of Ring and Rosing (1990: 71-74) scored above average for dissociative skills and a childhood marked by unhappiness or abuse. More than half of Stone-Carmen's subjects (1994: 313) reported suicidal feelings or attempts, a percentage far above the national average.

Combined with key characteristics of abduction such as amnesia, recurrent nightmares, panic reactions, intrusive imagery, and emotional swings between denial and acceptance, dissociative tendencies and self-destructive urges sweep abductees into a sphere of traits characteristic of Post-Traumatic Stress Disorder (PTSD) (Wilson 1990: 6). At one time PTSD seemed like proof that abductees experienced a literal and traumatic encounter, on the assumption that only genuine traumatic experience caused PTSD, but in fact similar symptoms may appear in fantasy-prone and possibly other vulnerable personality types without an experience of trauma (Brenneis 1997: 36-37). Even without fantasy-proneness the relationship between trauma and its consequences still takes twists and turns. Abductee trauma must necessarily be mild or else MMPI scores should register sharp deviations. This mildness also calls into question an alternative interpretation that positions child abuse as the core event and abduction as a screen memory to throw blame onto an external assailant, thereby sparing subjects the acknowledgement of betrayal by a family member (Powers 1994: 49). A history of abuse typically leaves a more distinctive psychological scar than abductees demonstrate (see, for example, Belkin *et al.* 1994: 540; Leavitt 1994: 389; Noblitt 1995: 745-746).

One possible explanation for a mixture of normal personality traits and signs of PTSD is a self-selection process among people who report abduction. Perhaps individuals who speak out – presumably a small fraction of a much larger group – recall rather than repress disturbing memories because the pain and stress of other life events have prepared them to weather emotional shock. When abduction strikes such people, they cope with better overall resilience than unprepared individuals. Another possibility is that traumatic forgetting is not the key mechanism behind time lapse. Many abductees describe the experience as frightening, but few seem scared out of their wits. Some people react with curiosity, awe, anger, annoyance – the full spectrum of human responses to a situation, not a uniform reaction that might dependably result in amnesia. Within the microcosm of the Hill story we see a division of reactions. Barney experiences intense fear and falls deeply under the entities' spell, whereas Betty expresses curiosity despite frightening moments, and successfully resists to some extent the efforts to control her. If abduction accounts are literally true, some sort of hypnotically induced amnesia or mind control technique seems a more likely cause for the time lapse than any form of traumatic shock.

Speculations along these lines entangle abductions in the labyrinthine and acrimonious dispute over recovered *versus* false memories (see Loftus and Ketcham 1994; Ofshe and Watters 1994; Nathan and Snedeker 1995; Pendergrast 1995). Reminders of the Salem witchcraft epidemic echoed through the 1980s as children across the country accused day-care center operators of sexual abuse and satanic rituals, leading to expensive trials, divided communities, and imprisonment for many of the accused. At the same time adult women entered therapy for minor problems and emerged with lurid memories of sexual abuse and rituals committed by their parents. A recovered memory movement urged women to believe they had been abused, to interpret vague and ambiguous feelings as well as every personal problem as evidence for abuse, and to seek the help of sympathetic therapists committed to wresting these repressed memories from their clients. *The Courage to Heal* (1988), a best-selling guide by Ellen Bass and Laura Davis, became the bible of this movement and encouraged thousands of women to discover apparent memories of incest.

The sincerity of testimony that convinced juries failed to impress scientists who studied the memories underlying these accusations. No persuasive physical evidence confirmed satanic rituals, and the allegations were implausible in the extreme and sometimes contradicted by demonstrable facts. Researchers challenged the videotape theory of memory with evidence that recall was a reconstructive process and subject to distortion by influence and expectation. They blamed the burgeoning docket of unsubstantiated accusations on zealots leading vulnerable individuals to believe in events that never happened, and identified the structured environment of therapy sessions and recovery groups as ideal for the creation and reinforcement of false memories. Supporters of repressed memory argued that the repeated trauma of the abused necessitated adaptive forgetting, but other researchers questioned the reality of massive repression on both experimental and historical grounds. As usual the truth may lie somewhere between these extremes, but the moral is abundantly clear: some people create memories out of suggestion and endow them with such emotional heft that these false memories become indistinguishable from the true.

If therapists created false memories of satanism, critics soon asked why not the same origin for an equally fantastic claim of alien abduction (e.g., Spanos, Burgess, and Burgess 1994; Paley 1997; Showalter 1997: 189-201)? Both accounts share an underlying thread of investigators with agendas and hypnosis or some other form of facilitated recall to uncover hidden memories. Dr. Simon took for granted that amnesia could hide traumatic events and hypnosis could break the block, but he cautioned at the same time that hypnosis was no "royal road to TRUTH" but led only to truth as the subjects understood it (Fuller 1966: 9), a personal or story truth rather than historical truth. Experts agree that hypnosis enhances suggestibility, role-playing, and uncritical thinking – in other words, the technique fosters a state of mind in which false memories thrive (Bullard 1989: 6-12). Experiments seem to confirm that non-abductees tell stories under hypnosis that differ little from accounts of real abductees (Lawson 1980: 201-205). Randle, Estes, and Cone (1999) draw the critical literature together in a powerful three-pronged attack. Natural but unusual occurrences like sleep paralysis lend abduction an experiential background, cultural influences from science fiction and media attention to UFOs provide plot and content ideas, but investigators perform the alchemy that transmutes mere raw materials into a full-blown abduction story. These authors uncover evidence that abduction investigators impose their expectations on hypnotized subjects through leading and suggestive questions, and dismiss abduction reports as nothing more than confabulated fantasies, the bad outcome of flawed procedures.

The case for false memory sounds better in the telling than under close argument. While the dangers of hypnosis are undeniable and faults of investigators may be legion, about one fourth of abductees keep full conscious awareness without hypnosis and most of them remember parts of the experience ranging from isolated sensations and images to extended narratives. The findings of a skeptical doctoral student at Concordia University are revealing. Hypnosis of eleven abductees brought out new episodes of the story in two subjects, elaboration of consciously recalled episodes in seven, and no new episodes in two (Day 1998: 119), hardly supportive of hypnosis as a creative mainspring. The Hills appear to have been receptive subjects capable of deep trance, but this ability does not generalize to the broader abductee population. As a group abductees are no more susceptible than the average (Rodeghier *et al.* 1991: 80; Spanos *et al.* 1993: 629). Some descriptions from non-abductees under hypnosis parallel the descriptions of real abductees, but conclusions based only on similarities overlook glaring differences – for example, each experimental subject describes a different type of entity while most real abductees describe humanoids. Day (1998: 144) experimented by suggesting medical motifs to one group of hypnotized subjects and they told stories enriched with medical references, yet another group planted with suggestions of message motifs returned no significant increase in references. Suggestion and story content interact in ways more complex than a mere deposit-and-return relationship.

No better instance of cultural influence presents itself than Barney Hill's descriptions of elongated and speaking eyes of the aliens, qualities so unusual and specific that they seem indisputable derivations from the Bellero Shield episode of *The Outer Limits* (Kottmeyer 1994). Sharpening the importance of this point is the fact that the Hills did not watch this series on a regular basis. Something as slight as a chance or passing observation planted these motifs as cryptomnesic memories, then, with the source promptly forgotten, they re-emerged as integral parts of Barney's story when he began hypnosis two weeks later. Here media images mutate into false memories before our eyes.

Yet two counter-examples illustrate that abductees also resist suggestion with equally little rhyme or reason. Critics have argued that Betty's nightmares contaminated Barney's memory with an abduction scenario, since his account remained a pale and passive copy of hers. This proposal ignores the uniqueness of his story. It corresponds to hers as long as they stay together but turns off on an independent course as soon as they part ways inside the ship. A pervasive semi-conscious state blunts the vividness and detail of his account but not its individuality, and original to his story are the sperm-taking and anal probe incidents omitted from the book, yet destined to become commonplace abduction motifs. Returning again to Betty's nightmares, she dreamed of aliens with large noses only to see small noses under hypnosis, as did Barney. Whether hypnosis cleared some dream-induced distortions of memory or falsified the imagery of a dream remains moot, but another lesson is plain enough: suggestion, even self-suggestion, holds nothing like absolute sway over the story. Far from spinning like weather vanes before every prevailing influence, abductees mingle some external elements into the account but block out others, with no obvious pattern in sight.

Malleability accompanies human memory as part of its baggage of imperfections. If abductees remember a genuine experience, this normal weakness should taint their recall, and any blanket exemption would be almost as remarkable as the abduction itself. Even vivid memories like those of John Kennedy's assassination are subject to distortion, though some research affirms that the central events of emotionally powerful memories resist change while peripheral details are vulnerable (Flathman 1999: 12). The basic fact of the assassination holds firm, or else memory would prove more treacherous than useful. We could expect the same for an event as impressive as abduction, if it truly happened.

A consideration of the Hills' performance under hypnosis casts further doubt on the creative role of this procedure. Critics have rightly condemned recovered memory therapists for their tenacity. Convinced that they will find abuse, these therapists coax accusations out of small children and build false memories in adults with dogged determination, refusing to take No for an answer. The typical adult client starts out with nothing more definitive than mild anxieties, low self-esteem, or ordinary troubles in personal relations. In the hands of a committed therapist these problems metamorphose into consequences of childhood sexual abuse, and lead to a regimen of suggestion as the therapist prods the client to describe ever more distinctive memories of this supposed abuse. An explosive onrush of emotions and vivid memories often occurs at some crisis point in the therapy, but as a rule these spectacular breakthroughs are a long time coming, and prior to the big revelation the memories creep out slowly, in the form of vague and indirect hints with a significance that only the therapist recognizes. This resistance comes not from absence of abuse, but because the client is in denial, according to the standard explanation, but the therapist can afford to be patient. With treatments lasting for months or years the therapist has ample time to dig out a life history of abuse – or, as critics see it, therapist and client co-operate in ongoing rounds of suggestions and interpretations that create an elaborate, elaborating horror fantasy out of innocent fragments of life history and borrowings from survivor doctrine (e.g., Ofshe and Watters 1994: 5).

The course of the Hills' testimony strikes a noteworthy contrast to this scenario. Their stories spilled out in a hurry, as if awaiting release once hypnosis broke through some sort of barrier. Barney's first hypnotic session revealed his terrifying capture experiences and the second brought out most of his onboard experiences. Betty recounted her abduction from beginning to end in her first session and later added only details. Neither of the Hills required prodding except with regard to isolated points, and many of their memories burst forth with immediate emotion. A certain unrehearsed quality characterizes stretches of the story where the descriptions include much puzzlement, surprise, and recognition from time to time that their behavior was unusual. These reactions seem characteristic of two people making discoveries rather than participating in make-believe. Not all supposedly repressed memories of sexual abuse require months of groundwork and buildup. Hence, the quick access of the Hills to their abduction memories does not in any way prove that those memories are literally true. What does seem reasonable is a conclusion that hypnosis sessions did not provide the creative workshop for the Hills to confabulate a story. Its source must be sought outside the therapeutic setting, either in experience or in a combination of Betty's dreams and various cultural sources.

Visions of the Night

Betty's unfolding series of nightmares began ten days after the interrupted journey and marked the first indication that something out of sight and conscious mind also happened that night. She kept a record of those dreams and they foretell her recollections under hypnosis with remarkable fidelity. Only a few changes in detail separate the two accounts. According to standard ufological interpretation, the blocked memories of Betty's abduction broke into conscious awareness during sleep and hypnosis simply lowered the barrier once again, allowing her to recall the same experience and set straight a few minor errors in her dreams. This explanation reflects a popular notion that frightening experiences replay in dreams with literal fidelity (see Fuller 1966: 342). Extensive publicity about repressed memories has reinforced this belief, but in fact it runs afoul of most dream research. Even everyday dreams incorporate a residue of the day by portraying concerns of the dreamer along with familiar characters and settings, but Freud's transformations of displacement, symbolization, condensation, and secondary elaboration mediate between any particular event and the dream that unfolds, so typical dreams are metaphoric and surreal rather than representational. When dreams mirror a supposed reality, alarms should ring that this is no reality at all.

Psychologists may set aside traumatic dreams as an exception to the rule. A hallmark of combat veterans suffering from post-traumatic stress is a recurring and intrusive nightmare of concrete, seemingly literal events played out with shattering emotions. Victims of accidents, disasters, and violent crimes often suffer from similar nightmares for a limited time. An extensive clinical literature enshrines these dreams as accurate replicas of the traumatic experience (e.g., Terr 1990: 210), or at least recognizes the possibility that dreamers relive the trauma in their dreams. This literal replay establishes one extreme on a spectrum of dream possibilities for traumatized individuals, where the next in line mixes actual scenes with life experiences unrelated to the trauma to create a plausible but fictitious scenario, and still more remote examples undergo thorough transformation to become mostly fantastic despite some realistic settings and events (Wilmer 1996: 88). The fracture between clinical and experimental psychologists over the issue of repressed memories also divides psychologists on the issue of literalness in dreams. Hard-nosed critics complain that clinicians present too little evidence to back their assertions. Claims for literalness need to provide the reader with full dream texts to judge, high standards for what counts as a likeness, and confirmation that the dream events truly reflect reality. The clinicians fail to meet these criteria (Brenneis 1997: 20).

No one questions that trauma stimulates dreams. They begin after a disturbing experience and continue for a few days or weeks, much the way that Betty reported. The dreams often dwell at first on events of the experience then evolve to deal with emotions, typical stages in the process of absorbing an external event into the inner life of the dreamer. In extreme cases associated with PTSD, the process sticks in the initial stage and the dream of a traumatic event repeats night after night with the vividness of the experience itself (Hartmann 1996: 100-103, 109). The literature abundantly confirms these observations. What remains in question is how closely the dream compares to reality. The weight of research affirms that traumatic dreams are homomorphic rather than isomorphic, analogous in some way to the experience but by no means a videotaped replica. These dreams track the mood and threat of the traumatic event, but they always transform the terms of representation so that reconstruction of the historical event is not possible from dream material alone. In comparisons of dreams with reality, even the closest approximations include alterations and distortions. The true isomorphic dream – one that faithfully mimics the traumatic event – does not exist (Brenneis 1997: 17-26), or at best is rare (Hartmann 1998: 224).

The dreams of PTSD sufferers may repeat unchanged for years, but not all recurrent dreams result from trauma. Recurrent dreams are common, with two-thirds to three-fourths of participants in surveys reporting one or more instances in a lifetime. Such dreams accompany times of stress then abate when the dreamer successfully copes with the stress, and most often befall people low in psychological well-being. Negative content predominates – it often takes the form of monsters in childhood, while the threatening figures naturalize into burglars, strangers, or members of a mob among adults. The external threat internalizes in adults as the dreamer assumes more and more responsibility for the action. Recurrent dreams are no more literal than ordinary dreams, and most of the content remains idiosyncratic. And yet themes common across individuals who report recurrent dreams have been noted. These include flying, falling, being chased, taking an examination, losing one's teeth, and nudity.

Feelings of fleeing, hiding, or watching helplessly are also common in such dreams (Zadra 1996: 231-232, 237, 241). Without reference to abduction when he compiled this list, the author nevertheless named motifs seemingly made to order for Betty's dreams, even down to the odd incident over Barney's false teeth. The similarities are undeniably striking.

Critics have emphasized Betty's dreams as the seed from which the Hills' abduction story grew, and the findings of dream research strengthen that argument at every turn. The evidence raises the likelihood that her dreams pictured fantasy events and built them from stock elements of dream content, while hypnosis simply gave her an opportunity to retell a well-rehearsed story. In this view Barney suffered from genuine fear of being captured and filled out these memories with Betty's dreams and cultural borrowings. If this explanation holds true, the Hill abduction and all its progeny follow from nothing more substantial than the airy vapors of a dream, and arguments in its favor are undeniably strong.

A final verdict would be premature, given the labyrinths of dream scholarship and certain possibilities it seems to allow. If recurrent traumatic nightmares differ from the literal truth, they may not differ by very much. Hartmann (1996: 105, 108, 112) argues that PTSD nightmares often vary from reality in one aspect or another but have none of the variable content of the ordinary nightmare. In fact they are not dreams at all; they are encapsulated memories that bypass the transformational processes of dreaming and intrude into sleep. These memories may impose themselves on dreams yet remain distinct from them, since memories of this kind break into any stage of sleep, not only the usual dreaming stage of REM (rapid eye movement) sleep or the non-REM sleep when night terrors occur. The same memories may also intrude in the waking state as flashbacks. People with thin boundaries are most likely to be subject to ordinary nightmares but not PTSD nightmares. The memory intrusions that comprise the latter often strike individuals with thick psychological armor, people who cope by walling off their traumatic experiences, though without success in this case since the memory forces itself into awareness despite efforts at isolation. Other researchers posit a strong tie between recurrent or traumatic dreams and specific personality traits – stress, neuroticism, depression, somatic symptomatology, and poor personal adjustment (Zadra 1996: 241), or fantasy-proneness and hypnotic susceptibility (Brenneis 1997: 36-38).

Whether exemptions from the transformational processes of dreaming apply to Betty's nightmares is a question that leads far down the long and twisted paths of speculation. She speaks of her dreams to say, "My emotional feelings during this part were of terror, greater than I had ever believed possible" (Fuller 1966: 342-343), suggesting an undercurrent of negative feelings that belies her apparent curiosity and self-control during captivity. Yet based on her narrative alone, her alleged experiences hardly seem horrifically traumatic, and Hartmann limits his concept of memory intrusions to the extremes of trauma that lead to PTSD. Barney's terror better qualified him for traumatic damage, but he reported no nightmares. Hartmann does not consider impressive or emotional but less threatening experiences as sources of encapsulated memories, though if an encapsulation process exists, perhaps it also operates outside of the extreme circumstances that Hartmann defines. Are extraordinary and uncanny experiences potent enough in their own way to trigger such an effect? The possibility is intriguing but untested, as far as I know.

A review of Betty's dream records shows that she dreamed of several literal elements – Barney, the dog, the car, the UFO, and the scene of asking Barney if he now believed in flying saucers. These literalisms anchor her dreams toward the isomorphic end of the spectrum, though of course they cannot vouch for the accuracy of her other descriptions. Certain inferences also suggest that her personality might be conducive to the encapsulation process. Her biography depicts a strong-willed and unconventional woman who set herself an independent course against prevailing norms. Her biracial marriage, profession, Unitarianism, and civil rights activities distinguished her as an out-of-the-ordinary individual in conservative, Protestant New Hampshire during a conformist 1950s era – differences that perhaps required her to cultivate a psychological thick skin and an ability to deflect the emotional sticks and stones tossed at her. With this adaptation well in place by the night of the interrupted journey, it is possible to imagine those memories lingering intact, unassimilated by the dream process and walled off but able to escape during sleep for five nightly forays.

In armchair analysis of her psychological profile, Betty stands out as something of a paradox. Her hypnotic susceptibility points to thin boundaries while her life history hints at thick. Distinctive personality traits do not apply to abductees as a group, but this population is diverse and includes some individuals with special characteristics. Out of a sample of 437 abductions reported between 1958 and 1998, 19 percent included mention of abduction nightmares. My 1987 sample of 103 high-information, high-reliability cases totaled 117 claimants who co-operated with investigators. Of this number, 20 or 23 – again about one fifth – described abduction-related nightmares. The record for after-effects is notoriously incomplete and the reports offer no way to judge personality correlates, but taken at face value, abduction-related nightmares seem to strike only a fraction of the abductee population. As one hypothetical way to explain this limited showing, perhaps relatively rare personal distinctions like Betty's contradictory mix of traits set preconditions favorable to a breakthrough of abduction memories.

A popular explanation holds that the Hills met spacemen equipped with some weird technology of thought control. However readily such visions dance in the heads of receptive believers, the fact remains that the proposition brings nothing of substance for building an argument. A rather more manageable proposal to save the extraterrestrial story suggests that the Hills fell under hypnotic influence or something akin to it. Their accounts are rife with references to intrusive eyes, repeated instructions, and a pervasive trance-like state that sapped their will. The alien leader's farewell to Betty included a statement that she would forget, similar to a post-hypnotic suggestion to restrict memories of the incident. Experts continue to dispute the nature of hypnosis, whether it represents a special mental state or a social-psychological interaction of role-playing, suggestion, and confabulation. The issue of separate cognitive modules versus inhibited expression may make no difference in terms of end results. Some people act as if they cannot or do not remember, and Dr. Simon's success when he induced post-hypnotic amnesia in Betty and Barney places the Hills among those people susceptible to hypnotic memory blocks.

What happens to memories restrained by hypnotic suggestion would be well worth understanding at this point. Do they ever emerge in sleep, and if so, how accurate are they? I have been unable to find research that addresses these specific issues. The closest relevant literature speaks only of tests involving readily forgettable lists of words or symbols. Dr. Simon's success in blocking the proceedings of hypnosis sessions will have to stand as evidence that suggestion could make the Hills forget extensive segments of experience. Much controversy surrounds the possibilities of memory repression, where a contingent of supporters credits massive repression for some traumatic memories, but a more persuasive contingent casts doubts on these suppositions. In any case hypnotic suggestion is not the mechanism at work. Studies treating dreams that arise from post-hypnotic suggestions affirm that the suggestions bear an influence on the subsequent dreams (Tart 1972: 139). On the other hand the suggested elements often mingle with the usual dream distortions and intrusions, until the final result leans closer to a typical dream than a copy of the suggestions.

Less certain in these experiments is the sleep status of the subject. The sleeper may dream while truly asleep, or may waken from true sleep and enter into hypnotic sleep in order to carry out the posthypnotic suggestions (Hilgard 1965: 160). Freud distinguished night fantasies as a form of imaginative thinking interspersed with sleep, with results often mistaken for dreams but without typical dream transformations. Lucid dreams designate a form of dreaming – or fantasy – in which the subject maintains awareness and control of the dream. Academic hair-splitting over the exact nature of these experiences may raise distinctions of little consequence in colloquial usage. Whatever happens at night in conjunction with sleep seems like a dream to most people, but only true dreams may require the transformation of contents. Betty's dreams may thus have seemed dreamlike without being the real thing in a strict sense. No studies that I have been able to find spell out any ties between dreaming and hypnotic amnesia, but the possibility is worth considering that memories blocked by hypnosis escape when sleep weakens the barrier, or if normal sleep gives way to hypnotic sleep.

Many aspects of psychology hinted at in the Hill case converge on the topic of dissociation, a splitting off of one aspect of consciousness from another. Dissociation can account for the forgetting of extensive experiences, since consciousness may resort to amnesia as protection from painful memories of trauma or stress, though this form of coping is extreme. One theory of hypnosis treats it as a controlled and structured type of dissociation (Cardeña 1994: 22). This view assumes the existence of subordinate cognitive systems, each with some degree of autonomy, integrated for many functions but capable of independent action as well. Suggestions from the hypnotist short-circuit the subject's mental chain of command, so that alterations of perceptual and motor functions observed in hypnosis result from external influence reordering hierarchical relationships among the various systems (Hilgard 1994: 38-41). Another phenomenon related to dissociation is state-dependent learning, where anything learned in one mental state is best — or uniquely — recoverable in that same state. Learning under hypnosis often involves dissociation of context and content. Temporal order is especially vulnerable, with the hypnotic subject recalling a series of events in random order, whereas everyday memory often depends on sequential recall as a retrieval strategy (Evans 1988: 177-178, 184-186). It may be remembered that Betty's dreams occurred in reverse order – not random, but not first-to-last, either. One explanation of post-hypnotic amnesia for a sequence of events thus blames it on a disruption of normal retrieval strategies. The memories remain always in mind, but they are inaccessible, dissociated until the subject re-enters the initial state, or a suggestion reassembles the cognitive modules and returns the memories to consciousness.

Much dissociation theory is as controversial as repression or the nature of hypnosis. I am well beyond my depth here, but dissociation scholarship is suggestive of several possibilities and deserves consideration in any effort to understand the Hills' story. Memories of a shocking experience may reside in a dissociated state inaccessible to consciousness except as a memory intrusion. Some sort of hypnotic control applied to the Hills might have set up a state-dependent situation that Betty's dreams or dream-like condition might have allowed her to re-experience, and thereby remember, her period of captivity. Hypnotic amnesia imposed on Betty may have encapsulated the memories until sleep lowered the barriers of resistance, or until normal sleep gave way to hypnotic sleep and the split-off memories reintegrated with conscious awareness. A study of dissociation among abductees finds that some 70% have this tendency (Powers 1994: 48), certainly far more than the 20% reporting abduction-related nightmares in my sample. The sample in Powers' study included only 20 individuals and may not be representative of the population as a whole, and dissociative skills alone may be insufficient to permit memories returning in nightmares. Still, where theory touches base with empirical reality, the relationship between dissociation and abduction dreams gains no apparent support. At best all these proposals are tenuous and speculative. I offer them only to avoid a rush to judgment and to point out possibilities by which Betty's dreams may have reflected reality after all.

In the End

The evidence at hand will not decide the nature of the Hills' interrupted journey, at least not to the satisfaction of everyone. Skeptics will dwell on Betty's dreamlike dreams and the fact that Barney had ample opportunity to learn their contents. A cogent argument will continue to center on the possibility that he recycled those dreams and borrowed cultural odds and ends to assemble his own account. The bizarre and unfounded tales of abuse that therapists have badgered out of children, or that adults have concocted out of suggestion and self-induced fantasies, will stand as a warning that human imagination can create false memories so circumstantial and emotion-laden that they solidify into personal realities, pivotal and redirecting events in the life of a person who in fact never lived them. The serious contender against either alien technology or memory loss through trauma is complex false memory, a situation in which suggestion, media-influenced content, and scraps of life experiences (e.g., dreams, visits to the doctor) join with personal needs and fantasy to create an elaborate memory of things that never happened. But it is probably impossible to distinguish true memory from false on the basis of narratives alone. No discernible line separates the two; no internal criteria divide them. Outside evidence is necessary to settle the issue, preferably physical. For external evidence, abductions have promised much and delivered little, leaving ufologists empty-handed of any persuasive physical proof.

The Hills brought back no direct physical evidence. Dr. Simon never accepted that they experienced anything as strange as they described. Barney spoke with quiet dignity to defend the memories recovered under hypnosis, saying they felt as real as any other memory; but research demonstrates that equalizing the feel of true and false memories is one peril of hypnosis. An intriguing clue like Barney's case of genital warts raises more questions than it answers. Here was another instance that seemed to point to psychosomatic reaction to the abduction, but in fact genital warts are not psychosomatic – they result from papillomavirus and nothing else. Here then is a delicate matter that may point to more stress in his life than emerged during therapy with Dr. Simon, or we must reach for such far-fetched ideas as aliens without sterile instruments, or a psychosomatic skin condition that a doctor misdiagnosed as genital warts. Neither of these alternatives scores many points for plausibility.

A sizable dossier of facts leaves the Hill case stranded in the limbo of surreal dreamscapes. Other facts and a richness of indirect evidence deserve consideration too. They back a conclusion that whatever happened to the Hills, it was more striking than an everyday fantasy, more substantial than dreams mistaken for reality.

So much uproar surrounding the abduction has overshadowed a close encounter that stands head and shoulders above most others on record. For half an hour the Hills watched a complex object that began with the apparent size of a nickel at arm's length and approached until it grew to the size of a dinner plate, or as wide as the distance between three telephone poles, when it hovered close by (Fuller 1966: 30, 42). The object seemed to maneuver and pursue the Hills' car in a purposeful manner, and showed structure. Under hypnosis Betty added that it passed before the face of the Moon, and blotted out the stars when directly above the car. The Hills observed the UFO from inside and outside their car, and with his binoculars Barney saw occupants through the windows of the craft. By any standard this report tallies a spectacular list of features.

While not proof, Barney's scuffed shoes and broken binocular strap attest to some uncommon event. Barney examined his lower abdomen and Betty refused to wear the clothes of that night again; both felt unclean. Betty's panic reactions, Barney's ulcers, and perhaps his reluctance to talk about that night, point to some sort of disturbing experience, not necessarily abduction, to be sure, and alternatives like an unsettling encounter with racist thugs (Matheson 1998: 55-56) have no leg to stand on in any testimony from the Hills. Such theories reflect only the fantasy-proneness of skeptics. The testimony of niece Kathy Marden throws another light on Barney's state of mind. She describes him as everybody's favorite uncle, always warm and jolly with the children of the family and consequently popular with them. After the night of the interrupted journey he changed to become distracted and moody, in notable contrast to his former manner. This state lasted until therapy with Dr. Simon brought out the abduction memories, and thereafter he became his old self once again. Was the abduction an elaborate fantasy to screen mundane stress? We will probably never know. What we see is a striking picture of a man afflicted with a period of acute stress – stress that began with the night of the interrupted journey and ended with release of the memories of that journey, in a relationship that seems notably sharp and clean.

In wider context the Hills tell a story cut from a common pattern, the first abduction to receive detailed investigation and widespread attention, but by no means the original. Crypto-abductions and Villas Boas affirm antecedents, while the subsequent flock of reports has strayed little from the Hill version. Impressions derived from selective reading can mar the image of consistency, but extensive comparisons confirm its shape. The core similarities have persisted before and after the story gained fame, alike with and without hypnosis, indifferent to the interests of investigators, and oblivious to cultural forces potent enough to redirect the story. Motifs like rejection of the infertile and harvesting of genetic materials, dying planets and hybrid-making, relate as different facets of the same theme. They demonstrate that whatever becomes a theme of the story, becomes a theme with depth, present from the early days and integrated into a pattern that escapes casual observation. Tales of ritual abuse seem more variable, more responsive to investigators, more wrapped up in the personal concerns of the subjects, whereas abductees never become the heroes of their own adventure. Their role remains that of impersonal objects used for the purposes of bland entities neither frightful enough to terrify, nor personable enough to become fleshed-out characters in the drama they instigate.

Unlike people reporting sexual and satanic abuse, abductees seem more like normal people troubled by a strange experience than like troubled people subject to strange fantasies. The overall normalcy of abductees repeats itself with every test (only Randle, Estes, and Cone [1999: 98-101] claim an exception, but they have not reported their psychological work in any systematic or detailed fashion). Neither fantasy-proneness nor suggestibility earmarks this population, and no other apparent psychological distinction predisposes abductees to false memories or fantastic yarns (see Appelle 1995-1996). An informal survey of the entities that appear in dreams or hallucinations reveals no typical alien form as a recurrent visitor – at least the bald, big-eyed image is not a default setting fixed in human imagery.

Cultural borrowings contaminate the story, but they alone seem unlikely to build it. Influences swarm in such abundance and variety that an argument for cultural models stabilizing abduction reports necessarily contradicts itself. The notion that investigators stitch the story into a whole must reckon with the number of investigators, each bringing different ideas and agendas to the task. So much consistency in the face of so much opportunity for variation stands at odds with the usual processes of human creativity, and stretches the credibility of any theory that the story is a whole-cloth product of false memories. Abduction opens a golden opportunity to fantasize, but abductees have not exploited it. Not even determined investigators seem able to rein in the creative impulse very effectively or for very long in comparable situations. UFOs have become mainstays of modern mythology. Beyond any question a great many mythic beliefs have accumulated around the subject, and abductions are bizarre enough to attract the most creative musings, but the uses humans make of the phenomenon do not explain the phenomenon itself. To recognize a rich structure of myths surrounding UFOs is to recognize how readily the subject of visitors from beyond grasps the human imagination, but to identify every parallel in the archives of human belief as proof that UFOs and abductions amount to psycho-social constructs simply goes too far. A search for parallels will always succeed, but mere analogies prove little. Only complex traits and meaningful evidence of influence builds a convincing case. "The Bellero Shield," as an influence on Barney's testimony, establishes just such a case, but most other arguments do not. An emphasis on content while ignoring narrative dynamics further undercuts the psychosocial argument. Variation is the true way of life for imaginative narratives, not the persistent consistency of abduction reports.

Our understanding of abductees and their psychology is too shallow, our knowledge of abduction reports too rife with error and false impression, for a literal interpretation to fall in our laps as a foregone conclusion. By the same token, no conventional alternative dissipates the multiple mysteries of the phenomenon. The Hills brought the modern era a myth it was waiting for, the right mix of technology and magic. The myth is so good that efforts to reduce it to any terms, conventional or otherwise, succeed only by whittling away the inconvenient evidence to fit a square peg into the chosen hole, of whatever shape. Yet in the end, behind the human uses and interests in the myth, the reports best make sense if some consistent experiential phenomenon underpins them, and make far worse sense if the story is only a story.

References

Angelucci, Orfeo. 1955. *The Secret of the Saucers*. Amherst, WI: The Amherst Press.
Appelle, Stuart. 1995-1996. *The Abduction Experience: A Critical Evaluation of Theory and Evidence*. Journal of UFO Studies 6 [new series]:29-78.

Bartholomew, Robert E., Keith Basterfield, and George S. Howard. 1991. "UFO Abductees and Contactees: Psychology or Fanstasy-Proneness?" *Professional Psychology: Research and Practice* 22:215-222.

Bass, Ellen, and Laura Davis. 1988. *The Courage to Heal: A Guide for Women Survivors of Child Sexual Abuse*. New York: Harper & Row.

Belkin, David S., Anthony F. Greene, James R. Rodrigue, and Stephen R. Boggs. 1994. "Psychopathology and History of Sexual Abuse." *Journal of Interpersonal Violence* 9:535-547.

Bloecher, Ted, Aphrodite Clamar, and Budd Hopkins. 1985. *Final Report on the Psychological Testing of UFO Abductees*. Mount Ranier, MD: Fund for UFO Research.

Brenneis, C. Brooks. 1997. *Recovered Memories of Trauma: Transferring the Present to the Past*. Madison, WI: International Universities Press.

Bullard, Thomas E. 1989. "Hypnosis and UFO Abductions: A Troubled Relationship." *Journal of UFO Studies* 1 [new series]:3-40.

Bullard, Thomas E. 1994. "A Comparative Study of UFO Abductions Update." In Andrea Pritchard, David E. Pritchard, John E. Mack, Pam Kasey, and Claudia Yapp, eds. *Alien Discussions*, 45-48. Cambridge, MA: North Cambridge Press.

Bullard, Thomas E. 1995. *The Sympathetic Ear: Investigators as Variables in UFO Abduction Reports*. Mount Ranier, MD: Fund for UFO Research.

Bullard, Thomas E. 1999. "What's New in UFO Abductions? Has the Story Changed in 30 Years?" In Walter H. Andrus, Jr., and Irena Scott, eds. *MUFON 1999 International UFO Symposium Proceedings*, 170- 199. Seguin, TX: Mutual UFO Network.

Cardeña, Etzel. 1994. "The Domain of Dissociation." In Stephen Jay Lynn and Judith W. Rhue, eds. *Dissociation: Clinical and Theoretical Perspectives*. New York: Guilford Press, pp.15-31.

Clark, Jerome. 1998. *The UFO Encyclopedia*, 2nd ed. 2 v. Detroit: Omnigraphics.

Clark, Jerome. 2000. "From Mermaids to Little Gray Men: The Prehistory of the UFO Abduction Phenomenon." *The Anomalist* 8 [Spring]:11-31.

Crabb, Riley. 1960. "The Director's Eastern Trip (continued from the June Journal)," *Journal of Borderland Research* [formerly *Round Robin*], July-August 1960

Day, Duncan J. A. 1998. *Psychological Correlates of the UFO Abduction Experience: The Role of Beliefs and Indirect Suggestions on Abduction Accounts Obtained During Hypnosis*. Montreal: Concordia University dissertation.

Druffel, Ann, and D. Scott Rogo. 1980. *The Tujunga Canyon Contacts*. Englewood Cliffs, NJ: Prentice- Hall.

Evans, Frederick J. 1988. "Posthypnotic Amnesia: Dissociation of Content and Context." In Helen M. Pettinati, ed. *Hypnosis and Memory*. New York: Guilford Press, pp. 157-192.

Flathman, Marcus. 1999. "Trauma and Delayed Memory: A Review of the 'Repressed Memories' Literature." *Journal of Child Sexual Abuse* 8:1-23.

Fort, Charles. 1959[1941]. *The Books of Charles Fort*. New York: Henry Holt and Company.

Fowler, Raymond E. 1979. *The Andreasson Affair*. Englewood Cliffs, NJ: Prentice-Hall.

Fuller, John G. 1966. *The Interrupted Journey*. New York: Berkley Medallion Books.

Gevaerd, A. J. 1984. "The Abduction at Jardim Alvorada: Investigation under Hypnotic Time Regression." *Flying Saucer Review* 30/2 (December):17-25.

Grinspoon, Lester, and A. D. Persky. 1972. "Psychiatry and UFO Reports." In Carl Sagan and Thornton Page, eds. *UFOs: A Scientific Debate*, 223-246. Ithaca, NY: Cornell University Press.

Gross, Loren. 1989. *UFOs: A History, 1953: March-July*. Fremont, CA: The Author.
Hartmann, Ernest. 1996. "Who Develops PTSD Nightmares and Who Doesn't." In Deirdre Barrett, ed. *Trauma and Dreams*, 100-113. Cambridge, MA: Harvard University Press.
Hartmann, Ernest. 1998. "Nightmares After Trauma as Paradigm for All Dreams: A New Approach to the Nature and Functions of Dreaming." *Psychiatry* 61:223-238.
Hilgard, Ernest R. 1965. *Hypnotic Susceptibility*. New York: Harcourt, Brace & World.
Hilgard, Ernest R. 1994. "Neodissociation Theory." In Steven Jay Lynn and Judith W. Rhue, eds. *Dissociation: Clinical and Theoretical Perspectives*, 32-51. New York: Guilford Press.
Hopkins, Budd. 1981a. *Missing Time*. New York: Richard Marek Publishers.
Hopkins, Budd. 1981b. "UFO Abductions: The Invisible Epidemic." *MUFON UFO Symposium* 1981, 44-58. Seguin, TX: Mutual UFO Network.
Hopkins, Budd. 1987. *Intruders*. New York: Random House.
Jacobs, David M. 1992. *Secret Life*. New York: Simon & Schuster.
Jacobs, David M. 1998. *The Threat*. New York: Simon & Schuster.
Jessup, M. K. 1955. *The Case for the UFO*. New York: Citadel Press, .
Keyhoe, Donald E. 1955. *The Flying Saucer Conspiracy*. New York: Henry Holt & Company.
Klass, Philip J. 1988. *UFO Abductions – A Dangerous Game*. Buffalo, NY: Prometheus Books.
Kottmeyer, Martin. 1988. "Abduction: The Boundary-Deficit Hypothesis." *Magonia* no. 37:3-7.
Kottmeyer, Martin. 1994. "The Eyes That Spoke." *The REALL News*. 2, no.7 [July]:1, 3, 6.
Lawson, Alvin H. 1980. "Hypnosis of Imaginary UFO 'Abductees'." In Curtis G. Fuller, ed. *Proceedings of the First International UFO Congress*, 195-238. New York: Warner Books.
Leavitt, Frank. 1994. "Clinical Correlates of Alleged Satanic Abuse and Less Controversial Sexual Molestation." *Child Abuse and Neglect* 18:387-392.
Loftus, Elizabeth, and Katherine Ketcham. 1994. *The Myth of Repressed Memory: False Memories and Allegations of Sexual Abuse*. New York: St. Martin's Press.
Lorenzen, L. J. 1962. "Where Is Private Irwin?" *Flying Saucers* 28 [November]: 17-26.
Luthi, Max. 1981. "Aspects of the Marchen and the Legend." In Dan Ben Amos, ed. *Folklore Genres*, 17-33. Austin: University of Texas Press.
Matheson, Terry. 1998. *Alien Abductions: Creating a Modern Phenomenon*. Amherst, NY: Prometheus Books.
Moseley, James. 1960. "Saucer Briefs," *Saucer News*, December 1960.
Nathan, Debbie, and Michael Snedeker. 1995. *Satan's Silence: Ritual Abuse and the Making of a Modern American Witch Hunt*. New York: Basic Books.
Noblitt, James Randall. 1995. "Psychometric Measures of Trauma Among Psychiatric Patients Reporting Ritual Abuse." *Psychological Reports* 77:743-747.
Ofshe, Richard, and Ethan Watters. 1994. *Making Monsters: False Memories, Psychotherapy, and Sexual Hysteria*. New York: Charles Scribner's Sons.
Paley, John. 1997. "Satanist Abuse and Alien Abduction: A Comparative Analysis Theorizing Temporal Lobe Activity as a Possible Connection Between Anomalous Memories." *British Journal of Social Work* 27:43-70.
Parnell, June O. 1986. *Personality Characteristics on the MMPI, 16PF, and ACL of Persons Who Claim UFO Experiences*. Laramie: University of Wyoming dissertation.
Parnell, June O., and R. Leo Sprinkle. 1990. "Personality Characteristics of Persons Who

Claim UFO Experiences." *Journal of UFO Studies* 2 [new series:45-58.
Peebles, Curtis. 1994. *Watch the Skies! A Chronicle of the Flying Saucer Myth.* Washington, DC: Smithsonian Institution Press.
Pendergrast, Mark. 1995. *Victims of Memory: Incest Accusations and Shattered Lives.* Hinesburg, VT: Upper Access.
Persinger, Michael A. 1990. "The Tectonic Strain Theory as an Explanation for UFO Phenomena: A Non-Technical Review of the Research, 1970-1990." *Journal of UFO Studies* 2 [new series]:105-137.
Powers, Susan Marie. 1994. "Dissociation in Alleged Extraterrestrial Abductees." *Dissociation* 7:44-50.
Randle, Kevin D. 1988. *The October Scenario.* Iowa City: Middle Coast Publishing.
Randle, Kevin D, Russ Estes, and William P. Cone. 1999. *The Abduction Enigma: The Truth Behind the Mass Alien Abductions of the Late Twentieth Century.* New York: Forge Books.
Ring, Kenneth, and Christopher J. Rosing. 1990. "The Omega Project: A Psychological Survey of Persons Reporting Abductions and Other UFO Encounters." *Journal of UFO Studies* 2 [new series]: 59-98.
Rodeghier, Mark, Jeff Goodpaster, and Sandra Blatterbauer. 1991. "Psychosocial Characteristics of Abductees: Results from the CUFOS Abduction Project." *Journal of UFO Studies* 3 [new series]:59-90.
Schmidt, Reinhold. 1958. *The Kearney Incident.* Hollywood, CA: The Author.
Showalter, Elaine. 1997. *Hystories: Hysterical Epidemics and Modern Media.* New York: Columbia University Press.
Spanos, Nicholas P., Patricia A. Cross, Kirby Dickson, and Susan C. DuBreuil. 1993. "Close Encounters: An Examination of UFO Experiences." *Journal of Abnormal Psychology* 102:624-632.
Spanos, Nicholas P., Cheryl A. Burgess, and Melissa Faith Burgess. 1994. "Past-Life Identities, UFO Abductions, and Satanic Ritual Abuse: The Social Construction of Memories." *International Journal of Clinical and Experimental Hypnosis* 42:433-446.
Stone-Carmen, Jo. 1994. "A Descriptive Study of People Reporting Abduction by Unidentified Flying Objects (UFOs)." In Andrea Pritchard, David E. Pritchard, John E. Mack, Pam Kasey, and Claudia Yapp, eds. *Alien Discussions*, 309-315. Cambridge, MA: North Cambridge Press.
Strieber, Whitley. 1987. *Communion.* New York: William Morrow/Beech Tree Books.
Tart, Charles T. 1972. "Toward the Experimental Control of Dreaming: A Review of the Literature." In Charles T. Tart, ed. *Altered States of Consciousness.* New York: Doubleday Anchor Books.
Taves, Ernest H. 1979-1980. "Betty Through the Looking-Glass." *Skeptical Inquirer* 4, no.2 [Winter]:88- 95.
Terr, Lenore. 1990. *Too Scared to Cry: Psychic Trauma in Childhood.* New York: Basic Books.
Webb, Walter N. 1961. *A Dramatic UFO Encounter in the White Mountains, N.H., September 19-20, 1961* (Report to the National Investigations Committee on Aerial Phenomena, October 26, 1961).
Webb, Walter N. 1965. *A Dramatic UFO Encounter in the White Mountains, New Hampshire: The Hill Case, September 19-20, 1961* (Final report to NICAP on the Hill case, August 30, 1965).
Webb, Walter N. 1994. *Encounter at Buff Ledge: A UFO Case History.* Chicago: Center for UFO Studies.
Wilkins, H. T. 1954. *Flying Saucers on the Attack.* New York: Citadel Press.

Wilmer, Harry A. 1996. "The Healing Nightmare: War Dreams of Vietnam Veterans." In Deirdre Barrett, ed. *Trauma and Dreams*. Cambridge, MA: Harvard University Press, pp. 85-99.

Wilson, John P. 1990. "Post-Traumatic Stress Disorder (PTSD) and Experienced Anomalous Trauma (EAT): Similarities in Reported UFO Abductions and Exposure to Invisible Toxic Contaminants." *Journal of UFO Studies* 2 [new series]:1-17.

Zadra, Antonio L. 1996. "Recurrent Dreams: Their Relation to Life Events." In Deirdre Barrett, ed. *Trauma and Dreams*. Cambridge, MA: Harvard University Press, pp. 231-247.

Thomas E. Bullard has had an interest in UFOs since childhood. He received his Ph.D. in folklore from Indiana University in 1982 with a dissertation treating mythic aspects of UFOs. Since then he has published UFO-related articles in the *Journal of American Folklore, Journal of UFO Studies, International UFO Reporter*, and the MUFON *UFO Journal*. He has made presentations at the 1987 and 1999 MUFON UFO Symposia, the 1992 Abduction Study Conference held at MIT, and a 2005 conference on false memories held at Niagara Falls. Under the sponsorship of the Fund for UFO Research, he completed a comparative study of alien abduction claims in 1987, *UFO Abductions: The Measure of a Mystery*, and in 1995 a comparative survey of UFO abduction investigators and their findings, *The Sympathetic Ear*. One of his papers appeared in the anthology, *UFOs and Abductions: Challenging the Borders of Knowledge*, published by The University Press of Kansas in 2000, and for the same press he is working on a full-length book that deals with the interplay of cultural belief and observation in creating the UFO mystery. He is a board member of the J. Allen Hynek Center for UFO Studies and the Fund for UFO Research, and toils day to day for the library system of Indiana University in Bloomington, Indiana.

CHAPTER FOUR

Beyond the UFO Horizon

A knowledge of a wide range of meetings with otherworldly beings is essential to a proper assessment of the Hills' abduction account

HILARY EVANS

On a dark September night, Barney and Betty Hill saw something in the sky; and what they saw changed their lives forever. If it was what they came to believe it was, that is understandable, for they had an experience that few if any mortals have been privileged to have: an encounter with beings from another part of the Universe. But even if no such encounter took place, the fact remains that their lives were changed, and that fact is central to any understanding of their experience.

Today, it is more than 45 years since Dr. Simon and the Hills mutually agreed to terminate their hypnosis sessions. During that period, the crucial question, the only one that really matters – did the encounter take place as ostensibly recalled? – has been left dangling, unanswered. With so much hanging on the answer to that question, it is astonishing that greater efforts have not been made to answer it.

It is particularly astonishing that there has been no in-depth re-appraisal of the case. Fuller, who authored the only full-length account of the matter, was a journalist; though we have no reason to question his integrity, and though his book is a creditable piece of reporting and, so far as I am aware, contains no major errors, it would be reassuring to have a second opinion in so serious a matter. Naturally the Hills' story is narrated, and to a degree commented on, in such publications as Clark's *UFO Encyclopedia*:

but the present compilation is the first attempt at a counter-investigation of the story, belatedly seeking to fill out the gaps that Fuller skipped over, perhaps because he did not even notice them, and to provide answers to the questions he left hanging, perhaps because he was in no position to answer them.

In these circumstances, we have no choice but to begin where Fuller left off. Perhaps our best starting point is this comment (Fuller 1966: 274) from his book: "Short of acceptance of the whole experience as reality, which contradictory evidence prevented the doctor from doing, the best alternative lay in the dream hypothesis."

That hypothesis, though it has never been formally set out, is to the effect that Betty's dreams were a fantasy: a fantasy that she communicated to Barney as the result of recounting her dreams to him, and that both would subsequently recall in the course of their hypnosis sessions.

For those who cannot bring themselves to accept the hypnotically-recalled scenario as fact, the dream hypothesis remains the option of choice. However, this alternative explanation has its own shortcomings: not least, that the part played by fantasy in human behavior, though it has been extensively explored, has yet to be precisely formulated. It is commonly accepted that we are all influenced by myths, archetypes, and stereotypes derived on the one hand from our cultural environment, on the other from our personal experience. But the processes are yet uncharted whereby the paths we tread through this labyrinth can, when the circumstances are appropriate, lead us to all kinds of anomalous experience ranging from simple misperception – an advertising blimp becomes an alien spacecraft – to total fabrication – the figure of an Old Hag enters our bedroom and seats herself upon our body.

The first step towards evaluating the explanatory power of the dream hypothesis for the Hills' encounter is, therefore, to set it in the wider context of anomalous experience. It needs to be considered in the light of other experiences where it seems possible that fantasy plays a crucial part.

This will not, of course, enable us to make an absolute yes-or-no judgment on the Hills' encounter. But it will enable us to gauge the probability that this is what set the process in motion. We shall then need to consider how such fantasy may be communicated from one person to another, and then, how it can re-emerge as ostensibly true memory.

Betty's Nightmares

Some ten days after their encounter – approximately September 29 to October 3, 1961 – Betty Hill experienced a series of remarkably detailed dreams that, when the disparate elements are brought together, rearranged and ordered, form a sequential narrative. This narrative offers a complete and coherent story in which the initial sighting, which they consciously remembered, leads seamlessly into related events of which they have no conscious memory whatever.

What makes the Hills' experience so remarkable – unique, it may be – is the fact that more than three years later, under hypnosis, not only would Betty recall events that match her dreams in detail, but Barney would echo her account. Understandably this would lead many to the conclusion that both the dreams and the hypnotic recall were literally narrating events that had actually taken place.

Could this be so? The interpretation of dreams had a long history before Freud used it as the title for his landmark book. Dreams requiring decoding are notable incidents in the Judeo-Christian Bible, the Roman statesman Cicero wrote a book about divination, and dream books are as popular today as they were with Victorian housemaids. But invariably we find it taken for granted that dreams are *not* to be taken at face value. They must be interpreted: you must read your Freud – or your gipsy astrologer – to learn what those extraordinary happenings really signify.

Nonetheless Fuller asserts: "It is not uncommon for dreams resulting from an experience of shock to be literal; i.e. a complete re-enactment, so to speak, of an event that actually took place" (Fuller 1966: 333). He provides no authority for this statement, which I suspect is open to question: I have found no confirmation of it in the literature. The general opinion, as expressed by John Antrobus of the City College of New York, is that "dreaming refers to a mixture of thought and emotional properties that are rare in normal waking, but common in sleep" (Antrobus 1993: 98).

Though I am not aware of any case in the literature of dreams, inquiry among my acquaintance elicited a case that at first seems to confirm Fuller's statement. A woman car passenger was involved in an accident in which a pedestrian was killed. Traumatized by the event, she had repeated dreams of it, night after night. She said the dream exactly matched the event.

However, there is a significant difference between this and the Hill case: this lady had consciously experienced her traumatizing event and retained conscious memories of it. The Hills, on the other hand, even if they lived their encounter on a conscious level – it is difficult if not impossible to learn from Fuller's account what state of mind the couple was in while participating in their adventure – they certainly had no conscious memories of it.

So even if we give Fuller the benefit of the doubt and accept as possible that Betty might be one of the exceptional people whose dreams are indeed a re-living of actual experience – or, at any rate, that on this occasion they were so – we must, because this is so exceptional an occurrence, consider the alternative as no less possible: that her dreams were – as most dreams are – a fantasy, making more or less use of veridical events, combined with material obtained, consciously or unconsciously, from every conceivable source to which she had ever been exposed, whether derived from her personal experience, from her cultural milieu, or from her imagination.

The Only Scenario

There is one aspect of Betty's dreams that is easily overlooked: veridical or not, the dreams made a highly significant difference to the couple's situation. Before the dreams, their experience comprised a UFO sighting, followed by a period for which they are amnesic. After the dreams, the Hills are provided with a possible account of what happened during that amnesic period. Moreover, it is an account that is remarkably detailed, remarkably coherent. We do not know whether Barney played any part in helping Betty organize the scattered incidents of her dream-content into a smooth-running narrative, but in the light of his dismissal of the dreams, it seems likely that it was Betty alone who arranged the disordered tableaux into a rational sequence. As set down by Betty, it is a complete and generally plausible story. Furthermore, it is a story that is rooted in known fact – or, at any rate, in the incidents related to the initial sighting and Barney's panic, details that the Hills regard as fact; so they can be forgiven for speculating whether the dream-narrative, containing both the initial sighting and the subsequent abduction, might be all fact.

Betty does not mention her dreams to their first interviewer Walter Webb on October 21, 1961. This is perhaps understandable in view of the fact that at this stage, though the Hills recognize a degree of amnesia in the course of their journey, they have not yet been confronted with the challenge of the two-plus hours of missing time. Though Betty found the dreams deeply disturbing, it is possible that she at this stage regards them simply as fantasy, without it even crossing her mind that they might bear some relation to real experience. Even if she does initially have any such thoughts, she might seek to put them out of her mind when Barney dismisses her dreams as nonsense.

The "missing time" mystery emerges a month later, in the course of the meeting with Hohmann, Jackson, and MacDonald on November 25, 1961. At once the amnesia is perceived to be greatly more significant. Betty says "This was the first time I began to wonder if they were more than just dreams. Then I really got upset over my dreams." It is at this point that hypnosis is suggested to aid recall, and both Hills favor the suggestion. Barney hopes that hypnosis "might clear up Betty and her nonsense about her dreams" (Fuller 1966: 47-48). In fact, however, the hypnosis proposal is not taken up at this point; on March 25, 1962 they decide against it, and the possibility will not be raised again until a year and a half later.

Nonetheless, it remains a fact that, irrespective of Betty's uncertainty about her dreams, and whether or not Barney regards them as "nonsense," they provide the couple with a possible scenario for what is otherwise a gap in their lives. Even if they do not accept it as a true account, *it is the only account they have*. It is inconceivable, therefore, that it is not in the back of their minds – to say the least – throughout the year and a half that elapses before hypnosis is undertaken, a period in which no alternative explanation is ever seriously considered.

Even if, in the light of Barney's dismissive attitude, neither of them had ever actually spoken of the dreams to the other, both of them must retain an awareness of the dream-story, if only as a terrifying scenario they would prefer to discard if only a better one were available.

Fact or Fantasy?

The question of whether those dreams were a factual replay of real events, or a fantasy in which fact and fiction are inextricably jumbled, is therefore a crucial one, but in the absence of any independent evidence or corroborative testimony, it is a question that is well nigh impossible to resolve. All we have by way of confirmation are a pair of subjective accounts, not consciously recalled but elicited under hypnosis. In support of their memories being true, there is the fact that both witnesses tell substantially the same story; against it, there is the fantastic nature of that story and the lack of any external corroboration.

However, these very facts place the Hills' experience in the same state of existential instability as a wide variety of other claimed anomalous experiences that, because they lie beyond the UFO horizon, are rarely perceived as relevant to ufological issues. Thousands of individuals have laid claims to have met the Virgin Mary, mother of the Christians' Jesus; thousands more have claimed to be, or have been diagnosed as being, possessed by evil spirits. Millions believe they communicate with spirits of the dead, and ghost stories are as widely reported today as they were 2000 years ago. Many of those who were burned as witches in the 15th through the 17th century believed they flew through the air to participate in sabbats; similar journeys are claimed by shamans in primitive cultures who travel to otherworldly destinations to consult with tribal deities.

By and large, these experiences are not today supposed to be literal accounts of physical events: alternative scenarios have been proposed, which are generally preferred by behavioural scientists. At the same time, they *are* accepted as literal fact by those who perceive them to be countenanced by a particular belief system. Some years ago, I attended a conference in Basel where a speaker told us about a case of diabolical possession in which he had been involved. To my astonishment, I suddenly realized that the speaker, though a university professor, believed implicitly in the literal reality of a possessing demon. Those who communicate with the dead round the séance table are not always the credulous victims of exploiting charlatans. Many of them are intelligent, educated people who believe they have sound and rational grounds for believing that they are truly doing what they think they are doing.

So an examination of other marginal experiences by no means implies that we are seeking to place the Hills' experience in a category occupied exclusively by fantasy. We must be prepared to accept that any of these claims may tip either way, this way into fact or that way into fiction. But, in the absence of either confirmation or rebuttal of the Hills' abduction scenario, at least a look at some of these other limbo cases may enable us to take a broader approach to their particular experience.

Case 1: Glenda and the spacewoman

In 1976 a 17-year-old girl from Dagenham, near London, England, told investigators of a series of strange experiences culminating in a cigar-shaped UFO that followed her along a city street. She revealed that five years earlier she had come home from school one afternoon and gone upstairs to her room, only to be joined by a spacewoman who walked in through the closed door, sat beside her on her bed and talked with her for an hour or so. Ever since then, the spacewoman had been a sort of companion, counselor, and friend – generally unseen, but always felt.

Glenda had no doubt of the woman's reality: I have the drawing she made of her visitor. Did Glenda's spacewoman exist? Probably not in the literal, physical sense. Yet, paradoxically, in another sense she did exist: for beyond question she played a significant role in Glenda's adolescent life, over a period of some five years. (Evans 1984: 15 *et seq.*). That is to say, the fact of an entity's *non*-existence must not be allowed to stand in the way of its ability to exert a very real influence on the individual who supposes her- or himself to have encountered it.

At the time, I was asked to provide an explanation for Glenda's experiences, and I failed, utterly. I did not believe that a spacewoman had visited Glenda, but neither could I say what had happened to her to make her think she had been visited. Then a year later I met a French girl who claimed to have met the Virgin Mary, and this not only provided additional incentive to find an explanation, but also suggested which way to look for one.

Case 2: Blandine and the Virgin Mary

In 1981, Blandine Piegeay was a 14-year-old Catholic French schoolgirl. One day, walking to school, she met an angel, who told her she would shortly receive a visit from Mary, the mother of Jesus, who died some 20 centuries ago. Two days later she did indeed experience the first of some 50 encounters. Every Saturday morning – for the Queen of Heaven agreed with Blandine that a weekend day would be more suitable than a study-disruptive schoolday – Mary would descend from Heaven and visit with Blandine in the family kitchen. No one else saw her, though her father claimed once to have heard her.

Her parish priest was skeptical, but thousands of pilgrims beat a path to her door: she was featured on television, a nine days' wonder. Today she is married, with a child, her adventure all but forgotten. But Blandine insists: "I know my apparitions were true. Why would I have invented them?" (Evans 1987: 9)

That question is the key to understanding her experience. Instead of asking: Why would the Virgin Mary come down from Heaven to meet with Blandine and tell her she eats too many bonbons? we should ask, Why would Blandine claim such an experience?

The conclusion must be that Blandine had a psychological need for such an encounter. She needed someone – and not just anyone, but an authority figure whose word she could accept – to tell her she was important, she mattered. If not to her fellow pupils or her teachers, then to the Queen of Heaven. Crudely put, the Virgin Mary came in answer to Blandine's identity crisis.

Looking back to Glenda's spacewoman, hindsight suggests that her manifestation took place for much the same reason. The 12-year-old English girl, like the 14-year-old French girl, needed an authority-figure to whom she could look for guidance, counsel, reassurance. Not for her, though, the Virgin Mary of Catholic Blandine: instead, a stereotype from her own cultural milieu, an extraterrestrial entity.

Each such encounter is both stereotyped and custom-made. The content is personal – each individual has his or her own agenda, but the format is largely cultural. In the history of Marian apparitions, the pattern has become almost as ritualized as a Japanese stage performance, with stock episodes – the apparition of the authority-figure in some isolated place, the conventionalized appearance, the formularized message, the healings limited to a certain range of ailments, the manifestation of a sacred spring. In similar fashion, stories of abduction by aliens have become stylized and run to a pattern with a greater or lesser degree of conformity (Bullard 1987; Brookesmith 1998).

This conformity has been seen as evidence both for and against the validity of the claimed experience. On the one hand, the fact that such narratives possess so many similarities, including very specific details with which an "innocent" experiencer could not reasonably be expected to be acquainted, has been taken as supportive of the view that the event was genuinely experienced. And indeed it is not easy to explain how such details could have been acquired unless the individual had been exposed to other experiencers' accounts. On the other hand, the inclusion of such details – if it can be shown that they could have been acquired in the course of the individual's casual daily reading or television viewing – could point to copycat replication. It is important to recognize that this would almost certainly have been an unconscious process: the acquisition of the details, and their assimilation into a personal experience, could perfectly well have taken place on a subconscious level – and indeed, more likely than not.

This issue remains unresolved, and those who make the case for the the reality of abductions seem to have as strong an argument as those who hold an "abductions-are-fantasy" view. This is why we must look beyond the immediate issue, the stylized pattern, to the individual encounter and the personal need to which it responds. For then we find that each case is both one of a class and one of a kind: both ubiquitous and unique.

Researcher D. Scott Rogo, investigating the 1953 Tujunga Canyon abductions, went so far as to suggest: "Each time an abduction experience is uncovered, a psychological inquiry into the life of the witness should indicate that he or she was undergoing a life-crisis at the time or was recovering from a psychological trauma" (Rogo 1980: 239).

The objection can be made that the Hills' encounter, being the first to be widely publicized, can hardly have been conforming to a pattern. If anything, it *set* the pattern. But this is to miss the point. If subsequent abductions have tended to follow in the same mould, it is because the Hills' experience was an acceptable model: it embodies elements to which later protagonists respond. Their story may seem to have been the first of its kind, but it is nonetheless a stereotype.

Case 3: Barbara and the Operators

The wisdom of Scott Rogo's admonition to look before as well as after is demonstrated tellingly in the book in which Barbara O'Brien, an American professional woman, records her encounters with otherworldly beings (O'Brien 1958). Following on personal problems, both domestic and at work, she begins to hallucinate a number of entities, who identify themselves as denizens of some kind of parallel world that interacts with ours. Although on one level she is aware that they are hallucinatory, they are at the same time totally real to her. She permits them to persuade her to leave home and work, and wander for many months, living in two worlds at once – the real world where she has to continue living as best she can, and this strange other level of reality. Apart from occasional breakdowns, she manages pretty well, and eventually she manages to resolve her situation.

What makes her story so remarkable is her ability to analyse it subsequently and to offer a diagnosis of what happened to her. In retrospect, she realizes that, triggered by her psychological crisis, her unconscious had taken control of her life and substituted its own unreal drama for the real play of events (O'Brien 1958: 5):

> The unconscious stages a play: the conscious mind is permitted to remain, an audience of one, watching a drama on which it cannot walk out....
> As you sit watching your Martian, it is your unconscious mind which is flashing the picture before your eyes... more than this, it is blowing a fog of hypnosis over your conscious mind so that consciously you are convinced that the hallucinations you see and hear, and the delusions that accompany the hallucinations, are real.

What happened to Barbara could be what happened to Glenda and Blandine: the illusion they take for reality is a presentation staged by their subconscious minds. Normally, the subconscious sits there in the background, letting our conscious self get on with things. But when the need arises, it steps in and makes its presence felt.

When that happens, the individual starts to function on two separate levels of reality. Sometimes for a single never-to-be-repeated occasion, sometimes over a long period. So Glenda, Blandine, and Barbara, each in her own way, function in this way: retaining their ability to live on the plane of everyday existence, but at the same time intermittently maintaining their otherworldly contact. (For a fuller presentation of these ideas, see Evans 1989.)

It is one thing to formulate a theory, quite another to apply it in practice. In November 1980 there was a notable case in England involving a police officer who, on patrol alone at night, encountered a UFO. Subsequently, under hypnosis, he recounted a horrific, dreamlike abduction experience. When I diffidently suggested that Alan Godfrey's abduction might be a fantasy triggered by psychological factors, he was indignant, rejecting my reading of his adventure, feeling I was accusing him of mental instability. Since then, however, he himself has come to question the physical reality of his experience: "It seemed real but it might have been a dream" (Randles 1988: 90). Investigator Jenny Randles (Hough and Randles 1991: 189) writes:

> Godfrey is commendably honest, pointing out that he read UFO stories between the sighting and the hypnosis sessions months later. He acknowledges this could have coloured what he said in an altered state, which might therefore be open to other interpretations. While nobody can prove what happened one way or another, if the witness himself is unsure of the objective reality of the abduction phase of his story, we must be wary of forming earth-shattering opinions about extraterrestrial life.

And she pertinently observes: "Of course, if it was a dream, the question is why it was so similar to everyone else's dream of abduction" (Randles 1988: 90).

Which brings us back to the Hills.

Case 4: Madeleine and Jesus

When popular fantasy author Whitley Strieber published his autobiographical *Communion*, the press release issued with it declared: "I was interviewed by three psychologists and three psychiatrists, given a battery of tests... and found to fall within the normal range in all respects," and carried an endorsement from the Director of Research at New York State Psychiatric Institute that stated: "I see no evidence of an anxiety state, mind disorder or personality disorder" (Strieber 1987a: 2). We can only assume that none of these highly qualified persons had considered it relevant to their examination to glance at Mr. Strieber's own non-fiction autobiographical writings. If they had, they would have come across his description of the security arrangements at the house where the alleged abduction took place, which by any standards approached paranoia – though if his story is as true as his dust-jacket says it is, perhaps, in the light of what was to occur, any paranoia was justified. They would have read of his erroneous belief that he was present at the 1966 Charles Whitman massacre at the University of Texas at Austin, when he undoubtedly was elsewhere (Conroy 1989: 120), of his prolonged amnesia in the course of a visit to Italy, and many other such incidents. Even from what he chooses to reveal about himself, we can see that "disordered" would be a mild description of both his mind and his personality, both at the time of his experience and, indeed, recurrently throughout his life. (Strieber 1987b)

Similarly, abduction researcher Budd Hopkins assures us (Hopkins 1987: 25), with regard to the abductees whose stories he recounts:

> Three psychiatrists and two psychologists have conducted hypnotic regression sessions over the years with a number of possible UFO abductees. Two other psychiatrists have interviewed our subjects.... None of these psychological professionals have presented to me, even tentatively, a psychological theory that might explain these bizarre accounts.

This is a truly astonishing assertion. One can only suppose that the psychologists in question had never taken the time to study the findings of their eminent predecessors. Simply among the best known, we can find similar behaviors described by Freud, Jung, and Janet. Pierre Janet, above all, laid the scientific foundations for such studies, based on his observations of hysterical patients at La Salpetrière, Paris. His patient Madeleine, a gifted and articulate lady, is convinced she makes periodical visits with Jesus – a spiritual activity she describes as "very rich and very beautiful," using language that verges on the erotic: "No, the state I enter isn't sleep: sleep is a kind of suspension of the life of the spirit, whereas mine is just the opposite.... my spirit and my heart soar over immense horizons into which they plunge and lose themselves in delight... no earthly pleasure can be compared to it! ... I am united to God and he to me !" (Janet 1926, volume 1: 68 *et seq.*)

There is no doubt in Madeleine's mind that her meetings with Jesus are real, or that he will, one fine day, fetch her to live with him permanently in Heaven. She speaks of her "life in common" with Jesus, and Janet describes it as "the life of a couple, even, dare I say it, a *ménage.*" While he had no doubt that none of this had any basis in reality, he sought to examine the process whereby she had come to make the claim, and how she was able to live simultaneously on two levels of reality – aware, indeed, of how remote one was from the other, yet unsurprised at her ability to pass easily to and fro between them. In so doing, he laid the foundations of the studies upon which we, today, are building. Siegel's exploration of hallucination (Siegel 1992), Hufford's study of "bedroom visitors' (Hufford 1982), and Schatzmann's account of his patient Ruth (Schatzmann 1980) all show that under appropriate circumstances sane, healthy people can have encounter experiences that are so vividly veridical that, if only for the time being, the witness sees no need to attempt any reality-testing, and unquestioningly accepts them as actual.

Case 5: The New Zealander and the flying saucer photo

The process of self-delusion is fascinatingly devious, as this trivial incident demonstrates. One day a gentleman from New Zealand, a total stranger, visited me on business. The conversation touched upon flying saucers, whereupon the visitor stated that he himself had not only seen but photographed one. When I expressed suitable amazement, he produced a glossy print and explained how, when and where he had taken it – on a given date, at a given place in his own country. However, I recognized it as a photo taken at an earlier date, in the United States, by an American photographer.

Beyond question, the man was lying, but was he lying knowingly? My guess is that my visitor had somehow acquired a glossy print of the photo and, from wishing he had taken it, he had come to convince himself that he was indeed the photographer. There must have been some part of him that knew perfectly well he had not taken that photograph. But, driven by whatever motivation, he chose to maintain the make-believe that to him was reality.

While we have no reason to suppose that the Hills had any wish to see a UFO, still less to meet its occupants, it is possible to argue that Barney's aggressive hostility to UFOs had its roots in a subconscious desire to do so. But this is pure speculation. What this anecdote reminds us, though, is that there are people whose unspoken motives can lead them to do and say things that consciously they would indignantly reject. Once again, only a detailed examination would disclose what motives were driving my visitor.

Case 6: Allan Kirk and his otherworldly life

A notable feature of O'Brien's experience is the way she accepts her otherworldly Operators into her life: their fantastic nature seems, at the time, something she can take in her stride. This seems to be generally true of those who meet with aliens. A Canadian lady, who described to me how aliens visited her every evening in her kitchen to report on the day's progress in helping the Mexican government perfect a cure for cancer, was well-dressed, articulate, seemingly normal in every other respect.

American psychoanalyst Robert Lindner had the opportunity to study at first-hand an extreme case of living on two different levels. (Lindner 1954). Not long after World War II he had a patient referred to him, a physicist engaged in highly classified government research, whose psychological condition was affecting the quality of his work.

What Lindner gradually unraveled was that Allen Kirk, aside from being a physicist on Earth, had been aware since childhood that he was also a prince on a distant planet, to which he would return on almost a daily basis. His written account of his other existence comprised some 14,000 pages, accompanied by hundreds of drawings, maps, and sketches.

The creation of imaginary worlds is nothing new. Apart from the many utopian writers who have imagined alternative civilizations, there are such people as the Bronte sisters whose fantasy creations went beyond literary invention to play a role similar to those imaginary playmates with whom many children enrich their childhoods. But Kirk's world surpassed these not only in the detail of the fantasy, but also the intensity with which he believed in it. He himself told Lindner (183-184):

> How can I explain this to you? One moment I was just a scientist, bending over a drawing board in the middle of an American desert; the next moment I was Kirk Allen, Lord of a planet in an interplanetary empire in a distant Universe, garbed in the robe of his exalted office, rising from the carved desk he had been sitting at, walking towards a secret room in his palace, going over to a filing cabinet, extracting an envelope of photographs, studying the photographs with intense concentration...
>
> It was over in a matter of minutes, and I was again at the drawing-board – the self you see here. But I knew the experience was real, and to prove it I now had a vivid recollection of the photographs, could see them as clearly as if they were still in my hands...

What puzzled Lindner was this: "The chief difficulty was that he regarded himself as completely normal, was thoroughly convinced of the reality of all that he experienced, and could not comprehend its significance in terms of his sanity" (Lindner 1954: 185).

In all such cases, if we look for a simple, blanket explanation, we shall almost certainly miss the point. Even if the fantasy itself falls into a specific category – the Münchhausen syndrome (Schnabel 1993: 26), say, which drives those it afflicts to claim false identities and experiences, or the Jerusalem syndrome (Sieveking 1999: 21), whose victims come to believe they are chosen to give an apocalyptic message to the world – even then, we have to ask why *that* particular individual developed the syndrome. Putting people into pigeonholes is a neat way of sorting them out, but more important is to find out what got them that way in the first place. Lindner was able to trace Kirk's fantasy back to childhood problems; the fantasy, for all its stereotypical nature, was custom-made for his personal needs.

Case 7: Christi Dennis's confession

Particularly revealing in this context is an incident that occurred at one of the Rocky Mountain reunions that Professor Leo Sprinkle used to hold every year at the University of Wyoming at Laramie. Most of those attending are abductees and contactees, who get together to compare notes and share experiences in a supportive environment. Experiencers tell their stories, and enjoy counseling from Leo and his colleagues and the sympathetic support of others like themselves.

In May 1981, one of the speakers was a college student, housewife, and mother from Arizona, named Christi Dennis. She told how she been confined to bed after an accident, practicing spiritual exercises such as Out of Body Experiences. One day she suddenly had the impression there were otherworldly entities in her room. She found she could talk with them. Subsequently she was transferred to their planet, where she met a female entity over 7 feet tall who gave her instruction.

Christi provided a detailed and coherent account of her experiences. She described her room, which contained, among other things, a television set where she could watch TV from Earth from any period in time, and much other sophisticated gadgetry. Her presentation was lucid, sensible, impressive. (*Proceedings of the Rocky Mountain Conference on UFO Investigation 1981*: 104). She was welcomed by the delegates, most of whom had passed through similar experiences, as one of themselves.

The following year, she wrote a letter to Sprinkle, which he in turn communicated to the conference, in which she confessed: "I am not a contactee. I have never had an extraterrestrial experience! The stories I have told and the book I have written are nothing more than fair science fiction" (*Proceedings of the Rocky Mountain Conference on UFO Investigation 1982*: 105). Her letter made it clear this was no crude, sensation-seeking hoax; rather, it was the outcome of some spiritual crisis. Christi had projected herself into this imaginary scenario as a way of working her way out of her personal psychological predicament. The abduction process provided her with a ready-made scenario onto which she could project her individual concerns.

Apart from vividly demonstrating the difficulty of distinguishing between a true and a false abduction experience, the Dennis case demonstrates the force – even the therapeutic value – of the authorized abduction myth. For Christi, as for Barbara O'Brien, the myth provided an existential framework for her personal situation. It could be reasonably suggested that, just as a medicine contains ingredients that the human biological system may from time to time require, so the encounter myth may contain elements for which the individual may have a psychological need. In the cases of Glenda and Blandine, that need was met relatively simply by the ostensible meeting and subsequent dialogues with a suitable authority-figure. In the cases of O'Brien and Dennis, more mature persons with more complex psychological needs, the psychodrama was more elaborate, but the process was the same. As to why it took the form it did, we are back with Scott Rogo's requirement for a before-the-event analysis. As to whether this has any bearing on the Hill case, this must remain an open question.

Case 8: The New Ager and the aliens

Few books about abductions are as revealing as Betty Hill's own aptly-titled *A Common Sense Approach To UFOs*. It includes several cautionary tales, among them this (Hill 1995: 75):

> Twenty years ago, a woman phoned to say she did not know if she was crazy or had been abducted by a ufo...
>
> Her problems began when she enrolled in a new age psychic development class. At every lesson they would lie on the floor and were put into a light trance. They were "connected" to different kinds of ufos... Over a period of time she began to think her fantasies were real.
>
> After these sessions ended she sought out hypnotists. Every hypnotist gave her a different abduction. She became fearful as she believed the "aliens" were watching her through her windows, unlocking her doors, coming in and giving her injections.
>
> She became suicidal... She was under the care of psychiatrists for fifteen years. She... had all kinds of delusions. She knew she was an alien who was forced to move to this planet...

Under hypnosis, it emerged that as a child she had been mistreated by her family: her grandmother continually hit her, and her mother followed the example. The resulting trauma was transferred to the aliens. She preferred to believe her anxieties were the result of UFO contacts, rather than the cruel treatment by her grandmother and mother.

In connection with the Hill case, the possibility of trauma stemming from the fact of their mixed marriage has inevitably been raised, and generally dismissed. Probably correctly, as there seems little doubt that their marriage – a second marriage for each of them – was a very successful one. But we do not know the circumstances under which their previous marriages broke up, and the possibility of trauma resulting from those circumstances cannot be entirely dismissed. Without going so far as to trace a cause-and-effect process along the lines of the case just cited, we should bear in mind that trauma may have been lying dormant in the subconscious of one or both of the Hills, and that they could have been transferred to the aliens in a similar way, as a contributory if not a causative factor.

Case 9: The party guest and the lost doll

The trigger for belief can be nothing more than simple suggestion, though that probably implies a suitably susceptible recipient. At a party at Betty's house, a hypnotist offered to uncover his guests' UFO abductions (Hill 1995: 77):

> They all laughed, for they knew they were never abducted. He requested a volunteer… A middle-aged woman volunteered. He put her into a light trance and began to question her. To our amazement, she told how she had been taken on-board a ufo, made pregnant, came home and later gave birth to a "big, fat baby girl," whom she named. Six months later the ufo came back and took the baby with them.
>
> None of this was true. She lived in the same neighbourhood all her life: no pregnancy, no birth, no police looking for the body of a missing baby. So why had she told this tale?
>
> …
>
> One day we were looking through her old family albums. Suddenly we saw a picture of her about the age of five sitting on the front steps. What was she holding? A big, fat baby doll. Name? The same as the one she used in her hypnosis. Where was this doll? She did not know, for this baby doll disappeared one day, and she was never able to find it. Finally, the solution to the tales she told under hypnosis were [*sic*] found. She took a real experience and turned it into a ufo abduction, while in a trance.

Yet again, only a study of the experiencer's past life could reveal the roots of the experience. But for the accident of the family album, Betty's question, "So why had she told this tale?" might have remained forever unanswered. While we have no reason to suppose that a glimpse of the Hills' family snaps would have been equally revelatory, such a possibility cannot be excluded.

Case 10: The abductee and the demons

Hypnosis is often fingered as the cause of fantasy and fabrication: but other and more down-to-earth factors can induce an altered state of consciousness. Fasting undoubtedly underlay many visionary experiences among religious people of the Middle Ages. For example, the 7th-century hermit Guthlac of Croyland left a sufficiently detailed account of his personal life for researchers to deduce that he probably suffered from protein and vitamin B deficiency, among whose likely consequences might be hallucinatory states: which could explain why he was continually troubled with horrifying visions of demons (Kroll and Bachrach 1982). In the 16th century, a similar factor led to outbreaks of convent hysteria, in which cloistered nuns would fancy themselves possessed by demons, causing them to indulge in a variety of behaviors ranging from outbursts of blasphemous language, to obscene gestures and orgasmic convulsions. The more open-minded doctors of the day traced it to the effects of diet and fasting, and of the cloistered and celibate lifestyle (Wier 1560).

Taking drugs, or not taking drugs, can have similar effects, as illustrated by another of Betty's cases (Hill 1995: 62-65). A woman told her doctor she thought she had been abducted by aliens. He referred her to Betty, who suggested she should be tested for her lithium level. She was given lithium treatment and became normal again. Then she said she didn't need lithium any more, but she ran naked round the garden, claiming the aliens were everywhere. She told Betty demons were in her basement, while the UFO people were in the back yard trying to get into the house to save her. The demons prevented them doing this. She started destroying the house, finally setting fire to it. She was sent off to a mental home while her husband faced a huge bill for the damage. In the end Betty convinced her to face facts, saying: "Ufos are real, but the aliens stay on board their crafts – remember you see them only when your lithium level is down."

While it would be naïve to suggest that the Hills ate something in the Colebrook restaurant that triggered a shared fantasy, Betty's common-sense diagnosis of this case reminds us not to ignore the possibility that a factor as mundane as body chemistry can have otherworldly consequences.

Case 11: Quintero and the thunderstorm

Clearly, there are many circumstances in which people will fantasize. Regrettably, fantasy is often associated with hallucination; and to many psychologists, especially in America, hallucination is perceived as an indication of a pathological condition. If you see a ghost or the Virgin Mary or an alien visitor, you are hallucinating; and if you are hallucinating, you must be mentally afflicted.

But what constitutes mental affliction? Studies by Israeli scientist Sulman show that "weather-sensitive patients encompass about 30% of any population," and other studies show that about 5% of the population are so sensitive to climate that an altered state of consciousness can be induced (Sulman 1980).

Consider, in the light of these findings, the case of Colombian cowman Anibal Quintero (Bowen 1977: 48):

> In 1976 Quintero told investigators how a luminous egg-shaped vessel landed close to him near his cowsheds. A number of people emerged, including three long-haired women. Though he knocked four or five down, they overcame him and took him into their spacecraft.
>
> When he came to, he found himself being massaged by the three females. They were naked, and behaved so provocatively that he started caressing one; she responded enthusiastically, and in no time they were making love. He described her as very hairy, with short legs, but very attractive, even if she communicated like a dog barking.
>
> Afterwards he was given an injection and everything went black. He woke to find himself lying on the grass, while dawn was breaking.

However, there is an interesting additional aspect (*loc. cit.*):

> His wife told the investigators Anibal had come home from work that evening in an unusual state, throwing himself into a hammock where he had fallen asleep. Shortly after, a violent thunderstorm occurred. Quintero woke, feeling queer, as though something was about to happen to him, and dashed out of the house. When the storm eased off, he walked towards the cowsheds, feeling that he was "controlled by some inexplicable external force."

This behavior makes no sense if what occurred was indeed a surprise visit by real aliens. On the other hand, it could be very relevant if Quintero was one of those who are strongly affected by meteorological conditions. If this was the case, the oncoming storm could have triggered an alternate state, in which he hallucinated the spaceship fantasy.

Case 12: Maureen and the broken date

While there is virtually no independent, external evidence for abductions taking place, there is evidence that some alleged abductions did *not* take place. The classic case is that of 37-year-old Australian housewife Maureen Puddy (Basterfield 1992: 13):

> On 3 July 1972 she had a UFO sighting while driving home from visiting her son in hospital – that is to say, at a time when we may reasonably

suppose that she was undergoing personal stress. Further odd experiences followed, then in February 1973 she alerted two prominent ufologists, Paul Norman and Judith Magee, that she had a rendezvous with the aliens. At the location, Magee and Norman joined her inside her car. She saw an alien figure, outside, beckoning, though her companions saw nothing. She then gave a detailed account of being aboard a spacecraft: yet all the time she was sitting right beside them.

During the witchcraft outbreak of the Middle Ages, skeptical observers would watch a supposed witch while she claimed to be attending a sabbat. (Spina 1523). Back in our own time, nine-year-old Gaynor Sunderland was witnessed by her mother, lying on her bed in a deep trance-like sleep; subsequently Gaynor described participation in an abduction. Jenny Randles, who investigated, concluded, "There is every reason to assume that these experiences were not objectively real, but were psychic in nature" (Randles 1981). Yet there is no reason to question the honesty of the witnesses who claimed these experiences: here again, their ostensible reality was totally convincing to the individual.

The Question of Communication

Every one of these case histories involves a single individual, without corroboration of any kind. What makes the Hills' case uniquely impressive is that Barney and Betty tell essentially the same story under hypnosis.

One way of looking at this would be to say that it was the Hills' exceptional good fortune that they had each other to provide corroboration. Perhaps many, if not all, of these other experiencers might have found corroboration if their experience had not taken place when they were alone. That is certainly a possibility, though we must bear in mind that there are tens of thousands of single-witness cases for each collective case, and that many collective cases are of questionable validity.

Alternatively, we should consider the possibility that the shared quality of the Hills' experience may point equally effectively against its being a real experience: the very fact that Betty's story is corroborated by Barney is an argument against its basis in fact. Fuller makes a significant observation (191) when he tells us:

> After the first sessions with Barney, Dr. Simon began to assume that the illusions and fantasies were his – and that Betty had absorbed them from him… With the completion of Betty's second trance, it appeared that the reverse of the doctor's initial assumption might be true. If the total experience were not true, a dream of fantasy initiated by Betty might have

been absorbed by Barney, who appeared to be more suggestible.

In fact, Dr. Simon noted that the things Barney experienced in the abduction portion of the incident were in Betty's story. On the other hand, very little of Betty's abduction sequence was included in his story. His recall of being taken through the woods was vague compared to hers. The details of the examination aboard the craft were much more extensive in Betty's story than in his.

Karl Pflock has pointed out that Simon was in error when he gave the impression that everything in Barney's narration can be found in Betty's: "There's a good deal of important material in Barney's recollections that doesn't appear in Betty's." [personal communication] Nonetheless, Betty's narrative was sufficiently richer than Barney's for Dr. Simon to arrive at his estimate of the process that probably took place.

The question of contagion in human behavior is a complex one, which has been insufficiently explored. If we knew more about it, we would be better able to interpret multiple-witness cases. The phenomenon known as *folie à deux*, though well known, is not well understood. A substantial number of well-attested ghost sightings are multiple in nature, but the mechanism of collective hallucination is as uncertain as the nature of ghosts themselves. The authors of the Society for Psychical Research's landmark study of apparitions (Gurney, Myers and Podmore 1886) were convinced that this could be explained – as could the apparitions themselves – by telepathy, though most researchers today would consider that this explanation is much too simple. Be that as it may, there is little doubt that what takes place in such cases is either some form of extrasensory communication, or some psychological process as yet unidentified that successfully transcends normal modes of communication. If the matter were better understood, we would find it easier to tease out the process that led from the Hills' experience, first to Betty's dreams, then to their independent recall. As it is, we can only speculate, balancing the probabilities.

As suggested above, some degree of open discussion of Betty's dreams must surely have taken place between herself and Barney, if only for him to reach the conclusion that they were "nonsense." We know, thanks to Karl Pflock's acquisition of an audiotape made of the couple speaking in November 1963, that Barney *had* heard Betty give a detailed account of her dreams and was no doubt aware that she had made a written version. It is hard to believe the subject would be dropped, never again to be raised between them throughout the months that followed. These were months, don't let us forget, when the couple were making repeated excursions into the New Hampshire countryside in search of topographical confirmation of their experience: the need to understand the experience led to the need to substantiate it, and the search for the geographical location was a primary requirement. But even though their efforts were directed at something as down-to-earth as the here or there of the experience, we must bear in mind that those efforts were directed towards finding the location of events for which there was no evidence outside Betty's dreams. This is to say that, even if we accept that it was tacitly agreed between them that the dream-scenario should not be openly discussed, that scenario must none the less have been in the back, if not the forefront, of their minds, since it was the only scenario they had, and thus was the only starting-point for their repeated car searches of the New Hampshire countryside.

My use of words "surely" and "must" underline the fact that this can only be speculation, but it is essential to appreciate the psychological context in which those searches took place.

The Deep Background

Dr. Simon himself seems to have recognized that the least improbable alternative was "that an actual experience had taken place on a sensitized background. A background existed on which could be imprinted illusions or fantasies, later to be re-experienced in dreams." (Fuller 1966: 190: these appear to be Fuller's words, though based on his interview with Dr. Simon.)

In considering what might constitute "a sensitized background" we run up against a crucial issue that divides the proponents of a psycho-social explanation for the UFO phenomenon from those who find the extraterrestrial hypothesis more probable. (For fuller discussion of these contrasting views, see Clark 1998: 749; Evans 1997; Evans 2001; Magonia, *passim.*). Several researchers, notably Méheust (1978; 1985; 1992) and Meurger (1995) have demonstrated the pre-conditioning created by the literature of science fiction, folklore, and suchlike cultural influences. Opponents have responded by pointing out that only a negligible fraction of flying saucer witnesses would be likely to have read pre-1939 popular fiction. Yet despite this objection, it seems unquestionable that cultural contamination does indeed take place. This is supported by the fact that there is no aspect of the flying saucer phenomenon that was *not* foreseen by the American pulps of the 1920s/1930s (Evans 1993: 4 *et seq.*). It is noteworthy that some of the details of the Hills' encounter – particularly the long-nosed, uniform-wearing aliens described by Betty (though not by Barney) – seem closer to those in *Amazing Stories* than to today's "greys."

So, when Dr. Simon suggests that "a background existed" onto which the Hills could impose their own personal encounter, he is not implying any out-of-the-way predisposition, but noting that no one, in America in 1961, could have escaped cultural contamination to the extent of being unaware of the possibility of alien visitation, or without having gained some subconscious ideas regarding what form the aliens, and any encounter with them, would take. The experiments of Lawson and McCall (Lawson 1983: 8), even though some researchers dispute their conclusions, provide ample demonstration of how firmly the abduction scenario is implanted in the minds of people who claim no interest in the subject, serving as the basis for fantasy "memories" whose only substance must be what has been more or less subconsciously picked up from their cultural milieu.

Despite his insistence that he was indifferent to UFOs, and that he and Betty had not talked about them for four years previous to their encounter, Barney could hardly have reacted to their sighting as strongly as he did unless he felt he knew what UFOs were and what harm they might do to Betty and himself. His actions in the course of the sighting point not only to a strong awareness of UFOs, but also to a strong fear – hence his sustained efforts to deny that it was a UFO at all, his determination to hide from Betty that he is scared, and his feeling that he must get a weapon.

His fear at the time seems in marked contrast to his subsequent indifference. This indifference may well be, as Karl Pflock has suggested [personal communication], a psychological defense position, adopted to conceal an underlying fear beneath a cloak of rationalization. None the less it remains a fact that, throughout, it is Betty who takes the initiative – it is she who goes to the library to find Keyhoe's book and who writes to him, it is she who suggests the return trips to the encounter location, and so on. Barney is presented as always reluctant, going along with Betty against his own feelings, and dismissing her dreams as nonsense.

Moreover, the dream scenario is largely, and probably entirely, Betty's handiwork. Her dreams, written up at an unspecified date, are given coherence only when she edits them into a sequential narrative. Her statement – "I will attempt to tell my dreams in chronological order, although they were not dreamed in this way. In fact the first dream told was the last one dreamed" – (Fuller 1966: 333) is extremely significant, for it implies an awareness that the dreams represent a sequence of events, a sequence that adds up to a plausible narrative. This could indicate a subconscious knowledge that the dreams are factual; or it could be her subconscious at work, forcing her to impose order on a jumble of dream incidents.

The Recall

The most remarkable element in the entire Hill case is that both witnesses, under hypnosis, should recall substantially the same events. But another feature is also worthy of remark: that both Betty and Barney should respond in the same way to hypnosis. Both recall a sequence of events seemingly devoid of fabulation. If they were indeed both recalling true fact, it is remarkable that they should both do so, given that most people introduce fantasy into hypnosis. To have one veridical recaller is unusual enough. To have two is remarkable.

On the other hand, if they were both recounting a fantasy, the fact that both narrated the same fantasy would be consistent with psychological experience. Material learnt in one altered state of consciousness (ASC) can be forgotten in the normal state, but recalled when again in an ASC, as this trivial anecdote illustrates: "An Irish porter to a warehouse, in one of his drunken fits, left a parcel at the wrong house, and when sober could not recollect what he had done with it; but the next time he got drunk, he recollected where he had left it, and went and recovered it" (Macnish 1834: 78).

The fact that both the Hills recall substantially the same events, and recall them as lived experience, proves nothing either way: it can be used to support either the veridical or the fantasy hypothesis. Indeed, the same is true of each of the paradoxes presented by their story.

Setting the Hills' adventure alongside other extraordinary experiences does not resolve the matter. But it does enable us to see that there exists in every one of us a faculty for mythmaking – that is, combining material derived from the individual's cultural framework with other material with personal content, to create an authorized yet made-to-measure myth. Each of us, given the appropriate circumstances, could find ourselves living a fantasy with the total conviction that we are really experiencing the events we are actually imagining, or recalling imagined experiences with such vividness that we are convinced they took place in reality.

Is this what happened to the Hills? We cannot say for sure, and perhaps we never will be able to say. But at least by seeing their story alongside other stories, we can see that the dream-fantasy scenario envisaged by Dr. Simon is a possible one.

References

Antrobus, John. 1993. "Characteristics of dreams." *Encyclopedia of Sleep and Dreaming.* New York: Macmillan.
Basterfield, Keith. 1992. "Present at the abduction." *International UFO Reporter* Vol 17 No 3.
Bowen, Charles. 1977. "Saucer Central, International." *UFO Report* Vol 5, No 1. New York: November 1977.
Brookesmith, Peter. 1998. *Alien abductions.* London: Blandford.
Bullard, Thomas E. 1987. *UFO Abductions: the measure of a mystery.* Bloomington, Indiana: Fund for UFO Research.
Clark, Jerome. 1998. "Psychosocial hypothesis.' *UFO Encyclopedia.* (2nd edition). Omnigraphics.
Conroy, Ed. 1989. *Report on "Communion."* New York: Morrow.
Evans, Hilary. 1984. *Visions, apparitions, alien visitors.* Wellingborough: Aquarian.
Evans, Hilary. 1987. *Gods, spirits, cosmic guardians.* Wellingborough, Aquarian.
Evans, Hilary. 1989. *Alternate states of consciousness.* Wellingborough: Aquarian.
Evans, Hilary. 1993. "Lo real y lo ficticio en el relato OVNI." *Cuadernos de Ufologia* No 15. Santander (Spain).
Evans, Hilary. 1997. "A Twentieth-century myth." Evans, Hilary and Stacy, Dennis (eds). *UFOs 1947-1997.* London: Fortean Tomes.
Evans, Hilary. 2001. "The psychosocial approach." Story, Ronald (ed). *The Encyclopedia of Extraterrestrial Encounters.* New York: Penguin Putnam.
Fuller, John G. 1966. *The interrupted journey.* New York: Dial Press.
Gurney, Edmund, Myers, F W H, and Podmore, Frank. 1886. *Phantasms of the living.* London: Trubner.
Hill, Betty. 1995. *A Common Sense Approach to UFOs.* Private.
Hopkins, Budd. 1987. *Intruders.* New York: Random House.
Hough, Peter & Randles, Jenny. 1991. *Looking for the aliens.* London: Blandford
Hufford, David J. 1982. *The terror that comes in the night.* Philadelphia: University of Pennsylvania.
Janet, Pierre. 1926. *De l'angoisse à l'extase.* Paris: Alcan.
Kroll, J. and Bachrach, B. 1982. "Visions and psychopathology in the Middle Ages." *Journal of Nervous and Mental Disease* Vol 170 No 1.
Lawson, Alvin H. 1983. "The hypnosis of imaginary UFO abductees" *Journal of UFO Studies* No 1.
Lindner, Robert. 1954. *The fifty-minute hour.* New York: Delta.
Macnish, Robert. 1834. *The philosophy of sleep.* London: Appleton.
Magonia. London: Quarterly journal. *Passim.*
Méheust, Bertrand. 1978. *Science-fiction et soucoupes volantes.* Paris: Mercure de France.
Méheust, Bertrand. 1985. *Soucoupes volantes et folklore.* Paris: Mercure de France.
Méheust, Bertrand. 1992. *En soucoupes volantes.* Paris: Imago.
Meurger, Michel. 1995. *Alien abduction: l'enlèvement extraterrestre de la fiction à la croyance.* Amiens: Encrage (Vol 1 No 1 of the collection *Interface* edited by Joseph Altairac for Scientifictions).
O'Brien, Barbara. 1958. *Operators and things.* Cranbury, NJ: A S Barnes.
Proceedings of the Rocky Mountain Conference on UFO Investigation, 1981: Laramie, Wyoming: 104.
Proceedings of the Rocky Mountain Conference on UFO Investigation, 1982: 105.

Randles, Jenny. 1988. *Abduction*. London: Hale.
Randles, Jenny. 1981. *Alien contact*. Suffolk: Neville Spearman.
Rogo, D Scott. 1980. *UFO abductions*. Signet: New York.
Schatzmann, Morton. 1980. *The story of Ruth*. New York: Putnam.
Schnabel, Jim. 1993. "The Münch bunch." *Fortean Times* 70. London: August 1993.
Siegel, Ronald K. 1992. *Fire in the brain*. New York: Dutton.
Sieveking, Paul. 1999. *Fortean Times* 118. London: January 1999.
Spina. 1523. "Quaestio de strigibus Venezia." Translated in Harner, Michael J. (ed) *Hallucinogens and shamanism*. New York: Oxford University Press, 1973.
Strieber, Whitley. 1987a. *Communion*. New York: Morrow.
Strieber, Whitley. 1987b. Press release issued with *Communion*. New York: Morrow, May 1987.
Sulman, Felix Gad. 1980. *The effect of air ionization, electric fields, atmospherics and other electric phenomena on man and animal*. Springfield: Charles C Thomas.
Wier, Jean. 1560. *Histoires, disputes et discours des illusions et impostures des diables &c.* Originally published in German; translated Paris: Bureaux de Progres Médical, 1885.

Hilary Evans has researched marginal human experiences for many years and has authored several books on the subject, including two in-depth surveys of visionary and encounter experiences with otherworldly beings. His most recent book at the time of the Indian Head Symposium, *From Other Worlds*, was a chronicle of the various beings who have reportedly visited our planet throughout human history. He does not believe any such visits have taken place, and this doubt includes the Hill case. Nevertheless, he considers the encounter experience to be of great interest, and that the Hill abduction, as the single most publicized case, is of paramount significance in helping to understand the processes, psychological and social, which have brought about the current proliferation of claimed experiences. Hilary Evans lives and works in London, England, where he is a partner in the Mary Evans Picture Library.

Chapter Five

Of Time and the River

*Why the Hills' abduction account should be viewed as
a landmark contribution to the mythic aspect of ufology*

Peter Brookesmith

In one sense, the legacy of the Hills' belief that they were abducted by aliens in September 1961 is plain, obvious, and all about us. Large numbers of people in the United States and the United Kingdom (and well beyond) believe much the same has happened to them, and many more people believe their stories to be true. The Hill case is the touchstone for these beliefs, and not only because it was the first such story to reach a wide audience. Subsequent abduction accounts have followed so similar a pattern to the Hills' reported experience that this consistency has become one test of an abduction report's validity – and indeed the claim to validity of *all* high-quality abduction reports (Bullard 1996; Mack 2000: 242–3).

For some of us, little inspires confidence in the notion that extraterrestrial aliens have ever visited Earth (Davis 1996; Brookesmith 2000). On the other hand, there can be little doubt that perfectly sane people have had abduction *experiences* of some kind, which are not explainable by appeals to psychopathology or the bias and/or incompetence of literalist investigators (Devereux & Brookesmith 1997; Persinger 2000). But an experience is a different thing from the narrative that represents it. Whether or not there is any substance to claims of alien abduction, and exactly what that substance consists of, are not trivial questions, but they are not the issue in this paper. The focus here is on the nature and significance of the narratives themselves.

The heart of the matter is surely *why* people, especially experients, should reject alternative explanations – of which there is no lack – for the basis of their narratives, and persist in believing in the literal truth of something that seems objectively so preposterous and is subjectively so distressing. Despite these obstacles, and the mockery they can expect from all sides, "abductees" will fiercely defend the validity of their accounts. This alone would suggest that they signify something crucial to the experients and to their supporters.

Mythology and the UFO

Mainstream scientists and social scientists have largely ignored this issue of belief and its tenacity. More energy has been expended on demolishing the plausibility of abduction stories than on pondering why they exist, why they appeal so widely, and what they may mean. The basis of the argument offered here is that alien abduction stories embody a modern mythology; and my essential theme is what that myth may mean. From this perspective, the underlying basis in reality or unreality of the ostensible subject of that myth is irrelevant to its meaning, its cultural significance, or the urgency of the issues it addresses. Rollo May (1993: 15) usefully defines myth as "a way of making sense in a senseless world. Myths are narrative patterns that give significance to our existence. ... Myths are like the beams in a house: not exposed to outside view, they are the structure which holds the house together so people can live in it." May here echoes Eric Dardel (1954): "Every period declares 'its' truth ... and is warmly attached to it. Our 'truth' of the moment is often only a myth that does not know it is one, and... we make myths every day without knowing it."

It is important to remember that living myths may be unrecognized as such. Consider the way that scientific (more often scientistic) and materialistic thinking redefined what may be regarded as acceptable objective "truth" in Western societies during the 19th and 20th centuries. For example, it is almost a point of honor among its devotees that Marxism is "scientific," although it is demonstrably no such thing (Popper 1934). This is what may be called a *conceptual* myth.

While myths are often oblique, metaphorical expressions of their true concerns, that does not prevent them from being taken as literally true by their adherents (Lévi-Strauss 1964). A tale about a man and a woman living in moral ignorance in a garden, beguiled by a serpent into stealing fruit from a magic but deadly tree, is both a thriller and a tragedy in miniature and grips its audience accordingly. It is also a metaphor for human development from the irresponsibility of childhood into adult self-consciousness, apprehension of right and wrong, and awareness of time and mortality. We might call this an instance of a *narrative* myth. Nonetheless the story of Adam and Eve has been taken to be historically factual by many and has traditionally been interpreted by Christians not as a tale of growth into maturity but to demonstrate the inherent, and inherited, wickedness and sinfulness of humanity. Narrative myths thus may be taken by their audience to be both literally true and metaphorically significant at the same time. One is reminded of T.S. Eliot (1933: 151-153):

> The chief use of the "meaning" of a poem, in the ordinary sense, may be ... to satisfy one habit of the reader, to keep his mind diverted and quiet, while the poem does its work upon him: much as the imaginary burglar is always provided with a bit of nice meat for the house-dog. [...] In a play of Shakespeare you get several levels of significance. For the simplest of auditors there is the plot, for the more thoughtful the character and conflict of character ... and for auditors of greater sensitiveness and understanding a meaning which reveals itself gradually.

Jerome S. Bruner (1960: 285) comments that "...when the prevailing myths fail to fit the varieties of man's plight, frustration expresses itself first in mythoclasm and then in the lonely search for personal identity." We may find that belief in a new *mythos* indeed involves an implicit attack on an older one – as when modern believers in Satan tacitly reject (post-) Enlightenment rationalism, or when adherents to the UFO *mythos*, more overtly, attack scientism, often mistaking it for the actuality of scientific method and pursuit (Brookesmith 1998a).

An alternative strategy – which the alien abduction myth follows – is the creation of a new mythology, or the resurrection of old myths that speak more plainly to prevailing conditions. C. Z. Nunn (1974), noting an increasing belief, in the U.S. during the 1960s and '70s, in Satan as an actual entity, wrote: "Instead of being viewed as random, irrational behavior, Devil-belief is an effort by the powerless to make sense of the world, to apply causality when disorder threatens, and to reduce the dissonance generated by their commitment to a social order that is incomprehensible and unresponsive to them" (May 1993: 24). Intuitively one senses that humanity prefers such a route. Even if successful, "the lonely search for personal identity" will not necessarily deliver that consciousness of connectedness with the rest of the tribe that seems to be fundamental to a sense of human completeness.

Nunn indicates above one of the functions of all myths – functions that are real and serious, no matter how bizarre or improbable their vehicle (their "ordinary meaning," or plot, in Eliot's sense) may seem to non-subscribers. Satan has made his way into UFO lore, and abductions have made their way into fundamentalist Christian millenarian thinking, and narratives of ritual satanic abuse bear certain structural and symbolic resemblances to abduction narratives. (Dean 1994; Melton 1994; Wright 1996; Randle *et al.* 1999). Conspiracy theories, which abound in ufology, fulfill much the same need as devil belief – and indeed often include it in one form or another. Dorothy Nelkin and Sander L. Gilman (1991) observed the same process at work in reactions to plagues, where "blaming" and conspiracy theories are "a means to make mysterious and devastating diseases comprehensible and therefore possibly controllable." When people are confronted by incurable, invisible and potentially universal afflictions like AIDS, say Nelkin and Gilman, they face

> situations where medical science has failed to serve as a source of definitive understanding and control, so people try to create their own order and to reduce their own sense of vulnerability. In effect, placing blame defines the normal, establishes the boundaries of healthy behavior and appropriate social relationships, and distinguishes the observer from the cause of fear.

Conspiracy theories may thus be seen as a form of mythic thought. The abduction myth not only contains conspiratorial elements but is a means both to make "the mysterious" comprehensible and to reduce social and political "dissonance." The abduction myth can be seen as a logical extension of the paranoia evident in ufology (Kottmeyer 1996), from which conspiracy theories are an organic outgrowth. Aspects of the abduction myth's social infrastructure, such as the "abductee support group" (Randle *et al.* 1999), also serve the "search for personal identity" identified by Bruner.

Although, chronologically, the alien-abduction myth is a subspecies and product of the much larger UFO *mythos*, it may well be displacing its parent as the dominant myth of its kind. At any rate the abduction myth is far richer and more suggestive than the context, and concept, from which it sprang and in which it remains embedded. But it is not wholly comprehensible (even as to its ostensible, "surface," meaning) without some awareness of the nature of the soil from which it has grown – soil that, in turn, the myth has modified.

The UFO *mythos* as generally understood presumes that UFOs and abductions are the product of an extraterrestrial, spacefaring, alien culture, and is usually known by the shorthand term "Extra-Terrestrial Hypothesis" (ETH), and sometimes as "the alien myth" (Peebles 1995). The loyal opposition to it is generally taken to be the fundamentalist "skeptical" or "debunking" (more accurately called "scoffing") position. The ETH is by no means the whole story in interpreting UFOs, but it underlies all contactee, close-encounter, and abduction accounts. Essential to the alien myth are the notions that ET aliens are surveying Earth, and that governments are probably aware that UFOs are ET craft but, for a variety of imputed reasons, are averse to revealing their knowledge publicly.

Watching Them Watching Us

As the myth evolved between 1950 and 1961, the perception of alien "surveillance" underwent these broad changes:

1. Neutral observation at a distance; daylight disks and lights in the night adduced as evidence.

2. Concerned observation and contact for the good of humanity, particularly in response to terrestrial atomic weapons programs; the aliens idealized, as in the contactee phenomenon.

3. A reversion to neutral observation, but now conducted from close quarters: close encounters of the third kind (CE-IIIs) adduced as evidence, in which UFO occupants were "surprised" while taking soil samples etc.

If, as Keyhoe (1950) and others insisted, UFOs were extraterrestrial craft, then it was in a sense logical they should have occupants. There was no consensus by 1961 as to their nature, and not everyone interested in ufology took every occupant case seriously. But heavily publicized accounts of close encounters such as those from the French wave of 1954, the tales of the much-maligned contactees, the Kelly–Hopkinson case of 1955, the Gill case of 1959, and even perhaps the Simonton case of 1961, along with seemingly "hard" evidence from the McMinnville photographs of 1950, accounts from Levelland in 1957, the Trindade photographs of 1958 – plus numerous South American cases – appeared to confirm the logic and to indicate that the saucers were at least "under intelligent control."

If there was a problem with the close-encounter stories, apart from the disparateness of the visiting aliens' appearance, it was their lack of finished plot *as stories*. It was impossible to gauge, from these tales, what the aliens were up to. This literary defect would also be characterized by ufologists as "absurdity," a favorite term of *Flying Saucer Review* editor Charles Bowen, and one echoed by Aimé Michel and Jacques Vallée. Almost no "serious researcher" in mainstream ufology was prepared to take the contactees' tales at face value. What was "really" happening remained enigmatic, even illogical.

The Hill case provided an answer to this question, in dramatic or narrative terms, and so gained a kind of authority. The Hill case achieved its status as "mythic first" (Thompson 1991: 62) because it both personalized the alleged alien presence and generalized it ("This could happen to me – it could happen to *anyone*"), and further generalized it by implicitly explaining the known inquisitiveness of alien visitors in a readily comprehensible fashion. Unlike the contactees' accounts, although intrinsically scarcely less absurd, the Hills' story fitted into the pre-existing pattern of CE-III accounts and extended them. The aliens' examination of their human specimens seemed to reflect a properly impersonal, scientific interest. There were no messianic messages for mankind in the Hills' experience, no moralizing, no extraterrestrial Utopia or Galactic Brotherhood to whose lofty standards Earthlings need aspire. This detached curiosity on the aliens' part also reinforced the authority of the story among those who were willing to subscribe to the UFO myth.

A further presumption, if often left unstated, of the UFO *mythos* is that the aliens were in some sense "superior" or "more advanced" than humanity. The basis for this notion was initially straightforwardly technological: we can't get to their planets, but they can get to ours. And furthermore, in craft that out-perform anything we have. The contactee movement added a moral dimension that, despite the mockery it routinely receives, has never quite been erased from wider ufological thinking: the spacemen were our guardians and advisors, and their civilizations were uniformly presented as more harmonious than our own. In the 1950s, scientific simplism equated technological progress with moral superiority; Earthlings became helpless, mystified savages in comparison to the aliens.

The abduction myth as we know it today builds on these foundations to offer aliens who are technologically advanced to the point of magic: they can read, edit, and wipe memories, "switch off" potential witnesses to their nefarious activities, ignore physical barriers such as walls and windows and float themselves and their captives through them, and make their craft invisible at will. These massive tactical advantages, along with their alleged "breeding program," have transformed their former benevolent guardianship into a cosmic threat to the human future. The aliens are morally superior only in some scientific, behaviorist or post-modernist sense – that is, they are amoral, treating us, not like the erstwhile benevolent paternalists of imperial or colonialist stripe, but like vivisectionists to whom all moral schemes are merely relativistic. We are no longer simple savages: we are more like laboratory rabbits. Between the contactees and the abductees, the myth shifts from a scheme in which humanity is in a childlike or primitive state and has yet to pass certain tests to become accepted into the Galactic Federation, to one in which people are simply victims – and victims who have no power at all over the aliens, their intentions, or the outcome of their activities. (Hopkins 1987, 1996; Jacobs 1998)

This version of the alien agenda seems to have attracted a rather larger following than the more benign one promulgated by abductologists such as Mack, Sprinkle, Boylan, *et al.* The public (or that proportion that is interested) would appear to *prefer* an apprehension of their own individual condition that entails casting themselves as victims. This is as informative as it ought to be alarming.

Beyond the Aliens

If abduction narratives do not describe veridical four-dimensional events but are essentially mythic in nature, then their history is extremely rare in the annals of folklore and anthropology. For, unlike urban legends, and unlike most mythic tales from the past or from other cultures (an exception being cargo cults), we can pinpoint their origin. Although the Villas-Boas case of 1957 was the first abduction to be recorded, it was the 1961 Hill case that brought the phenomenon to public attention and that has largely shaped the cases that followed it.

The questions then arise: what, in terms of specific ingredients, inspired their particular story? And what cast the Hills into the unusually sensitive position of being able to create a myth that spoke to the condition of a large segment of their society? For answers, we need first to look at what the abduction myth may mean – at what its metaphors reveal of its underlying human concerns.

Relatively little of the skeptical and none of the literalist literature on abductions has addressed this issue. One of the earliest surveys (Rimmer 1984) hinted that projections of fears for the environment lay at the heart of abduction narratives. However, neither that hint nor any general thematic analysis is developed in the book.

Rogerson (1990:10) and Devereux (1993) have suggested that the impersonal soullessness of modern Western civilization is reflected in and accommodated by abduction stories. In this view the aliens are projections of our social selves: *alien*-ated, *dis*-eased with ourselves and one another and with the dis-*spirit*ed, impersonal, conformist, bureaucratically invasive and uncontrollable elected dictatorship of a society that we have created and, more important and more depressingly, apathetically sustain. Rogerson wrote:

> ... the ufonauts do not represent aliens, but are perceived as non human (or at least non humane) aspects of ourselves and our society. The 'greys'

are surely personifications of 'little grey men' – that stock term of abuse for petty, colourless, hidebound bureaucrats – an apt image of 'only doing my job' cosmic social workers. I would go further, and say that there is being made here an identification between the impersonal forces of mass society and the impersonal forces of wild nature.

Devereux echoes this, thus:

> The reality of UFO abductions is, I suggest... to do with altered states of consciousness. These states were known of in earlier cultures, but today... we have no cultural context for experiences of the Otherworlds – which... can appear totally real, with all senses involved. Rather than spirits and ancestors [encountered during altered states of consciousness in shamanic societies], our modern altered states of consciousness are peopled by aliens and machines. While shamanic initiates experience death and rebirth, we experience invasive examinations at the hands of impersonal beings. The machine is within the modern soul. And the ET robot or alien could be the very image of our estrangement from our own inner selves and from nature itself.

Chronologically separating these two characterizations, Thompson (1991) drew attention to the mythic nature of UFO and abduction accounts, and for the exercise did not distinguish between solved, unsolved, or hoax reports on the grounds that all contribute to the mythopoeic mix. Thompson offers no interpretation of the material. But he usefully points to many parallels between various aspects of the UFO and abduction myths and various figures from ancient Greek mythology to demonstrate that, regardless of "UFO reality" (or not), ufological "knowledge" is mythic in nature.

In an attempt to account for the extraordinarily large numbers of potential abductees supposedly revealed by a Roper poll of 1991 (Hopkins *et al.* 1992), Stacy (1992, 1993) proposed a radical psychosocial hypothesis that would also explain the aliens' reported appearance and behavior. Stacy contended that the Grays of abduction lore are, in effect, exactly what they look like: dead human fetuses. Stacy proposed that the abduction experience was a way to expiate guilt over abortions. He first noted that what he called the New Revised Abduction Scenario, the version promulgated by Hopkins and Jacobs, differed from the Old Standard Scenario described by Bullard (1987) in two crucial respects. Bullard's scenario had no hybrid children and no claimed cases of missing fetuses. As claims for the number and extent of abductions do not stand up to common sense, we should seek a terrestrial cause for reports of hybrid babies and missing fetuses.

Medical termination of pregnancy has been legal in the U.S. since 1972, and in the U.K. since 1967. Stacy noted that since 1972, some 30 million American women had had abortions. The proportion of the U.S. population thus potentially affected far outstrips even the wildest claims for the number of "probable" abductees. Polls showed that Americans held contradictory opinions on the subject. While 73 percent of Americans supported abortion rights, 77 per cent viewed the operation as a form of murder. Thus, most people managed to endorse both ideas at once. Clearly, this was fertile ground for internal conflict, guilt, and shame. Stacy pointed to the many fetus-like physical attributes of the aliens, and suggested that out of powerful emotions they had metaphorically become "avenging angels":

> The hybrid baby... is nothing less (or more) than the aborted foetus brought to life. The 'missing' fetus is no longer dead, then, but lives on in a 'heaven' (outer space) from which it can never physically return, perhaps even aboard a 'Mother' ship. And the only way it can be revisited is for the abductee to be 're-abducted'. ...Allegorically, [the Grays] represent the souls of all departed, or aborted, fetuses. And the fact that the Grays are now responsible for the 'missing' fetus – both literally and figuratively – absolves the aborter of the original sin, that is, it reduces any guilt attached to abortion per se.... The abduction experience, then, serves a fundamental purpose, namely, the reduction of psychological tension occasioned by guilt.

Stacy pointed out that men may feel as guilty and confused over their role in an abortion as women, and members of both sexes could be morally appalled and bewildered by abortion without having been directly concerned with one. In the New Revised Abduction Scenario, the victim of the termination becomes the victimizer, punishing the guilty. But, justice having been done, the abductee is once more free to grow — as expressed in post-abduction "rebirth" or "psychological resurrection." Signs include "an increased appreciation of life, greater self-acceptance, a deeper concern for others, an expanded level of spirituality, and a heightened level of concern with social/planetary issues." In light of Stacy's hypothesis, the abduction experience is comparable with the shaman's spiritual rebirth, whose narrative structure parallels the abduction scenario (Méheust 1985; 1987) and could be seen as a restatement of it in contemporary, technological dress.

By the early to mid 1990s commentators with no previous ufological connections had become alert to the abduction phenomenon. Newitz (1993) suggested that the aliens represent an imperialist tendency shared by all humanity:

> One might say the alien abduction story is too allegorical to be true. It is as if, hundreds of years later, white people are experiencing a return of the repressed – suddenly they are having fantasies in which they imagine themselves victims of the same uncontrollable injustices suffered by non-whites for centuries under Western imperialism. ...But [as] Jacobs and other UFO researchers like Budd Hopkins point out, people from every racial and class background are being 'abducted'. In fact, the famous Barney and Betty Hill case involved an interracial couple. ... If the alien abduction narrative is merely fantasy, then this would seem to indicate that one of our basic fears as human beings is a fear of being colonized. This is not a fear specific to any race, class or nation. ...
>
> Danger doesn't always wear a white face – it may not even wear a human face. ... If we render invisible the 'white person' in everyone, that white person will come back – right back to the white people's old place – in the form of 'aliens', perhaps, who are so like ourselves.

A related, if more tightly focused, idea was proposed by Mizrach (1994):

> The U.S. is currently dealing with the fact that its white majority is decreasing, thus provoking all the debates about "multiculturalism." White supremacists take to the talkshow airwaves every day to proclaim the dangers of "race betrayal" by those who "miscegenate" and "pollute" the white race. And Budd Hopkins tells us that women – the majority of whom are white and WASP, heartland, middle-America types – are being carried off by aliens to achieve a "hybridization" of them and us. ...[The abduction investigators'] focus on the "hybridization hypothesis" shows the extent to which race fear may be one of the unconscious logics behind the UFO abduction panic.

Mizrach was at pains to insist that the investigators were not racist, only that they and their subjects were articulating an unconsciously perceived threat to their cultural identity. He noted that black nationalists too have conscripted the abduction phenomenon to their own cause, alleging it is part of a genocidal plot. What Mizrach calls "race fear," however it is expressed, manifests a sense of threat to the secure future of a culture and a way of life.

The emphasis in abduction lore on reproduction, birth and death suggests a deep and widespread deep anxiety about the future, whether that means the human future or the immediate fate of the individual experient. Newitz's and Mizrach's commentaries confirm that principle.

Peebles's study (1994) was one of the most theoretically generalized analyses of UFO mythology. He calls throughout on such hoary themes as the "UFO cover-up" and notes an increasing paranoia in American ufological discourse in the late 1980s and early '90s, finding its roots in political nihilism born of the Viet Nam conflict. Each chapter summarizes the particulars of the developing UFO mythology, but Peebles leaves specific interpretations to the reader. His closing paragraphs are uncontentious, but also aloof from any detailed exegesis:

> Each person goes through life attempting to make order of the events and phenomena around him. Humans need order, which comes both from knowledge and [from] myth. The flying saucer and alien myths are really about how one makes order out of his world. The idea of disk-shaped alien spaceships becomes the symbol for hopes and fears about the world.
> We watch the skies seeking meaning. In the end, what we find is ourselves.

Thus – for example – the roots of the paranoia that Peebles identifies, and quite why it should increase in its power of enchantment over the decades following the end of the Viet Nam war, are left unexamined. Peebles' theme that UFO flaps and major shifts in ufolore are reactions to social crises is suggestive, but the significance of individual motifs and images is not explored. Nor does he examine ufology or social conditions outside the U.S., so leaving unexplained the attraction American developments might have for markedly different societies such as Mexico, Brazil (a major UFO hotspot), France, Spain, the Scandinavian countries, or the U.K. – which all have strong traditions of UFO reporting, investigation, and analysis.

James Lewis (1995) published a collection of essays by various hands proposing that ufology, and in particular the contactee and abductee movements, were religious in nature. In this collection John Whitmore makes a convincing case for seeing, in abductions, parallels to religious imagery, practice and belief. Whitmore's self-confessed reliance on a Jungian vocabulary does not require an endorsement of Jungian beliefs to appreciate his case; the terms can be taken as useful shorthand. For instance, he writes (79–80):

> Whatever else UFO abductions may be, they are an encounter with the Other. Every detail of an abduction story emphasizes the idea of otherness. Abductees are subjected to an otherness of space, taken aboard an extraterrestrial spacecraft and even at times pulled out of their bodies, isolating them from a sense of the familiar. They experience an Otherness

of time, which does not seem to flow at the same rate or with the same laws as in day-to-day experience. They are surrounded by Other beings, aliens with visages and powers which are simply not human. The aliens are physically Other, with their short statures, enormous eyes, and oversized heads. They are sexually Other, arousing the abductee and sparking feelings of love. They are spiritually Other, superintelligent and either morally superior or clinically amoral. The abduction experience is a very condensation of the strange and unfamiliar.

As encounters with the Other, UFO abductions are essentially religious. Humanity seems to innately separate the prosaic from the unfamiliar, and the sacred from the profane. Things which do not fit into the definitions of the familiar, humanity tends to sacralize. The sacred, the numinous, is that which is "wholly other," completely beyond the pale of human experience as normally considered. Abduction by aliens certainly fits into that category, and this is perhaps the reason for the tendency of abductees to interpret their experiences within some sort of religious framework. Researchers who devise interpretative scenarios tend to encounter religion whether they mean to or not, and even resort to theologizing about alternate realities and the final goal of human history. The otherness of the abduction phenomenon makes religion impossible to escape, and no understanding of the phenomenon can be complete without a consciousness of its religious nature.

The Irrelevance of Reality

Matheson (1998) treats abduction narratives as just that – narratives – and discerns several major themes in them. The very arguability of the reality of abduction is taken as a sure sign of their mythic status. Matheson cites Day (1984) – "scientifically, [a myth] cannot be proved" and neither can it be "properly reconciled with phenomenological facts" – and quotes Gadamer (1980): "A myth which can be proved or verified by something outside of the living oral tradition or written religious tradition is not really myth. Thus *the only good definition of myth is that myth neither requires nor includes any possible verification outside of itself.*" [Emphasis in original] This describes abduction mythology and its self-reinforcing elements (which include the narrators and their audience) fairly precisely. Ufology's treatment of the notorious Roswell Incident also illustrates the pattern. That case long ago forked into rational attempts to discover what really happened on one hand, and on the other into an extraordinary collation of truths, half-truths, tendentious claims, and wild fictions, all of which continue to grow with each passing day. And it is the latter, with its alien bodies, MJ-12 farrago, six alleged crash sites, fake autopsy movies, and monstrous cover-up – not the wreckage of a Mogul balloon train – that means "Roswell" in the vulgar mind.

Matheson's analysis of the abduction myth emphasizes that it is a response to (or, I would note, in structuralist terms, a mediation of) conflicting human apprehensions of developing technology, which is seen as an agent of both potential liberation and potential oppression (296):

> ...the abduction narrative presents a confused and confusing picture of the potential within our technological world for both evil and good. It depicts in a deliberately ambiguous manner the possible effects on the quality of life in a technological environment, by presenting us with beings whose power is practically magical, but who are virtual slaves to the society that has attained this state. ...For if the myth presents the aliens as technocrats *par excellence*, it also reveals them as beings who possess little else of meaning in their lives. In those versions where aliens take their subjects on tours of their craft, it is almost as if... they have nothing else they could point to in their *milieu* such as art, music, or literature that would demonstrate an enriched state of being. Here the myth's message is pretty obvious: ...in a totally technological society *all* opportunities for the creative functions will be lost; there will simply be no room or time for the exercise of the emotions, the passions, empathetic responses, or even love.

Like Rogerson and Devereux, Matheson too draws attention to the ramifications of abduction imagery for social and political life (300–301):

> Practically speaking, the aliens' power bears an unmistakable resemblance to the ubiquitous tentacles of modern bureaucracy. Just as no place is safe from the intrusions of technology-assisted statecraft, so no human is beyond the reach of the aliens and their inscrutable designs. ... In keeping with the theme that modern bureaucracy is intrinsically dehumanizing, the aliens as representatives of a technocratic/bureaucratic *milieu* remain steadfastly insensitive to human needs, an insensitivity they never seem to overcome.

From such seeds, Matheson observes, conspiracy theory naturally springs.

Whitmore's 1995 essay crystallized various nascent ideas in my own mind, which resulted in a series of articles (Brookesmith 1995, 1996, 1998a) exploring the religious connotations of ufological lore. My essential thesis there followed Bloom's (1992) delineation of an "American Religion," to observe that abduction imagery and alien attributes were strikingly related to concepts of divinity in versions of Christianity native to the U.S. Important aspects of the aliens' profile were their magical ("miraculous") technology, their inescapable nature, their arbitrary and inscrutable behavior, their indifference, and their victims' utter powerlessness. Published at much the same time as Matheson's, my book (Brookesmith 1998b) surveying the abduction phenomenon also explored abduction narratives' relation to mythic thinking. Like Thompson and Matheson, I regard all abduction reports, regardless of their credibility, as grist for a mythopoeic mill. Those writings inform the view of the alien-abduction myth offered here.

This is the Way the World Ends

A theme rarely examined by critical analysts of either ufology or abductions is their connection with millenary or apocalyptic lore. An exception is Bullard (Jacobs 2000: 176–184) who notes (182): "The contours of apocalypticism show like ribs stretching through the flanks of UFO lore." The topic deserves exploration.

By the end of the 1980s the UFO *mythos* had in place a treasury of images, rumours, symbols, folklore, encounter reports – and a few facts – from which to coin a response to the next great sea-change in American politics – the end of the Cold War. But by then (1989) other looming cosmic threats had emerged to decrease the gaiety of nations. In the U.S., there was the discovery of other "enemies within" – ritual satanic abuse, and recovered memories of incest, both of which so strikingly echo the motifs of abduction lore. The global dimension was sabotaged by pollution to such an extent, according to some environmentalists, that it threatened not just wildlife but the future of humanity itself: human fertility was being disrupted by hormones and antibiotics clinging to the very food we ate (Colborn *et al.* 1996). In other words, the notion of imminent threat (secular Armageddon) shifted from nuclear annihilation to a no less comprehensive and, crucially, *less visible* ecological doomsday. Westerners increasingly presented themselves as powerless victims of indistinct forces beyond their control.

The themes emphasized by UFO researchers shifted to match this politico-socio-psychological change of gear. The nightmares of paranoid "Dark Side" ufologists became absorbed into established ufological wisdom: even reptilian aliens now crawl through the narratives endorsed by "mainstream" abductologists. A remarkable proportion of those devoted to ufology (and many outside it) believe everything connected to the U.S. space program is a cover-up. The abduction scenario came to feature three motifs patently related to End-Time fears: the scenes of future devastation played to abductees, the aliens' messages of concern over the Earthly environment, and the idea that the Grays were a dying race.

Besides revealing an unmistakable link between the 1950s' contactees and today's abductologists' interpretations of abduction reports (even as those same abductologists scoff at the contactees' claims), these themes alone powerfully suggest that the Grays of abduction lore are not objective "aliens" but projections of humanity's own inhumanity. Mack – environmental and anti-nuclear campaigner – is clearly in millennial mood when he ties abductions to a divinely ordered Universe thus (Jacobs 1992):

> Is it possible that… an effort is being made to place the planet under a kind of receivership? This would… arrest the destruction of life and make possible the evolution of consciousness or whatever the *anima mundi* has in store. … [T]his scenario is consistent with the facts of the abduction phenomenon.

For Hopkins (1996), ecological collapse, alien interference in genealogy and genetics, and a global cover-up of the alien presence are woven together. Jacobs (1998) takes the victimization of humanity one stage further, declaring that within five to 50 years the aliens will reveal themselves and their (by then successful) plot to remake humanity in their own image. In these ufological musings, the immediate future is quintessentially the same as that of Christian Fundamentalists: the end of human history and of humanity's engagement in its own destiny. Outside forces will intervene. And all these myths involve things that no one can see, or is permitted to see – such as "alien implants" – while Hopkins maintains that UFOs can make themselves "selectively invisible." Likewise, in thematic parallel, no one can actually *see* the dire fate allegedly concealed in the real Universe, such as creeping ecological disaster, the hidden world of child abuse, the financial tentacles of the Mafia, or the spread of a plague like AIDS.

The unfolding of the UFO *mythos*, whatever else it may signify, seems to be inextricable from a presentiment of a doomed humanity, a doomed social fabric and very possibly, at the bottom of this inverted pyramid, the fragility of personal identity (Kottmeyer 1988). Some ufologists do retain a touching faith in the salvific efficacy of the ufonauts. The contradiction is only superficial: both facets reflect the character of conflict that is at the heart of the apocalyptic vision. In some versions of the UFO *mythos*, this is specifically presented as a "war in heaven" between rival ET civilizations, in which Earth is a disputed territory (Branton 1999).

In a century that has seen previously unimaginable cruelty and destruction, in which both religion and humanism have failed to save humanity from its incomprehensible self, it should be no surprise that a frustrated craving for the transcendental might elaborate on technologically otherworldly elements in contemporary culture and combine them with elements from established religious imagery to explain, or redeem, the human predicament. The apocalyptic aspects of abduction narratives, too, clearly derive from themes in the "American religion" (Strozier 1994) and are an organic development of the paranoid pedal note of ufology.

A myth, let us repeat, will bear more than one meaning. The abduction scenario meets that criterion, for it can be interpreted as a religious fable for a godless and anxious age, a hero myth, a shamanic ritual, the purging of a specific guilt, or a technologized version of millenniary hopes and fears – among other things. Any one of these generalized psychodramas may be adopted and varied so that they speak to the peculiar needs of a particular individual's condition.

The Hills' Stories

In many, although not all, respects (Barney Hill had his own takes on the aliens' appearance and on the medical examination phase), the Hills' accounts of their abduction bear a strong resemblance to Betty Hill's nightmares. The content, her detailed notes tell us, did not surface in sequential order. The record we have – and it is the earliest available to us, as Betty confirmed that she no longer had her original handwritten notes (Hill 2001) – is a *consciously organized* series of events. She made her notes sometime in November 1961, and we cannot be sure whether they represent the felicitous marshalling of dream fragments, or the simple chronological (re)ordering of whole episodes. The resulting story may be the outcome of logic or intuition, but it has a dramatic coherence (Kottmeyer 1990). But if Betty Hill's narrative, in her dreams or emerging under hypnosis, is not veridical but in effect a work of folk art, then it's reasonable to look for possible sources and influences – from which not even the most original artist is free. Kottmeyer and Randle *et al.* have pointed to the possible influence of various science fiction movies on the Hills' accounts, although no one seems to have enquired whether the Hills actually saw any of those cited besides the "Bellero Shield" episode of *The Outer Limits* TV series.

However, it is a matter of record that, at a sitting, Betty read *The Flying Saucer Conspiracy* (Keyhoe 1957) – *after* the encounter, but *before* her nightmares began. If we grant Betty Hill the ability to tell a good story well – which is not difficult for those who met her – then we may be able to find in Keyhoe's book some material that contributed to her account – or not.

Keyhoe has this to say (51):

At eleven minutes past two [on August 6, 1953] the pilot of a TV-1 jet sighted a strange, glowing object streaking up from directly behind. When approximately 100 feet astern, the UFO shot to starboard and paced the TV-1 for four seconds. It then accelerated swiftly to an estimated speed of 1,000 miles per hour – and disappeared.

According to ground crew and officer, the pilot was very pale and frightened when he landed. He kept saying, "I actually saw him."

A credible observer reports seeing the occupant of a craft. All in four seconds, perhaps, but that may have provided authority, or perhaps was a confirmation, for what Barney Hill said under hypnosis that he saw.

A reported discussion follows (52) between Keyhoe and broadcaster Frank Edwards about the physical appearance of creatures from other worlds. Keyhoe dismisses stories about "monsters" from outer space, but does not quibble with the idea that intelligent beings exist on other planets or that they may well look rather different from humans.

Keyhoe reports (107-8) a conversation with a "Paul Redell." (This, like "Ed Stone" [see below], was actually an *alter ego* of Keyhoe himself, a dramatic device the pulp-fiction writer used to air, eliminate, and refine various ideas he was entertaining. French ufologist Aimé Michel used to perform similar, if less devious, mind experiments in reporting conversations he had had with an alien creature of superior intelligence, namely his cat.) In this imaginary dialogue Keyhoe initially confirms his notion that "some advanced race" of ET visitors – who, he agrees, would "certainly be ahead of us technically" – might be concerned with "helping us out." But then he is left to ponder the thought, which "could be right," that ETs may regiment humans, because "to them we might seem like infants that had to be brought up the right way." We may note here how the notion of "superior" ETs is taken for granted, and that Keyhoe, after some thought, endorses the idea that ETs' own view of what is right and proper would take precedence over ours – for our own good, in their eyes.

Betty's dream notes tell how the aliens reassured her: "All they want to do is make some tests; when these are completed in a very brief time, they will take us back to the car and we will go safely on our way home. We have nothing to fear" (Fuller 1981, 380). The theme is constant throughout later abduction narratives. Its ultimate inspiration may be Keyhoe's 1957 book, as transmuted by Betty's imagination.

Keyhoe (116–7) and former *True* magazine editor John du Barry discuss the possible nature of ET visitors, agreeing that the contactee stories are "a cruel hoax" but leaving it open as to whether they may be benevolent or dangerous: "After all," writes Keyhoe, "what did we really know about the mysterious creatures who controlled the flying saucers?"

A solution to this problem – "controlling creatures" being taken for granted – is implicitly invited. A mediating resolution is actually found in the Hills' narratives, in that their ETs are seen to be neither utopian missionaries nor predatory abominations. They are indifferent, impartial scientists, determined to do what they have to do, occasionally bewildered by what they find and willing to explore issues they find problematic (such as dentures), and even hospitable to a degree. Following the logic of the soil-testing, plant-sampling aliens of other CE-IIIs, they treat human beings like field specimens, testing them but meaning them no harm. It could even be said that the Hills' ETs want their subjects to think well of them. But that does not inhibit their investigations. Keyhoe gently insists that whoever is watching Earth need not be hostile (144).

He reports (144–5) a conversation with "Ed Stone" speculating about the possibility of separate races of aliens living on the Moon and on Mars, and the pair then discuss what might affect the physiology of Moon beings. This passage is important insofar as it dismisses space-monster yarns, but (especially if one has been infected by Keyhoe's eccentric methods of alogical inference) could be taken to allow the possibility that the spacefarers are indeed humanoid.

Keyhoe considers CE-IIIs from the 1954 European wave to be "wild tales…with weird creatures" (162). From France, we hear of "a small creature wearing a 'crash helmet'" and, from Portugal, of "two small creatures in shiny metallic outfits" seen collecting grass and stones – the classic CE-III scenario. Other descriptions from the French wave are admittedly bizarre. A German witness describes "four small, peculiarly-shaped creatures with 'thick-set bodies, oversized heads and delicate legs'" (163). Keyhoe also mentions (191–2) two Venezuelan reports featuring "a dwarfish creature" in one and "four little men" in the other, and an Italian report of "three or four small creatures wearing transparent helmets." Keyhoe says the Venezuelan entities were "hairy dwarfs" but does not quote all the witnesses on this feature. All these reports reinforce a notion of UFO-related entities as diminutive creatures. This is the one repeated, if not consistent, feature in Keyhoe's mentions of CE-IIIs. The standard image of the ufonaut is seen in the process of creation. Sheer repetition might create an aura of plausibility onto which Betty Hill's imagination could latch.

Keyhoe's final chapter (228–36) raises some themes that later were to be incorporated into the abduction myth. "Colonel W.C. Odell, U.S. Air Force Intelligence, had said that an unknown race might be planning to migrate from some dying planet" (228). This is also a staple motif in science fiction, and it was the 19th-century astronomer Percival Lovell's belief that the "canals on Mars" were evidence of a dying civilization. "Redell" is quoted (229) saying that "a race advanced enough for space travel would certainly have means and weapons far beyond ours," and Keyhoe responds: "All right... I agree that we're in their power." The idea that the 1953 Kimross F-89 crash could have been a capture of both plane and pilot – in other words, an abduction on the aerial hoof – is canvassed in a conversation with "Redell" (230). The exchange includes Keyhoe's belief that the "saucer creatures" are "trying to prepare for a peaceful contact with the earth" (another science fiction motif). The (in)famous disappearance of Flight 19 of Bermuda Triangle fame, it is likewise suggested, was really a capture of the aviators and their planes by aliens (232–6).

Keyhoe's book presents a fair summary of the UFO myth as it stood in 1957. He presumes throughout that UFOs are piloted by "superior" ETs, and that their mission is some kind of surveillance of Earth. Although he generally dismisses most CE-IIIs as fantasies and tall tales, he also equivocates over some of them (51, 191) and dwells on the possibility that humans have been captured by UFO entities. He insists too that the ETs are not ultimately hostile, although "we're in their power." These themes, and the febrile paranoid style of his prose, tend to outweigh Keyhoe's ostensible caution over "space monster" stories.

There would appear to be sufficient raw material in Keyhoe's book alone on which Betty's creativity could go to work. Quibbling over particular details misses the point; Betty Hill was never a slave to other people's take on things. Keyhoe supplied themes, images, and a framework that she could "dress" in specifics. Webb had it right the first time when he concluded in 1961 (Chapter Eight) that Betty's dreams were a creative answer to the question "What if...?" – that is, *what if* we were captured by aliens? What would they do?

In still broader terms, Keyhoe stimulated her (and she had the imagination) to answer the questions posed by the dramatically unsatisfactory, somewhat absurd CE-III scenario, and give point and purpose to alien contact reports – and all without contradicting UFO experts and upsetting their emerging myth, at least in spirit. Webb (1965: 12) comments that "Betty Hill picked up several books on UFOs" including Keyhoe's, after the Indian Head encounter. Their titles are unknown, so the triviality or profundity of their effect on Betty's dreams cannot be gauged. The important point is that Betty was freshly primed with a range of ideas, of who knows what richness or oddity, from UFO mythology shortly before she had her dreams.

If the Hills' story is indeed a mythic construction, we are still left with the problem of why Betty, in particular, created it. Do any of her circumstances or concerns match any of those discussed earlier?

On the Fringe

Barney had a secure job at the Post Office, then one of the best-paying divisions of the U.S. Civil Service; Betty, from a long-established New Hampshire family, was a social worker for the State. Both had wide intellectual interests and were intensely politically aware. Barney was a voracious reader. Before they were married, Betty sold the land on which her house stood to an oil company for a gas station development and had the house (which dates to the early 1800s) moved to its current location. They had extra income from renting out parts of the house. Financially, they were probably noticeably better off than the average, especially if one includes the value of their Post Office and New Hampshire State health benefits.

From the perspective of the early 21st century, the Hills were unexceptional people of impeccable respectability. There seems to be no reason to invoke any Lenskian status-inconsistency theory (Lenski 1956; Warren 1970) to rationalize the Hills' experience in psychosocial terms. But in 1961 the Hills were an anomaly in U.S. society and would be uncommon even today [2000] in New Hampshire. The 1990 U.S. Census showed that state's population to be 98 percent white; blacks made up 0.6 percent (just 7,198 people) – fewer than both Hispanics (1 percent) and Asian and Pacific Islanders (0.8 percent). In 1970, black/white marriages represented 0.146 percent of all marriages in the U.S.; by 1995 the proportion had risen to 0.545 percent (Wright 1995). A mixed-race couple like the Hills was thus unusual enough in the U.S. as a whole in the early 1960s, but would have been particularly noticeable in New Hampshire.

Betty told me in 1997 that her marrying Barney had lost them no friends except those they "didn't want to know anyway," and she enquired rhetorically why, if her mixed-race marriage had somehow contributed to her imagining her abduction, all mixed-race couples weren't claiming to be abductees? Leaving aside the undistributed middle in that logic, Fuller's account and common sense both would suggest that the issue of race was of considerably greater moment to Barney than to Betty, particularly on the night of their UFO encounter. It was he, after all, who was the member of the minority ethnic group. There is some evidence (Pflock 2000) that because he was black Barney had been thwarted in his hopes of a career in the U.S. Army; he was very probably underemployed as an assistant dispatcher in the Boston post office. Possibly his civil rights work and the distinctions he achieved through it made up for any other, prior lack of recognition through prejudice. But by undertaking his civil rights work he was inviting attention to, even emphasizing, his liminal status or "difference." New Hampshire, then as now, was politically conservative and had preferred Richard Nixon by 157,989 votes to 137,772 over Kennedy in the 1960 presidential election. Race was about to become literally a burning issue in the U.S., and 1961 saw riots greet black "Freedom Rides" organized by the Rev. Martin Luther King in Anniston and Birmingham, Alabama.

In this context, Barney had chosen a distinctly exposed, outsider's position, which was surely accentuated by having a white wife. He had reason to be stressed quite apart from his grueling commute to and from Boston. Betty, although she glossed over such problems later, most likely shared that stress, certainly shared Barney's outsider status, and must have identified easily with black powerlessness, disenfranchisement, and victimization.

We have observed the themes of powerlessness and victimhood in the abduction myth. The civil rights campaigns of the 1960s inevitably dealt in images of colonization and slavery, as well as being explicitly concerned with the future. Given the Hills' location, we should look to the increasingly deranged rhetoric of those who opposed "integration" to gain an insight into the daunting prospect faced by civil rights campaigners of the era. The Nazi-like black jackets and perceived threatening mien of the aliens as Barney saw them suggest plainly enough a sense of "difference" and exposure, which also would reasonably account for his acute sensation that he was the centre of hostile, white human attention earlier on the night of the encounter. That in turn probably contributed to his sense that the UFO was following them, and its occupants were gazing at him (Fuller 1981: 37).

Resurrected by the activities of integrationist campaigners were segregationists' fears of miscegenation and of black men's sexual prowess. Perhaps the semen sample taken by the aliens, according to Barney's testimony under hypnosis, related to this racist imagery. Webb (1965: 11) relates how Barney felt "a cup-like device placed around his genitals and believed a sperm specimen was somehow withdrawn." Shortly afterwards, in a development heavily disguised in Fuller's book, a "cylindrical object" was inserted into Barney's rectum, and he "believed something was extracted." The "sperm sample" has since become a staple of the New Revised Abduction Scenario.

Martin Kottmeyer (2001; 2002) has suggested that Barney's hypnotic memory may have derived from a method of extracting sperm from bulls for artificial insemination, which involves inserting an electrode into the bovine rectum to stimulate ejaculation. Barney, who spent time on a farm as a child, may have known about this or seen it happen. It doesn't require much wit to see that such a demeaning image of the archetypally powerful bull may readily be turned into an icon of humiliation and helplessness. Nor is it exactly difficult to convert the image into a metaphor for the situation in which Barney recalled finding himself, and then to incorporate it into the imaginative experience of an hypnotic memory. Even if the scene did not have its source in agricultural actuality, the reported event reeks of symbolism in purely human terms. The degradation and powerlessness embodied in the account are intimate, radical, and comprehensive.

On the basis of this incident, Dr. Simon diagnosed Barney Hill as latently homosexual (Webb 1965, 15), which reeks of crass boilerplate Freudianism and is an unnecessary multiplication of entities. Barney's reiterated fear, almost amounting to expectation on that particular evening, that he was about to be victimized because of his color (a concern accentuated by being in Betty's company in strange terrain), may have been an intensification of his everyday attitude – unless this was his customary level of sensitivity to the issue. But with that level of tension in the background, one might expect Barney to represent his sense of being utterly at the mercy of any hostile entity with the most drastic image he – perhaps anyone – could find in his imaginative repertoire. And given the ineluctable underlying theme of powerlessness in the abduction myth, the similar scenes that have cropped up in later abduction accounts may be no more than a readily accessible metaphor for extreme victimization, a direct equivalent of rape for women.

Barney Hill, as a relatively powerless black man, may have been the first to grab at the imagery, but its repetition (or independent ideation) by later abduction claimants proves nothing more than that the pool of male nightmares is unsurprisingly small. In the Hills' case, there is certainly a good case for saying that their circumstances anterior to their conscious experiences that night in September 1961 provided nourishing soil for archetypal imagery. One could push the psychological envelope further: September 19 was the birthday of one of Betty's adopted children. Barney felt considerable guilt about leaving his own children, and his former wife was antipathetic to their having any contact with Betty – who in turn was unable to have her own children. Just possibly Barney felt "unmanned" by these unfortunate circumstances, which thus may also have informed the creation of the imagery of this episode in his hypnotic recall.

To Beat the Devil

The nature and interpretation of Betty's dreams *qua* dreams is problematic, as are the related matters of post-traumatic amnesia and repression. Space precludes discussing them fully here. But if the dreams were purely imaginative, and if Betty's recall under hypnosis was no more than a reconstruction and reinforcement of them, then the distinctive elements in Barney's account under hypnosis need addressing. The differences in the aliens' appearance and details of the capture and release episodes are almost trivial enough to be expected. What is intriguing is Barney's reaction to his experience as recalled – or relived, or created – under hypnosis. To follow my argument here, we should recall Whitmore's comment (Lewis 1995: 79): "Whatever else UFO abductions may be, they are an encounter with the Other. Every detail of of an abduction story emphasizes the idea of otherness." After September 20, 1961 Barney was facing an Otherness of a peculiarly disturbing kind: an amalgam of a terrifying event – the encounter at Indian Head – and after it, a monumental hole in his recall. All that filled that chasm were Betty's dreams, which had an emotional and psychological logic in light of Barney's conviction that the ufonauts were bent on capturing them, and one would think the dreams unnerving for their potential plausibility. Certainly the issue deeply troubled Barney: at our meeting at Indian Head, his niece Kathy Marden testified that after that Canadian vacation he became listless, distracted, and depressed, a "different man" from his usual self. Under hypnosis – which in this case might be considered the functional equivalent of directed dreaming: Simon constantly leads the Hills to develop their narrative, albeit for purely therapeutic purposes – Barney looks into the abyss, to find not only that the abyss looks back at you, as Nietzsche warned, but that it puts you through the mangle, and so thoroughly that it turns you metaphorically inside out in the process.

Now consider Hartmann's view of dreams: "Dreams make connections in the nets of our minds more broadly than does waking thought. Not randomly, however, but guided by the emotion or emotional concern of the dreamer. Dreams 'contextualize' emotion. They do this in the form of 'explanatory metaphor'" (Wilkerson 1998). And, says Hartmann elsewhere (1999):

> Roughly, the most basic function can be called reweaving or interconnecting. Returning to one of the many series of dreams after trauma, we have found that the person first dreams about tidal waves and gangs, then gradually more and more about other related material from

his or her life. The dream is making connections and tying things together. It starts with a new piece of distressing information – in an extreme case, trauma – and ties it in, connects it with other images of trauma, other memories related to the same feelings, etc. This process interconnects and cross-connects the material so that next time something similar happens, it will not be quite so frightening since it will be part of a woven pattern in the mind. The dream reweaves a torn net or redistributes excitation, to use two very different images. Over all, we can talk about the dream as calming by cross-connecting.

For Barney Hill, the hypnotic process, inspired if not controlled by Betty's dream material, can be seen as a resolution in several ways. First, the hiatus in his memory is confronted and its enigma unraveled. Providentially, if predictably, the imagery is consonant with his wife's, who has much invested in the veracity of her dreams. As Hilary Evans notes (Chapter Four), "Even if they do not accept [the dreams' scenario] as a true account, *it is the only account they have.*" An already long-running and potentially corrosive conflict between the couple is thus voided. And there is this, from Barney's second session with Dr. Simon, on February 29, 1964 (Fuller 1981: 156–7):

> I was lying on a table, and I thought someone was putting a cup around my groin, and then it stopped. And I thought: How funny. ...If I keep real quiet and real still, I won't be harmed. ...And it will be over. And I will just stay here and pretend that I am anywhere and think of God and think of Jesus and think that I am not afraid. And I am getting off the table, and I've got a big grin on my face, and I feel greatly relieved. [Barney then tells how he was led back to the car.] And I see Betty coming down the road, and she gets in the car, and I am grinning at her and she is grinning back at me. And we both seem so elated and we are really happy. And I'm thinking it isn't too bad. How funny. I had no reason to fear.

He then describes how he felt when they regained US 3:

> And Betty and I feel, I feel real hilarious, like a feeling of well-being and great relief. ...I am relieved because I feel like I've been in a harrowing situation, and there was nothing damaging or harmful about it. And I feel greatly relieved.

To reprise: "The dream reweaves a torn net or redistributes excitation, to use two very different images. Over all, we can talk about the dream as calming by cross-connecting." Barney has confronted the Other, and found it innocuous. Whether the Other is the conventional (white) social world distinct from his liminal status, or a gang of threatening young men in Montreal, or merely a generalized sense of potential uproar, even personal harm, because of his marriage to a white woman, the cross-connections symbolically meet in the abduction psychodrama and resolve his fear – despite the grotesque and humiliating treatment he has undergone. Barney would appear, and not entirely irrationally in his circumstances, to have suffered a fair degree of allophobia (fear of the other – in Barney's case, particularly fear of other people). In a poetic, Empsonian ambiguity that is typical of dreams, Barney's rectal probing is certainly a violation, but it is also a clearing and cleaning out – a catharsis in its most literal sense – as is suggested by his belief that "something was extracted".

An Alien Infestation?

The psychosocial factors rehearsed above may account for the sexual and "political" elements in Betty's dreams and in both the Hills' hypnotically retrieved or induced memories. But they will not explain Barney's genital warts.

Genital warts (*condylomata acuminata*) are caused by about 30 of the more than 60 wart-producing kinds of human papillomary virus (HPV), of which there are about 100 known varieties. They are remarkably widespread. It's thought that some 75 percent of Americans are infected with warts of one kind or another, while 40 million Americans are estimated to carry genital HPV, with 1 million new cases occurring annually. One source notes: "Infection with HPV is very common, although the majority of people have no symptoms (asymptomatic). In several studies done on college women, nearly half were positive for HPV; although only between 1% and 2% had visible warts and [fewer] than 10% had ever had any visible genital warts." In those cases in which the symptoms of HPV infection do become visible, growths may occur within three weeks of infection, but equally may not appear for several years.

In the overwheming majority of cases, genital warts are acquired through sexual contact, although according to the American Cancer Society and the Centers for Disease Control, recent research has shown that HPV can be transmitted through any skin-to-skin contact with any HPV-infected area of the body. For instance, the virus can be transferred from the fingers via an open scratch in the genital area. They are usually associated with other genital infections, and some varieties are associated with cancers in the genital region, especially in women. For what it is worth, Betty Hill suffered from just such a cancer in her latter years. There is no cure for HPV infections. The warts may go into spontaneous remission, and then reappear after a period of time. They may be invisible to the naked eye, or emerge smooth, round, raised or flat, stalked, or in clumps as cauliflower-like excrescences. Colors range from gray to yellow or pink (Martin 1994; Smith 1990; Warts Web references).

The implications of this hardly need elaborating but, if any recent episode had contributed to the warts' appearance, shame could have reinforced Barney's self-consciousness, guilt, and sense of powerlessness on the night of the Hills' close encounter, and might likewise have affected his testimony under hypnosis. This could explain why Barney spontaneously and for no conscious reason inspected his genitals on returning from the trip to Canada. On the other hand, the potentially lengthy incubation period for HPV infections and their frequent asymptomism mean that Barney could have been infected quite innocently by a long-term, conventional partner, possibly years before September 1961.

There is no particular significance, I am told by experts (Baxter & Skew 2000), in the warts' emergence in a circular pattern around Barney's groin, although this could conceivably reflect the spread of body fluids around the genital area. Barney's warts were diagnosed and treated as an HPV infection. Besides, no other growth, pustule, chancre, or zit, besides cancers, is so long-lived, and they reappeared shortly before his death. Garden-variety warts caused by a terrestrial virus are thus indicated. Occam's razor slices off, if not the growths themselves, the notion of alien contamination. Although there remains the dim possibility of a psychosomatic connection (it would be a unique case), there is anything *but* a firm physical link between Barney's warts and the Hills' abduction experience.

As Time Goes By

What *did* happen that night? The central issue is whether or not there was an appreciable period of "missing time." Karl Pflock (Chapter Seven) has made his own calculations of the time the Hills spent watching a UFO before they reached Indian Head. While I would quibble over details in Pflock's figures – for example Webb (1965: 3) says that, from spotting the UFO until stopping at Indian Head, Barney never *exceeded* 30 mph, so that their overall average speed for this part of the journey would be expected to have been significantly lower than that – I am happy to accept his calculation of the mileage and his argument about the route the Hills took. Where we differ is over interpretation.

Rather remarkably, no analyst of this case since Walter Webb seems to have thought to recheck Barney's (or Fuller's) calculation of the miles the couple had to cover to reach home from Colebrook. This measure is critical because the "missing time" element depends on Barney's reckoning that it would take 4½ to 5 hours to cover "the 170 miles" (Fuller: 25) from Colebrook to Portsmouth. After much discussion, Karl Pflock and I agreed that the planned route down US 3, US 3B/NH 132, NH 104, I-93, and US 4/202, covers 189 miles, and that the detour onto minor roads added only 2.75 miles. Thus we are asking, from our different perspectives, why it took the Hills seven hours to cover 191.75 miles.

It is difficult to gauge how fast Barney generally drove, and therefore whether his estimate of the traveling time from Colebrook to home was accurate or optimistic. The distance from the Hills' motel 11 miles east of Montreal to Colebrook was approximately 105 miles, and we do know how long one section of this trip took. The Hills crossed the border into the U.S. at about 9:00 p.m., and arrived in Colebrook half an hour later. We know that they entered the U.S. on Provincial Route 22 (now 147), which joins VT 114 just north of Norton, Vermont. They therefore covered the approximately 20 miles from the border to Colebrook at about 40 mph. This may indicate Barney Hill's driving habits more accurately than Fuller's vague remark that Betty was always complaining about Barney driving too fast. If he was to reach Portsmouth in 4½ to 5 hours, he was reckoning to maintain an average speed of between 42 and 37.8mph, giving a median projected average of 39.9mph. This closely matches his speed from the Canadian border to Colebrook.

In the table on p.180 I show the distances as measured between various key points on the Hills' route, the time to the nearest minute taken to travel them at Barney's lower average speed for each stage of the 189-mile journey, and the time I calculate they may actually have taken. I have used the lower projected average because to maintain even this speed over nearly 200 miles in the dark on the kind of road under discussion calls for driving for extended stretches at considerably higher speeds. Any experienced driver can confirm that observation. Recent experience of my own on a regular 110-mile journey between Wales and England, all but 9 miles of it on two-lane roads, driving hard – wherever possible at or above the legal speed limit in the U.K. (60 mph) – never produced a journey time of less than 2 hours 35 minutes (42.58 mph), and more frequently it was between 2 hours 45 minutes and 3 hours, an average speed of between 40 and 36.67 mph. And this was in a modern vehicle with hard European suspension, on better maintained, less slippery and less sinuous roads than US 3 (let alone NH 175).

I suggest that two stages of the journey were slower than Barney had estimated. The first is the sighting and first encounter stage (Groveton—Indian Head), for which I allow a minimum of 2 hours 43 minutes and a maximum of 3 hours 12 minutes, reckoning that the Hills' average speed would (respectively) have dropped to no more than 25 mph, and could have been as low as 20 mph. This is based on the same reasoning as that above, in taking the lower average projected speed as the more likely, and from our knowledge that Barney Hill never exceeded 30mph once the sighting began. If this was his maximum pace, his average would have been appreciably slower. I also allow 60 rather than 48 minutes for the stage that included NH 175. This comes from reckoning that the nature of the road, the stops and starts Barney engaged in, and his exhaustion (about which, more below), could fairly be expected to have reduced his average speed to 32.75 mph. The estimate may be overgenerous. This part of the journey may have taken a few minutes longer, and that between Groveton and Indian Head may have been covered marginally more quickly. Nonetheless, the results bring the total calculated journey time so close to that of the Hills' actual homeward trip that the mystery of their "missing time" is, I believe, in effect solved.

The Hills arrived home at 5:05 a.m. The longer estimated journey time in the table is thus clearly too long. But if one grants the reasonableness of the shorter journey time (Estimate A), and allows a fraction more time for stops and starts, slowing down for speed limits in the more than 20 towns through which the Hills passed, and for the leg from Ashland to Plymouth (which included more stops and starts), one should easily account for the remaining 21 minutes. Just one 10-minute rest stop in a seven-hour trip seems either frugal or merciless, but again would eat up half the time remaining unassigned. The official histories delicately avoid mention of such exigencies of nature. In addition, Barney spent *some* time accelerating, swerving, decelerating, and stopping and then burning rubber in attempts to make the mystery "beeps" recur. Such activity can wreak havoc with an average speed.

Asleep at the Wheel

The Hills' late arrival home, then, can be attributed largely, if not with absolute precision, to their stop-go observations of a UFO between Groveton and Indian Head on US 3, then straying down the minor roads of New Hampshire, followed by more stopping and starting after hearing the second set of "beeps." No missing time means no abduction, leaving the Hills' story wide open to psychosocial vulturization.

This still leaves the gap in the Hills' mutual recall unresolved. But not quite. The 105-mile journey from their motel near Montreal to Colebrook can be reckoned to have taken at least 3 hours. For the sake of the argument I will be conservative and kind to those who argue for an actual abduction, and assume the Hills woke up no later than 8:00 a.m. If they left

Timing the Hills' Trip Home

Barney Hill's Stage of Journey	Distance in miles	Projected time (at 37.8mph) (in hh:mm)	Est. time (a) (speeds vary) (in hh:mm)	Est. time (b) (speeds vary) (in hh:mm)
C'brook-Groveton	27.0	00:43	00:43	00:43
Groveton-Ind Head				
(a)	48.0	01:16	02:43	
(b)				03:12
Ind Head-Ashland				
(a)	30.0	00:48		
(b)	32.75		01:00	01:00
Ashland-Concord	40.0	01:03	01:03	01:03
Concord-Portsmouth	44.0	01:10	01:10	01:10
TOTALS	189.0	05 hr 00 min		
	(a) 192.75	06 hr 39 min		
	(b) 192.75	07 hr 08 min		

ETAs at Portsmouth   Barney 3:00am Earliest 4:44am Latest 5:13am
(depart Colebrook 10:05pm)

NOTE
Speculative allocation of time spent, Groveton to Indian Head (48 miles)
(adapted & recalculated from Pflock: see Chapter Seven):

Six stops @ 5 min each	30 min
CE-III	10 min
0.8 mile @ 5 mph	10 min
a) 47.2 miles @ 25 mph	1 hr 53 min
b) 47.2 miles @ 20 mph	2 hr 22 min
TOTALS	a) 2 hr 43 min
	b) 3 hr 12 min

Colebrook at 10:05 p.m., and maintained Barney's estimated average speed until the sighting began at Groveton, they would have left Indian Head at about 1:30 a.m. By my estimate, they had thus already been awake for 17½ hours, perhaps longer, by the time they left Indian Head. Adding to an already long day, the miles between there and Groveton had been full of unwonted excitement, to say the least. Darkness had fallen before they reached the Canadian border. The Hills should have been exhausted physically, while Barney, who carried on driving, should have been emotionally depleted in addition. Robert Baker (1995: 122) reminds us that periods of amnesia while driving long distances are extremely common, and those "who drive at night [when] their range of vision is restricted to the area of the headlight beams" are especially vulnerable to having large stretches of a journey blanked from memory. Baker notes that passengers as well as drivers are susceptible to this effect. The reason:

> Reed, in his *Psychology of Anomalous Experiences*, discussed this missing time experience at length and explained it in terms of the mental organization or schematization required by a situation. While the task of driving a car is itself highly skilled, its component activities are all overlearned and habitual to the experienced driver [and] ...do not require focused, conscious attention. Furthermore our experience of time and its passage is determined by events – either internal or external.
>
> So when a person reports a 'time gap,' he is not saying that a piece of time has disappeared, but that he has failed to register a number of *events that normally serve as time markers*. [Emphasis in original] ... The time gap is experienced when no events of significance occur – when there is nothing unusual about the traffic, there is clear visibility and a smooth unchanging road surface, there are no warning signs, and the demands of the driving task are few and unchanging.

The time gap, and a subjective distortion or suspension of the passage of time (I speak again from experience), also occurs when driving tired on an unfamiliar, empty, featureless, winding minor road in the dark, when attention is concentrated on anticipating and then negotiating the next bend, and relentlessly focused within the headlamps' hypnotic pool of light. It would be my guess that this is what happened to the Hills, their energy drained after the encounter at Indian Head (whatever may have stimulated that). According to Fuller (38) they felt "an odd tingling drowsiness" and "a sort of haze" come over them shortly after they set off on this stage of their journey. We might recall in this connection that both Hills were remarkably susceptible to hypnosis.

From just south of Woodstock, State 175 roughly parallels US 3 on the other side of the Pennigewasset River until it rejoins US 3 just north of Ashland. To my eye, this road is sinuous and undulating enough both to slow down and to entrance a thoroughly fatigued driver at night. And in 1961 this was an "almost uninhabited region," while State 175 was a "lonely wilderness road," (Webb 1965, 3; 7), offering few markers to the memory until it terminated at its T-junction with US 3. Even today, dense, featureless forest grows right up to the roadside for miles on end. It seems persuasive that a combination of weariness, vision limited to the not very lustrous pool of light produced by the headlamps of American cars, and the unvarying prospect they illuminated, slowed Barney's driving and put him and (if she did not just doze off) Betty into a mild trance.

This interpretation would account not only for an appreciable dent in the Hills' average speed on the highway mentioned earlier, but also for their vagueness about this part of their journey. It may, indeed, explain Barney's going off his intended route in the first place. The first turning off US 3 to State 175 is just about gentle enough a bend to have been taken in error, particularly if the Hills were more preoccupied with what might have been above them rather than with the road in front of them.

In conclusion I might note that, with so much that is missing, confused, or ambiguous in the record, any analysis of the Hill case rests in some measure on conjecture. All one can do after so many years is attempt, honestly and rationally, to construct the most credible hypothesis from the available materials. The interpretations offered here are thus inevitably as speculative as even the truest of True Believer's conviction that the Hills were insouciantly inspected by off-world visitors. It may prove impossible to arrive at a commonly agreed account, but that constitutes no reason to evade the attempt. Long experience of the *soi-disant* "UFO research community," however, permits one safe prediction. Even if it is universally accepted that the Hill case, denuded of its crucial element of "missing time," has bitten the dust, there will be no lack of voices clamoring to propose a throng of alternative candidates for the title of First Abduction. The myth will not die.

References

Appelle, Stuart. 1996. "The Abduction Experience: A critical evaluation of theory and evidence," *Journal of UFO Studies* ns6.
Baker, Robert. 1995. "Alien Dreamtime." *The Anomalist*, No 2, 94-137.
Baxter, Dr. Richard, and Skew, Dr. Barbara L. 2000. Personal communications with the author.
Bloom, Harold. 1992. *The American Religion*. New York (USA): Simon & Schuster.
Branton [Bruce Alan Walton]. 1999 (access date). http://www.eagle-net.org/dulce.
Brookesmith, Peter. 1995. "Holy Violence," *Magonia* 54.
Brookesmith, Peter. 1996. "The Godlings Descend," *Magonia* 56.
Brookesmith, Peter. 1998a. "Meanwhile, Back at the Ranch," *Magonia* No 63.
Brookesmith, Peter. 1998b. *Alien Abductions*. London (UK): Blandford Press; New York (USA): Barnes & Noble.

Brookesmith, Peter. 2000. "Elephants on Mars," *Fortean Times* 134, 135, 136.
Bruner, Jerome S. 1960. "Myth and Identity" in H.A. Murray (ed), *Myth and Mythmaking*. New York (USA): George Braziller.
Bullard, Thomas E. 1987. *UFO Abductions: The measure of a mystery*. Mt Rainier (USA): Fund for UFO Research.
Bullard, Thomas E. 1996. "Abduction Phenomenon" in Clark, Jerome. *High Strangeness*. Detroit (USA): Omnigraphics.
Bullard, Thomas E. 2000. "Lost in the Myths," in Jacobs, David M. (ed). *UFOs And Abductions*. Lawrence (USA): University Press of Kansas.
Colborn, T., Dumanoski, D, & Myers, J.P. 1996. *Our Stolen Future*. London (UK): Little, Brown.
Dardel, Eric. 1954. "The Mythic," *Diogenes* #7.
Davis, Mike. 1997. "Cosmic Dancers on History's Stage?" *The Anomalist* No 5.
Day, Martin S. 1984. *The Many Meanings of Myth*. Lanham (USA): University Press of America.
Dean, Gwen. 1994. "Comparisons with Ritual Abuse Accounts," in Pritchard *et al*.
Devereux, Paul. 1993. "Beyond Ufology: Meeting with the alien." Paper presented at UFOIN Conference, Sheffield (UK), August 1993.
Devereux, Paul, and Brookesmith, Peter. 1997. *UFOs and Ufology: The first fifty years*. London (UK): Blandford Press.
Eliot, T.S. 1933. *The Use of Poetry and the Use of Criticism*. London (UK): Faber & Faber.
Fuller, John. 1981. *The Interrupted Journey*. Page references are to the Revised (1979) edition. London (UK): Corgi Books.
Gadamer, Hans Georg. 1980. "Religious and Poetical Speaking" in Olson, Alan M. (ed), *Myth, Symbol, and Reality*. Notre Dame (USA): University of Notre Dame Press.
Hill, Betty. 1995. *A Common Sense Approach To UFOs*. New Hampshire: Private printing.
Hill, Betty. 2000. Private communication with Karl Pflock, July 2000.
Hill, Betty. 2001. Private communication with Karl Pflock, March 2001.
Hartmann, Ernest. 1996. "Outline for a Theory on the Nature and Functions of Dreaming." *Dreaming*, Vol. 6, No. 2.
Hartmann, Ernest. 1999. "The Nature and Uses of Dreaming." *USA Today*. March 1999. (http://www.findarticles.com).
Hopkins, Budd. 1987. *Intruders*. New York (USA): Ballantine Books.
Hopkins, Budd. 1996. *Witnessed*. New York (USA): Pocket Books.
Jacobs, David. 1992. *Secret Life*. New York (USA): Simon & Schuster Foreword by John Mack.
Jacobs, David. 1998. *The Threat*. New York (USA): Simon & Schuster.
Jacobs, David. 2000. (editor). *UFOs And Abductions*. Lawrence (USA): University Press of Kansas.
Keyhoe, Donald. 1950. *Flying Saucers Are Real*. New York (USA): Fawcett Publications.
Kottmeyer, Martin S. 1988. "The Boundary Deficit Hypothesis," *Magonia* 32.
Kottmeyer, Martin S. 1990. "Entirely Unpredisposed," *Magonia* 35.
Kottmeyer, Martin S. 1996. "UFO Flaps," *The Anomalist* No 3.
Kottmeyer, Martin S. 2001. Personal communication with the author.
Kottmeyer, Martin S. 2002. "Probing Exosemination," REALL *News* Vol 10 No 3, March 2002.
Lenski G.E. 1956. "Social Participation and Status Crystallization." *American Sociological Review*, Vol.21, N 4. pp458-464.
Lévi-Strauss, Claude. 1964. *The Raw and the Cooked*. Trans. pub. 1969: London (UK):

Jonathan Cape.
Lewis, James (ed). 1995. *The Gods Have Landed*. Albany, NY (USA): State University of New York Press.
Mack, John E. 1994. *Abduction*. New York (USA): Charles Scribner's Sons.
Mack, John E. 2000. "How the Alien Abduction Phenomenon Challenges the Boundaries of Our Reality," in Jacobs 2000.
Martin, Elizabeth A. 1994. (editor) *Oxford Concise Medical Dictionary*. Oxford (UK): Oxford University Press.
Matheson, Terry. 1998. *Alien Abductions*. Amherst (USA): Prometheus Press.
May, Rollo. 1993. *The Cry for Myth*. London (UK): Souvenir Press.
Méheust, Bertrand. *Soucoupes volantes et folklore*. 1985. Paris (France): Mercure de France.
Méheust, Bertrand. 1987. "UFO Abductions As Religious Folklore" in Evans, Hilary & Spencer, John, *UFOs 1947–87*. London (UK): Fortean Tomes.
Melton, Gordon G. 1994. "Religious Reflection on UFO Stories: Contactee to Abductee" in Pritchard *et al*.
Mizrach, Steve. 1994 "UFO Abductions and Race Fear," *Bulletin of Anomalous Experience*. Vol 5 #3.
Nelkin, D. and Gilman, S.L. 1991. "Placing the Blame for Devastating Diseases," in Mack, Arien (ed), *In Time of Plague*. Albany (USA): New York University Press.
Newitz, Annalee. 1993. "Alien Abductions and the End of White People," *Bad Subjects* #5. *Bad Subjects* is available on the World Wide Web, URL: http://english-www.hss.cmu.edu/BS/issues.html.
Nunn, Clyde Z. 1974. "The Rising Credibility of the Devil in America," *Listening: Journal of Religion and Culture* No 9: 84-100.
Peebles, Curtis. 1994. *Watch the Skies!* Washington (USA): Smithsonian Institution Press (cited edition: 1995. New York (USA): Berkley Books).
Persinger, Michael. 2000. "The UFO Experience: A normal correlate of human brain function" in Jacobs, David M. (ed) *UFOs and Abductions*. Lawrence (USA): University Press of Kansas.
Pflock, Karl T. 2000. Personal communications with the author.
Popper, Karl. 1934. *Die Logik der Forschung*. Vienna (Austria). Translated 1958: *The Logic of Scientific Discovery*.
Pritchard, Andrea *et al.* (eds). 1994. *Alien Discussions*. Cambridge (USA): North Cambridge Press.
Randle, Kevin; Estes, Russ; William P. Cone. 1999. *The Abduction Enigma*. New York (USA): Forge/Tom Doherty Associates.
Rimmer, John. 1984. *The Evidence for Alien Abductions*. Wellingborough (UK): Aquarian Press.
Rogerson, Peter. 1990. "Northern Echoes," *Magonia* 35.
Smith, Tony (editor). *The British Medical Association Complete Family Health Encyclopedia*. London: Dorling Kindersley 1990.
Stacy, Dennis. 1992. "Abductions and Abortions," *Bulletin of Anomalous Experience*. Vol 3 #5.
Stacy, Dennis. 1993. "Alien Abortions, Avenging Angels," *Magonia* #44.
Strozier, Charles B. 1994. *Apocalypse: On the psychology of Fundamentalism in America*. Boston (USA): Beacon Press.
Thompson, Keith. 1991. *Angels & Aliens: UFOs and the mythic imagination*. New York (USA): Addison Wesley.
Warren, Donald L. "Status inconsistency theory and flying saucer sightings." *Science* 170

(November 6, 1970), 599–603.
Warts: source material on the World Wide Web, accessed July–August 2000:
National STD Hotline (USA):
http://www.unspeakable.com/facts/warts.html.
Arnot Ogden Self Help Library: http://www.aomc.org/hpv.html.
Planned Parenthood of Western Washington:
http://www.ppww.org/warts.htm.
Planned Parenthood Federation of America:
http://www.plannedparenthood.org/sti/HPVfacts1.htm.
Yahoo.com: http://health.yahoo.com/health/Diseases_and_Conditions/Disease_Feed_Data/Genital_warts.
US National Institute of Health: www.niaid.nih.gov/factsheets/stdhpv.htm.
Webb, Walter N. 1965. *A Dramatic UFO Encounter in the White Mountains, New Hampshire*. Cambridge (USA): The Author (Report on the Hill case to NICAP).
Wilkerson, Richard Catlett. 1998. Interview with Dream and Nightmare Authority Ernest Hartmann, M.D. *Electric Dreams* 6 (7), 12 Nov 1998. (http://www.dreamgate.com/electric-dreams).
Whitmore, John. 1995. "Religious Dimensions of the UFO Abductee Experience" in Lewis 1995.
Wright, John W (editor). 1995. *The Universal Almanac* 1996. Kansas City (USA): Andrew and McNeel.
Wright, Lawrence. 1996. *Remembering Satan*. New York (USA): Alfred Knopf.

Peter Brookesmith was co-creator with Karl Pflock of the Indian Head Symposium. He spent some years as an advertising copywriter, and then took a degree at the University of York, England, in English and French literature; his D.Phil. thesis concerned anthropological, musicological, and sociological connections between pre-industrial Anglo-American folk music and rock music of the 1960s and '70s. He next worked for the Nuffield Foundation, editing science texts for schools, before going into mainstream publishing. He has written books on firearms and shooting techniques, past and future plagues, domestic bugs and bacteria, and equine psychology, as well as four (one co-authored with Paul Devereux) largely skeptical books on UFOs. He is also a regular if infrequent contributor to *Fortean Times* and *Magonia*, and lives and works in rural Shropshire, England.

Chapter Six

There Were No Extraterrestrials

*The compleat skeptic's case against the reality
or likelihood of the Hills' abduction by aliens in 1961*

Robert Sheaffer

The purpose of this book is to examine an incident that became the most famous UFO case of its time: the supposed "abduction" of Barney and Betty Hill. I will not repeat the details here, except to illustrate the differences between the story as it is commonly told, and the facts.

The Canonical Version of the Story

Let us inquire whether or not the account of this fascinating incident, as popularly given, is actually correct.

Between 10:00 p.m. and midnight on September 19, 1961, the Hills were driving south along U.S. Route 3, nearing New Hampshire's White Mountains. They reported that the sky was perfectly clear. A gibbous Moon (more than half full) was shining brightly low in the southwest. As they passed the town of Lancaster, Betty Hill reported seeing a "star" or planet below the Moon. Soon afterward, she reportedly spotted a second object, which she described as a bigger or brighter star, above the first object (Fuller, 1966: 171). This was the object that she believed to be a UFO.

They watched this object, or "craft," for at least 30 minutes. It appeared to be following their car. Barney believed it to be an ordinary object, perhaps a satellite or airplane; but Betty quickly decided that it must be a flying saucer, and she fervently attempted to convince her husband that it was. "Barney! You've got to stop!" she shouted. "Stop the car, Barney, and look at it. It's amazing" (Fuller, 1966: 179). Her near-hysterical excitement proved contagious. Barney stopped the car to get out for a better look. He believed that he saw menacing alien faces peering at him. Now he, too, was terrified. He got back into the car and drove off. It was at about this point that the supposed "two lost hours" are said to have begun.

What Did the Hills Actually See?

The Moon was in a region void of any conspicuously bright stars. However, at midnight the planet Saturn was a highly conspicuous first-magnitude object almost directly below the Moon, as seen from the White Mountains. But there was a second planet present – Jupiter, two and a half magnitudes (12 times) more brilliant than Saturn, looking "like a star, a bigger star, up over this one," which parallels Betty Hill's description of the UFO (Fuller, 1966: 171). The Hills reported seeing two starlike objects, one of them the UFO. But two starlike objects were indeed near the Moon that evening – Jupiter and Saturn. Betty's description of the relative positions and brightness of the objects matches well with the two planets. If a genuine UFO had been present, there would have been three objects near the Moon that night: Jupiter, Saturn, and the UFO. Yet they reported seeing only two.

Some have objected that Saturn, less bright than Jupiter, would not have been easily visible so close to a nearly full Moon. As fate would have it, at the time of our gathering at Indian Head, not only were Jupiter and Saturn quite close to each other just as they were in September of 1961, but over the several days of our symposium the nearly-full Moon passed directly through the area of the Saturn-Jupiter pair. While the weather did not always co-operate with our attempts to settle the question empirically, I, as well as two of my colleagues who did happen to chance upon seeing the Moon and Jupiter in a clear sky (you had to wait until about midnight for them to get up high enough to see), not only had no difficulty seeing Saturn but even spotted the nearby star Aldebaran as well, almost two magnitudes fainter than Saturn.

Further evidence that the "UFO" was a distant celestial object (at least during the initial part of the incident) is found in Barney's observation that the object stopped when he stopped and started moving again when he did, exactly as the Moon or other celestial body appears to "follow" a vehicle (Fuller, 1966: 143). What Betty was initially calling a "UFO" must have been the brilliant planet Jupiter. She described it as moving in a sawtooth pattern, a typical description arising from the autokinetic phenomenon, when the eye tries to follow a bright point source of light against a dark background (Hendry 1979: 26). It is true that Betty told John Fuller that, looking in the binoculars, she saw the UFO pass in front of the Moon (Fuller 1966: 27), a detail that first came up when she was under hypnosis by Dr. Benjamin Simon, and which, if correct, would rule out the object being Jupiter. However, this seems to be contradicted by her statement under hypnosis that "all I did was to see it flying through the air and over the front of the car. And you know, I didn't get much of a look at it" (Fuller 1966: 215). In any case, so many details reported by Betty are exceedingly implausible, if not downright impossible, that one must be cautious in considering which of them to accept.

To some it will seem incredible that any sane person could misperceive a distant (if brilliant) planet as a close-in structured craft, complete with portholes and alien faces peering out. But the examples of numerous other UFO cases prove conclusively that this does indeed happen. Philip J. Klass documents how three educated adults, including the mayor of a large city, observing the re-entry of a piece of space debris nearly a hundred miles over their heads, described it as a mysterious craft, with square "portholes," passing less than a thousand feet overhead (Klass, 1974: 9). Allan Hendry's data compiled at the Center for UFO Studies shows that well over half of all so-called close encounters of the first kind can be attributed to either advertising aircraft or stars, with one "third-kind" encounter – an alleged occupant sighting – attributed to each of them (Hendry, 1979:72-74; 85-86).

Betty's description of the UFO sounds very much like a brilliant point-source of light such as Jupiter: "Even when it was coming in, it still looked like a star. It was a solid-light type of thing ... you couldn't see it too clearly without the binoculars" (Fuller, 1966: 175; 179). Barney Hill was the only one who thought he saw aliens "in real time."

It must be noted, however, that Jupiter cannot account for the complete story of the Hill "encounter." When Barney stopped the car just south of Indian Head, right in the middle of the road (near the present-day site of the Mountaineer Motel, just north of the interchange of Exit 33 of Interstate 93, which did not exist at that time), the UFO was still on the right-hand side of the car, toward the southwest, near the Moon. This was the position of Jupiter, where the object had been since the "encounter" began. At this point, the Hills allege that the object crossed over the road and hovered over the left side of their car, much closer than it ever had been before. This is where Barney got out of the car while Betty remained inside – "flopping in the front seat," according to Barney (Fuller, 1966: 146).

Given that Jupiter and the Moon were sinking lower, it is entirely likely that they lost sight of the planet behind the hills at this point and transferred their attention to something else. Most likely they saw an aircraft or a bright satellite crossing the sky from west to east, causing the Hills to confuse it with the original object that was no longer visible and to transfer their attention to it. Whatever the "something else" on the left may have been, it was not Jupiter, and no other astronomical object seems to be a likely candidate. Whatever the object may have been that Barney was looking at during the "close encounter," his state of mind was anything but objective and calm. He looked at the object through binoculars and fancied that he could see a row of lighted windows with alien faces peering out. The aliens appeared to be busily engaged in pulling levers and quickly turned their backs to him, except for the "leader." Barney was horrified to see that the leader of the aliens appeared to be a "Nazi," as he described it (Fuller, 1966: 115). Betty described him as "in a hysterical condition, laughing and repeating that they were going to capture us" (Fuller, 1966: 47). He rushed back into the car, and they drove off.

What About the Two "Lost Hours"?

The two "lost hours" were said to begin when the Hills drove off after Barney's terrifying face-off with spacemen. In the canonical version of the story, a short series of beeping or buzzing sounds was heard, apparently coming from the rear of the car. The first set of beeping sounds caused the Hills to lose consciousness, while the second caused their conscious recollection to return, roughly 35 miles down the road. Each beep caused the car to vibrate. One possible explanation for the "hypnotic beeps" would be some kind of flaw or corrugation in the pavement, such as often is encountered in construction zones or before reaching a tollbooth. Another is that the trunk latch apparently was not fastened tightly, and the trunk lid was rattling around, as considered by Karl Pflock in his chapter in this volume.

Even after the Hills had returned home, it was not evident to them that two hours had been "lost." Several weeks afterward, they were subjected to intense cross-examinations, lasting up to 12 hours, by UFO proponents seeking to squeeze from them the last drop of recollection. Only then, from their inability to account accurately for every minute of the evening, was it concluded that two hours had mysteriously gone "missing."

But the Hills' account of that evening's timetable has never been fully consistent. In their report to the Air Force (their earliest account) they gave the time of the reported close encounter as between midnight and

1:00 a.m. In *The Interrupted Journey*, we read that it took place not long after 11:00 p.m. In *The Edge of Reality* there is a transcript of a conversation from a radio show in which Betty Hill says, "We estimated the UFO started to move in close to us right around 3:00 a.m." (Hynek and Vallee, 1975: 9). Which of these times is correct? It is obviously impossible to establish the existence of two lost hours when we have this uncertainty ranging over nearly four hours. If Betty and Barney were unable to give an accurate chronological account of the night's events, how can anyone else hope to do so?

A few other facts will help us view the question of the "lost hours" in perspective. Barney said that prior to the "close encounter," as the UFO seemed to be moving in closer, "I became slower in my driving...I must have been driving five miles an hour, because I had to put the car in low gear so it would not stall" (Fuller, 1966: 143). Under hypnosis, the Hills told Dr. Simon of leaving the main road and driving down some side roads, where they reportedly encountered a roadblock set up by UFO aliens – although it is difficult to say how much of that part of their story is fact and how much is fantasy. Still, it is likely that they made some detours from the direct route home. Barney also relates sitting in the car much later, motionless, watching an orange light that presumably was the Moon setting (moonset was at about 1:25 a.m., although it would have disappeared behind the mountains well before that time). He says, "I just wasn't driving ahead at this time" (Fuller, 1966: 287). He does not recall how long they sat there, or why he had stopped in the first place. Since that event supposedly occurred after the UFO abduction, we still have a problem with the timeline. If the supposed UFO abduction was over by 1:00 or 1:15, early enough for Barney to watch the Moon set, then why did they not arrive in Portsmouth until the light of dawn was seen, around 5:00 a.m.? (Sunrise was not until 6:35 a.m.) Even after allowing for a supposed two-hour UFO abduction, the three-hour trip from Indian Head to Portsmouth still seems to have taken at least four hours. One thing is clear from the confused scenario above: the Hills appear to have used up a great deal of time doing something other than driving directly home.

In any case, the exact route driven by the Hills to the supposed "capture site" is highly problematic. Remember that the "close encounter site" marks the transition from the largely uninhabited White Mountain forest area to the familiar, Norman Rockwell landscape of picturesque New England villages. The towns of North Woodstock, Woodstock, West Thornton, and Thornton lie along Route 3 between the first close-encounter site and the second, the claimed "capture site." The speed limit is generally 30 mph along this portion of Route 3, although to be fair Karl Pflock pointed out in discussion that these limits were not necessarily in place outside of townships in 1961. Depending on exactly where the Hills left the main road (an issue still unresolved), they would have had to drive directly through the main street of one or more these towns. Almost immediately after the frightening "close encounter," the Hills would have found themselves slowing down to negotiate the winding streets of the town of North Woodstock. In Webb's 1964 report, Barney indicates a "capture site" near Waterville, due east of North Woodstock, which would suggest that they left Route 3 just past that town. However, Betty disagreed that this was the correct site (Webb 1965:7). In September 2000 Betty guided the symposium members to what she believes to be the "capture site," not far off New Hampshire State Route 175, near Thornton, considerably further south. Betty's "capture" site is approximately 11 miles from the "close encounter" site, and implies that they likely stayed on Route 3 a greater distance. In 2000 Betty herself was no longer certain (if she ever was) of the exact point where they left Route 3.

What Does the Hypnosis Testimony Prove?

What about the hypnosis testimony itself? When the late Dr. Benjamin Simon placed Barney and Betty Hill under hypnosis separately, they each told of being "abducted" by alien creatures and then being released with no conscious memories of the incident. This is considered by many to be the strongest evidence supporting the reality of the alleged UFO encounter.

However, psychologists generally agree that what a person says while under hypnosis need not necessarily be actual fact. Often it may be a fantasy believed by the individual. Hypnosis is of little value in separating fantasy from fact (Baker, 1990).

How did the Hills each come to tell essentially the same story? Shortly after the alleged UFO incident, Betty began having a series of dreams about being abducted by the supposed UFO occupants. She wrote down these dreams and discussed them with anyone who wanted to listen (there were many who did). Barney had heard these accounts many times. The "abduction" story told under hypnosis was simply a retelling of these dreams. Under hypnosis, Barney admitted to Dr. Simon that Betty had told him "a great many details of the dreams." This prompted Dr. Simon to ask Barney, "How do you account for the fact that you know nothing about Betty's experiences, yet she seems to know everything about yours?" (Fuller, 1966: 237). Dr. Simon's statement is not literally correct, since Barney has "remembered" (or "invented") some details that are not in any of Betty's narratives. Nonetheless, Dr. Simon's point is well-taken. If Barney was in fact just repeating and expanding upon the dreams his wife had often described, that would explain why she knew (almost) everything about his experiences, while he seemed to know next to nothing about hers.

But the most significant fact to be noted about the hypnosis testimony is that Dr. Simon himself did not believe it. A careful reading of *The Interrupted Journey* clearly reveals Dr. Simon's skepticism. Dr. Simon indicates what he believes to be the most tenable explanation for the "abduction" story: the dreams of Betty had "assumed the quality of a fantasized experience" (Fuller, 1966: 327). Appearing on the NBC-TV *Today* show the morning before the Hill TV movie *The UFO Incident* was shown (Oct. 20, 1976), Dr. Simon reaffirmed his opinion: "It was a fantasy ... in other words, it was a dream. The abduction did not happen." Dr. Simon expressed this same opinion to Philip J. Klass, who quotes him at length in two UFO books (Klass, 1974: 252-4; Klass, 1968: 229). Dr. Simon was a man eminently qualified to distinguish between fantasized and real events, that being one of the principal tasks of the analyst.

Painstaking experimental research on human memory, taking place in the years since the Hill incident, casts serious doubt upon the entire concept that human memories are formed by something like a photographic process, and that details not at first remembered have been accurately stored and can be later recovered. It is now known that memories are malleable and that remembering is process of active reconstruction. Subsequent information and ideas are frequently confabulated together with original material, so that an individual may gradually come to "remember" events that never in fact occurred (Loftus and Ketcham, 1996).

How Accurate is the Reconstruction of the Event?

A calibration of the accuracy of the witnesses' descriptions can be made by comparing their description of the weather conditions at the time of the incident (one of their few observations that can actually be checked) with official weather records. This comparison reveals that the Hills' recollection is seriously in error. In their report to the Air Force and in their discussions with John Fuller, the Hills stated that the sky was perfectly clear at the time of the sighting. Yet the official weather station atop nearby Mt. Washington, tallest of the White Mountains, recorded that high, thin cirrus clouds covered more than half the sky at the time of the incident, and this is confirmed by the records of other weather stations throughout New England. Such clouds, while thin and wispy, would be extremely conspicuous in the bright moonlight. Thus we see that one of the few statements in the Hills' account that can he verified turns out to be inaccurate. Furthermore, the weather observers on Mt. Washington reported a visibility of 130 miles (!), yet did not report seeing any unusual objects.

Is There Any Independent Corroboration of the Story?

Another often cited "proof" of the Hill incident is the supposed "radar confirmation" of the sighting, reportedly showing that an unknown craft did indeed take off at the very time of the supposed UFO abduction. Betty herself has repeatedly made this claim, which has now become widely accepted in UFO circles.

Appearing on the Lou Gordon show in Detroit (WKBD-TV, November 9, 1975), Betty alleged: "When the UFO was coming in around midnight, it was picked up on seven different radars, all along the New England coast." Very impressive, if true. In another TV appearance, on the NBC-TV *Today* show (October 20, 1975), Betty Hill once again claimed that seven different radars had seen the object land about midnight, and she added, "The Air Force in our area released a radar report of it being seen leaving the area at 2:14 a.m.," which appears to confirm beyond any doubt the reality of the alleged abduction. Unfortunately, with just one exception, all the records alleged to support this truly remarkable claim have accidentally been "lost."

I am indebted to the late Philip J. Klass for his assistance in tracking down the claims about radar. Klass was also a guest on the Lou Gordon show when Betty Hill repeated her claims about the radar sighting. He asked her if she could provide him with a copy of the documents that are alleged to support them. She readily agreed to do so, but said regretfully that she had only the documents pertaining to one of the radar sightings in her own file – the Air Force radar that reportedly showed the object leaving the area – and that a newspaper reporter had the others. A few weeks later, she informed Klass that the newspaper reporter was unable to provide any documentation supporting any of the seven alleged radar sightings, because records of them had all reportedly been "lost."

The only piece of evidence in existence that in any way supports the supposed radar confirmation of the sighting is a brief paragraph from Pease Air Force Base in Portsmouth, New Hampshire, that is contained in the Air Force Project Bluebook report on the Hill case: "06142 observed unidentified A/C come on PAR 4 miles out. A/C made approach and pulled up at 1/2 mile. Shortly afterward observed weak target on downwind, then radar CTC lost. TWR was advised of the A/C when it was on final, then when it made low approach. TWR unable to see any A/C at any time."

Translating the official jargon, the report says: "At 2:14 a.m. E.D.T., an unidentified target was observed on the Precision Approach Radar 4 miles out." (This is a type of radar that sends out its signals in a narrow beam, directly down the runway. It has an extremely narrow field of vision, seeing only those objects that are in a direct line of sight with the runway.) "The object appeared to approach the runway, but left the beam of the radar when it was about one-half mile away. Shortly afterward, another, weaker target was observed, then nothing more was seen. The control tower was twice told about the object, but they were never able to see it."

One highly significant factor is missing from this account – the Airport Surveillance Radar. This is the wide-angle radar that scans the entire region around the airport, keeping track of all aircraft in the area; the Precision Approach Radar is used to help guide the aircraft onto the runway once the Airport Surveillance Radar has been used to steer it into the general area. As far as the USAF records indicate, the Airport Surveillance Radar saw no unidentified objects at any time. This suggests that the other radar unit was not detecting an actual aircraft when it briefly showed an unknown target. (Sometimes even birds and insects are registered as targets on radars such as the PAR.) The second false target, weaker than the first, confirms the suspicion that the PAR was not detecting any actual craft. Radar "angels," as these false targets are called, give rise to many spurious UFO reports.

Even if we bend over backwards to grant that the Pease radar sighting did indeed represent a genuine UFO near Portsmouth, New Hampshire (along the Atlantic Ocean), there is no reason to connect it with the UFO reportedly seen two hours earlier in the White Mountains, many miles away. Why didn't the observers in the control tower see the UFO if it approached within one-half of a mile? Even more puzzling, why would a UFO enter the runway approach pattern of Pease Air Force Base, imitating an aircraft about to land?

What About the "Alien Star Map"?

What does the now-famous "star map" prove? Much attention has been focused on this supposed star pattern, which Betty claims to have seen aboard the UFO and subsequently sketched by posthypnotic suggestion. The reason for most of this attention has been the work of Ms. Marjorie Fish. Using the most accurate star catalog then available, Ms. Fish strung colored beads on a 3-D frame. She claims to have matched the "stars" drawn by Betty Hill with a group of nearby stars that are all similar to the Sun, and which appear to be likely places to find habitable planets.

One of the biggest boosters of the Fish map has been Stanton Friedman, a well-known professional UFO lecturer who billed himself as "The Flying Saucer Physicist" for decades after he stopped doing any physics. He writes, "There can no longer be any doubt that the Barney and Betty Hill kidnapping by aliens did occur, and we now know exactly where those particular extraterrestrials originated from, thanks to the inspired and intensive research by Marjorie Fish" (Friedman and Slate, 1973). When Friedman and Betty Hill appeared together on the Tom Snyder Show on NBC-TV (October 22-23, 1975), he went on to say: "The chances that the Fish map would grab 15 and come up with the right kind are, well, ... astronomical." "Every one of the stars on the map are the right kind of stars, and all the right kind of stars in the neighborhood are part of the map," he told an amazed Tom Snyder.

Another well-known proponent of the Fish map has been Dr. David Saunders, a psychologist formerly of the University of Colorado and the University of Chicago, who was a dissident member of the Condon Committee. Dr. Saunders, a specialist in statistics, has estimated that the odds against a random pattern of stars matching Betty's sketch as well as the Fish map is "at least 1000 to 1" (Saunders, 1975). The only problem with statements such as these is that they are incorrect and misleading. All 15 stars have been identified, according to Friedman, but he neglects to mention that Betty's original sketch contains 26 stars, not just 15. Why doesn't the Fish map identify the remaining 11? Three of Betty's background stars (those unconnected by lines) are included in the Fish map, because they fit nicely, but the other 11 are ignored. This hardly constitutes a valid scientific procedure.

As for the claim that all the stars that fit the pattern are exactly the right kind for supporting planets with life, Fish excluded other stars on theoretical grounds, as being unsuitable for supporting life-bearing planets, and hence uninteresting to extraterrestrial travelers. So using the Fish approach, there could not have been any other kind of "match." Betty Hill shows a star between the points represented on the Fish map by Tau Ceti and Gliese 86, but Fish does not. Nu Phoenicis, a star missing from the Fish map which is even more favorable for life than some stars which are included, ought to appear at the bottom of the map, where Betty Hill drew nine stars. But Fish, apparently realizing that if she identified one of these stars she would have to identify the other eight – an impossible task – chose to ignore Nu Phoenicis.

Two of the stars that are part of the Fish map (Tau 1 Eridani and

Gliese 86.1). are not even included in the list of 46 nearby favorable stars which were published in the issue of *Astronomy* discussing the Hill "star map," as they lie just outside its definition of a "favorable" star (Dickinson, 1974). However, this expanded definition of what makes a star "favorable" will bring in a number of new stars, and no attempt has been made to deal with the rest of them. There are 106 nearby non-binary stars of spectral types F6, F7 and K2 in the current Gliese catalog. Obviously not all of these lie within the volume of space of the Fish pattern. However, since these types of stars must rightfully be included among the "favorable" (given that Fish has already expanded the definition of "favorable" to include one star of F6 and one of K2 in her map while ignoring the rest), the inclusion of even a few new stars will wreak havoc with the tenuous "correspondence" claimed to exist.

Zeta 1 and Zeta 2 Reticuli on the Fish map (the supposed home base of the ufonauts) are shown as giant globes on Betty's sketch, supposedly because they are high above the rest of the map in the third dimension and hence appear larger. Yet other stars on the map, such as Tau 1 Eridani and Gliese 95, are equally high above the rest of the stars, but they appear as tiny dots, not as giant globes. Furthermore, although the globes in Betty Hill's sketch are widely separated, on the Fish map Zeta 1 and Zeta 2 Reticuli are so close as to be inseparable without a magnifying glass (though of course they are never drawn that way). In an attempt to resolve these problems, Kent C. McColloch has suggested that the star in the lower right foreground of the Fish map is not Zeta 2 Reticuli, but instead Zeta 2 Doradus, 12 light years from it. "The other large foreground star is both Zeta 1 and Zeta 2 Reticuli, which are too close together to be resolved" (McCulloch, 1982). The apparent validity of the Fish map is due to selective inclusion of data and by mis-drawing the map to make it appear to match Betty Hill's sketch.

Subsequent astronomical discoveries have raised additional issues concerning the Fish map. In 1981, Allan Hendry, then of the Center for UFO Studies, wrote "the Fish thesis has been demolished by French astronomer Daniel Bonneau, who used speckle interferometry to prove that Zeta 2 Reticuli, supposedly one of the aliens' homes, is in reality a binary pair of stars and is incapable of supporting life as we know it" (Hendry 1981b: 111). If so, it ought to have been excluded from the Fish map. However, Bonneau has since expressed doubts about the validity of this observation, which has not been repeated, suggesting that the existence of the close companion of Zeta 2 Reticuli is "doubtful." The matter has not yet been fully settled.

Another investigator of the Hill star-map is Charles W. Atterberg, then of Hanover Park, Illinois. Generating a mathematical representation of the Fish map, which is far more accurate than stringing up beads, Atterberg found that the orientation of Zeta 1 and Zeta 2 Reticuli, as given in the star catalogs, is totally out of line with the corresponding giant globes of the Hill sketch. The lines connecting Betty's globes slant northwest and southeast, but a line through the two Zetas actually slants northeast and southwest (although the distinction is largely academic, since magnification would be required even to see Zeta 1 and Zeta 2 as separate objects were the Fish map drawn accurately). Thus on the two most critical points of the map, the supposed "home base" stars of the ufonauts, the Fish map is totally wrong in the orientation and separation of these stars.

As astronomers Steven Soter and the late Carl Sagan pointed out (Soter and Sagan, 1975), the only reason that there appears to be any resemblance at all between the Hill sketch and the Fish stars is because of the way the lines have been drawn. View the two patterns simply as dots, without any lines to help the reader visualize the resemblance, and the two patterns look about as different as can be.

Not only is the resemblance between the Fish map and the Hill sketch questionable, but more than one pattern of stars has been found that appears to match the sketch. At least three other such "identifications" of the Hill sketch had thus far been proposed.

In 1965 a map of the constellation Pegasus appeared in the *New York Times*, showing a location of a strange astronomical object designated CTA-102, which a Russian radio astronomer claimed was an artificial radio beacon in space. Upon seeing the map, Betty Hill noted a striking resemblance between the stars of the constellation Pegasus and the stars she had drawn on her sketch. She then proceeded to fill into her sketch the corresponding star names from the *New York Times* map. (Of course, these are entirely different stars from the ones on the Fish map.) The supposedly artificial radio source, CTA-102, appeared very near the ufonauts' supposed home base, the star Zeta Pegasi. Was it a beacon to guide the UFOs home from their explorations? This Pegasus map so impressed author John Fuller that he included it in *The Interrupted Journey*. It appeared to provide strong evidence in support of Betty's story. But the case for the Pegasus map quickly fell apart. Other astronomers soon refuted the sensationalist claims that had been made about CTA-102. This supposedly artificial object turned out to be an unusual quasar, and that was the end of the Pegasus map.

A third supposed identification of Betty Hill's star map was proposed by Atterberg. He computed the patterns made by certain groups of stars when viewed from various perspectives in space. After much labor, Atterberg discovered that there exists a point in space, along the southern boundary of the constellation Ophiuchus, from which the stars in the Sun's vicinity appear to match almost exactly the pattern of the Hill sketch. The Atterberg map fits the sketch much more closely than does the Fish map, identifying 25 of Hill's 26 stars, instead of just 15. Atterberg did not restrict himself to just the stars favorable for life. He started out by plotting all the stars in the Sun's vicinity, which makes it all the more remarkable that the majority of the stars supposedly selected for visitation by the aliens (according to this map) are quite favorable for life. Of the 11 stars supposedly visited by aliens (not counting the Sun), seven of them are listed in Stephen H. Dole's Rand Corporation study, *Habitable Planets for Man*, as stars "that could have habitable planets." Not a bad percentage for stars selected at random from the solar neighborhood!

Even more surprising is the fact that the three stars that form the heart of the Atterberg map – Epsilon Iridani, Epsilon Indi, and Tau Ceti – which are connected by lines supposedly representing the major trade routes of the ufonauts, have been described by Carl Sagan as "the three nearest stars of potential biological interest" (Sagan and Shklovskii, 1966). Surely this is more remarkable than any of the evidence supporting the Fish map.

Yet a fourth interpretation of the Hill star Map was developed during the 1990s by the prominent German ufologists Joachim Koch and Hans-Juergen Kyborg. They wrote: "We present here a new interpretation of Betty Hill's map: that it is a view of our solar system at the time of the abduction, from a viewpoint slightly beyond Saturn, looking towards the Sun. We believe that this interpretation fits more of the data than the Fish interpretation. We also believe, in the context of Betty's abduction experience, that it is more rational for the alien to first use a display of the local solar system to determine Mrs. Hill's astronomical knowledge" (Koch and Kyborg, 1993). In the Koch-Kyborg interpretation, the objects in the map are not stars but the major and minor planets of our solar system, set for some reason not to the date of the supposed "abduction" itself, but exactly one month afterward. The large globes, which seem to have equatorial rings (unexplained in the Fish map), are Jupiter and Saturn, which in fact do have rings, although according to Betty the "rings" were sketched into the map not by her but by Dr. Simon!

A fifth and thus-far final interpretation of the Hill sketch has been developed by Yari Danjo, whose theories build upon those of Zechariah Sitchin. In this interpretation, the large connected globes represent the double star Alpha Centauri, the closest star system to our own, with the small connected star representing its fainter companion Proxima Centauri. Other points on the map represent nearby stars such as Sirius and Procyon. He hypothesizes that our Sun has an as-yet undiscovered companion, which periodically comes into the inner solar system and is recorded in human history. It, of course, is depicted on the map (Danjo, 1994).

The purpose of this discussion is not to convince you that Atterberg or the German ufologists or Danjo have unraveled the mysteries of Betty Hill's supposed alien map, but to show that an impressive-sounding case can be made for more than one map. There are simply too many possible ways to interpret Betty Hill's sketch. Random star or planetary positions, when rotated, sorted, and manipulated by choice of position, date, or criterion for inclusion, can be made to match any pre-established pattern, as long as we are willing to expend enough time and effort to obtain a match. This is much like the contemporary practice of searching for hidden messages in the Bible; the same techniques uncover hidden messages equally well in Moby Dick, and even in the Sears Roebuck catalog! (Thomas, 1997)

How Credible are the Statements of the Principal Witness?

After their "abduction," Betty and Barney Hill would go out looking for UFOs and were to see them many more times. In fact, Betty reports that "every night UFOs paced us. Sometimes it was only one, sometimes it was four" (Hill, 1995: 39). This makes it very difficult to avoid the conclusion that what Betty Hill calls "UFOs," other people would call "stars, planets, and airplanes." She acknowledges that some of the UFOs she regularly watches "appear as planes with the same lighting and the sounds of airplane motors" if skeptics are present. "Then I know the night is over, and we leave" (Hill 1995: 147).

About 1977, Betty Hill began talking about a "UFO landing spot" in southern New Hampshire, where she would go as often as three times a week to watch UFOs. Its exact location is a loosely kept secret, since numerous reporters and UFO watchers have accompanied her to the site. Betty claims that close encounters are such frequent events at this site that she has made up names for some of the more frequently appearing UFOs: one she calls "the military" because of its allegedly hostile activity, and another is "the working model" (Wysocki, 1977). Betty explains that "the 'new' UFOs aren't friendly as the 'old' ones were. Whereas before they would buzz cars, flying over the roofs and behaving almost playfully, now they sometimes shoot beams, and dart at cars in menacing fashion ... once they even blistered the paint on my car" (Clark, 1978). Betty also has asserted that the aliens sometimes get out and do calisthenics before taking off again (Jones, 1978; Hill, 1995: 106). John Oswald, a field investigator for CUFOS, accompanied Betty on a vigil at her now-famous UFO landing spot. He reported that, on one occasion, she was unable to "distinguish between a landed UFO and a streetlight" (Burke, 1977). Nonetheless, Oswald still believed that Betty Hill was abducted by aliens in 1961.

In a long, three-part article by Dr. Berthold E. Schwartz, a New Jersey psychiatrist formerly with APRO who has spent much time interviewing Betty, numerous paranormal events allegedly experienced by her are related. She reportedly has encountered a "Pumpkin Head" form that glides beside her car as a UFO hovers above. Afterwards, she is "filled with electricity," setting off airport security devices and resetting electric clocks. She has also performed babysitting chores for a troublesome ghost named Hannah to give her sister a respite from a long and tedious haunting. After the ghost had reportedly settled in at Betty's home in Portsmouth, "Hannah would walk in the room, cough, and you'd see the rocking chair rock but nobody was in it," Betty stated (Schwartz, 1977). Betty has also stated that she believes herself to be receiving telepathic messages from her alien abductors (Fowler, 1976).

Betty made other pronouncements that caution us against assigning too high a probability that her statements corresponded to physical reality. In a conversation taped for publication, Betty was asked "What ever happened to the tapes of your regressions, yours and your husband's?" She replied, "Dr. Simon has one, John Fuller has one, I do, and there's a copy in the Library of Congress in Washington" (Hynek and Vallee, 1975: 96). Being very interested in researching the case, I contacted the Library of Congress to arrange to listen to them. I contacted a number of persons in the Recordings Department, and also in the Gift Department, who catalog all materials donated. However, I was informed that the Library of Congress has no such tapes in its possession. There were no such donations from Barney or Betty Hill, Dr. Simon, John Fuller, or anyone else.

When James Moseley printed a letter from Betty in his publication *Saucer Smear*, in which she cites a court decision that cautions against relying upon hypnosis for "recovered memories," he noted, "We agree with Betty Hill's remarks here, but we recall that in her own UFO abduction case, she and her late husband Barney were only aware of 'missing time' until they were repeatedly hypnotized separately over a period of time. In this way they gradually remembered their experiences aboard the craft." Betty promptly wrote him back, and said in a letter published in the very next issue, "Incidentally, we did NOT have missing time. We clearly remembered the UFO men standing in the road, blocking our way. We clearly saw the equipment they used to stall our car motor. We could not remember what happened on board the craft, but we clearly remembered their pacing our car for awhile after we left them" (Moseley, 1995). This of course flatly contradicts the story that Betty and Barney Hill told John Fuller in *The Interrupted Journey*, and indeed everything she had said previous to that time. When one individual gives two narratives of the same event containing major discrepancies, neither should be believed.

Since so many statements made in public by Betty can easily be shown not to correspond to reality (although few have taken the trouble to check this out), we are left with absolutely no reason to credit any bizarre tale she tells that has no proof. Indeed, it would be most unwise to base any theories about the Universe and what creatures it may contain upon Betty Hill's uncorroborated statements.

The Effects of the Hill Case on Ufology

Prior to about 1966, when the Hill abduction story became well known to the public, accounts of "UFO abductions" were virtually unknown. (A 1957 case involving Brazilian farmer Antonio Villas Boas, who claimed to have been abducted by UFO creatures and then seduced by an alluring, nude extraterrestrial female, produced more snickers than genuine interest, although it is more widely believed today given ufology's inexorable trend of steadily increasing credulity.) The Hill case, with its seemingly high degree of credibility, broke new ground in terms of its acceptability to ufologists. It was the first claim of face-to-face contact with UFO aliens that was embraced by the mainstream of the UFO movement. NICAP – the largest and most influential UFO group then in existence – had previously rejected all cases in which direct contact with extraterrestrials had been claimed. The Hill case turned out in retrospect to have been a watershed event, opening the floodgates for a torrent of subsequent "UFO abduction" claims, contributing significantly to the climate of ever-increasing credulity that has characterized the UFO movement.

A flood of "abduction" stories followed in the wake of the NBC-TV telecast of the movie dramatization of the Hill case *The UFO Incident* on October 20, 1975. A minor "UFO flap" in certain areas of the country occurred as well.

A significant portion of the book *Abducted* by APRO's James and Coral Lorenzen consists of spin-off cases generated in the wake of the movie. Some of the cases derived from alleged sightings from a few months earlier, whose "missing hours" and "abduction" aspects were only recognized after the supposed abductee watched *The UFO Incident* on October 20. The Lorenzens write, "the summer and fall months of 1975 appear to have been a busy time for whoever and whatever was generating the reports of abduction" (Lorenzen and Lorenzen, 1977). That the Hill TV movie and its related publicity may have been the "generator" seems not to have occurred to them. Among the best-known spin-off cases were Mrs. Sandra Larson of Fargo, North Dakota; two young men in Norway, Maine; the celebrated *Fire in the Sky* Travis Walton abduction; and Judy Kendall, a legal secretary living in northern California. In addition to the spate of "abduction" cases, the Hill movie seems to have triggered a respectable, if not overwhelming, flap of UFO sightings. A Defense Department memo, dated November 11, 1975, declassified under a Freedom of Information Act request, reads: "Since 28 OCT 75 numerous reports of suspicious objects have been received at the NORAD COC (Combat Operations Center)..." (*NY Times Magazine*, Oct. 14, 1979). The reports originated from military personnel at bases in the northeastern United States and adjacent regions of Canada. Note that the "flap" began exactly eight days after the Hill movie was shown. In the period of November 4–9, a UFO "flap" reportedly associated with cattle mutilations broke out in Wisconsin, and a police sighting was reported in Ohio.

The late Richard Feynman, the Nobel prize wining physicist, had this to say about UFO cases: "Almost everybody who observes flying saucers sees something different, unless they were previously informed of what they were supposed to see" (Feynmann, 1998). The historical significance of the Hill case is that, because it was the first account of its kind, and because of the massive publicity that followed in its wake, it informed those who came later of what they were supposed to see.

Subsequent Replacement of the Hill Abduction Paradigm

A typical "UFO abduction" scenario from the 1960s through the early 1980s runs like this: a sighting of an unidentified object; wondering about a possible abduction; regressive hypnosis leading to "discovery" of previously forgotten memories of physical examination aboard a UFO by alien beings; finally, subsequent experience of paranormal events. The debt to the Hill case is obvious. Several major "abduction" cases were reported before the Hill movie was telecast but had already been widely disseminated in print. Patty Price first believed she might have been abducted after reading a *Saga* magazine article on UFOs. Sgt Charles I. Moody first speculated he might have been abducted after happening upon a copy of *Official UFO* magazine (Lorenzen and Lorenzen, 1977).

The "UFO abduction" scenario changed significantly after the publication of Budd Hopkins's book *Missing Time* in 1981, which made a lasting impression upon the UFO community. The alien abductors became more sinister, their intentions frankly more sexual. Hopkins's most significant innovation was to sever completely the link between UFO sightings and UFO abductions. Hopkins wrote of a new "abduction scenario that is, if anything, even more disturbing to contemplate. Many people have simply been taken from their homes while they were either asleep, or engaged in some quotidian activity, like watching television or reading" (Hopkins, 1981: 79). The supposed alien abductors discovered by Hopkins's hypnosis no longer need to have any link to UFO sightings whatsoever. The aliens may simply show up without warning anywhere, at any time, and carry you away for bizarre medical procedures and sexual acts. Budd Hopkins believes that the space aliens are conducting genetic experiments on humans. When the view of UFO abductions promoted by Hopkins (along with his colleagues David Jacobs and John Mack) became the dominant paradigm in ufology, the Hill case began to fade in significance. Henceforth, major UFO abduction cases almost invariably tended to fit the Hopkins pattern rather than that of the Hills (which in itself strongly suggests the entire "abduction" scenario to be of psychological origin).

In her book *A Common Sense Approach to UFOs* Betty Hill strongly rejects the new Hopkins paradigm for UFO abductions, arguing that such cases are indeed psychological in origin. Her arguments against relying upon hypnosis-enhanced "memories" are surely valid. However, to argue against others' unsupported claims does not automatically validate one's own. Betty writes, "Real abductions have the same characteristics. The event happens in a rural, isolated area usually between dusk and 4 a.m." (Hill, 1995: 81).

As the originator of a now-largely-discarded paradigm for UFO abductions, Betty may be suspected of having personal motives for trying to stop the further dilution of her own once-unique claimed experience. But setting aside speculation about motives, "common sense" tells us that Barney and Betty Hill were not paced by UFOs "every night" as she claims; that they and others did not see UFOs by the dozens or even hundreds flying in formation nightly, even in New Hampshire; that she did not observe formations of "mystery black helicopters" in areas of UFO visitation (Hill 1995: 48); or a huge trailer truck airborne above the turnpike (Hill 1995: 124). Whatever factors may be shaping Betty's views on UFO visitations and abductions, "common sense" is not among them.

Many factors clearly denote the subjective nature of the entire "UFO abduction" phenomenon. The appearance and behavior of supposed UFO occupants varies greatly with location and year. UFO abduction claims have been made much less frequently outside North America, especially in non-English-speaking countries, although foreign reports have started to catch up since the overseas publication of Whitley Strieber's *Communion*. The descriptions of supposed UFO aliens contain clear cultural dependencies; in North America large-headed gray aliens predominate, while in Britain abducting aliens have been mostly tall, blond, and Nordic, while South Americans tend to be abducted by more bizarre creatures, including hairy monsters. If we are to believe that such reports reflect reality, then the Galactic High Command must have divided the earth into Alien Occupation Zones whose boundaries reflect those of human culture.

Also, the demeanor and activities of supposed UFO occupants depend greatly on which abductionist "uncovers" the story. Each abductionist has a unique "agenda" representing his or her own expectations concerning a UFO abduction, and each case investigated has a tendency to confirm that "agenda." Planting his tongue firmly in cheek, Philip J. Klass gives the following advice to those who think they may have been abducted: "If you are considering contacting an abductionist to undergo regressive hypnosis, ... I strongly recommend Dr. Leo Sprinkle. Under his guidance you are more likely to encounter a gentle and spiritually uplifting type of UFOnaut than one who takes flesh samples, ova, or sperm, or removes unborn children from their mothers' wombs" (Klass, 1988: 194).

Ripple Effects from the Hill Case in the Culture at Large

Starting in the 1980s, dramatic events discovered via supposedly "recovered memories" began to receive widespread attention. When these cases began being reported, the only precedent in the culture at large for "recovered memories" was in UFO abduction reports, which in turn was built upon the seeming credibility of the Hill case. The increasingly sexual content of reported UFO abductions fed this trend. Issue 38 of the British publication *Magonia* (January 1991) was mainly devoted to analysing stories of alleged satanic child abuse and their links with UFO abduction reports. The immediate trigger of the Satanic molestation scare is generally recognized to be *Michelle Remembers* (Smith and Padzer, 1980), in which Michelle claims to have been molested not merely by a Satanic cult, but also by Satan himself. Roger Sandell notes that many of the elements in Michelle's lurid story "closely parallel UFO abduction claims," adding: "It seems likely that had Michelle approached Budd Hopkins instead of Lawrence Padzer, she would have been cited as one of his abductees" (Sandell, 1991).

Given this cultural background, a small number of women began "recovering" memories of supposedly being raped, usually by a family member during childhood. Strongly embraced by the feminist movement, the original few grew into a small torrent. Prodded by the best-selling *The Courage to Heal* (Bass and Davis, 1988), millions of women worldwide imagined themselves to be "recovering" memories of supposed sexual abuse. Soon "recovered memory therapy" was all the rage in therapy. Thousands of families were devastated by mostly-groundless accusations, and few gave such claims the critical examination they required.

Around the same time, lurid accusations began circulating about organized child sexual abuse that was supposedly occurring nationwide in daycare centers. Often supposed "satanic cults" were claimed to be involved, with claims of victimization ranging from the implausible to the completely impossible. A number of innocent persons spent years in prison, usually because of bizarre testimony coerced from small children. The fad grew quickly until the mid-1990s, when several persons whose lives had been ruined by false accusations of rape or "satanic rituals" fabricated during therapy successfully sued for damages the "therapist" who instigated the supposed "recovered memories." With "therapists" suddenly being held accountable for the harm resulting from the delusions they had implanted, the fad for "recovered memory therapy" faded as quickly as it had begun.

In Elaine Showalter's study of modern hysterical epidemics, in which "alien abductions" are featured as a prime example, the delusion is considered in a broader societal context. Noting that the great majority of supposed UFO abductees are female, as are 90 percent of those who claim to have recovered memories of childhood sexual abuse and 90 percent of those who are diagnosed with Multiple Personality Disorder, she views the hysteria as serving the function of a kind of "women's protest against patriarchy" (Showalter, 1997: 10). Showalter argues that if we want to understand the cause of these hysterias, we cannot do so by ignoring the social context in which they occur, and the "empowering" role they play.

Conclusion

With the excesses and absurdities of the Hopkins/Jacobs/Mack UFO abduction paradigm becoming increasingly obvious with each passing year, some ufologists have seized upon the Hill case as perhaps the one true instance of claimed alien abduction. However, in view of the evidence cited here, it must be painfully evident to any fair-minded person that the credibility of this classic case is essentially nil.

The reasons below summarize why the Hill case does not provide convincing evidence of any extraterrestrial encounter:

1. We have seen that Betty's observations and recollections have sometimes been quite inaccurate, implausible, and/or confused (the confused timeline, the weather conditions, claims of radar confirmation of her UFO, the Library of Congress papers, etc.). This prevents us from having any confidence in those aspects of her remarkable tale that cannot be directly proved or disproved.

2. There is no physical evidence whatsoever supporting any aspect of the supposed UFO sighting or abduction. We hear of spots on their car's trunk, of warts on Barney Hill's groin, of holes in her dress, etc. However, none of these phenomena, even granting their description to be accurate, can be shown to have any necessary connection with supposed alien visitations. Betty claims to have obtained several physical samples from UFO landing sites, but she suggests that a conspiracy of ufologists, academics, and government agencies has caused all of the samples to "disappear" before they could be analysed (Hill 1995: 127-31). This allegation of a vast conspiracy to suppress her UFO evidence should serve as a red flag against accepting her statements as literally true. The supposed "star map" proves nothing.

3. We have also noted quite a number of instances in which Betty has shown a tendency to tell fanciful tales: the ghost, the floating pumpkinhead, the window-peeping aliens, levitating trucks, seeing UFOs by the hundreds, the mystery black helicopters, etc. This is fatal to the credibility of someone who would convince us that she has truly experienced something extraordinary, especially if just once. To state the matter bluntly, it is far more likely that Betty's imagination would embellish a sighting of a bright celestial object than that extraterrestrials pursued her and her husband and interrupted their journey.

4. From the perspective of the year 1965, a remarkable tale that surfaced via intense interrogation and was later enhanced by hypnosis, containing supposedly recovered memories of extraordinary and remarkable events, might sound new, exciting and possibly plausible. However, from the perspective of the year 2001, having seen the rise and fall of hysteria over "repressed rape," "Satanic cults" and "daycare molestation," generated in exactly this same manner, such a tale must be judged implausible in the extreme.

Occam's Razor compels us to attribute the complex Hill incident to psychological causes and to classify it along with other recent high-profile hysterical accounts such as *Michelle Remembers*, rather than to "multiply essences" and invoke otherwise-unknown extraterrestrial beings as the cause.

References

Baker, Robert A. *They Call it Hypnosis*. Buffalo, New York: Prometheus Books, 1990.
Bass, Ellen and Davis, Laura. *The Courage to Heal*. New York: Harper and Row, 1988.
Burke, George. "UFO Investigator Refutes Betty Hill's Recent Claims." *Foster's Daily Democrat*, Dover, N.H., October 15, 1977.
Clark, Jerome. interview with Betty Hill. *UFO Report*, January 1978.
Danjo, Yari. *ASTRO-METRICS Of Undiscovered Planets And Intelligent Life Forms*. Privately published, 1994 (ISBN 0-9638989-0-6). Introduction by John Lear.
Dickinson, Terence. *The Zeta Reticuli Incident*, Astronomy, December, 1974.
Feynman, Richard P. *The Meaning of it All: Thoughts of a Citizen Scientist*. New York: Addison Wesley, 1998.
Fowler, Raymond. "Telepathy and a UFO." *Official UFO*, January 1976.
Friedman, Stanton and Slate, B. Ann. "UFO Starbase Discovered," *Saga*, July, 1973.
Fuller, John G. *The Interrupted Journey*. New York: Dell, 1966.
Gliese and Jahreiss, *Preliminary Version of the Third Catalogue of Nearby Stars*, 1991. On-line at the University of Heidelberg, http://www.ari.uniheidelberg.de/aricns/ .
Hendry, Allen. *The UFO Handbook*. New York: Doubleday, 1979.
Hendry, Allan. "UFO Newsfront," *Frontiers of Science*, Jan.-Feb., 1981. (1981a)
Hendry, Allan. "Anti Matter UFO Update," *Omni*, Nov., 1981, (1981b)
Hill, Betty. *A Common Sense Approach to UFOs*. Privately Published, 1995.
Hopkins, Budd. *Missing Time*. New York: Ballantine Books, 1981.
Hynek, J. Allen and Vallee, Jacques. *The Edge of Reality*. Chicago: Regnery, 1975.
Jones, Mike. "Abducted by UFOs?" An account of a lecture by Betty Hill. Centralia, Illinois *Sentinel*, June 27, 1978.
Klass, Philip J. *UFOs Identified*. New York: Random House, 1968.
Klass Philip J. *UFOs Explained*. New York: Random House, 1974.
Klass Philip J. *UFO Abductions: A Dangerous Game*. Amherst, N.Y.: Prometheus Books, 1988. p. 194.
Koch, Joachim and Kyborg, Hans-Juergen: "New Discoveries in Betty Hill's Star Map," 1993. English translation by Doug Girling, Canada, 1995. On the Internet at http://www.shoah.freeonline.co.uk/801/Abduct/HillMap.html.
Loftus, Elizabeth and Ketcham, Katherine. *The Myth of Repressed Memory*. New York: St. Martin's Press, 1996.
Lorenzen, James and Coral. *Abducted! Confrontations with Beings from Outer Space*. New York: Berkley, 1977.
McCulloch, Kenneth C. "A New Look at Betty Hill's Star Map." Paper given at the 1982 MUFON Conference, Washington, DC.
Moseley, James. *Saucer Smear*. Volume 42, No. 6 July 5th, 1995; Volume 42, No. 7, August 10th, 1995.
Pflock, Karl. Chapter Seven in this volume.
Sagan, Carl and Shklovskii, I. S. Intelligent Life in the Universe. San Francisco:

HoldenDay, 1966.
Sandell, Roger. "From Evidence of Abuse to Abuse of Evidence." *Magonia* 38 (January, 1991).
Saunders, David. *Astronomy*, August 1975.
Schwartz, Berthold E. "Talks with Betty Hill." *Flying Saucer Review* 23, nos. 2,3,4(1977).
Showalter, Elaine. *Hystories – Hysterical Epidemics and Modern Media*. New York: Columbia University Press, 1997.
Smith, Michelle and Padzer, Dr. Lawrence, M.D. *Michelle Remembers*. New York: Congdon & LattËs, Inc., 1980).
Soter, Steven and Sagan, Carl. *Astronomy*, July 1975.
Thomas, David E. "Bible Code and Hidden Messages." *Skeptical Inquirer* 21:6 , (November, 1997).
Webb, Walter. *A Dramatic Encounter in the White Mountains, New Hampshire*. Submitted to NICAP, Sept. 11, 1965.
Wysocki, David. "Reporters join UFO trackers in N.H. Woods." *Boston Herald American*, Oct. 10,1977.

Robert Sheaffer is a writer and Silicon Valley data communications engineer with a lifelong interest in astronomy and the question of life on other worlds. He is a founding member of the UFO Subcommittee of the Committee for the Scientific Investigation of Claims of the Paranormal (CSICOP). He is also a founding director and past chairman of the Bay Area Skeptics, a local skeptics' group in the San Francisco area pursuing aims similar to those of CSICOP. He is the author of *UFO Sightings* (1998) and a regular columnist for the *Skeptical Inquirer*, and has contributed articles and reviews to such diverse publications as *Omni*, *Scientific American*, *Spaceflight*, *Astronomy*, *The Humanist*, *Free Inquiry*, and *Reason*. He contributed to the book *Extraterrestrials—Where Are They?* and wrote the articles on UFOs for the *Encyclopedia of the Paranormal* and for Funk and Wagnall's *Encyclopedia*. He was an invited speaker at the Smithsonian UFO Symposium and has spoken at a number of UFO conferences, as well as at the First World Skeptics' Congress. Robert Sheaffer lives and works near San Diego, California.

CHAPTER SEVEN

A Singular Visitation

*The Hills' abduction really happened the way they described it
– and may well have been the only case of its kind*

KARL T. PFLOCK

Ufologist Stanton Friedman declares: "There can no longer be any doubt that the Barney and Betty Hill kidnapping by aliens did occur, and we now know exactly where those particular extraterrestrials originated from..." (Friedman and Slate, 1973). Ufological skeptic Robert Sheaffer asserts, "[I]t must be painfully evident to even the staunchest UFO believer that the credibility of the one 'true' classic CE-III case, the Hill 'UFO abduction,' is essentially nil" (Sheaffer, 1981: 43).

What Really Happened to Barney and Betty Hill?
Despite such unqualified pro and con declarations about the reality and nature of the Hills' experience, the simple truth is that we are unlikely ever to know with objective certainty exactly what happened to the Hills on the night of September 19-20, 1961. Of course, this is far from saying that it is not possible to draw reasonable, supportable, and convincing conclusions about the case from the sighting – and abduction-specific evidence and relevant related information. Quite the contrary, and after carefully considering everything – including the arguments of the skeptics – I am convinced that what happened was essentially what the Hills reported.

As the couple drove south on U.S. Highway 3 through the White Mountains of northern New Hampshire, they were spotted and stalked by the crew of a vehicle hailing from an extra-solar planet. Near North Woodstock, about a mile and a half down the road from where our September 2000 symposium was held, the stalking ended in an initial attempt to bag the hapless aboriginals. The "flying saucer" swooped down in front of the Hills' car, beginning a very close and frightening encounter that convinced Barney they were about to be "captured like a bug in a net" (Webb, 1961: 3). As the terrified couple tried to escape, they were compelled by some means – for the sake of convenience, call it "mind control" – to drive to a secluded spot a few miles south of the first encounter site to a secluded spot just off and to the east of State Route 175. There they were taken aboard the landed craft, physically examined and, in Betty's case at least, communicated with in a peculiar, almost playful fashion, an interaction that included showing her a star map with the explanation that it depicted where her captors' race had journeyed among the stars as traders and explorers, and implying it also revealed whence they had come, as well as the relative location of our own solar system.

Released to go on their way, with their conscious memories somehow curbed concerning everything shortly after their attempt to avoid being "netted," they drove off with their immediate awareness still mostly impaired. A while later, they emerged from their mental fog, though apparently not fully, to discover with some bemusement that they were well south of the first close-encounter site, some 35 miles down the road toward their home in Portsmouth, with only vague recollections of traveling those 35 miles.

Both Hills vividly remembered everything up to a point moments after a panicked Barney had slammed their '57 Chevy Bel Air into gear and torn off down the highway – the point when they heard and felt a series of strange beeping-buzzing sounds and slipped into a trance-like state. All after that was mostly a misty blank, until they seemed to be returned to near-normal consciousness with the sounding of another series of weird beeps. From the gloom of shrouded memory, a few fleeting images emerged: an orange Moon-like shape looming on or by the road ahead ("Oh, my God, not again," Barney exclaimed), closed diners, darkened village streets, road signs, and, perhaps, an encounter with a group of strange men blocking the road.

When the Hills arrived home, they were still dazed and uneasy. Glancing at the kitchen clock, Barney noticed distractedly that they had gotten in considerably later than he had anticipated, about two hours later (Fuller, 1966b: 17-18). This was a wrinkle that in time would become central to both an understanding of and the controversy surrounding the couple's experience, as well as becoming a recurring element in many subsequent claims of abduction by aliens from space.

Many objections have been raised against the view that the Hills not only saw a real alien flying machine but also were captured, taken aboard, and briefly held by the extraterrestrials operating it. Instead, it has been suggested that the Hills' merely saw and misidentified a bright planet "made mobile" and at one point seemingly brought very up close and very personal by their excitement and quirks of atmospheric optics and physiology. Their abduction story arose from psychological factors, with Betty as the "prime mover."

According to the skeptics, what happened could not have been what it manifestly purports to have been. An array of alleged factual difficulties, inconsistencies, and the like, Betty's prior paranormal experiences and apparent belief in the reality of flying saucers, personal problems and fears of the Hills, notably Barney's with respect to racism, and seeming absurdities in the couple's account are adduced to sweep the case into the rationalist dustbin. According to the debunkers, Betty was primed for such an experience, and Barney, despite himself, caught the contagion from her – via her enthusiasm to pursue answers and talk about the experience and, especially, her repeated recounting of her dreams of abduction in his presence.

In truth, this does not hold up, as I will demonstrate here. Other ufologists besides myself, more cautious than Friedman, acknowledge we are unable to make a case for the reality of the Hills' experience that rises to the beyond-reasonable-doubt standard of criminal law. However, I am confident that were we trying a civil action the aim of which was to establish that, other than a natural reluctance to accept such an incredible account, there is no good reason not to believe the Hills' story, we would have no trouble meeting to the satisfaction of judge and jury the preponderance-of-evidence standard that prevails in such proceedings. With that aim in mind and asking the reader to stipulate the same standard for purposes of argument, here is my case, followed by what I think the Hill incident means – or should mean – to ufology and more conventional disciplines.

The Not-So-Reluctant Hills

Beginning with John Fuller, proponents of the Hill case have made a particular point of the Hills' reluctance to "go public," arguing that this bolstered their credibility. Fuller asserted that, with two exceptions, other than discussions confined to a close circle of friends and family, Barney and Betty kept their story to themselves. These two exceptions, he wrote, were an informal, essentially private talk given to a church discussion group in September 1963 at the urging of the Hills' minister, and a closed-door presentation to a group of "technical people interested in the UFO portion of the story," arranged by Walter N. Webb, the original investigator of the Hill case, date not mentioned. (Fuller, 1966b: 56, and 1966a: 192). This is not quite true.

The first public discussion of their experience by either of the Hills was an anonymous telephone call from Barney aired the evening of August 21, 1962, on Boston radio station WBZ. Walter Webb was a guest that night on WBZ's *Program PM* show, and he had arranged for Barney to make the call. Barney briefly discussed what he consciously recalled about his and Betty's experience, but at Webb's suggestion, made no mention of the figures he had see peering down at him from the hovering UFO (Webb, 2001; Hill, 1962).

According to Webb, over the next few months, the Hills gave two semi-private presentations about their sighting to small groups at their church (Webb, 2001). Just when the first of these was is not clear, but the second, to the Couples Club, took place on March 3, 1963, not in September of that year, as Fuller had it. In November 1995, Webb told me this was in conjunction with a talk he gave on life in the Universe, which the Hills had invited him to present to the club.

As for the private gathering of "technical people," this actually was a November 3, 1963, open-to-the-public meeting of the Two-State Unidentified Flying Object Study Group, in Quincy, Massachusetts. This was about a month before Barney first contacted Dr. Benjamin Simon and less than six weeks before the Hills' initial appointment with Simon on December 14. In 1995, Webb told me that, while he is reasonably sure he attended the meeting (he gave me a copy of the postcard meeting notice), he did not arrange it. Neither did he set up any other meeting of the sort described by Fuller. Betty Hill also has told me there was no such closed-door event with technical people.

I have on file two partial copies of the audio recording made of the Hills' November 1963 presentation. These include the last few minutes of Barney's talk, Betty reading in its entirety her written account of her abduction dreams as Barney sat on the platform beside her (more on this important point below), and both Hills fielding questions from the audience at the end of their presentation. It was this meeting that got *Boston Traveler* reporter John Luttrell interested in the case and ultimately led to his series of feature articles in October 1965, "outing" the Hills to the general public. In a November 4, 1995, telephone conversation, Luttrell, now deceased, told me he was at the study group gathering, invited by a neighbor who was a group member. In 1996, Luttrell gave me one of the partial recordings I have of the Hills' remarks.

(An aside: Fuller's highly inaccurate characterization of the study group gathering and his factual slip regarding the date of the church-group meeting are just two of more than a few instances of either literary license or sloppiness on his part, giving all with a serious interest in this case good reason to consult other sources in addition to *The Interrupted Journey* and relevant references in *Incident at Exeter*. Another particularly egregious problem is his unacknowledged editing of Betty's September 26, 1961, letter to Donald Keyhoe, as presented in *The Interrupted Journey*, eliminating her reference to her and Barney's consideration of "the possibility of a competent psychiatrist who uses hypnotism" to break Barney's amnesia. To be fair to Fuller, near the conclusion of *The Interrupted Journey*, he does mention the Quincy event, but puts it in September 1962 and with no apparent realization of the problem this "third" meeting represents for his claims about the Hills' reluctance to speak publicly about their experience [Hill letter in Webb, 1965, and in Fuller, 1966b: 29-30, 284; Rodeghier, 1994]).

Fuller reports in his foreword to *The Interrupted Journey* that he first heard about the Hills' case in October 1965 from Derry, New Hampshire newspaper editor-publisher Conrad Quimby, while he was investigating the sighting reports in the Exeter area that he chronicled in *Incident at Exeter*. Quimby "mentioned the fact that an extremely intelligent and reliable couple he knew had encountered a UFO in the White Mountains back in 1961.... He further said that they had been very reluctant to discuss their case except with a few close friends because they did not want to be considered eccentric, and the subject was so controversial that they thought it might interfere with their dedicated work in the Civil Rights movement" (Fuller, 1966b: xiii).

Days later, Fuller received a message at the Exeter police station, which he used as a sort of base of operations for his investigations and which, as a state social worker, Betty Hill visited regularly (Fuller, 1966b: xiv):

> ...Mr. and Mrs. Hill would appreciate it if I'd call them in nearby Portsmouth.... The Hills had indicated that they might be able to supply me with some helpful information on the UFO research.
> Later that day, I talked with Mrs. Hill, who felt the subject was becoming important and needed exploration by responsible research. She gave me the names of some people in the area who had come to her with reports of seeing the objects....
> But she said nothing whatever of her own case. It was obvious to me that she was reluctant to discuss it, and knowing her attitude from Conrad Quimby, I did not press the subject.

A few days later (not "several weeks" as Fuller wrote), Luttrell's series began in the *Boston Traveler*.

It is obvious that a good number of persons outside the Hills' immediate social and family circles were aware of their experience for quite some time before Luttrell's series appeared. People in the Portsmouth-Exeter area knew to go to Betty Hill with their UFO reports. The Hills had spoken at a public meeting of UFO enthusiasts and investigators two years before Fuller heard about their experience, and it is more than likely that some of those attending the semi-private church-group meetings had talked to others about what they had heard. So it is clear that, while the Hills were not exactly shouting their story from the housetops, neither were they making every effort to remain anonymous.

Barney's Knowledge of Betty's Dreams

Clearly, Barney was fully aware of the content of Betty's dreams as she recalled and recorded them. We have proof positive of at least one instance in which he listened to a full, verbatim presentation by Betty, and both he and Betty admitted he was privy to at least partial accounts on other occasions.

Superficially, this would seem to bolster critics' contentions, and the conclusion of Dr. Simon, that Barney "absorbed" Betty's dreams and regurgitated a sketchy version of them under hypnosis. As we shall see, however, this is not any more true than the skeptics' and Dr. Simon's assertion that Betty's dreams matched her recall under hypnosis in precise detail. Nonetheless, there is no doubt that Barney had heard the dream tales in their entirety at least once before undergoing hypnotic regression.

A Possible Source of the Mysterious "Beeps"

An element of the case generally accepted by those who believe the Hills were captured by extraterrestrials, including the Hills themselves, is that the beeps the couple reported hearing were connected with the trance-like state they experienced or perhaps, as Betty suggested to me, was involved in the aliens' tracking their two subjects. The generally accepted view – or, more correctly, speculation – is that the first set of beeps somehow was involved in the induction of the state and the second set with its being lifted. The Hills described the sounds variously as "electrical," like "a tuning fork being dropped," a "buzzing vibration," and so on, always emanating from the rear or trunk of their car. Sheaffer has made a point of APRO member C. W. Fitch's report that Barney said the beeping kept up for a distance of 35 miles rather than being heard twice, once at the beginning of that segment of the journey and once again near Ashland, suggesting to the skeptical Sheaffer that Barney had mis-remembered his lines (Fitch, 1963; Sheaffer, 2000).

Taking the latter point first, Fitch's article in the March 1963 *A.P.R.O. Bulletin* was lifted in only slightly rewritten form from Walter Webb's initial report to NICAP on the case, a copy of which that organization's headquarters secretary Richard Hall provided Fitch in July 1962, against Webb's advice (Webb, 1965b; Hall, 1965). In his efforts to make Webb's work his own, Fitch sometimes failed to get things right. This is what Webb wrote about the beeps: "The car had traveled only a short distance ('five or six blocks') when the Hills heard a series of beeping or buzzing sounds.... About 35 miles further south, at Ashland, Mrs. Hill asked her husband for the first time, 'Do you believe in flying saucers?' and he replied, 'Don't be ridiculous. That wasn't a flying saucer.' Both claim that at once they heard five or six beeps on the rear trunk" (Webb, 1961). Here is how Fitch garbled this, while implicitly attributing it to Barney: "They had traveled only a short distance when they heard a series of beeping sounds.... These kept up for approximately 35 miles until they reached Ashland when they ceased as suddenly as they had commenced" (Fitch, 1963). Clearly, we need to be careful about whom we rely upon for accurate reporting, regardless of our position on the case.

After the second series of beeps, Barney wondered out loud if something might be shifting in the car. He even tried to reproduce it by speeding up, slowing down, and weaving a bit, without apparent success. He and Betty eventually connected the odd sounds with their trance-like state and control (or tracking) of their actions by the aliens.

However, there is another *possibility*. Discussing the beeps during her November 1963 remarks to the UFO study group, Betty mentioned that when she and Barney got home, they discovered the car's trunk lid was closed but not latched. It will be recalled that shortly before the first close encounter began, Barney was fearful enough to retrieve a .22 pistol from the trunk. (Fuller changed the .22 to a "tire wrench" in *The Interrupted Journey* because of a concern that there might a problem for the Hills if it became known they had innocently but illegally transported the handgun into Canada and back again.) In his fearful state of mind, Barney may well have failed to close the trunk lid with enough force to latch it. The bouncing of the lowered but not locked lid as the car traversed rough spots in the road *might* have been the source of the sounds and vibrations, or beeps, which the Hills consistently described as coming from the rear of their vehicle. Their noticing the sound-vibration when they did would be sharply remembered in the first instance because of its coincidental timing with the clearly terrifying close encounter and, in the second, because it harked back to the first: It's those same weird sounds again! In the circumstances, every out of the ordinary thing became important to them, more salient.

If it appears I am giving away too much here, it should be remembered that while he stood in the field beside the lonely, deserted highway, staring up at the looming ship and under close, cold observation by the being he thought of as the craft's captain, Barney felt very strongly under the influence of some compelling personality, and that this is something he mentioned in his first interview with Webb just a month after the incident. (Webb, 1961: 3). During his first hypnotic regression, on February 22, 1964, Barney told Dr. Simon, "And he's [i.e., the captain] looking at me. And he's just telling me: Don't be afraid.... Stay there – and keep looking. Just keep *looking* – and stay there. And just keep looking. Just keep looking.... It's pounding in my head!!" So it would seem that the process of putting the Hills under some form of control had begun before any beeps were heard.

In any case, I am not asserting that a loose and bouncing trunk lid definitely is the explanation for the odd sounds heard and felt by the Hills that fateful night. I merely offer it as a possible and plausible answer, making it necessary to temper any conclusions about the beeps being connected with the actions of the Hills' pursuers with caution and qualification.

Who Were the Hills?

One of the weakest reeds on which to lean in any UFO investigation usually is that of the character and community standing of the witnesses. (They are fine, upstanding citizens with no reason to make up such a crazy story!) While it helps to have some idea what sort of persons you are dealing with, easing the task of sorting the ufological wheat from the chaff, that is about as far as it goes.

Usually.

Like other serious researchers on both sides of this case, I completely agree that the Pease Air Force Base radar contacts had nothing whatever to do with the Hills' experience. Claimed physical evidence – the heavy scrapes on the tops of Barney's dress shoes, burrs on the cuffs of his trousers, the broken binocular strap, the Hills' simultaneously stopped wristwatches, the spots on the car's trunk lid, the ring of warts in Barney's genital area, and the peculiar residue on Betty's dress – is for the most part meaningful only if we can be confident of the Hills' truthfulness.

All this evidence is interesting, suggestive, and consistent with the Hills' testimony. However, except for the warts and the spots, we only know of it from the Hills themselves. The warts, while independently verified, offer nothing other than the likelihood that their recurrence was psychosomatic. This tells us that Barney was having a very strong emotional reaction to what he was going through during therapy with Dr. Simon, but, objectively, nothing more than that. The spots were seen by the Hills' tenants and their niece Kathy and perhaps others. However, as Webb has pointed out, they could have resulted from some natural source, becoming important only when Betty Hill began looking for some supporting evidence of the frightening UFO encounter. Thus their importance may be "acquired" in much the same sense as that accorded to the mysterious beeps.

Which brings us to who the Hills were at the time of their experience. Betty, from the old and respected Barrett family of Kingston, New Hampshire, was a state child welfare caseworker. Child abuse, abandonment, and worse were her beat. Her credibility was central to her professional success. Her mother, a member of the New Hants Dow clan, had been a union organizer during the Great Depression, and her father, a civic leader in Kingston, had served as the town's mayor. Both her parents had strong political views and social consciences, which Betty emulated. She was and remained a devoted social and political liberal, firmly committed to such causes as the civil rights movement and support for the United Nations. At the time of the 1961 incident, she was serving as assistant secretary and community coordinator of the local chapter of the National Association for the Advancement of Colored People and as a UN "envoy" for the Unitarian-Universalist Church, to which both she and Barney belonged. Betty had divorced her first husband some years before meeting Barney and was devoted to her adopted son and daughter, her first husband's children from his first marriage and both adults at the time of the Hills' UFO encounter (Fuller, 1966b: 4).

Barney, originally from Philadelphia, black, two years younger than Betty, and the father of two sons, had divorced his first wife sometime after meeting Betty through mutual friends about four years before the UFO incident. He and Betty were married in 1960. It would be too strong to say he divorced to be with Betty, but it is likely this was a factor, and in September 1961, he was still working through his guilt about the matter. He was a highly intelligent man who seems to have chosen not to develop his intelligence formally through higher education or to pursue a professional career. He worked as a supervisor for the U.S. Post Office in Boston, preferring the security and lesser demands of such work, which freed him to pursue his own intellectual interests (one of the reasons he was drawn to Betty), as well as causes about which he felt passionately. Like Betty, and with her, he was very active in the civil rights movement and was a UN booster. The couple traveled the state speaking on behalf of both causes, and Barney had served as the political action chairman and in September 1961 was the legal redress chairman of the Portsmouth NAACP and a member of the State Advisory Board of the U.S. Civil Rights Commission and the board of directors of the Rockingham County Poverty Program. Sargent Schriver had presented him with an award for his work on the latter (Fuller, 1966b: 4).

Barney and Betty were high-profile people involved in things that demanded unquestioned integrity and credibility. They outspokenly espoused causes that were not exactly at the top of the political hit parade in a politically and socially conservative, almost entirely white, very Republican state, during a turbulent time in American politics and social affairs, particularly with respect to racial matters and the Cold War. And she was white and he was black and they were married.

Not only were the Hills solid citizens – if too politically and socially liberal for most Granite Staters. Not only were they the sort of people generally unlikely to cook up and report a flying saucer tale just because it was not something one did. But their situation was such that they simply could not afford to be thought dishonest or loony publicity seekers. Other pillars of the community might be tempted to tell a tall tale for the fun of it, do so, and get away with it with little more than a bit of cluck-clucking and kidding. The Hills, on the other hand, could easily have faced not only a collapse of their personal reputations but also the undermining of the causes they so strongly believed in. They had to be and were concerned that their ideological opponents would seize upon any opportunity to cut them off at the knees of credibility.

Moreover, while Barney had no trouble speaking out in public about political and other issues, he was a rather private man, not given to wearing his personal concerns and quirks on his sleeve. This is reflected in his initial embarrassment and reluctance to talk about the experience, even privately on the telephone with a U.S. Air Force investigator.

Betty seems to have believed in UFOs as extraterrestrial craft before the events of September 19-20, although with no more than a passing interest in the subject. Her sister Janet had an interesting multiple-object sighting *circa* 1953, and the Barrett family took it seriously. In addition, there was a family ghost – not all that unusual in New England. The family called this spook Hannah, and Betty claims to have experienced its presence. Clearly, she was quite open to accepting a UFO sighting as something other than a misidentified planet, as well as to the reality of other sorts of anomalous phenomena. This is something that must be taken into account in assessing her and Barney's claims, but it hardly calls for dismissing them out of hand.

For his part, Barney was adamant in rejecting the reality of flying saucers. In conversation with Dr. Simon, he mentioned that he had been present on occasions when Betty and members of her family discussed Janet's sighting and flying saucers in general. The last time he recalled such a conversation taking place was in 1957, right after the Soviets launched Sputnik I. Discussion of this event led first to talk about life on other worlds and then to chatting about flying saucers. When the latter came up, Barney said, he merely listened and maintained polite silence, as he had always done in the past (Fuller, 1966b: 81-82).

Barney's skepticism about UFOs as alien spacecraft is evident throughout his and Betty's accounts of their experience, with him dismissing and arguing against Betty's views. He continued in his skepticism even after his frightening close encounter at Indian Head. Quite simply, it took a lot of doing for him to accept that he had seen, let alone been taken aboard, a flying saucer. Flying saucers were not something he believed in before that fateful night, and they were not something he wanted to believe in afterward.

Betty's openness to the reality of UFOs and other anomalous phenomena was strongly counterweighted by Barney's skepticism. The couple's positions in their city and state and their professional and political activities militated very heavily against concocting a UFO-encounter tale, let alone making it public. In short, they were highly credible witnesses reporting incredible things.

White Mountains Weather on the Night of September 19-20

Sheaffer has asserted that the Hills' insistence that the night sky was clear proves they made up their story or, at the very least, that they were poor observers. He cites weather observation data from the Mount Washington Observatory, located not far from where the Hills encountered the UFO, which shows that there was 50-to-60-percent cloud cover. He has "interpreted" this data in a sketch of the southwestern quadrant of the sky, where the UFO first was seen, as he thinks it would have appeared to the Hills – five- to six-tenths cloud shrouded, indicating the clouds as opaque and quite obvious in the bright light of a 10-day-old Moon (Sheaffer, *circa* 1975; 1981: 36).

In fact, according to a November 19, 1980, letter from John B. Howe of the Mount Washington Observatory to Walter Webb, "For the entire night of 19-20 Sept. 1961, sky cover was 5 to 6 tenths. At sunset on the 19th the clouds were cirrostratus and at sunrise on the 20th there were 2 tenths lenticular alto cumulus with the remainder of the 5 tenths being cirrostratus. Since humidities were low and *visibility excellent*, it seems safe to say that clouds during the night were primarily cirroform *(high thin clouds)* [emphasis added]."

So the clouds that night were high and thin and thus not particularly noticeable – a night a non-scientific observer might well call clear, especially with a bright Moon shining. Moreover, the weather data makes no mention of the *distribution* of the clouds, so it is quite possible the southwestern quadrant was entirely or mostly cloud-free.

The Dancing Planet Jupiter and its Coquettish Partner Saturn

Sheaffer and Philip Klass have contended that what the Hills thought was a UFO actually was the planet Jupiter (Sheaffer, 1981: 35-36; Klass, 1989: 12-14). Betty reported seeing a bright star near the Moon and, a short time later, another much brighter starlike object higher up – "like a star, a bigger star, *up over this one*" (emphasis added). (Fuller, 1966b: 136). Sheaffer and Klass note that Saturn was "almost directly below the Moon" – Betty's first star, they say – and claim Jupiter, much brighter than Saturn, was "up over" Saturn. Jupiter was Betty's UFO, these two skeptics assert, probably occulted by a cloud – one of those anomalous very dense cirrostratus clouds – when Betty first noticed Saturn, then unveiled when Betty looked again.

Actually, Jupiter was located to the lower left of the Moon and Saturn to the lower right. The Moon, waxing gibbous, brightly illuminated the night sky. Saturn, with an apparent magnitude that night of +0.6 and always much fainter than Jupiter (exactly 12 times fainter that night), was just 4.5 degrees from the Moon, making it quite difficult to see. Jupiter, -2.1 magnitude and about 3.5 degrees to lower left of the Moon, would have been conspicuous and easily visible even to the casual observer (U.S. Naval Observatory, 1961; Webb, 1976).

Nothing suggests Betty Hill does not know left from right, so there is no good reason to doubt she saw another object *above Jupiter*, not Jupiter above Saturn – which it was not. I have observed these two planets and the Moon in similar configurations, at similar magnitudes and lunar phase, and under closely similar sky conditions. I am a casual amateur astronomer, and in every instance, I had to make a point of finding Saturn, while Jupiter shone forth like a beacon.

It is also important to note that at first Betty "wasn't quite sure" that the new object she saw was moving. Soon Barney stopped the car and both got out to watch the UFO free of the movement of their vehicle. It was then, Betty recalled under hypnosis, that "I noticed that the star was definitely moving.... *It was moving fast,* but *it went in front of the Moon.... I saw it travel across the whole face of the Moon,* and it was odd shaped. And it was flashing different colored lights [emphasis added]" (Fuller, 1966b: 136). Planets do not pass across the face of the Moon.

Sheaffer and Klass have attempted to explain the close encounter with a craft "at least as large as a four motor plane" at an altitude of from 50 to 80 feet and at a distance of 50 to 100 feet, complete with humanoid beings peering out from behind a brightly lit double row of windows, as a product of atmospheric refraction and autokinetic effects of the sort applicable to stationary celestial objects, the illusion of being followed by a star or the Moon when riding in a moving car, etc. (Betty Hill, 1961a; Sheaffer, 1981; Klass, 1989). Sheaffer and Klass also cite examples of instances in which witnesses reported distant objects as being quite close and thinking they saw windows, etc., on what proved to be large meteors or other prosaic objects.

The magnitude of illusory motions and apparent angular jiggles reasonably attributable to refraction and autokinesis are minuscule compared to what the Hills actually reported seeing. Observed with two pairs of unassisted, normal-vision eyes and through binoculars, the Hills' UFO was unequivocally seen to enormously increase its angular size and shape, to dramatically decrease its separation from the Hills, and to stray at least 90 degrees from Jupiter's position in the southwestern sky. Betty Hill said (albeit under hypnosis) that she watched it cross the face of the Moon. The Hills stopped their car several times and saw that the UFO definitely was moving in an erratic, pronounced step-like flight pattern and that it appeared to be spinning about its vertical axis. It eventually swooped down to about 100 feet above a point just to the right (west) of the road and ahead of the Hills, stopped in mid-air, glided across the highway out over a field on the left (east), and hovered again. It grew from a distant point source to a clearly structured flattened disk ("like a big pancake," according to Barney) with a double row of windows that ultimately filled the entire field of view in Barney's binoculars (Fuller, 1966b: 85; Webb, 1988). That's interesting maneuvering and apparent shape-and-size changing for a gas giant in an orbit millions of miles away.

When the participants in the Encounters at Indian Head Symposium visited the site of this first close encounter with Betty Hill, Robert Sheaffer was astounded to learn that the UFO had crossed the road from west to east before taking up a position low over the field in which Barney confronted it. After years of studying and attempting to debunk the Hills' experience, he somehow had missed this reported maneuver, a key and widely reported feature of the case! To his credit, Sheaffer admitted that, if the UFO had indeed crossed the highway as the Hills reported, then Jupiter could not be the answer. He then suggested without much conviction that it was possible the Hills unwittingly transferred their attention from the distant planet to the lights of a much closer earthly aircraft flying south of them on a west to east course. When I pointed out this would not explain the two hovers and the lack of sound – teasingly suggesting that any airplane far enough away not to be heard also would be obscured from view by Sheafferian cirrostratus – Sheaffer agreed, shaking his head in puzzlement.

It is worth noting, too, that Dr. Simon, though a UFO skeptic and convinced that the Hills were not captured and taken aboard a craft from another planet, was quite sure the Hills saw a real flying machine, not a peripatetic planet. He preferred to believe it was something of this earth, perhaps some sort of classified experimental device, but he had no doubt about its objective reality (Webb, 1965a: 14).

Dreams and Reality

Sheaffer, Klass, Dr. Simon, and even John Fuller have claimed that Betty's dreams, which began about 10 days after the UFO incident and continued for 5 days, almost precisely matched – Simon and Fuller said they were "identical" to – what she recounted under hypnosis (Fuller, 1966b: 31, 227, 279). In fact, while there is a general similarity, there are several key differences.

Just one example, or set of examples, is the appearance of the Hills' captors. In her dreams, Betty tells us their "hair and eyes were very dark, possibly black." Their "complexions were of a gray tone; like a gray paint with a black base; their lips were of a bluish tint." Most interesting were their noses, which "were larger (longer) than the average size although I have seen people with noses like theirs – like Jimmy Durante's." She also described uniforms "of a light or navy blue color with a gray shade in it. They wore trousers and short jackets, that gave the appearance of zippered sports jackets..." (Fuller, 1966b: 296).

Yet in her description that arose from hypnosis, "In a sense they looked like mongoloids, because I was comparing them with a case I had been working with, a specific mongoloid child – this sort of round face and broad forehead, along with a certain type of coarseness. The surface of their skin seemed to be a bluish gray, but probably whiter than that. Their eyes moved, and they had pupils. Somehow, I had the feeling they were more like cats' eyes" (Fuller, 1966b: 264). Neither she nor Barney recalled large noses, but rather only something vestigial, nor any hair. Nor did they recall lip color or even seeing lips. Barney recalled, "[Their mouths were] much like when you draw one horizontal line with a short perpendicular line on each end. This horizontal line would represent the lips without the muscle that we have.... I didn't notice any hair.... Also, I didn't notice any proboscis, there just seemed to be two slits that represented the nostrils" (Fuller, 1966b: 260). As for uniforms, both remembered them as being black and recalled no specific details (Fuller, 1966b, *passim*).

Both Betty and Barney said that once inside the craft, they were taken to separate compartments. Each recalled significantly differing experiences while they were apart. There was the general similarity of a physical examination, but most of what happened to Barney was quite different from Betty's experience. For example, he said something cup-like was placed over his "groin area," and he believed a semen specimen was taken. He also felt something being inserted into his anus, and again believed a specimen was taken. (In deference to the Hills' and public sensibilities, Fuller finessed these details in his book.) Betty recalled nothing in the way of a genital or anal examination. And so on. Of course, the major difference was Betty's "conversation" with the being she called "the leader." The only communication Barney received from his examiners was a continuing "telepathic" direction to remain calm, keep his eyes closed, etc. When they spoke among themselves, he said, all he could discern was a sound like "mmm-mm-mm-mm-mmm-mm" (Fuller, 1966b: 187).

If Betty merely were repeating her dreams under hypnosis, we reasonably could expect her to relate all or most all of the same important details about the aliens. She did not. If Barney simply were regurgitating what he had heard about Betty's dreams, we quite fairly could expect him to have provided details matching or closely matching those in Betty's dream recollections. He did not, not even in response to specific questions from Dr. Simon, more than a few of which were intended to elicit parrotings of bits and pieces from Betty's account of her dreams. As a matter of fact, Barney quite explicitly contradicted important features of Betty's dream aliens – e.g., with reference to the aliens' noses, which he remembered as totally lacking or vestigial (Fuller, 1966b: 260).

What actually emerges from the hypnosis sessions is closely similar information from two points of view on shared experiences and utterly individual descriptions of events that took place separately and were experienced by each party out of the sight and hearing of the other. This is just what could be expected in the wake of a real event.

It is true that Betty's dreams and the story that surfaced during her hypnosis sessions are similar. However, they are not by any means identical. Again, this is something we might reasonably expect when dreams actually are imperfect recollections of repressed memories of a traumatic event or memories confused or blocked by some outside agency. Dr. Simon chose to focus on the similarities and ignored the dissimilarities because this suited his diagnosis. After all, psychiatrists are human, too.

The branch of psychology dealing with dreams and their meanings and, more important in this case, whether or not dreams can bring forth accurate and complete or nearly complete recall of real experiences of the dreamer, especially of memories lost to the dreamer's conscious mind, is fraught with controversy and conflicting theories. Thus, or so it seems to me as a layman highly skeptical of the at best imperfect arts of clinical psychology and psychiatry and their practitioners, what might be said about such matters, even by "experts," offers us little to go on here, one way or the other.

Moreover, if one accepts, as I do, that their captors, through some means unknown to us, induced the Hills' amnesia, we can only speculate about how recall resulting from the failure of that induced memory repression would manifest. Would it be total and entirely accurate, or would it be partial and inaccurate in some respects? Could it emerge via dreams? Would the flawed barrier be susceptible to hypnotic intervention? Would the aliens' "amnesia ray" be more effective with some subjects than with others?

That Betty's dreams are very similar to, but do not exactly match, her hypnotic recall suggests to me that both were somewhat flawed memories of a very real experience. So, too, does the fact that what Betty and Barney said under hypnosis sounds exactly like what we would hear from two people who were involved in the same incident, with two points of view and some separate, "compartmented" experiences along the way. Barney's less detailed and more dreamlike recall may have been a consequence of his being more susceptible than his wife to his captors' technique. (Were his eyes *really* closed during most of the couple's captivity?)

"What We Have Here is a Failure to Communicate"

Betty Hill had a fairly lengthy communication with the being she called "the leader," including a discussion involving food, physiological aging, color ("What is yellow?"), and his and our people's places among the stars. Betty had the sense that he spoke to her in English in a voice with a slight foreign accent of some kind. Yet upon reflection, she came to conclude the communication, at least from the alien, was not verbal but mind-to-mind, telepathic, and that the alien's words were not English but that she "could understand what was being said to me as if it *were* in English. But whether it was English or not English, verbal or nonverbal, I understood clearly.... [But w]hen they talked among themselves, they were entirely impossible to understand" (Fuller, 1966b: 264).

There also were jarringly odd gaps in the alien's understanding of such seemingly simple concepts as color, time, food, and physiological aging. For example, with respect to time, he seemed not to understand what a year was, yet at one point he said, "Wait a minute." The skeptics point to the apparent absurdity of this, as did the Hills themselves. (Fuller, 1966b: 265). If Betty had had the presence of mind to explain a year was our term for the length of time it took our planet to make one complete revolution around the Sun, the leader is likely to have gotten it. But this does not explain "Wait a minute." There are similar difficulties with other issues that Sheaffer and Klass have seized upon as reasons to dismiss Betty's account, and by extension Barney's, as at best fanciful.

However, it is clear from Betty's recollections that no small part of the communications difficulty arose from Betty's inability to come up with ways to explain what she was saying so her interlocutor could "get it." Moreover, if some sort of translation device was being used, as it is reasonable to assume, it well could have been doing a less than perfect job. As for the "Wait a minute" problem, perhaps the thing was doing its job well, translating the alien version of "Stop!" into colloquial terms.

The history of human exploration and (non)communication upon first contact – and sometimes long after – between cultures with different languages is replete with examples not dissimilar to those described by Betty, some hilarious, some tragic. Contrary to being evidence of a non-real event, these failures to communicate suggest to me quite the opposite.

The Book and the "Mutiny"

Betty asked the leader to be allowed to take something from the craft as proof of the experience. He told her to pick something. She chose a book, filled with "writing, but nothing like I had ever seen before." Betty carried the book with her as she and the leader prepared to exit the vehicle, along with Barney and two other beings escorting him. Then, Betty reported, "some of the men are talking. I don't know what they are saying, but they are very excited. And then the leader comes over and takes my book.... And I said, 'You promised that I could have the book.' And he said, 'I know it, but the others object.' But I said, 'This is my proof.' And he said, 'That is the whole point. They don't want you to know what has happened. They want you to forget all about it'" (Fuller, 1966b: 173-178).

Skeptics such as Klass have laughingly noted that, if indeed Betty's "leader" was captain or at least a senior officer of the ship, members of the crew would not have, in effect, mutinied, and if they had, no senior officer would have put up with it as the leader did. Martin Kottmeyer follows a similar argument in his contribution to this book (Appendix).

Dare I say that the dismissal of the incident as inconsistent with military discipline is just a tad anthropocentric? Perhaps the Hills' captors are a race of extreme collectivists, running everything by committee. More seriously, the skeptics have a valid point – or would if we knew Betty's leader indeed was the UFO captain or a superior officer of some sort. Which we do not. We have only Betty's impressions to go on. It was she who tagged him "the leader." Ironically, the skeptics rely upon Betty's say-so on this point in their attempts to refute the rest of her testimony.

Suppose Betty's leader actually was a mushy-headed xenologist, a supernumerary on the ship with no command or line authority, who in giving Betty the book overstepped the rules governing contact and communication with the locals? Those actually in charge certainly could and would have overruled him. Perhaps the excited group of aliens were not ship's crew but scientific colleagues of Betty's xenologist, and they collectively prevailed upon him to correct his error. As may be, this episode in no way undermines the credibility of the case.

The Eyes Say Very Little

In his fascinating essays "The Eyes That Spoke" and "The Eyes Still Speak," self-described "psycho-social [UFO] theorist" Martin Kottmeyer contends that Barney Hill's obsession with controlling eyes arose from a television science fiction program. On the evening of February 10, 1964, an episode of *The Outer Limits* entitled "The Bellero Shield" aired. This was 12 days before Barney's initial hypnotic regression session with Dr. Simon, when he first made specific mention of the compelling, slanted eyes of the entity who stared down at him as he stood in the field at Indian Head, eyes which stayed with him through much of the capture experience, disembodied but very real, and dominating.

Kottmeyer notes that the alien from Bifrost featured in "The Bellero

Shield" had compelling eyes and, telling a human character he does not read minds, the Bifrostian says, "I cannot even understand your language. I analyse your eyes. In all the universes, in all the unities beyond all the universes, all who have eyes, have eyes that speak." Kottmeyer then contends that the close parallel in what emerged from Barney's subconscious under hypnosis on February 22 was a product of his having viewed the program less than two weeks before (Kottmeyer, 1994).

Subsequent to Kottmeyer's theory being published, I asked Betty about this. She told me she and Barney never watched *The Outer Limits*, that they had absolutely no interest in science fiction. She also pointed out that Barney worked nights and so could not have watched the show even if he had wanted to. Barney's shift was from midnight to 8:00 a.m., and it is conceivable, but given the exigencies of everyday life, highly unlikely, that he could have seen the show. Of course, we cannot be certain that Barney did not see the program. Stretching a bit to accommodate Kottmeyer, perhaps a friend, impressed with the episode, described it to Barney in vivid detail. However, does this mean that Barney's intense feeling of being mentally dominated, being compelled to do another's bidding, being about to be "snatched like a bug" is merely a product of the television production, first- or secondhand? (Barney Hill, 1963)

It is clear from the earliest, pre-hypnosis, pre-*Outer Limits* accounts that Barney felt under particular scrutiny from the commanding figure, "the captain," he observed in the craft at Indian Head. For example, Walter Webb's initial report to NICAP on his October 21, 1961, interview with the Hills states: "The 'leader' at the window held a special fascination for the witness and frightened him terribly. The witness said he could almost feel this figure's intense concentration to do something, to carry out a plan. Mr. Hill believed he was going to be captured 'like a bug in a net'" (Webb, 1961: 3). There are no eyes in this, but there is a clear sense of intense, concentrated menace, emanating from a being whose attention Barney felt was focused directly and powerfully on him.

We will never know if Barney Hill watched or was told about "The Bellero Shield" before he first so dramatically spoke under hypnosis of the speaking, controlling eyes. If he did, there is another interpretation that is just as valid as Kottmeyer's: Barney did, indeed, come under the close scrutiny of the captain and an attempt to establish control over him, an attempt that very nearly succeeded at that moment and did so later. When he watched or heard about the *Outer Limits* alien with the thing for eyes, it subconsciously struck very close to home, and when Dr. Simon took him back to the night of September 19-20, Barney's mind confabulated the two memories into one. His recollections of the actual experience were filtered through his memories of the really rather impressive "Bellero Shield."

Missing Time

When he and Betty left Colebrook at 10:05 p.m., Barney estimated they should cover the 189 miles (Fuller inaccurately reported the distance to be 175 miles) to their home in Portsmouth in 4.5 to 5 hours, an average speed of between 37.8 and 42 mph, a quite reasonable estimate. This would have gotten them home between 2:35 and 3:05 a.m. Skeptics argue that the Hills' arrival at shortly after 5:00 a.m. on September 20, two to two-and-a-half hours later than Barney had estimated, can be explained by their slowing and stopping as they observed the UFO and a period of wandering around back roads, temporarily lost (Sheaffer, 1981: 36-37).

Taking the later point first, Barney's recollections during hypnosis and afterward show that, after rushing away from the Indian Head site, he all but certainly turned left about 3 miles south, just beyond North Woodstock, onto southbound State Route 175 (Fuller, 1966b: 228), and after proceeding about 12.5 miles, turned left again, onto Mill Brook Road, traveling not more than half a mile before encountering the aliens' roadblock. What happened after the capture experience is not quite as clear, but once again the recollections of both Hills strongly suggest they proceeded south on 175 and returned to US 3 at one of several possible points north of Plymouth. They then made their way via US 3 and 3B and a very short segment of State Route 104 to a finished stretch of the then-under-construction I-93 expressway, which they took to Concord. There they picked up US 4 eastbound to Portsmouth (Hill, 1961b; Fuller, 1966b: 21 and *passim*). If we assume this is the route they took without a capture experience but, to err on the generous-to-skeptics side, including the jog up Mill Brook Road and back to Route 175, it would have added about 2.75 miles to their trip and thus about five minutes or so to their total time on the road.

Simply stated, the debunkers' notion that, after Barney panicked at Indian Head, he managed to get lost in his attempt to avoid being captured by the ufonauts, is something concocted out of thin air, or to be a bit more polite about it, a result of lack of careful study of known facts and testimony. So that chunk of "recovered time" is lost to the skeptics.

It is unknown how many stops the Hills made before the close encounter at Indian Head – we know with certainty that there were four – but once again to give the skeptics the benefit of the doubt, let us say Barney pulled over six times for an average of five minutes each, a total of 30 minutes. Then add an additional 10 minutes for the 20 miles or so they traveled at about 30 mph as Barney reported (just 7.8 mph under the average speed they would have made on a 5-hour trip from Colebrook to Portsmouth) and an additional 10 minutes for the stretches were they crawled along at 5 mph. Then factor in 10 minutes for the close encounter at Indian Head.

The total additional time on the road reasonably attributable to the initial sighting and close encounter, plus a detour over to Route 175 and a side trip up Mill Brook Road and back, is 62 minutes. This means that, without being captured, taken aboard a flying saucer, and so on, the Hills should have arrived home between 3:37 and 4:07 a.m. Thus, even employing calculations quite generous to the skeptical side, between 60 and 90 minutes remain "missing" and available for the capture and examination of the Hills.

For what it may be worth in considering this issue, I have twice driven from Colebrook to the Hill home in Portsmouth, following the same route the Hills would have taken had they not detoured to the abduction site, the only exception being through Franconia Gap, just above Indian Head, where I had no choice but to travel on I-93 for a few miles. I made a point of not pushing it, driving at speeds consistent with road conditions, making brief "call of nature" stops, and so on, even keeping my speed down to the minimum allowed on the stretch of I-93 through Franconia Gap, 45 mph, which is about what one could have done on Route 3 through the same area in 1961. One of these trips was driven in daylight, the other at night. In the first instance, my elapsed time was 4 hours and 11 minutes (average speed, 45.18 mph). The second – night – trip took 4 hours 37 minutes (40.94 mph), almost exactly Barney's estimated minimum on the much less heavily trafficked and built-up roads of 1961. In truth, I probably averaged very slightly better speeds, as construction of I-93 required some rerouting of the roughly parallel U.S. 3, adding perhaps a mile or two to the overall distance .(To my embarrassment, I must confess I did not take down the distance covered as recorded by my vehicle's odometer!)

Betty Hill Today and the Day Before Yesterday

Skeptics make much of Betty Hill's outlandish claims of secret UFO landing sites, her clinging to the Pease AFB radar unknown and other "missing" radar reports as proof of her and Barney's encounter, and the like (Hill, 1995). It is not so gently suggested that Betty's pronouncements mean that nothing that has gone before – specifically the 1961 incident – can be taken seriously (Sheaffer, 1981: 38-39, 43-44). This is far from fair or wise.

Walter Webb has pointed out that "persons involved in UFO close encounters often suffer a variety of traumatic aftereffects.... Obsessional behavior is not uncommon among such witnesses (and perhaps understandably so). Betty is a classic example" (Webb, 1986). Often, this obsessional behavior is focused, consciously and unconsciously, on finding evidence to back up or "prove" what the witness reported experiencing and to counter ridicule. In the Hills' case, their lives were turned upside down in the wake of publication of *The Interrupted Journey* in 1966 and, once again for Betty, by the airing of the television movie *The UFO Incident* in October 1975. It was not easy to cope, even for Betty, who certainly was less reluctant to accept the role of celebrity than was Barney, and in fact came to enjoy it.

With Barney's unexpected and untimely death in February 1969, Betty lost her life partner and the person with whom she had shared her remarkable encounter less than eight years before. I know this deeply affected Betty. I am sure that her continuing hope that her captors might return, her efforts to learn more about them, and her seeing such everyday things as airplanes, house lights, and railroad signals as UFOs were in some sense something she was doing for Barney. If Betty could have *proved* she and Barney really did see and experience what they said they did, it would have been a great tribute to him and would have brought closure – I hate this use of the word, but it fits here – for her.

The reality of what happened that night in September 1961 does not depend upon what Betty said and did in the years since. No amount of pointing and snickering from the skeptics' gallery can change that.

The Star Map

Those who have sought to debunk Marjorie Fish's analysis and interpretation of the map recalled and sketched by Betty Hill conveniently disregard the most fundamental of facts. They wave off Fish's stringent criteria and her meticulous, persistent, six-year effort and the methodology that eliminated random star patterns with dismissive comments characterizing her models as "colored beads hung on thread." Nothing could be further from the truth.

After spending literally thousands of hours conducting photographic and visual inspections of the three-dimensional models she constructed of our Sun's neighborhood out to 10 parsecs, only one view angle emerged that included:

(1) all the candidates for life-as-we-know-it included in Betty's sketch out of more than 256 stars of various types found in the volume of space

encompassing the pattern stars in the sketch;
(2) all the trade, expeditionary, and occasional-visit (the Solar System is at the end of one of the latter) route lines connecting only stars that are candidates for life as we know it;
(3) all the stars in the pattern recalled by Betty being connected in a logical, progressive, energy-use-minimizing travel sequence from one to the other, with the "home" star (Zeta 2 Reticuli) linked only with the nearest stars having spectral classes that favor life as we know it. (Webb, 1976; Dickinson, 1974, 1976, 1980); and, last, but not least,
(4) a reasonable match with Betty Hill's sketch.

Let's re-examine the Hill Star Map and the Fish Star Map with these criteria in mind.

First, how did the Hill Star Map originate? Betty drew the map in 1964 under posthypnotic suggestion. She was told to draw the map only if she could remember it accurately and she was not to pay attention to what she was drawing. This puts it in the realm of automatic drawing – a way of getting at repressed or forgotten material that can result in unusual accuracy. She made two erasures, which could indicate that her conscious mind took control a part of the time (Dickinson 1980).

After realizing that Betty Hill's map might just possibly provide an opportunity to verify at least a portion of the couple's abduction story, Marjorie Fish set out to thoroughly research and thoughtfully review the steps that would be necessary to recreate the Hill Star Map. She recognized immediately that the star pattern was not one that would be reproduced in conventional astronomical charts, since it was purportedly a view of a set of stars shown from a position deep in space, rather than from an earth-oriented position. Thus, it was apparent that only a three-dimensional model would be able to capture the patterns of the stars accurately.

Her choice of stars for her three-dimensional model were logically limited to known stars, those stars already shown in detailed star catalogues, which go out to about a 55-light-year radius from the Sun. It was necessary for her to refine her choice of stars further on the basis of their distance from the Sun, their known composition, and the very general guidelines produced by those who are considered experts in the relatively inexact science of exobiology (the branch of astronomy that deals with the possibility of life in other areas of the Universe). Further assumptions were made about logically linked trade and expeditionary routes, based on the conversations with their captors repeated by Betty Hill.

The exobiological guidelines indicated that the stars must be neither too hot, nor too cold, neither too large, nor too small, and must show stability for a long enough period of time for carbon-based life to have evolved. (There is rampant speculation about silicon-based life, or life based on the ammonium hydroxide molecule, but since, so far, it is only speculation, it was excluded in the Fish exercise.) The crew members were reportedly roughly humanoid in appearance and able to operate on Earth without protective clothing or other supportive devices, so another logical assumption was that they must have come from a planet similar to our own.

It is thought that to sustain life, a star should give off steady heat with little or no fluctuation. When a star is on the main sequence – that is, its hydrogen-burning phase – it is burning at its steadiest for the longest period of its existence. Life as we know it would exist only when the star is on the main sequence, or possibly in the very beginning of the subgiant state, and only if the star stays on the main sequence long enough for life to emerge.

So, how did Fish identify the stars are on the main sequence most likely to have a possibility of life as we know it?

Unusual Suspects

There are seven main spectra groups of main-sequence stars. These are – from most to least massive, hottest to coolest, and bluish to red – OV, BV, AV, FV, GV, KV, MV. Each group is further divided into ten subgroups of descending size. Star types O, B, A, and down to F2 are massive hot stars. They burn faster and last for a shorter length of time on the main sequence – probably not long enough for life to form as it did on Earth. Most of these stars are rotating fast, indicating little probability of planets around them.

F2V to F5V might support planets with the beginnings of life – but not all of these stars are rotating slowly, thus indicating that it is unlikely that many have planets. F5V to F7V have more stars rotating slowly, which might indicate the presence of planets.

From F8 on, all main sequence stars are rotating slowly, indicating they may well have planets. As a matter of fact, Carl Sagan himself speculated that F8 is the point at which intelligent life would have time to emerge. Main-sequence stars from F8 through the Gs to the Ks have a possibility of intelligent life. But many exobiologists mark K2 as the end point for life since, as stars get cooler, their planets must be closer to their Sun to garner the heat needed to allow life to develop. A planet's proximity to its Sun brings its own challenges, including synchronous rotation (similar to our Earth's relationship to the Moon) and solar flaring: either of which would preclude the development of life as we know it.

So, applying these criteria, Fish identified 256 stars within a 10-parsec distance of the Sun. She constructed several three-dimensional models between August 1968 and February 1973. She checked and re-checked her data, researched additional data, and re-checked her model again. Fish's three-dimensional model included 256 beads, hung on thread, representing the angular direction and distance of the star from the Sun. The beads were of different colors, representing the different types of stars. But, identifying a specific star pattern within the cubic space occupied by 256 stars would prove not only to be extremely difficult but also could have raised the ugly specter of identifying more than one group of stars that would be roughly similar to the Hill Star Map, which would be positive proof of... nothing.

Marjorie Fish again went to work to refine the candidates for credible stars even further. If the aliens the Hills claimed to have met were humanoid in appearance, then their home planet would likely be similar to Earth, and their 'base stars" would resemble our Sun. Likewise, the planets on their trade routes might logically be assumed to be similar to Earth. Those on the expeditionary or occasional-visit routes might diverge a bit, but should still have characteristics close enough to those of Earth to qualify for inclusion the model.

After applying these additional criteria, the number of stars considered appropriate to include in the model was reduced to 62, and a pattern of stars corresponding to a portion of the Hill Star Map became apparent. "Portion" is the operative word here, since the pattern roughly matched 9 of the 12 stars in the map originally sketched by Betty Hill while under hypnosis. But three stars (the so-called "triangle stars") were not visible in the pattern produced by Fish's model.

Into the Missing Dimension

Disappointing? Somewhat...but the partly complete pattern led to the first meeting between Marjorie Fish and Betty Hill. It was during that meeting that Betty Hill explained that the Star Map she was shown was three-dimensional, not two-dimensional as reported in *Interrupted Journey*. She also provided enough information to allow a calculation of the dimensions of the volume of space containing the stars she was shown, which is shown in the sketch on the following page (234):

The top and bottom surface of the cube are squares and the height of the map is the size of the square – which seems too tidy to be a coincidence (Fish 1974).

Walter Mitchell, professor of astronomy at Ohio State University in

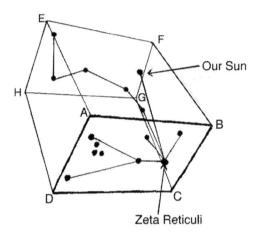

Columbus, examined Fish's model in detail and said "The more I examine it, the more I am impressed by the astronomy involved in Marjorie Fish's work." (Her work was hardly just stringing "colored beads on a 3-D frame" as ungenerously characterized by Robert Schaeffer in Chapter Six of this book.) In continuing his examination of the Fish Star Model, Mitchell, together with some of his students, did a computer analysis of various star alignments as though they were out beyond Zeta Reticuli, looking toward the Sun. This computer analysis came up with a nearly exact duplicate of the Fish Star Model. However, it also revealed an extremely important fact, previously unknown. The stars in the map are nearly in a plane; they fill a wheel-shaped volume of space, which would make travel from one to another both easy and logical!

David Saunders, a statistician at the Industrial Relations Center of the University of Chicago and an unenthusiastic member of the Condon Committee, concluded that "the odds are about 10,000 to 1 against a random configuration matching perfectly with Betty Hill's map. But the star group identified by Marjorie Fish isn't quite a perfect match, and the odds consequently reduce to about 1,000 to 1" (Dickenson, 1976).

No other model or map that was created with the intent of showing that Fish's pattern could easily be the product of random chance – including the oft-cited map produced by Charles W. Atterberg of Elgin, Illinois – matches all of the critical criteria laid out by Fish. But the stars in the Atterberg map are not suitable for life as we understood such suitability at the time he and Fish did their work. They are either red dwarfs or double stars. Based on the most reliable information available at the time, Fish very reasonably ruled out both these classes of star in establishing the criteria and methodology of her study.

Some astronomers have suggested Zeti 2 Reticuli should be also be rejected as the home star of the Hills' captors because it supposedly is a close binary, a class of star system thought not to favor the formation of life-bearing planets (Hendry, 1982; Sheaffer, 2000). However, Daniel Bonneau, the French astronomer who identified Zeta 2 as a close binary later retracted his findings as having resulted from an artifact (known as "Mickey's ears" to astronomers) in the diffraction pattern of the telescope that he and his colleagues used in the observations (Bonneau, 1988).

Now let us turn to those three missing "triangle stars" referred to previously. After the publication of the 1969 *Catalogue of Nearby Stars* (commonly referred to as the *Gliese Catalogue*), more detailed and accurate data were available; and those three stars were identified. The parallaxes of two of the "triangle stars" on the map were wrongly calculated before 1969, and the third (Gliese 86.1) was entirely unknown until then. In 1961 and even in 1964 when Betty made her sketch, *no one on this planet could have known where these stars would appear on any map.*

Some, such as Mark Steggert of the Space Research Coordination Center at the University of Pittsburgh, challenged the accuracy of the Gliese catalogue, citing the substantial variation in catalogue material, which uses photometric, trigonometric, and spectroscopic parallaxes and derives a mean from all three after giving various mathematical weights to each value. Dickenson (1976) quotes Steggert as saying: "The substantial variation in catalog material is something that must be overcome. This must be the next step in attempting to evaluate the map." However, the scientific director of the U.S. Naval Observatory, K. A. Strand, who numbers among the world's foremost authorities on stellar distances for nearby stars, cites the Gliese catalogue as "the most complete and comprehensive source available."

Finally, skeptics, notably Sheaffer, criticize the Fish model for not identifying the background stars in Betty's sketch. (Sheaffer, 1981: 40). The reason for this, which has been known for more than 24 years, is that Betty included them randomly to show the existence of a background of stars in the map she was shown. Except for the so-called triangle stars, the positions of which were easily recalled because of their configuration – and which Fish seems to have identified – none of the background objects were intended to represent actual star positions as seen and remembered by Betty Hill (Webb, 1976).

I am not suggesting that the Hill and Fish Star Maps are *proof* of the Hills' capture experience. It is impossible entirely to rule out coincidence, but the case against the map's authenticity and congruence with celestial reality is not, by a long shot, as strong as those who seek to debunk it would have us believe. In addition, the inclusion in the map of three stars unknown to the astronomical community before the publication of the 1969 Gliese Catalog is significant and should not be summarily dismissed. To put it succinctly, we did not have the data to draw the map in 1961 or in 1964 (when Betty's sketch was done). The data became available only after the 1969 Catalog was released.

So What Does It All Mean?

As Terence Dickinson has put it, "the Zeta Reticuli star map is provocative evidence – not proof – that extraterrestrial intelligence is visiting Earth..." (Dickinson, 1980: 4). I would say "has visited," and argue that this is the significance of the entirety of the Hill case, of which the map is a key element.

For my part, I am *subjectively* quite certain that the Hill incident happened essentially as Barney and Betty have told us, and that their captors were visitors from an extra-solar planet. However, as with so much in ufology, *objective proof* of this remains just beyond our grasp.

This being so, what the Hills' experience means – or should mean – to ufology and other fields of study is that there is good reason to believe we have been visited, and visited recently by beings from another world. For ufology, this should be taken as an admonition to never give up – but to be dramatically more careful about what is claimed, what evidence is made to do, what is acceptable research and what is not, and to focus on UFO phenomena and not imaginary if titillating cover-ups and other distractions.

More conventional disciplines should take this as a call to unblinker, to consider well-documented, well-researched, well-worked-up evidence of visits by extraterrestrial spacefarers and reflect upon what such visitation means for mankind and what it could mean should the visitors return. "There are more things in heaven and earth, Horatio, than are dreamt of in your philosophy."

So speaks the Hill case to me.

References

Bonneau, Daniel. Letter to Robert M. Collins, April 19, 1988. Copy in author's files.
Dickinson, Terence. "The Zeta Reticuli Incident." *Astronomy*, December 1974.
Dickinson, Terence. *The Zeta Reticuli Incident, with Related Commentary by Jeffrey L. Kretsch, Carl Sagan, Steven Soter, Robert Sheaffer, Marjorie Fish, David Saunders, and Michael Peck*. Milwaukee, Wisc.: AstroMedia, 1976.
Dickinson, Terence. *Zeta Reticuli Update*. Fredericton, New Brunswick: UFORI, 1980.

Fish, Marjorie E. "Journey Into the Hill Star Map." *MUFON 1974 UFO Symposium Proceedings.* Ed. by Walter H. Andrus, Jr., Quincy Il. MUFON 1974.

Fitch, C. W. "The Experience of Mr. and Mrs. Barney Hill." *The A.P.R.O. Bulletin,* March 1963: 7.

Friedman, Stanton, and B. Ann Slate. "UFO Star Bases Discovered." *Saga,* July 1973: 36-38, 54, 56, 58.

Fuller, John. *Incident at Exeter.* New York: Putnam, 1966a.

Fuller, John. *The Interrupted Journey.* New York: Dial, 1966b.

Hall, Richard. Letter to Walter N. Webb, November 17, 1965.

Hendry, Allan. "UFO Road Map: Or, Lost in the Stars." *Fate,* February 1982: 56-63.

Hill, Barney. Anonymous telephone call-in to "Program PM," WBZ Radio, Boston, Mass., August 21, 1962. Audio tape in author's files.

Hill, Barney and Betty. Presentation to the Two-State Unidentified Flying Object Study Group, Quincy, Massachusetts, November 3, 1963. Audio tape in author's files.

Hill, Betty. Letter to Donald E. Keyhoe, September 26, 1961[a] (in Webb, 1965a).

Hill, Betty. Letter to Walter E. Webb, November 27, 1961[b]. Copy in author's files.

Hill, Betty. *A Common Sense Approach to UFOs.* Greenland, New Hampshire: The author, 1995.

Klass, Philip J. *UFO Abductions: A Dangerous Game.* Amherst, N.Y.: Prometheus Books, 1989.

Kottmeyer, Martin. "The Eyes That Spoke." *The Reall News,* July 1994.

The Nautical Almanac for the Year 1961. Washington, D.C.: U.S. Naval Observatory Nautical Almanac Office, 1960.

Rodeghier, Mark. "Hypnosis and the Hill Abduction Case." *International UFO Reporter,* March-April 1994: 4-6, 23-24.

Sheaffer, Robert. Sky sketch made for Philip J. Klass, ca. 1975. Copy in author's files.

Sheaffer, Robert. *The UFO Verdict: Examining the Evidence.* Amherst, N.Y.: Prometheus Books, 1981.

Sheaffer, Robert. "There Were No Extraterrestrials." Encounters at Indian Head Symposium paper, 2000 (Chapter Six in this volume).

Webb, Walter N. "A Dramatic UFO Encounter in the White Mountains, N.H., September 19-20, 1961," report to the National Investigations Committee on Aerial Phenomena, October 26, 1961.

Webb, Walter N. *A Dramatic UFO Encounter in the White Mountains, New Hampshire: The Hill Case, September 19-20, 1961.* Final report to NICAP on the Hill case, August 30, 1965[a].

Webb, Walter N. Letter to Barney and Betty Hill, November 20, 1965[b]. Copy in author's files.

Webb, Walter N. Letter to the editor, *Official UFO,* July 13, 1976. Copy in author's files.

Webb, Walter N. "Betty Hill." *MUFON UFO Journal* ("News'n'Views"), March 1986: 16.

Webb, Walter N. "Reflections on the Hill Case." (Chapter Eight in this volume.)

Webb, Walter N. Letter to Philip J. Klass, November 19, 1988. Copy in author's files.

Karl T. Pflock was co-creator with Peter Brookesmith of the Indian Head Symposium in 2000. He was a writer, consultant, and UFO researcher, and at various times served as a CIA intelligence officer, congressional staffer, and deputy assistant secretary of defense. He held a degree in philosophy and political science from San José State University. His articles on UFOs appeared in such journals as *Omni*, *Fortean Times*, the *International UFO Reporter*, *The Anomalist*, *Fate*, the MUFON *UFO Journal*, *Cuadernos de Ufología* (Spain), and the *MUFON 1995 International UFO Symposium Proceedings*, and he contributed a chapter to *UFOs 1947-1997* (Evans and Stacy, eds.). His *Roswell in Perspective*, a book-length monograph on his investigation of the Roswell "crashed-saucer" incident through March 1994, was published by the Fund for UFO Research in 1994. His *Roswell: Inconvenient Facts and the Will to Believe* (Prometheus, 2001) is now in its second printing, and a French edition is planned. *Shockingly Close to the Truth! (Confessions of a Grave-Robbing Ufologist)*, written in collaboration with James W. Moseley, was published by Prometheus Books in 2002. In 1998, he was named Ufologist of the Year by the National UFO Conference. His interest in UFOs was virtually lifelong, inspired in part by his own sighting as a boy in 1951 or 1952. In latter years Karl Pflock lived and worked near Albuquerque, New Mexico; he passed away at home on June 5, 2006.

CHAPTER EIGHT

Reflections on the Hill Case

The original chronicler of the Hills' story considers his investigation, its aftermath, and the impact of the case

WALTER N. WEBB

As the original investigator of the Barney and Betty Hill case, I was invited to participate in the Indian Head conference in New Hampshire in September 2000. Therefore, it wasn't easy for me to respectfully decline the invitation. After all, the Hill case remains to this day the prototypical UFO abduction episode and thereby constitutes one of the most significant events in UFO history. That said, however, the Hill affair had consumed me for a great many years, with all of its permutations, fascinations, and distractions. Eventually, I chose to move on and in the process uncovered a major encounter case that I felt superseded the Hill event (Webb 1994a).

Nevertheless, I did offer to contribute some commentary for this book. The conference organizers asked me, and I agreed, to write a chapter discussing my personal reflections on the case after 40 years, giving my assessment of the historic event and the witnesses, as well as the impact of this single episode upon the UFO abduction stories that followed in its wake. Additionally, I was asked to comment upon some of the specifics and ideas enunciated at the conference.

How I Became Involved

The story of my involvement with the Hill incident has been well documented in Fuller (1966). Dennis Stacy's paper (Chapter One) also summarizes the steps in my investigation of the affair. Here, I expand and flesh out the details of my exposure to the case. Betty Hill kindly gave me permission to use excerpts from some of her letters to me.

Six days after the Hills' experience, Betty wrote her now-famous letter to Major Donald E. Keyhoe (USMC, ret.), Director of the National Investigations Committee on Aerial Phenomena (NICAP). In the letter (see Chapter One for its content), Mrs. Hill described the consciously remembered first-encounter phase of the UFO experience. Three weeks later, on October 17, 1961, NICAP's Secretary Richard Hall typed two letters – one to me and the other to Betty. At the time I was Chairman of the Boston NICAP Subcommittee and NICAP's Special Adviser in Astronomy. Hall's letter to me (Hall 1961a) read, in part:

> I hate to burden you and the Subcommittee, but after reading the enclosed letter [Betty's] I suspect your curiosity may be aroused enough to plan an excursion to Portsmouth, N.H. ... I realize Portsmouth is about 60 miles from Boston, and hope you will be able to talk to Mrs. Hill.
> Two gentlemen from IBM in N.Y., one Robert Hohmann [and C. D. Jackson], may contact you about going along on the investigation. They learned about the case from Maj. Keyhoe on a recent visit here. They could be helpful, and if you are unable to make the trip they might be willing to investigate it for us. I am giving Mr. Hohmann your name, address, and home phone number. Please let me know one way or the other, because we don't want the trail to get too cold....

Simultaneously, Hall alerted Betty of NICAP's interest (Hall 1961b), introducing my name as a UFO investigator for the organization:

> Major Keyhoe ... wanted me to send you this reply to your letter of September 26.
> We were greatly interested in your report and we are making preparations for an investigation. Our Boston Subcommittee (investigative unit) will probably contact you in the near future. The Chairman is Walter N. Webb, but any of our subcommittee investigators will be carrying identification cards signed by Major Keyhoe. Mr. Webb is a close friend and an adviser to NICAP, and you may trust him completely.
> One thing that the subcommittee undoubtedly will want to do is to pinpoint the exact location of the incident. Perhaps you would have some maps, which would be helpful to them. .
> Thanks for reporting your experience to us. We hope to be able to gather more details from you very soon.

Having read Keyhoe's *The Flying Saucer Conspiracy* (1955) following the encounter, Betty wished to find out more about unidentified flying objects. "Any suggested readings would be greatly appreciated," she had written in her letter to Keyhoe. "Your book has been of great help to us and a reassurance that we are not the only ones to have undergone an interesting and informative experience."

A reference to UFO occupants piqued both my curiosity and suspicion. Betty reported that her husband Barney was close enough to the approaching unknown object that he could peer inside it and "see many figures scurrying about. ... One figure was observing us from the windows."

When the Hills reported their experience to an Air Force officer the next day, Mrs. Hill said they pointedly omitted Barney's observation of the figures "as it seems too fantastic to be true." Furthermore, it was at this point in the UFO encounter that Barney suffered an odd memory lapse. "His mind has completely blacked out," Betty wrote in her letter. "Every attempt to recall leaves him very frightened."

Despite the sensational nature of the story, I decided to approach the claim critically and with proper scientific skepticism. I telephoned the New Hampshire couple and arranged to meet with the Hills at their Portsmouth home that Saturday, October 21. A friend, Cheryl Wellock, accompanied me on the one-and-a-half hour drive.

The Interview

My interview with the Hills took place 31 days after the couple's experience. Again, Fuller's book and Stacy's paper cover my six-hour interview with the Hills in some detail. Five days later I typed my six-page report to NICAP, submitting copies to the Hills and to Hohmann and Jackson. It will be recalled that the latter gentlemen knew about the case through a meeting with Keyhoe. Jackson called me after I returned from Portsmouth, saying he was sorry he had missed joining me for the interview. During a visit with me in Boston in early November, Jackson told me he and Hohmann still hoped to meet with the Hills.

My perceptions of Barney and Betty and their amazing story were perhaps best expressed in a paragraph from my November 4 post-interview letter (Webb 1961b) to NICAP's Dick Hall:

> The N.H. sighting was one of the most interesting & impressive UFO cases I've worked on (and my first involving occupants), and I have you to thank for alerting me about it. The Hills were anxious to talk to someone with some knowledge & interest in UFOs and so I had no trouble extracting info from them. They were eager to learn more about the strange object they had seen. So engrossed were we all that no one was conscious

that six hours had passed during the interview. The couple was extremely patient to survive the ordeal of my barrage of questions. They did not seem overeager in describing the sighting – they were not trying to sell me on anything; they even played down the more startling portions of the incident. At any rate, I am convinced of their honesty & sanity, that they were telling me the complete truth.

I overlooked a number of clues in my interview. Had I known exactly what I was dealing with then, I would have handled many aspects of my investigation quite differently. No one at the time realized the truly historic import of the Hill case and what would become an abduction scenario. The Barney and Betty Hill affair proved to be my very first exposure to a report of close-encounter occupants, not to mention the virtually unprecedented abduction claim. My skeptical mind tended to be somewhat selective during the Hill inquiry, and not everything was explored that should have been. Nor did we early UFO investigators always take advantage of such equipment as tape recorders. One can only imagine the significance today of having a recording of my initial interview with the Hills.

During that first meeting with the witnesses, Barney admitted feeling a special fascination for the figure ("the leader") peering back at him through the windowed craft. Indeed, as he looked through his binoculars, Barney sensed in this figure an intense concentration to carry out a plan, to somehow capture the witness "like a bug in a net."

It was at this point in his testimony that Barney showed evidence of suffering a mental block, for no matter how hard he tried he was unable to describe this figure's appearance. There was a puzzling contradiction here: even though by this point the descending UFO had filled up the entire field of view of Barney's binoculars, the witness insisted that he wasn't close enough to detect any facial characteristics on the figures. And yet he referred to one of them looking back over his shoulder and grinning, and to the leader's expressionless face. Barney and Betty's hypnotic revelations were still more than two years in the future. I summarized my opinion of Barney's block in October 1961 this way (Webb 1961a):

> It is my view that the observer's blackout is *not* of any great significance. [Emphasis added.] I think the whole experience was so improbable and fantastic to the witness – along with the very real fear of being captured added to imagined fears – that his mind finally refused to believe what his eyes were perceiving and a mental block resulted.

The Hills said they were consciously aware of the strange beeping sounds that occurred twice on the rear trunk – once just after they drove away from the descending object near North Woodstock, and again in the Ashland area some 30 miles to the south. But they were puzzled as to why they were unable to recall the interval between the two sets of beeps nor which road they traveled in that interval, except that they vaguely remembered turning off U.S. Route 3 at some point. At first, Betty thought they had turned off U.S. 3 onto State Route 3B, which started at Ashland. Later, the Hills believed their initial turnoff was onto State Route 175. As I remembered it, nothing emerged in our meeting with reference to a later-than-expected arrival home.

The two witnesses also remembered seeing trees silhouetted in front of a bright orange object in the woods, which I took to be the setting Moon. The sighting of the orange object, the Hills thought, occurred sometime after the first series of beeps. Since the time of their highway encounter could only be approximated, it seemed entirely reasonable to me at the time that the gibbous Moon was the culprit. (Atmospheric refraction would have caused reddening of the setting lunar disc.) The Moon would have set behind the White Mountains much earlier than its sea-level disappearance time of around 1:30 a.m. Thus, I selectively (and improperly) excluded any reference to this component from my initial report.

Then there were the alleged "shiny round spots" on the Hill car. Reportedly, on the same day the Hills arrived home, Betty found a cluster of more than a dozen shiny, circular spots the size of a half or silver dollar on the rear trunk. She claimed that a compass needle behaved differently when it was placed over the spots than over other parts of the car. If the spots were mentioned during our interview, I must have minimized their importance as well as that of the beeps supposedly connected with them. Passing a compass over any large metallic object such as an automobile will cause the needle to move. So I was skeptical to begin with. Also fully a month had elapsed since the detection of the spots. As a consequence, I simply omitted any reference to the spots in my 1961 report. (They were incorporated, however, into my 1965 revision.)

Four years later, NICAP's Richard Hall prepared a list of questions about the case, asking me to respond to them. One of the queries involved whether I had previously observed the circular markings on the trunk of the Hill car. The only clarification I could produce, besides what was already in Fuller's book, came in my reply to NICAP, dated September 17, 1965 (Webb 1965b, 1994b):

> Concerning the circular spots on the car, I unfortunately failed to attach

much importance to the "beeps" in '61 and it seems to me that I casually looked at the car [as I left the witness interview] but recall seeing nothing out of the ordinary. I believe there were spots on the trunk, but they didn't impress me at the time as being of suspicious origin.

Much later I recall viewing similar silver round spots on my own vehicle and realized that these had a natural cause due to some sort of weather-related or road precipitate. It had been raining when Betty discovered the spots on her car. As she noted to me in 1962, "this agent [the spots] deteriorated over time." I believe Betty's description of the spots may have been somewhat exaggerated. In her excitement following the UFO encounter, she quite naturally was looking for some sort of proof of their experience, and she found something on the car that she thought might have had a connection with the beeping sounds.

Another detail I actually *had* known about from my initial interview but had neglected to include in my first report was Betty's dreams. (She hadn't yet typed her five-page dream narrative. That would be sometime in November. A copy of the narrative became part of the Appendix to my revised 1965 NICAP report.) Of course, Betty thought her unusual "capture" dreams after the encounter might possibly explain what had happened to her and Barney during the gap between the sets of beeps. It is impossible now to recall any variations or comparisons between her written account and what she told me. I remember that she felt the dreams were different from any others she had had before: they seemed so vivid and real to her that she wondered aloud if they might not have represented a real capture down the road, following the couple's first encounter. I failed to attach much importance to the dreams. I dismissed them as sort of a projected fantasy extension of the initial close encounter event, pointedly explaining that they could just as easily be explained in conventional terms as a wish-fulfillment fantasy or some similar projection.

Subsequent Events

In her September 26, 1961, letter to NICAP, Betty asserted that while both witnesses were frightened by their experience, at the same time "we feel a compelling urge to return to the spot where this occurred in the hope that we may again come in contact with this object." But, she added, "We realize this possibility is slight." The blend of both repellent fear and gnawing attraction to the UFO site is not at all unusual in close-encounter participants. The urge to return to the scene and engage again with her captors would haunt Betty for the rest of her life.

Three weeks after my interview, the Hills returned to the first-encounter area along U.S. Route 3. They chose to arrive in the Indian Head vicinity about midnight, the supposed time frame of their closest highway contact with the UFO – just in case! Although they saw nothing out of the ordinary, the main purpose anyway was to better locate where the event took place.

In the meantime Hohmann and Jackson had arranged to meet with Barney and Betty on November 25. While going over the timeline of the couple's journey home that night of September 19-20, one of the two questioners asked the Hills why it took them so long to reach their home in Portsmouth. Suddenly Barney realized at least two hours appeared to be unaccounted for on the journey home. From then on, the concept of "missing time" would forever alter the landscape of UFO abduction reports.

A friend of the Hills, Major James MacDonald (USAF, ret.), also attended the meeting. He suggested that Barney and Betty consider the services of a psychiatrist using hypnosis in order to unlock their apparent amnesia and treat any repressed trauma resulting from the UFO experience. This proposal was not new since, in her letter to Keyhoe, Betty herself had mentioned the possibility of using a psychiatrist skilled in hypnosis to uncover the cause of Barney's mental block. Following the Hohmann-Jackson-MacDonald gathering, I received a letter (Hill 1961) from Betty, dated November 27. She wrote that she and her husband now questioned whether the orange object in the woods really was the Moon. Mrs. Hill wanted to know when the Moon had set that morning, and then she commented on the new developments emerging from the meeting just ended:

> Saturday while Mr. Hohmann and Mr. Jackson were visiting us, we recalled something that we had not discussed before.
> This had happened in the Ashland area before we heard the beeping sound the second time. We were riding on Route 3B – a short cut to avoid going into Laconia. This narrow twisting road is quite dark. We had driven up a hill and were going down a sharp decline in the road when we saw a huge glowing red-orange object directly in front of us. It appeared to be ground level and we could see the outline of trees in front of it. At that point the road branched and we followed Route 3B to the left, and away from it.
> We believed that it was the Moon setting. Mr. Hohmann and Mr. Jackson questioned this, in view of the time. This event occurred somewhere between 12:30-1:30 a.m.
> This Saturday [December 2] we plan to return to the area again. One purpose is to determine the time needed to drive from Ashland to Portsmouth, and the mileage involved. It appears that this part of the trip

took 3¹/₂ hours, and is quite puzzling to us, as we believe we drove quite rapidly toward home.

Also Mr. Hohmann is going to send us the names of competent psychiatrists who use hypnosis. In this way we may be able to determine the cause of Barney's black-out.

Despite the new concept of missing time entering the picture, and the implication that the Hills took longer than they had anticipated to get home that morning, I remained skeptical about it. After all, the couple had stopped their car a number of times to observe the unknown object through binoculars and had turned off onto a "twisting" back road "to avoid going into Laconia." This activity and the slowdowns, it seemed to me, certainly could have accounted for the extra time to arrive home. I also thought the setting Moon still offered a better explanation than a landed UFO. But I had to admit the "beeps" continued to baffle me.

The Barney and Betty Dynamic

Fuller, Karl Pflock, and Peter Brookesmith (the latter two in their papers in this book) are among those who have detailed the Hills' careers and family backgrounds. To their discussions, I now add my own personal perspective on the two witnesses. I am one of very few individuals left in the UFO field who were present at the outset of the Hill experience, interviewing both Barney and Betty and thus able to observe their interaction together. In addition, I still have my correspondence with Betty (who was the letter-writer of the couple).

First of all, Barney and Betty Hill were held in high regard as responsible citizens in their community. Barney worked a night shift as a postal dispatcher at Boston's South Station Annex. This forced him to commute long distances daily, from Portsmouth, New Hampshire, to Boston, Massachusetts, and back. In 1965 he managed to secure a transfer to Portsmouth as a rural mail carrier. Mrs. Hill was employed at Portsmouth as a child welfare worker for the New Hampshire Department of Public Welfare. Both were active in civil rights. During the 1960s Barney was appointed to a number of county and state positions. He was a member and eventually the Chairman of the Board of Directors, Rockingham County Community Action Program; on the Board of Directors of the County Poverty Program; on the U.S. Civil Rights Commission, eventually for a third term; and appointed by the Governor to the State Advisory Board of the Economic Opportunity Program. Betty participated in a Governor's Conference on Drug Abuse.

Betty brought to the marriage (the second for each partner) an openness and curiosity about life. As was true for many people, she certainly was aware of the UFO subject prior to the 1961 encounter. Betty had read newspaper accounts of UFO sightings, heard references to sightings on the radio, and heard her sister Janet's report of her own sighting about eight years previously. (Webb 1961a, 1965a). Except for her sister's observation, Betty's exposure to the UFO topic appeared similar to that of everyone else. But she was much more receptive to paranormal phenomena in general than her husband.

Barney, on the other hand, had a total lack of interest or curiosity about UFOs before the 1961 experience. He had been a complete skeptic. Even after his UFO encounter, he still despised the popular term "flying saucer." During the actual encounter, Barney constantly tried to explain away what he was seeing. Viewing the figures in the approaching craft, he exclaimed repeatedly, "I don't believe it!" and "This is ridiculous!" Toward the end of the experience near Ashland – when Betty turned to her husband and asked, "Do you believe in flying saucers now?" – he retorted, "Don't be ridiculous – that wasn't a flying saucer!" (At that point both claim to have heard the second set of beeping sounds on the rear trunk.)

When Betty posed her question to Barney, most likely she had been referring to their first encounter of which they both had retained conscious memory, and to Barney's constant denials that the object was anything but a conventional craft. At that stage early in the experience, Betty had the binoculars most of the time and had the best view of the object, while her husband watched the road ahead as he drove along Route 3.

It was clear in my meetings with the couple that Betty was the dominant and more talkative of the two. When Barney spoke, however, I recall that the force of his understated testimony impressed me considerably. His remarks were carefully and intelligently measured. At the same time he did not give me any reason to believe he was being manipulated or controlled by Betty. Without his supporting testimony, this case might have taken a different turn. Despite Barney's reluctance to accept what his eyes and brain had perceived, obviously he too was very curious about what had happened to them that night. He, however, still believed, as I did then, that Betty's dreams were fantasy, having no connection with the reality of the conscious experience.

In a revealing letter (Hill 1965c) to me after she received a copy of my revised 1965 investigation report, Betty devoted a paragraph to my comments about her dominating presence and her husband's apparent passivity:

I never considered Barney as passive – if anything, he is quite aggressive.

So we have been asking friends about this. The consensus seems to be that at the first meetings he gives this impression, but not for long. I will agree that I am dominating – this is always the personality structure of the oldest child in a family, and one of the most important factors in a happy marriage is to marry the youngest child in his family – which I did with Barney. Apparently I have developed some possessiveness – which I have been striving for for a long time, which also can be a fault in the oldest child. This child is always encouraged to give to the younger ones, so they grow up finding it difficult to say "mine." In my honest opinion, I do not feel that Barney is highly suggestible. He does listen carefully to suggestions, evaluates them, and then does as he pleases....

As a mixed-race married couple (he was black; she was white) and highly visible in trustworthy positions in a conservative state, the Hills had a lot of credibility to lose by fabricating a story about meeting up with a flying saucer and its occupants on a Granite State highway. As a matter of fact, it is important to emphasize that in the beginning the Hills never wanted their experience publicized.

Recently I discovered among my old reel-to-reel radio program UFO tapes what I believe is the earliest public airing by the witnesses of their UFO encounter. On August 21, 1962, I appeared as the guest "UFO expert" on Boston's WBZ radio talk show *Program PM*. (Webb 1962). I had arranged beforehand for Barney to call in anonymously during the broadcast to relate his and Betty's UFO experience. Barney spent five minutes describing the couple's conscious experience without mentioning (at my suggestion) the entities he had reportedly seen through binoculars. Since I hadn't tape-recorded my initial meeting with the Hills, the 1962 audio recording of Barney's description becomes an invaluable historic resource. Other significant mileposts of this recording lie in the fact that it occurred 1) only 11 months after the UFO encounter, 2) 14 months before the couple's recorded narratives at Quincy, Massachusetts, and 3) nearly one and a half years prior to the start of the Hills' hypnosis sessions.

Subsequent to Barney's anonymous radio call-in, the couple restricted any comment about their experience to family, a few friends, and two small intimate groups of their local church. The Hills invited me to lead a discussion on life in the Universe at the second church-related home meeting (Couples Club) at which we also heard Barney and Betty's story. That was on March 3, 1963. Eight months later, on November 3, 1963, Barney and Betty agreed to share their sighting at the monthly meeting of the now-defunct Two-State (Massachusetts and Rhode Island) UFO Study Group in Quincy, Massachusetts. Although my memory isn't too clear about the

Quincy gathering, I was invited to attend and believe I probably did. I know that afterwards the Hills joined me at my apartment.

Of course, it was the Hills' appearance at that meeting that changed everything! A tape-recording of the couple's talk eventually came into the hands of a Boston newspaper reporter, the late John Luttrell, and led directly to his five-part series in the *Boston Traveler* in October 1965. (Lutrell 1965). The Hills knew the *Traveler* story was coming a few months before it appeared, because the reporter called them, their employers, and acquaintances in an attempt to assemble background information about the two witnesses and their sighting. The Hills and I refused to give Luttrell a copy of my investigation report, since doing so would have violated Barney and Betty's wish to keep the report confidential with me and NICAP.

Despite the couple's desire to keep knowledge of their UFO experience confined to trusted friends and small groups which might be interested in hearing their dramatic story, their effort to avoid publicity proved somewhat naïve and in the end impossible to maintain. As telling evidence of their wish to shun the limelight back then, I cite the following excerpt from a letter (Hill 1965b) that Betty typed two months prior to publication of the explosive *Traveler* story:

> We have decided that we are NOT going to be involved in his [Luttrell's] story. ... When he talked with Barney, he revealed that he knew most of the facts of our personal life. So we are letting people know that we do not want the story published. ... If it were ever published in a Boston newspaper, with all the publicity, I would probably be fired from my job. [This didn't happen.] Generally, people would question my sanity....
>
> Also I do not know what effect publicity would have on Barney's position in so many of the things he is doing. There is a possibility he *might* [her emphasis] be appointed to the State's Human Rights Commission which is being set up here; and he has just been appointed to the U.S. Civil Rights Commission, and he is Director on the Board of Directors of the Poverty Program, and several other things…

The Abduction Scenario Emerges

The entire UFO experience had a profoundly traumatic effect upon both witnesses, particularly Barney. In the wake of the encounter, he returned to drinking (a problem that had been absent for about 10 years), developed an ulcer and high blood pressure, and eventually underwent long-term psychotherapy in an effort to alleviate his emotional difficulties. At least some of Barney's anxieties appeared to be associated with the UFO episode. Betty remained concerned about her abduction dreams.

Ultimately, the Hills were referred to Dr. Benjamin Simon, a Boston psychiatrist specializing in the use of hypnosis to treat his patients.

The Portsmouth couple proved to be good subjects for hypnosis. From January to June 1964 the Hills drove to Dr. Simon's Boston office once each weekend and were hypnotically regressed to the time and place of their UFO encounter. Each witness repeated the Route 3 first-phase in vivid detail. More importantly, Betty recounted as part of her experience something quite similar to her dreams of being abducted by the UFO entities, as if it had been the recall of an actual capture event. And, for the first time, Barney appeared to confirm an abduction scenario as well. Dr. Simon regressed each witness separately and told them they would not remember the content of each session until the treatment program was finished and the recorded hypnosis sessions were played back. That way Simon would be able to evaluate their statements as a whole, while at the same time keep the Hills from comparing their accounts between sessions.

I was in contact with Barney and Betty during this period. On occasion, after meeting with Simon, they would drop by my Cambridge apartment or the planetarium where I worked. I especially remember their excitement and disbelief when they paid me a visit immediately after hearing together the first tape playback of their hypnosis. It had been at Barney's initial session in Simon's office, and listening to his (Barney's) emotional revelations astounded him. During that session, as he approached the point in his account where he knew his mental block has occurred, under hypnosis Barney screamed and sobbed hysterically, apparently clutching his face and shaking uncontrollably. With the psychiatrist's guidance, this critical point was passed, and he recalled what had frightened him that night two and a half years before. Later that week Barney would spontaneously begin to remember more details, including his own abduction and examination aboard the landed UFO.

Now, the Hills were more interested than ever in finding the spot where they believed they had been kidnapped by alien entities. I accompanied them on three of their searches for the second encounter site.

The Abduction Site

On April 18, 1964, I joined the couple, along with a fellow investigator Harold McCormack, on their return to a candidate back road off U.S. Highway 3. Following their first encounter, they believed they had turned left, or east, off Route 3 not too far south. On an earlier visit to the area, the Hills found the State Route 175 exit off Highway 3 about three miles south of their first encounter site. Once on SR 175, Barney and Betty thought that on the night of the encounter they had made a second left somewhere off that road. Thus began a series of probings of back roads that exited eastward from SR 175.

Their first selected stretch – Tripoli Road – had been impassable because of a snow barricade. Now, however, we were able to travel the same road all the way to the Waterville Valley ski area. Near there, Barney found a clearing in the woods where he thought the abduction could have taken place. But Betty disagreed with the choice. Six weeks later, on May 30, I accompanied them again on another hunt for the kidnap site. A friend of Betty's, Gail Peabody, also came along. This time we traveled the full length of Tripoli Road, which looped back to Route 175. The Hills discovered another potential capture site, but once again Barney and Betty failed to come to a consensus on it.

It was on this drive that I had Barney re-enact his first encounter along Route 3 while I photographed him. (The car wasn't the same vehicle from the original episode.) The color-slide sequence pictured the car stopped on the highway north of North Woodstock; Barney standing outside his vehicle, peering through binoculars "at the UFO"; rotating his body southward as the object crosses the highway from right to left; and the witness standing in the field and looking through his binoculars as the UFO descends toward him.

It wasn't until Labor Day of 1965 that the Hills finally stumbled on an agreed-upon kidnap site. Barney's sketch in Fuller's book is an overhead view of the UFO abduction location as he remembered it. In his drawing the "men in the road" block the Hills' stalled car. Leaving the road to the right, the path along which the two captives were taken leads directly to the landed craft.

A problem arises for those who have visited the couple's preferred site for the second encounter, which is in rural Thornton, New Hampshire (about 12 miles south of the first-encounter spot). If it is assumed that the Hills' car turned off SR 175 and headed east on Mill Brook Road, the selected path and clearing where the craft allegedly rested is on the left or north of the road, not on the right or south of the road (as Barney drew the location sometime after the sessions with Dr. Simon). Betty attempted to explain this inconsistency in a letter to me (Hill 1965c), dated September 22, 1965, in which she announced the discovery of the "true" abduction site:

> We are quite sure that we have found the spot where the second encounter took place. It is off Route 175, a sharp turn to the left. We were riding in

that area on Labor Day [September 6] with my parents when we found it. Also it resembles Barney's aerial map very closely. There is one puzzling aspect – it is on a dead end road. That night after the second encounter I was well aware that the car had been moved for it had stalled in the middle of the road. When I returned, the car was pulled off the road – I am positive of that. Now I believe that *the car had been turned around and headed back towards Route 175* [Emphasis added]....

Supporting Betty's contention that somehow the car was turned 180 degrees from its original position, under hypnosis she mentioned being led to the car after their release from the craft: "We were walking, and the path – just a short distance – it doesn't seem as long as it did going in. Going in seemed awfully long" (Fuller 1966: 178). This tiny, seemingly insignificant detail of the witness implying that she walked a shorter path back to the car than on the way to the craft has the ring of truth, in my judgment. In a typical abduction scenario, one might reasonably expect the witness to state that he or she returned along the same pathway.

Mass displacement of automobiles in connection with UFO close-encounter episodes, while uncommon, has been reported in other cases (Rodeghier 1981; Keyhoe and Lore 1969). The implication here is that if the entire experience truly happened as the Hills reported, then their vehicle was deliberately repositioned, perhaps to help the two dazed witnesses return to the route from which they had come. In being moved, the car may have been relocated along the road somewhat closer to the landed craft. This could account for Betty's shortcut back to the car. If the car had remained in its original position, pointed east instead of west, the couple would have driven about three miles to a dead-end, forcing them to turn around and head back toward Route 175. Yet neither Barney nor Betty mention having to turn around to resume their homeward journey.

Is it possible that Barney's sketch actually represents a combination of before and after memories of the capture site? Perhaps his drawing depicts two orientations instead of one – that of the figures in the road at the outset of the abduction, with the path and UFO actually off *to the left*, and that of his last memory of the landed craft appearing *to the right* after the car had been turned 180 degrees. Of course in the end, this mental exercise is purely speculation. But it is one attempt to resolve the dichotomy between Barney's sketch and the Hills' kidnap site selection.

Betty invited me to come along on their return to the new capture location on Mill Brook Road. So on October 9, 1965, I joined them once again. At the chosen spot we parked and walked the sandy path through the woods into a roughly circular clearing surrounded by tall pines. I recollect that both Barney and Betty did seem to agree on the location north of the road as being the actual abduction site.

Astronomical and Meteorological Questions

In their papers Karl Pflock and Robert Sheaffer debate the role celestial objects and the sky played in the Hills' sighting.

Prior to the onset of the first phase of their experiences, Betty said she noticed an especially bright star or planet to the lower left of the nearly full Moon. (This object was the planet Jupiter.) As the couple continued their drive, suddenly Betty spotted another, even brighter starlike object above the other one, and it was moving upward to the left of the Moon. The sky was reported to be clear.

Sheaffer attempts to explain the UFO by combining a witness misidentification of Jupiter above the "highly conspicuous" planet Saturn, and an illusory motion and erratic behavior caused by the movement of the Hills' car and the phenomenon of autokinesis (the perceived motion of a stationary point source due to involuntary eye and neck movement). Pflock, on the other hand, offers what I believe are valid arguments opposing the celestial/physiological hypotheses. Since he already has covered this issue in some detail, using and crediting my past rebuttals to Sheaffer and Philip Klass, I will only summarize the main points that I believe dismantle the Sheaffer–Klass rationale.

First of all, while both Jupiter and Saturn might have been visible near the brilliant 10-day-old Moon, Saturn would not have been "highly conspicuous," as Sheaffer suggests. Jupiter would have been much more easily discerned than Saturn, particularly under conditions of bright moonlight. And the UFO itself was reportedly even brighter than Jupiter.

When the Hills stopped their car on several occasions to view the unknown object, both eyewitnesses noted that it was definitely moving and therefore not an illusion of motion caused by the car's travel.

How does Sheaffer account for the point source becoming a structured craft of large angular diameter? He compares the Hills' description to that in a case where several individuals visualized the fiery re-entry of space debris as a strange craft with portholes along its side. I don't doubt that this misidentification occurred as reported in that instance. Speeding fireballs (bright meteors) have, on rare occasions, produced similar descriptions. But it is quite a leap to compare a short-duration space re-entry to the Hills' long-term observation, in which the object gradually expanded to a huge flattened disc filling Barney's binocular field, and moved away from Jupiter's position by at least 90 degrees!

In his paper (Chapter Six), Sheaffer describes the night sky as he saw in it New Hampshire in September 2000. But in September 2000 Jupiter and Saturn were 1.5 and 1.7 times brighter, respectively, than during the same time frame in 1961. The angular separation between the three celestial objects was different; the Moon's shape and phase *were* similar. Sky clarity, cloud cover, planet magnitudes, and angular elevations above the horizon all play a part in visibility.

As for the couple's claimed clarity of the sky during the sighting, Sheaffer objects to this as inaccurate, thereby impugning the credibility of the Hills' testimony. He justifies his comments by citing information from the official weather records of Mount Washington Observatory (located east of U.S. Highway 3). The records indicated that high, thin cirrus clouds covered "five to six tenths" of the sky on average during the night of September 19-20. (I also possessed the same data in a letter from the mountaintop's observer.)

Cirrus sometimes is thin enough to go virtually unnoticed by the average observer, especially at night. We do not know from the records, however, whether the cloud coverage was a general five-to-six tenths scattered over the whole sky, or confined to one half of the sky as opposed to another half. For all we know, it might have been totally clear in the southwest sky where the UFO first appeared.

Concerning the radar report made at Pease Air Force Base the same morning as the Hill sighting, I agree with Robert Sheaffer and Philip Klass that only a single radar report of unidentified targets could be confirmed and documented that night, and that observation was most likely the result of atmospheric-caused anomalous propagation. Air Force Intelligence reported the existence of an atmospheric temperature inversion prevailing in the area on the morning of the radar observation. (Webb 1972). Such conditions can cause radar waves to bend earthward to pick up stationary or moving ground targets, producing false objects on the radarscope. Moreover, the Pease radar observation happened some 80 miles southeast of the Hill first-encounter location. There is no justification for connecting the two events.

Missing Time

It is generally agreed that the element of missing time in connection with UFO abduction reports commenced with the Hill case. Though unrecognized during my first Hill interview, certainly the clues were there: Barney's mental block, the amnesic gap between both sets of beeps, the round orange object in the woods, Betty's series of unusual dreams. Not quite appreciating memory loss or abductions as something new and possibly real on the UFO scene, I naturally tended to be skeptical and to discount these problem areas in the testimony as having convenient rational explanations.

Barney's mental lapse, embracing his observation of the "leader," was dismissed as some sort of traumatic forgetfulness (which indeed it may have been). For me the beeping sounds existed as an embarrassing unexplained feature of the case. Although the couple had mentioned a seeming inability to remember the interval between the sets of beeps, I convinced myself that, since it is entirely normal to lose track of time on a long drive, I was justified in omitting the "beep gap" from my 1961 investigation report.

Although I was aware of both the reported moonlike orange object and Betty's dreams during my interview, neither detail was included in my initial report. In my own mind I had rejected the orange object as the setting Moon (the time of moonset was approximately "right") and the dreams as a "what-if" fantasy extension of the first-encounter phase. At the time neither component seemed important enough to include in the report, since each appeared to have a perfectly logical, mundane explanation. Hindsight would indicate that, regardless, these features should have been part of my first investigation report. Even after Hohmann and Jackson raised the question about the witnesses' late arrival home, I maintained my skepticism, blaming any additional time to get home on stops, slowdowns, and travel along an unknown secondary road.

With the realization that between two and three hours were somehow "missing" from the time it should have taken to drive between North Woodstock and their home in Portsmouth, Betty and Barney began to remember some odd details that allegedly occurred upon their return – a broken binocular strap, stopped watches, Barney's scuffed shoetops and his genital inspection, and pink residue on Betty's dress, which she subsequently packed away and never wore again. Some details arose spontaneously in memory during the ensuing weeks and months; others emerged during Dr. Simon's regressive hypnosis.

Even as the Hills were hearing the playback of their hypnosis tapes for the first time, Dr. Simon simultaneously shared the same recorded testimony with me – all 11 hours of it! I spent seven evenings at his home, listening in fascination as the couple relived their emotional journey and recalled long-buried elements of their UFO encounter and *apparent* abduction. The tapes became quite an eye-opener for me. The raw emotional power of the Hills' reliving of their experience was impressive, to say the least. Of even greater importance to me, this ostensible release of suppressed information, in my view, pointed strongly to the reality of an additional second encounter – the kidnap sequence first hinted at in Betty's vivid dreams.

Under hypnosis, the unexplained memory gaps were nicely filled in, like pieces of a puzzle, and both witnesses, for the most part, corroborated each other's accounts.

Barney Hill appeared to uncover the cause of his mental block as he observed the leader through binoculars. This figure's large eyes (depicted under hypnosis in a sketch) and a "voice" in Barney's head instructed him to move closer and keep looking. As he obeyed, a ladder began to descend from the UFO coincident with the lighted "fins" sliding outward from opposite sides of the craft. (The finlike structures and their extension outward were also part of his conscious recall.) At this point Barney broke the spell, forcibly dropping his binoculars and breaking the strap around his neck. (Prior to hypnosis, he could not remember how or where he had broken the strap.)

Previously Barney had been unable to describe the central figure's appearance, even though his binocular view should have furnished some clues at such close range. Under hypnosis, he drew a sketch of an alien face. As he listened to the tapes, Barney drew a sketch of the leader's face, depicting a countenance possessing large elongated eyes, two nasal apertures, and a greatly diminished mouth. With the aid of hypnotic recall, the end of the first encounter transitioned smoothly into the beginning of the second encounter phase, while the end of the abduction scenario flowed into that portion of the trip home where the two witnesses once again became consciously aware.

If one regards the two sets of beeping sounds on the car as an integral part of the scenario, then they may have served as some sort of control mechanism over the witnesses. After hearing the first beeps, Barney now reports that the "mind-voice" tells him to turn off the main highway onto a secondary road that eventually leads to another. Ahead the couple spots a bright orange glow in the woods and a cluster of figures in the road. All at once the car's engine dies and won't restart.

As the two abductees are removed from their vehicle, the "mind-voice" instructs Barney to close his eyes and tells him no harm will come to him. Betty is left in a semiconscious state. They are led to the landed craft and then on board. Once inside the witnesses are guided to separate rooms where their medical examinations are conducted. (The exam details are covered in Fuller's book and in Stacy's paper as well as in my 1965 revised

NICAP report.) At the conclusion of their abduction experience, the Hills say they are returned to their car. The couple watches as the darkened craft once again begins to glow orange, becoming brighter and brighter, and then lifts off, disappearing rapidly into the night sky.

Memories of the capture events fade as the Hills drive away. Somewhere in the Ashland area, Betty breaks the silence, asking her husband: "Do you believe in flying saucers now?" He replies: "Oh, Betty, don't be ridiculous. That wasn't a flying saucer." Both claim at once to hear and feel another series of codelike beeps on the rear trunk. From that point on, conscious memory resumes during the rest of the homeward journey. When they finally arrive home, Barney looks at the kitchen clock and realizes that their trip has taken much longer than expected. At least two hours seem to be unaccounted for.

Critics often attribute the Hills' lost hours to a combination of travel slowdowns and stops in order to observe the UFO, and to Barney's "decision" to turn off Route 3 and wander the back roads to "escape" the UFO. Barney's testimony, however, indicates his obvious *puzzlement* and apparent *involuntary* action in turning onto the back roads, rather than making a conscious decision to do so. Furthermore, slowdowns, several brief stops, and a 30-mile side trip down a rural road still don't add up to between two and three hours of missing time. Pflock's analysis of the witnesses' possible driving time frame clearly demonstrates this fact.

Suggestions also have been made that perhaps the beeps were caused by the car encountering rough or corrugated stretches of pavement, particularly since the couple later found the trunk lid not securely latched. I would make two points about the rough road/loose trunk lid speculation:

First, after hearing the last series of beeps, Barney said he tried to reproduce the sounds by deliberately accelerating and suddenly decelerating the car, swerving from one side of the road to the other, and abruptly accelerating from a stop. In all instances, he was unable to recreate the enigmatic noises. (Fuller 1966: 125)

Second, it is intriguing that the two sets of beeps closely bracketed the Hills' time/memory lapse. The onset of the lapse coincided with the initial series of beeps, and then memory returned with the last set of beeps. In my opinion, it seems beyond coincidence that the road surface could have generated sounds in the vehicle that appeared only at the precise moments when conscious memory faded and later returned.

Hypnotic Regression

The Hill episode became not only the first widely publicized UFO abduction case in history but also the first such incident to employ hypnosis in an effort to retrieve suppressed details of the experience. Fortunately, Dr. Simon was a trained clinician skilled in this approach.

The goal in regressive hypnosis is to take the entranced subject back in time in order to recall forgotten or repressed traumatic experiences. In ideal circumstances, past events may be relived with the same associated emotions felt at the time. Clinical hypnotists frequently are able to dissolve a patient's phobia by regressing him or her to an earlier period of life and having the subject confront and re-experience the original traumatic incident that triggered the irrational fear.

We know now that the hypnotic state produces a mixture of both true memories and fantasized material; therefore, information elicited in this way must be carefully sifted and evaluated. Despite the pitfalls, I believe hypnotic regression can be helpful in probing *multiple-witness* close-encounter/abduction claims. Independent verification of specific details in these cases by witnesses who have undergone hypnosis separately is not easily dismissed – especially in the rare instances where the participants have not communicated with each other since their experience.

In the Buff Ledge episode (Webb 1994a), for example, neither individual had communicated with the other between the end of their UFO experience and the initiation of my investigation 10 years later. Yet despite their years of separation accompanied by periods of missing time, both witnesses independently filled in their time lapses with a shared abduction scenario during isolated hypnosis sessions, with an astonishing agreement in many major and minor details.

Such circumstances, however, are exceedingly rare. In nearly all multiple-witness abduction reports, the principals involved are friends, family members, or married partners who already have shared remembered particulars of their experiences prior to undergoing hypnosis. Thus their hypnotic testimony is potentially contaminated. This, of course, probably happened to some degree between Barney and Betty.

The Simon Dream Hypothesis

Dr. Simon agreed with me that the first encounter along Highway 3 actually occurred, and that Betty and Barney Hill had been frightened by an occupied craft of some kind. The psychiatrist, however, believed the sighting likely involved the perception of an unidentified earth-based military aircraft of either classified or conventional type. While conceding that Barney may very well have seen figures in the craft as he looked through his binoculars, Simon reasoned that the description could have been distorted by Barney's underlying anxieties, which the psychiatrist believed were uncovered during hypnosis.

As for the abduction story itself, Dr. Simon decided that the second encounter happened only in Betty's dreams, which he surmised were triggered by the initial experience. A kidnapping by space beings, in his view, had all the bizarre earmarks of a nightmare. Dr. Simon further hypothesized that Betty's retelling of her dreams to Barney, and in Barney's presence, caused her husband to imagine during hypnosis his capture as well.

Certainly it is apparent that Betty's account of the alien kidnapping and physical examination aboard the craft was much more elaborate and detailed than her husband's rather sketchy narrative of his own alleged on-board experience. To Dr. Simon, this seemed clear evidence that the entire abduction scenario originated in Betty's mind and was transferred by suggestion to Barney.

With respect to Dr. Simon, it should be kept in mind that, as a psychiatrist, his primary objective was to alleviate the anxieties of his two clients. To a great extent, he succeeded in achieving that goal. Nevertheless, it has always been my feeling that had he made an honest effort to acquaint himself with the UFO phenomenon, he might have altered his views somewhat about the nature of the Hills' experience. As it was, he had no interest at all in the UFO subject, even refusing to read my personally investigated case reports that I made available to him. Typifying what little he understood about UFOs, Simon labeled the extraterrestrial hypothesis "supernatural."

I will agree that contaminated testimony between Barney and Betty no doubt played some role in the retelling of their experience. Having said that, I also remain convinced to this day that, for the most part, both phases of the UFO encounter happened generally as the couple reported them.

If we are indeed dealing with an actual alien abduction, it is clear that the participants were compelled to forget parts of the experience through the imposition of some form of hypnotic amnesia. Betty's more elaborate description of her capture might be explained by her desire to stay aware during the abduction and by her stubborn refusal to forget the on-board events that happened to her. A good example of her strong determination to remember allegedly took place after the "leader" took away the book he had given her. Under hypnotic recall, she said to the leader: "I won't forget about it! You can take the book, but you can *never, never, never* make me forget! I'll remember it if it is the last thing I do. ... I won't forget. I will remember it somehow" (Fuller 1966: 178).

According to this speculation, Betty succeeded enough in fighting the controls imposed upon her that she later recalled the abduction in her dreams.

Barney, by contrast, obligingly did what he was told – to keep his eyes closed and to forget his experience. (Although at least once he did open his eyes long enough to glimpse his abductors and his strange surroundings.) During the playback of their recorded hypnoanalysis, Barney began to comprehend and remember: "And I was able to realize that these men made me forget what happened. They told me to. They told me to forget, *and I wanted to forget*. [Emphasis added.] And I think this is why it wasn't too difficult for me to put this whole thing out of my mind for so long" (Fuller 1966: 256).

Thus, Barney's account of his abduction shouldn't have been expected to be as detailed as his wife's. Unlike Betty, he seems to have made no effort to block his imposed amnesia. He wouldn't have been able to recall much of what happened on the craft.

Even so, under regressive hypnosis Barney reported elements unique to his examination and not to Betty's. Though only hinted at in Fuller's book, Barney told me, with some reluctance, that his exam had included the withdrawal of sperm and rectal samples from his body. Since his eyes were closed at this point, he had only tactile sensations of a cuplike device placed around his genitals ("cup around my groin" in Fuller, p.123) and believed a sperm sample was subsequently removed. Additionally, he said, a cylindrical device had been inserted in his rectum and "something" extracted. To spare the witness any public embarrassment, Fuller replaced the rectal episode with "felt something at the base of my spine, like a finger pushing" (p.187).

Bullard and Pflock point out in their papers the uniqueness of Barney's story when the two witnesses separated inside the craft. Also see Brookesmith's paper, which quotes the paragraph from my 1965 NICAP report, briefly describing the above two alleged procedures.

I have been asked why Barney thought a sperm specimen had been withdrawn. Attesting to the case's total novelty back then, I can't say I pursued why Barney felt that a specimen had been taken. I am sure he did not volunteer much more about either the genital or rectal procedure, and no doubt I believed it prudent not to delve further into either aspect. Perhaps Barney simply thought a sperm-sampling exercise would have been a logical consequence of feeling a device around that part of his anatomy.

Intriguing similarities exist between the narratives of the Hills and the Buff Ledge witnesses – the two UFO abduction cases with which I am especially familiar. One of the two partners in each incident (Betty and "Michael") appeared to remain more consciously aware of the abduction phase than the other (Barney and "Janet"), and they were thereby able to furnish more information during postencounter hypnotic recall.

Early in the Buff Ledge experience, Janet entered an altered trancelike state prior to her capture. Once inside the craft, she said she was instructed telepathically to keep her eyes closed. Most of her on-board memories were tactile sensations. This circumstance compares favorably with Barney's situation. (Both abductees opened their eyes briefly to see their captors.)

Michael's intense curiosity, on the other hand, seemed to overcome his fears and his own semiconscious state to such a degree that he broke through his controls. His account implied that his alien "guide" was cognizant of this and may have permitted Michael to remain partially aware. Both he and Betty Hill happened to share exploratory minds, which were open to confrontations with esoteric phenomena. By contrast, Janet and Barney revealed more conservative personalities, and each was a complete UFO skeptic prior to the encounter.

I had promised Janet a copy of Fuller's book when all hypnosis sessions ended. Reading about the Hill case for the first time, Janet felt immense relief upon discovering that she was not alone in her incredible experience. She noted with amazement the similarities between Barney's testimony and her own, including the use of the same words and phrases to describe similar aspects of their abductions. *The Interrupted Journey* reaffirmed for Janet that "I was *not* [her emphasis] 'making up' my story or relating a dream under hypnosis" (Webb 1994a: 156).

Could Betty's reading of *The Flying Saucer Conspiracy* (Keyhoe 1955) have led to the alien abduction sequence featured in her dreams? It is a legitimate question, and Brookesmith's paper attempts to show that Keyhoe's book provided "sufficient raw material to form the basis of Betty's nightmares." He cites a number of examples from the book where Keyhoe mentions various UFO entity reports from around the world and the possibilities of extraterrestrial contact.

When I perused my copy of *The Flying Saucer Conspiracy*, I found extremely little in its pages that matched anything in Betty Hill's dreams. Virtually all of the entities mentioned in the book were quite different from Betty's gray-skinned, five-foot-tall, humanoid abductors. Keyhoe's alien reports were either ambiguously defined ("gruesome creature," "fearsome creature," "small creature") or didn't resemble the Hill beings at all. References included a "creature nine feet tall," "space man 13 feet tall," "zebra-striped space man who changed color like a chameleon," and "gigantic creature wearing what looked like a diver's suit." When shorter beings were cited, they were reported as either wearing shiny metallic suits with transparent helmets or as "hairy dwarves" – neither fitting the Hill abductors. Many of the entity reports in the 1950s, when Keyhoe's book was written, consisted of small silver-suited figures exhibiting "discover-and-escape" behavior, not kidnap activity. Upon being detected outside their landed or hovering craft, the occupants quickly retreated, according to these accounts, making a hasty escape in their vessels.

The only suggestions of UFO abductions that Brookesmith can find in *The Flying Saucer Conspiracy* are two controversial cases – the 1953 Lake Superior F-89 episode and the 1945 disappearance of Flight 19 off Florida. The former involved the jet pursuit of an unknown radar target. Both the plane and unidentified target were alleged to have merged on the ground radarscope. No trace of the pilot and his crewman, or the plane, was ever found. Keyhoe implies that in both cases a UFO might have executed an aerial seizure of planes and pilots. Even if a genuine UFO happened somehow to be connected with either incident (particularly unlikely in the second instance), it seems quite implausible to me that either case could have inspired Betty Hill's extremely detailed abduction dreams.

Even a year after Barney and Betty's hypnotic interviews with Dr. Simon, both participants suffered varying degrees of distress while listening to their copies of the taped sessions. One evening in March of 1965 I visited Portsmouth with my brother so that he could meet the Hills and hear a couple of the tapes. On this occasion I noted how disturbed and even hostile Barney appeared as we listened to the recordings.

In her reply (Hill 1965a) to my letter in which I brought up Barney's apparent hostility that evening, Betty commented on her and her husband's reaction to the tapes and to Simon's explanation of the UFO experience:

> In your last letter, you referred to Barney's upset in listening to the tapes. And you are right, as he does become very upset, and angry at times. My reaction is to break out in hives, but I did not the last time I listened to them.... In my own mind, I am convinced that those tapes are true. I am also convinced that I did dream about my experience, which was a form of hypnotic recall.... I do get somewhat upset in hearing the tapes because I do have an emotional reaction to the actual experience, as I feel some of the same feelings that I did that night. In other words, I relive the experience.
>
> Barney has a different reaction. In fact he has several. First of all the experience is very painful to him still. We have talked about this with a friend, a psychiatric social worker, on several occasions, and she feels that

Barney gets upset because of his reactions on the tapes, which are contrary to the way he thinks of himself. On the tapes, he is fearful, crying, helpless, frightened, etc. In other words, he is not very "masculine," to his way of thinking. Because of this sensitivity, we do not play the tapes very often – actually only when there is a specific reason to do this....

When Barney becomes upset, he seeks approval by asking if the person believes the tapes. Actually he is asking that the person understand his position. ... He is asking if the other person might react in the same way in the same experience....

And he always becomes angry with Dr. Simon. ...Barney feels that Dr. Simon deceived him by assuring us on several occasions that the truth ... would be on those tapes, and then at the end, he decides that it was a dream I had. ...Then he explains Barney's part of the sessions by saying that he was suggestible to my dream! ... So you can see, Walter, that the whole experience has been an upsetting, time consuming and expensive project. I personally am very glad that we did it, for now I know without any doubt what happened.

Star Maps and Night Vigils

My ongoing contact with the Hills essentially ended at the close of 1965. In the occasional letters that Betty wrote in the late 1960s, I could see that she seemed to be enjoying her celebrity status as a consequence of "going public," while Barney maintained a lower-key presence with regard to the UFO affair.

My interest in the case was rekindled briefly in 1973 when I began to hear about the work of Marjorie Fish. An Ohio schoolteacher at the time, Marjorie sought to identify the stars in Betty's star map by building three-dimensional models of our stellar neighborhood. (See Fuller, 1966: 175, 218-19, 300; papers in this book by Pflock and Sheaffer.) After an exhaustive six-year search, Fish believed she had discovered the identities of the 12 key stars in Betty's sketch – the ones linked by curved lines (routes) between the alien captors' home star (Zeta Reticuli) and the planetary systems they visited, including our Sun (and Earth).

After interviewing Marjorie in July 1974, I wrote a two-part analysis of the Fish model for the Aerial Phenomena Research Organization (Webb 1974, 1975, 1976). I still believe Marjorie's work signifies a potentially important discovery that could be a vital key to unlocking the UFO mystery. Her model should now be reexammed in light of today's enormous strides in astronomy and astrophysics and the greatly improved distance measurements to thousands of stars, including those in the Hill-Fish pattern.

In April 1978, I had my first reunion with Betty in many years. One purpose of my meeting was to visit the purported "secret UFO site" where Betty claimed to have spotted UFOs frequently. Several years after Barney's sudden death in 1969, Betty had found an open but secluded area about 20 miles from her home where she hoped she might somehow make contact with her alien kidnappers. The spot actually had been selected for her by John P. Oswald, a UFO investigator familiar with sighting activity in southeastern New Hampshire (Oswald 1987). Betty drove to this site several nights a week and invariably observed "unknown" objects in the sky. I accompanied her to the area, equipped with binoculars and a telescope. Unfortunately, every single object in the sky pointed out as anomalous was in fact identifiable – either as aircraft lights or distant ground lights.

Betty was a classic example of the altered life that so often results from such otherworldly close encounters. Long after their experiences, these individuals may sustain after-effects ranging from unnatural fears (of specific locations, being alone, UFO or alien images) to obsessive behavior, heightened psychic abilities, and permanent life changes.

I knew both Barney and Betty before the general public learned of their abduction story. At that time the couple generally rebuffed publicity about the UFO incident. Then Fuller's book placed the quiet couple on the world stage, making them international celebrities. Subsequently, Betty lost the one person who had shared her original UFO experience; Barney's death came as a terrible shock to her. Through it all, she continued to hope that her UFO captors would someday return. It is likely that her weekly vigils in the New Hampshire countryside served as an outlet for her obsessions.

I think in many instances Betty fooled herself into believing she was seeing real UFOs. At the same time, I get the impression she believed she had a public image to uphold at all costs, even if it meant exaggerating her sighting claims. Regrettably, her later extravagant stories and alleged UFO sightings only served to undermine her credibility with respect to her and Barney's original experience. Debunkers delight in using Betty's later pronouncements in their attempts to refute her 1961 episode – without, of course, taking into account the post-encounter changes that 40 years wrought in the witness.

The Historical Impact of the Hill Case

The Hills' experience had the distinction of being the first UFO abduction account to receive extensive public coverage. But it was not the first such story. In February 1958, a Brazilian investigator interviewed farmer Antonio Villas Boas, who claimed to have been snatched aboard a UFO four months earlier and forced into a sexual liaison with a female alien being. The provocative story was withheld from public view, except for a pidgin-English account of it in a 1962 Brazilian UFO newsletter limited to its subscribers.

Not until May 1965 did Barney and Betty become aware of the "AVB" incident. (This would have been a year after the end of their hypnosis sessions.) I sent the couple and Dr. Simon copies of a *Flying Saucer Review* version (Creighton 1965) of the Brazilian abduction in order to point out, especially to Simon, certain similarities between the Villas Boas case and the Hill encounter. I also included the *FSR* piece in my August 1965 final Hill report. While Dr. Simon never replied (no surprise) after I sent out the *FSR* article, Betty responded in a June 1, 1965, letter (Hill 1965a). She proceeded to make comparisons between their experience and Villas Boas's. She also noted the differences, including the fact that "there was no girl present to my knowledge." Betty concluded by stating: "There is no doubt in my mind but this man had the same type of experience as Barney and I had."

Bullard has documented the history of UFO abduction reports in his paper (Chapter Three) and in several comprehensive surveys. He points out that, despite the enormous publicity accompanying the 1966 release of Fuller's book, additional stories of UFO capture were rarely reported until 1975. That year, on October 20, the Hill case burst upon the scene once again in an NBC-TV docudrama starring James Earl Jones and Estelle Parsons and called *The UFO Incident*.

Critics believe the 1975 NBC movie had much to do with generating other "copycat" abduction accounts that appeared later that year, including the Travis Walton episode. It should be noted, however, that while the Hill movie may have encouraged the reporting of these cases (as well as a number of episodes from prior years), at least some of the UFO kidnap incidents alleged to have happened in 1975 are known to have been reported in the months prior to the NBC telecast. For example, Moody's and Larson's initial reports were made in August 1975.

As the years rolled on and more and more UFO capture stories were reported, the prototypical Hill abduction scenario repeated itself in case after case and virtually in the same ordered sequence. Characteristically, this sequence begins with the approach of a disc-shaped craft or its occupants, described as short, big-eyed, gray-skinned humanoids. Exerting some form of mind control on the witness, the entities transport their captive into the craft. The abductee is placed on a table in an examination room where a medical exam is administered, with apparent emphasis on the genital area of the body. After communicating mind-to-mind with the human captive, he or she is returned to the original abduction site but with memory of the on-board experience blocked (the time lapse). Often abductees are plagued with both short-term and long-term aftereffects.

First utilized in the Hill case as a therapeutic tool – with unintended investigative benefits – hypnotic regression continues to be the method most commonly used to uncover details of the abductee's missing-time interval and to help mitigate associated anxieties produced by the abduction experience. Because of the risk of creating pseudomemories under hypnosis, it is important to consider that a surprising number of capture scenarios are recalled without the aid of hypnosis. In an examination of several studies using collections of well-documented abduction reports, I found that an average of about 30 percent of these scenarios – nearly one third – were said to be remembered naturally with no hypnosis employed (Bullard 1987: 322; Webb 1994: 198–202).

During the 1980s and 1990s – though the sequence of internal events in the abduction scenario remained essentially the same – Bullard indicates a number of changes in the stories. These comprised such situations as a capture location shift from outdoors to indoors; multiple abductions spanning an individual's lifetime; alien messages altered from warnings of nuclear destruction to ecological concerns; hybrid breeding; and implanted objects in the captive's body.

Proponents of UFO abductions as real objective events representing something new to science must concede that there still is no conclusive physical proof for these alleged occurrences (despite some claims to the contrary). Yet, as Bullard points out, abduction stories are incredibly consistent and have remained so over a time span of four decades. Not only are the same elements – first brought to the world's attention by the Hill affair – still being reported, but these components follow the same order time after time, regardless of the storytellers or any potential influence from investigators. Given the opportunity for creative variation in abduction accounts, spurred by Hollywood's and television's fictional portrayals of aliens, "variants should be many if fantasy lends a hand in formulating these narratives, yet variants are few" (Bullard 1995). Moreover, abduction stories often contain recurrent insignificant details unlikely to catch another narrator's attention. Some abductees who have never met relate identical details that have never been made public by investigators so as to help authenticate these experiences.

Most psychological studies of abductees show these individuals as more or less normal personalities except for symptoms of post-traumatic stress disorder (PTSD) as a consequence of their emotionally disturbing encounters. According to Bullard, "abductees seem more like normal people troubled by a strange experience than like troubled people subject to strange fantasies."

From my personal observations, both Barney and Betty matched the above profile – normal responsible individuals who were forced to confront a bizarre and frightening unknown event, which led to stressful post-encounter effects. Even 40 years later, I believe Betty's somewhat eccentric behavior toward the UFO subject demonstrated her continuing struggle with the effects of her original experience.

If by this point I haven't made my position clear on what happened to the Hills that September night in 1961, permit me to clarify the matter now. At the time of my final report to NICAP, I felt that the New Hampshire witnesses *were* telling the truth with respect to the first encounter along Route 3. Strange though their story was, I nonetheless was quite impressed by their testimony, particularly Barney's understated, measured, reasoned response to the experience. Without his credible corroboration, I doubt that I would have accepted the story as genuine. Also the couple had a lot to lose by concocting such a fantastic tale. Both had been active politically. During the 1960s Barney held county and state appointments in civil rights and poverty programs.

In 1965 I was less certain about the second encounter or abduction phase but could not rule out the possibility that it might in fact have occurred. On the other hand, I was far from convinced by Dr. Simon's dream hypothesis. Though some of Barney's hypnotic recall might have emerged strictly through hearing Betty repeat her dreams, he also reported features of the experience that happened uniquely to him and not to Betty. The Hills' hypnotic testimony appeared nicely to fill in their amnesic time lapses, linking both conscious and "forgotten" aspects of the episode into a logical continuum – from first encounter through capture sequence through restoration of awareness. And Barney and Betty's gut-wrenching hypnotic responses to the presence of their nonhuman captors strongly suggested a real objective event.

For some time I have believed compelling circumstantial evidence exists supporting an extraterrestrial origin for the residue of UFO sightings not explained as misidentified known objects and phenomena. When the evidence is carefully and objectively sifted, the residue, in my judgment, points to a totally unique phenomenon indicative of intelligent activity. I feel that the probability is high that the Barney and Betty Hill case represents a genuine physical abduction by extraterrestrial visitors to our planet.

This belief is based not only upon my own firsthand investigation into the principals and their accounts, but also upon my 50 years of experience researching UFO sightings, commencing with my own anomalous observation and encompassing interviews with witnesses in some 50 close-encounter episodes.

Some Final Words

Until the scientific community at large recognizes the UFO topic as something worthy of professional study (an inquiry that quite frankly is long overdue), the burden must fall on citizen investigators and a few courageous professional researchers to scrutinize this stubborn enigma.

In order to bolster support for future scientific inquiries, UFO investigators need to exercise much more care in documenting their cases. This is especially true for abduction investigators.

The task facing the abduction researcher is formidable, starting with the fact that the majority of these types of experiences involve critical delays in being reported. The reasons center upon the abductee's partial or total amnesia of the experience or, if remembered, an unwillingness to reveal the incident for fear of ridicule. Therefore, the age of many abduction accounts, along with the vagaries of human perception, memory, and testimony, inflicts severe penalties upon attempts at carrying out truly scientific probes into such claims. And so the goal remains to always investigate a UFO kidnap story – indeed any UFO report – as soon as possible, while memories still are fresh.

It is extremely important to record the witness's conscious memories of a UFO experience *before* considering hypnotic procedures. If careful guidelines are followed, I believe hypnotic regression can be a beneficial adjunct in exploring close UFO encounters and abduction stories, especially multiple-witness accounts. The investigator, however, must be aware at all times of the entranced subject's suggestive state, conscientiously avoiding leading questions or inadvertent cues. And the process demands a very cautious interpretation of the elicited information.

For an abduction case investigation to be of potential use someday to science, *everything* must be documented throughout the probe, including keeping a log, tapes of witness interviews, transcripts of taped hypnosis sessions, witness drawings, photographs, correspondence, background character responses, and records of tests performed or physical traces found.

Ideally, obtaining the witness's psychosocial and medical histories should be part of every abduction investigation. Perhaps with grant assistance or other funding, professional analysts can assist in this phase by administering personality tests and employing the polygraph to help in appraising the truthfulness of the witness's story. And since confirmatory physical evidence as yet is missing in abduction cases, the investigator must be alert to any prospect of discovering and substantiating reports of UFO-associated injuries, implants, residues, ground traces, and the like. Any such legitimate finds, of course, should receive the highest priority and be carefully protected until analysed by trustworthy authorities.

Finally, abduction researchers and mental health professionals need to become familiar with clinically recognized phenomena that resemble some elements reported in abduction experiences. Among these masquerading phenomena is a relatively common but little studied syndrome – sleep paralysis imagery.

With now more than half of UFO abduction events alleged to begin in a bedroom setting, knowledge of sleep paralysis (SP) is vital. Those who suffer SP attacks frequently describe symptoms akin to bedroom UFO entity reports – sensations of feeling fully awake, being unable to move, sensing a presence in the room, feeling pressure on parts of the body, and floating. The "presence" sometimes assumes a visual form, most often dark and shadowy but occasionally more sharply defined as a humanoid shape with large dark or red eyes.

Studies now suggest that SP may strike up to 40 percent of the general population at least once in a person's lifetime. The phenomenon's frequency has serious and troubling implications for the increasing numbers of UFO alien encounters being reported in the bedroom. This is not to say that SP hallucinations can explain multiple-witness "visitor" encounters, outdoor abductions, entity episodes with physical traces, or even all bedroom intrusions. (The claimed durations of UFO abductions exceed the very short periods of most SP events.) But such imagery may resolve some of the simplest indoor experiences in which bedroom entities are "observed" by a single witness. In worst-case scenarios, investigators might unknowingly support a witness's belief in an alien visitor intrusion when in fact the cause is sleep-related hallucinatory activity.

The problem of SP imagery is recognized in an excellent guide for UFO investigators and mental health professionals working with those reporting abduction experiences. The "Ethics Code for Abduction Experience Investigation and Treatment" was developed by a committee formed at the landmark Abduction Study Conference held at MIT in 1992 (Gotlib et al. 1994). This document should be in the hands of all abduction investigators and scrupulously followed in their inquiries.

References

Bullard, Thomas E. 1987. *UFO Abductions: The measure of a mystery*. Mt Rainier (USA): Fund for UFO Research.
Bullard, Thomas E. 1995. *The Sympathetic Ear: Investigators as Variables in UFO Abduction Reports*. Mt. Rainier, Md.: Fund for UFO Research.
Creighton, Gordon. 1965. "The Most Amazing Case of All." Part I. *Flying Saucer Review* 11, no. 1: 13-17.
Fuller, John G. 1966. *The Interrupted Journey*. New York: Dial Press.
Gotlib, David, Stuart Appelle, Georgia Flamburis, and Mark Rodeghier. 1994. "Ethics Code for Abduction Experience Investigation and Treatment." *Journal of UFO Studies*, n.s. 5: 55-81. (J. Allen Hynek Center for UFO Studies).
Hall, Richard. 1961a. Letter to Walter N. Webb, October 17, 1961.
Hall, Richard. 1961b. Letter to Mrs. Barney Hill, October 17, 1961.
Hill, Betty & Barney. 1961. Letter to Walter Webb, November 27, 1961.
Hill, Betty & Barney. 1965a. Letter to Walter Webb, June 1, 1965.
Hill, Betty & Barney. 1965b. Letter to Walter Webb, August 23, 1965.
Hill, Betty & Barney. 1965c. Letter to Walter Webb, September 22, 1965.
Keyhoe, Donald E. 1955. *The Flying Saucer Conspiracy*. New York: Henry Holt & Co.
Keyhoe, Donald E., and Lore, Gordon I.R. Jr, (eds). 1969. *Strange Effects from UFOs*. Washington: National Investigations Committee on Aerial Phenomena.
Luttrell, John H. 1965. "Did THEY Seize Couple?" *Boston Traveler*, October 25-29, 1965.
Oswald, John P. 1987. Letter in *MUFON UFO Journal*, June 1987: 17–18.
Rodeghier, Mark. 1981. *UFO Reports Involving Vehicle Interference: a Catalogue and Data Analysis*. Evanston, Ill.: Center for UFO Studies.
Webb, David F. 1994. "The Use of Hypnosis in Abduction Cases." In Pritchard, Andrea *et al.* (eds), *Alien Discussions*. Cambridge, Mass.: North Cambridge Press.
Webb, Walter N. 1961a. "A Dramatic UFO Encounter in the White Mountains, N.H., September 19-20, 1961." Cambridge, Mass.: by the author. (Report to the National Investigations Committee on Aerial Phenomena, October 26, 1961).
Webb, Walter N. 1961b. Letter to Richard Hall, November 4, 1961.
Webb, Walter N. 1962. *Program PM*, WBZ Radio, Boston, Mass., August 21, 1962. (Bob Kennedy, host; audiocassette copy from reel-to-reel tape).
Webb, Walter N. 1965a. "A Dramatic UFO Encounter in the White Mountains, New Hampshire: The Hill Case September 19-20, 1961." Cambridge, Mass.: by the author. (Final report to NICAP, August 30, 1965).
Webb, Walter N. 1965b. Letter to Richard Hall, September 17, 1965.
Webb, Walter N. 1972. Supplement to final report to NICAP, May 29, 1972.
Webb, Walter N. 1974. "An Analysis of the Fish Model." *The APRO Bulletin* 23, No. 2 (September-October): 8-9; No. 3 (November-December): 3-7. (Aerial Phenomena Research Organization).
Webb, Walter N. 1975. Ibid. *Pursuit* 8, No. 3 (July): 55-62. (Society for the Investigation of the Unexplained).
Webb, Walter N. 1976. Ibid. Chapter 7 of *Encounters with UFO Occupants* (Coral & Jim Lorenzen, eds). New York: Berkley Medallion.
Webb, Walter N. 1994a. *Encounter at Buff Ledge: A UFO Case History*. Chicago: J. Allen Hynek Center for UFO Studies.

Webb, Walter N. 1994b. "Postscript to the Hill Case." Letter in *International UFO Reporter* 19, No. 6: 6. J. (Allen Hynek Center for UFO Studies).

Walter N. Webb has been involved in UFO research for over half a century, following his own sighting in 1951. During that time, he has been associated with four national UFO organizations, three of them as an astronomy consultant and the other as a senior research associate, and served on the conference committee for the Abduction Study Conference held at MIT in 1992. Over the years, he has interviewed several hundred UFO witnesses, utilizing his professional background in science to interpret the phenomena reported. He holds a degree in biology from Ohio's Mount Union College, but a continuing interest in astronomy developed into a career. He served under the late J. Allen Hynek, founder of the Center for UFO Studies, in the Smithsonian Astrophysical Observatory's Optical Satellite Tracking Program (1957-58), where among other things he tracked the world's first artificial earth satellites. Subsequently, he spent 32 years at Boston's Charles Hayden Planetarium as senior lecturer, assistant director, and operations manager. Walter Webb lives in Westwood, Massachusetts.

Appendix

"No One Should Know of This Experience"
Paradoxes, ironies and contradictions in the Hill abduction story

Martin S. Kottmeyer

In Betty Hill's notes describing her dreams of being abducted, she tells the leader of the saucer crew that her experience has been "so unbelievable" and, implying she might talk about it, says that "no one would ever believe me... they would think I had lost my mind." What she needs is absolute proof that the experience happened. She looks around the room and finds a large book. The leader lets her take it, and she thanks him. She is happy even when she realizes the symbols look unreadable. It is her absolute proof. As she leaves the craft, however, one of the crew evidently notices the book and there is an excited conversation. The leader finds he is forced to take the book back. Betty objects that this is her only proof. While he saw no harm in her having it, the majority feeling among the crew was that "no one should know of this experience." They decide they will also take her memory. She gets angry and vows she will remember somehow. The leader laughs and agrees she might, but he would do his best to prevent this, since this was their final decision. Whether she forgot or not, no one would believe her (Fuller, 1966: 349).

A Book of Puzzles

Everyone familiar with the history of UFO experiences knows that aliens have a poor record at predicting the future (Kottmeyer, 1998). Their failure to foresee Betty would be believed is, from that perspective, not much of a surprise. Yet, there are surely puzzles and irony here. Though they took back the book, the story of her encounter became a book. My Dell paperback of *The Interrupted Journey*, bought back in 1966, sported a red-lettered description of it as "One of the most fascinating bestsellers of the decade." The journalistic truism comes to mind – the big mistake is trying to cover things up. Would people much care about such things as a poorly executed medical exam if it weren't for the fact that aliens tried to make a secret of it? Great numbers of people paid money to read her book. Odds are the aliens' own book would have been a dud in the market. The fact that the leader was willing to let his copy go, I take as a bad omen of its value.

Stranger, though, is the fact that the leader finds himself in disagreement with the crew over the matter. Saucers had been flying around our world for at least a decade with no open declaration of their intentions. One would think the clandestine nature of their operations was understood by all involved. Most assuredly a leader should have an understanding of the policy regarding the parameters of what can be revealed and what cannot. So how does this scene come to happen? The leader should not have any question in his mind over the matter of Betty not having any proof. When she asked about the book, then was the time to declare firmly it was of no concern to him whether she has proof or appears crazy. It would be unfortunate for her, but that was the way things were going to be.

Regard it as a puzzle, too, that our leader puts himself in a position where his authority was challenged by the crew. When one thinks of the military, we have the impression that orders are orders and nobody second-guesses the people up the chain of command. At minimum, you don't do it to their faces and you never do it in front of others. Barney remarked, early on, that he felt the leader was a capable person who behaved like the group had business to attend to – "there can be no nonsense here" (Fuller, 1966: 67). Yet, letting Betty have the book was a bit of nonsense. The leader should have known better and the crew must correct him about it. Bit of an embarrassment, you would think. This might be possible, but it doesn't sound likely, does it?

The Sound of Memory Control

How the saucer crew intended to make Betty and Barney forget is an even thornier paradox. Given the chemical nature of memory, the method of choice one would think would be the injection of a chemical that interferes with the short-term memory buffers. This would mean that the memories will be unable to be processed into the long-term memory. (Siegel, 1989: 242-3). Throughout the book, however, people link the forgetting to a pair of beeping noises. Her dreams shortly after the encounter end with the observation. "Then we heard the beeping on the car again, and I thought, good luck, good-by, and I am going to forget about you. If you want me to forget, I will, and I will not talk." Her letter to Keyhoe of September 26, 1961, mentions this noise: "As we started to move, we heard several buzzing or beeping sounds which seemed to be striking the trunk of our car. We did not observe this object leaving, but we did not see it again, although about thirty miles further south we were again bombarded by those same beeping noises…There does not appear to be any damage to our car from the beeping sounds" (Fuller, 1966: 47).

Elsewhere in the book, though, she does wonder if some dozen or so shiny circles she finds all over the trunk are connected (Fuller, 1966: 39). To an Air Force investigator the beep is described as "sounding like someone had dropped a tuning fork" (Fuller, 1966: 47). To Dr. Simon, Barney said the second beeping occurred just as he tells Betty not to be ridiculous when she asks him if he believed now in flying saucers. He "heard a beeping and the car buzzed, and I kept silent." He thought he felt a vibration when he touched the steering wheel with his fingertips. As it continues he slows down and stops. He said he asked Betty, "Is there something shifting in the car?" Delsey, their dog, reacted to the sound by pricking up her ears (Fuller, 1966: 158-60).

Betty confirmed to Simon that she heard and felt the whole car vibrate a little. She initially wondered if it was an electrical signal, Morse code maybe. Continuing the electrical line of thought she wondered if there was perhaps a shock hazard. When she touched the metal, however, nothing happened (Fuller, 1966: 182-4). Barney tried to reproduce the sound by experimenting with the speed of the car, braking, swerving (Fuller, 1966: 182-4). Simon wondered about the possibility of the beeping come from the radio (the 1957 Chevrolet Bel Air Hard Top, the type driven in the case, is a model that can have rear stereo speakers, which could account for the trunk direction), but Barney firmly denies the possibility, saying he never had it on when driving (Fuller, 1966: 159). According to Fuller, the Hills concluded after therapy that the initial beeps "put them in a trance-like state." The second set of beeps "seemed to restore them to consciousness," albeit they remained dazed throughout the rest of the trip home

(Fuller, 1966: 217).

Some ufologists concurred in that interpretation. The Lorenzens wrote, "So it is more possible that the beeping sounds set up some type of control by which the Hills were guided to the spot where they were taken aboard the ship. The same type of beeping sounds which were heard hours later when they came out of their somnambulistic state in the car could have been a release from 'control'" (Lorenzen, 1967: 80-1). They expand on this in a later book: "This naturally sounds like the rankest kind of science fiction; nevertheless, in view of what is known about the human brain, the device apparently used by UFO occupants to lure humans or control them may merely be a device which, when we thoroughly understand the brain, could be devised and used by us. It has been learned that the brain is nothing more or less than a very complex computer through which electrical impulses are constantly flowing. Could it, then, be affected by, for instance, a magnetic field?" (Lorenzen, 1968: 206-7). Hans Holzer took the same line a few years later: "Obviously, they had been put under hypnosis by the aliens through an electrohypnotic device, not unlike some of the devices in use among human hypnotists, except that we prefer optical devices to sound apparatus" (Holzer, 1976: 131).

Holzer's comment is precious precisely because it admits what it denies. Hypnotic devices usually invoke the visual senses and are indeed unlike what is being proposed. The rhythmic induction process tends to involve watching pendulums or candles or shiny things go back and forth. The hypno-disc involves watching a slowly spinning spiral. The usual auditory input only has the hypnotist reinforcing the rhythmicity with a soft sing-song voice. If anybody uses beeps to induce hypnosis, it is little known. The notion that a second set of beeps would restore consciousness and release control of the subject is unlike earthly hypnosis also. A snap of the fingers or a sharp clap 'awakens' the subject from the trance. In the interest of causal consistency, a second set of beeps should induce a second episode of hypnosis, not break a trance.

Lorenzen's and Holzer's discussions also toy with the notion that Barney was controlled in part by the eyes of the leader and that is why his trance seemed deeper. This however highlights a striking disparity between Betty and Barney's regressions. Barney puts much emphasis on the eyes and their magical qualities – their "burning into his senses," their existing unconnected to a body, their ability to talk to him (Fuller, 1966: 300, 124, 126). Betty however experiences nothing like this. In the dream, she almost casually notes the "eyes were very dark, possibly black" (Fuller, 1966: 344). But there is nothing else. The regression by Simon adds a new detail:

"And the examiner opens my eyes, and looks in them with a light" (Fuller, 1966: 193). But he moves on to the mouth, throat, teeth, and ear, with no emphasis. There seems to be no special reason to think Betty's amnesia was in any way connected to the magical eyes of the aliens. This is a troubling incongruity if one hopes to fit the case in with modern cases where alien eyes bode large for their supernatural abilities to control all aspects of the human mind and body, notably in those of David Jacobs and his thinking about mindscan (Jacobs, 1998: 83-7). Too bad also for abduction apologists that Barney's descriptions of the eyes do not show them to be all-black, as in present cases of mindscan. Betty also indicates the eyes "had pupils...I had a feeling they were more like cat's eyes" (Fuller, 1966: 309).

Other UFO cases are not much help in understanding the beeping sounds. Though there are dozens of missing-time cases subsequent to the Hill case, they rarely seem to link the amnesia to a beeping sound. I suppose apologists will tell us the aliens opted for a new method of induction. They surely either realized the method was a spectacular failure or they needed to cover their tracks. This is not to say beeping never happened in other types of UFO cases.

On May 18, 1964, a ten-year-old named Mike Bizon of Hubbard, Oregon saw a bright silvery object, 3 meters long, 1.5 meters high, with a cone-shaped front part, resting on four legs, in a wheat field. It made a beeping noise, rose first to the altitude of telephone poles, then took off vertically. Wheat was found flattened in all directions (Vallée, 1969: *Magonia* catalog #606). Four students working on a farm near Cherry Creek, New York noted radio interference and a peculiar "beeping sound," then saw an object at low altitude. It was shaped like two saucers glued together, had a shiny chrome-like surface, diameter of 15 meters, height of 6 meters, and left a trail and smell of burned gasoline. It rose straight up into the clouds, which were illuminated with green light. Five minutes later it came down again over a wooded area, rose, and finally flew off to the southwest. Some animal effects were noted: a barking dog and milk production in cows markedly decreased (*Magonia* catalog #684). Neither of this pair mentions any missing time or abduction, and the UFOs don't resemble or even behave like the UFO in the Hill case.

In 1993 we finally get another case of an abduction with beeping and missing time. K.O. talks about how he is recording some strange beeping sound that appears to be coming from a cattle barn north of their house. They saw a light shoot behind them from the west, heading southwest. This light turned a deep, blood red before it shot out of sight. Back in the house, K.O. and another person reviewed what happened and realized there was some time missing – and several minutes of video, too. It's interesting to some degree, though we aren't told if there is a second set of beeps or if there are sensations of vibration nor even if there was an alien experience underlying the amnesia. According to the author, "To this day we still aren't sure what happened to the rest of the time – or to us" (Jordan & Mitchell, 1994: 300-1). Some sources allege there were beeping sounds in the Herbert Schirmer abduction (McCampbell, 1976: 53-4). Transcripts and other sources do not bear out this contention (Norman, 1973: 141-62).

An Alien Owl

Roy Craig of the Condon investigation visited Washington state in May 1967 to look into reports of strange beeping at treetop level with no visible source. They were described as unearthly. Amateur ornithologists stated the sounds were definitely not those of any bird, and officials felt they were electronically generated. Because of similar reports of strange beeping sounds received by the project, it was decided to check it out. A Civil Defense person briefed him and he subsequently interviewed the ear-witnesses and some who had seen flying objects. The accounts of sightings were vague and generally inconsistent. One technician reported radio interference in conjunction with a beeping event. An instrumented field trip to record the beepers at a site by a tree where it was regularly heard almost every night did not get results though faint sounds in the distance were briefly heard. A guide told them that a young boy climbed a tree on one occasion there was beeping there. The source of the sound seemed to leave the tree and circle around still beeping. The boy saw nothing in the darkness. It seemed rather bird-like to the investigator and he made the mistake of making a flippant comment in the morning. "The bird didn't show." One of his companions took offense and accused him: "You're calling it a BIRD!" They go to another site the next night and there are several cars there. Locals were tramping through the woods. Some with guns. The next morning they make contact with the Skagit County sheriff who was handling a local investigation of the sounds. They learn he had been handed a dead saw-whet owl that was said to have been shot down after the field party left. The man said he lived on the edge of the woods and shot the owl to get rid of all the people milling around his yard. There were no further reports. He adds that the end of the beeping also coincided with the end of the owl-mating season (Craig, 1995: 3-13). The particular owl that was shot was rather unlucky, for he was going to stop anyway. Audio recordings made before and during the investigation were analysed sonographically and compared to recorded bird calls of pygmy, saw-whet, and ferruginous owls from both Peterson's *Field Guide to Western Bird Calls* and recordings from Cornell University's Laboratory of Ornithology. The sound structure matched those of saw-whet owls (Gillmor, 1969: 310).

An investigation into a beeping UFO seen at close range near Bragg Creek, Alberta, Canada in 1968, found that tapes of the sound were similar to a Pygmy Owl though the ornithologist remarked he had never heard one beep so regularly. The investigators felt this made the solution inconclusive but allow it is possible the "presence of the UFO caused a resident Pygmy or Saw-whet Owl to become excited and make beeping sounds" (Regan & Williams, 1997: 177-93).

Such findings had me gravitating to the notion that owls were somehow also involved in the Hill case, pointing to a detail where it is stated they did not hear the beeps until they were "in the woods" (Fuller, 1966: 160). Reading things again however caused me to ponder the detail of their accounts where both felt vibrations associated with the beeping-buzzing sound. Just before the noise began, Barney had ripped off the binoculars and in near hysteria ran back to the car. He "jammed the car into first gear, spurted off down the road" (Fuller, 1966: 32).

What Were the Beeps?

Let's propose this scenario. Upon spurting off, a spray of small rocks is kicked up by the tires. One of the rocks gets wedged between a pair of surfaces that are moving relative to each other. This could be the gap between the rolling brake drum and the stationary brake unit; perhaps in the gap by the rim or inside wedged in front of the brake shoe. Alternatively, the rock could be caught within or behind the universal joint next to the rear axle. The rock abrades and vibrates between the metal surfaces creating the buzz or beeping. Perhaps the hollow of the drive shaft contributes to the sense of a tuning fork sound. It abrades smooth and the noise ceases for a while, but then shifts and it starts up again. When Barney stops, the rock gets a solid grip on the surfaces and cracks apart upon slightly rolling back. The pieces fall away and nothing remains to reproduce the noise when Barney experiments later. Variations on this scenario may also exist, but this seems the more probable form of explanation among several considered.

But what of the presence of the flying saucer? In fact, there was no saucer sighted when the second set of beeps was heard. The assumption that the saucer was causing the noise should probably be discounted from that fact alone. The assumption of a causal connection may only reflect a reasoning based on analogy. In 1957 Russia had sent up a spacecraft called

Sputnik that made headlines as the first orbital satellite. It sent out a beeping signal to aid in its tracking. If it beeps, it must be space-related – maybe the unstated logic. This was an equation reinforced by movies. The cue-ball-like alien satellite in *Attack of the 50 Foot Woman* (1958) was among the first to have beeping sound effects associated with it.

This however leaves us a bit of a vacuum concerning how the aliens made Betty and Barney forget. If the beeping noise was irrelevant, what did they do it with? Not their eyes, given that Betty was little impressed by them. Not injections – I doubt Betty's needle in the navel counts here – and Barney didn't seem to get one. There's nothing about helmets being put over their heads as happened in several abductions (Bullard, 1987: 87, 101). Their brains weren't taken out and put back in as happened in the Sandra Larson case (Lorenzen, 1977: 59). If it was done with some sort of long-range amnesia ray, there was evidently no visual beam associated with it. Mind altering rays are usually visible in other UFO cases like those of the Stanford brothers, Eugenia Siragusa and Chuck Doyle (Kottmeyer, 1994). Interesting trick if that amnesia ray can work through a car body, but if it must, it must. Actually though, it didn't – at least not very well – for, we are told, the memories welled up in Betty's dreams and Barney's regression.

Drama and Dream Logic

And here we come up against another problem. Is there any compelling reason to believe Betty's dreams actually represent an experience deleted from her awareness? There is of course no doubt that dreams do utilize material forgotten by the dreamer. Strumpell avers the depths of memory in dreams extend to people, things, and events from the earliest times that "never possessed any psychical importance or more than a slight degree of vividness" (Freud, 1965: 49). Volkelt agrees: "Dreams are continually reminding us of things which we have ceased to think of and which have long ceased to be important to us" (Freud, 1965: 50). This cuts slant from the thrust however. Hildebrandt remarks, dreams often by-pass stirring, powerful, compelling and major events for their material, preferring worthless fragments of the recently experienced. A family bereavement that occupies all one's waking thoughts can be blotted from memory in favor of thoughts of the wart on a stranger's forehead. Dreams, even vivid dreams, are virtually never undistorted replays of some memory videotape of prior experience. As Strumpell remarks: "Dreams do not reproduce experiences. They take one step forward, but the next step in the chain is omitted, or appears in altered form, or is replaced by something entirely extraneous. Dreams yield no more than fragments of reproductions; and this is so general a rule that theoretical conclusions may be based on it." When it actually happens, it is exceptional (Freud, 1965: 54).

The material in Betty's dreams contains a number of elements that seem unreal. I direct attention to the dramatic high point involving the alien examiner picking up a very long needle and inserting it with "a sudden thrust." The examiner had said it would be "a very simple test, with no pain" (Fuller, 1966: 346). But it does cause pain – "great pain, twisting and moaning." The examiner "looked very startled." The leader waved his hand in front of her eyes and "immediately the pain is completely gone." Betty is grateful and "lost all fear of him." He says they didn't know she would suffer pain from this test or they would not have done it.

The obvious question is how could they not know thrusting a needle into someone's belly would cause pain? Are they total idiots? We can't say the aliens have no experience with the concept of pain for they tell her beforehand to expect none. Similarly, how would the leader know to wave his hands to remove the pain? And that brings us to the puzzle of why does this pain-removal procedure work? Waving one's hands over a person's eyes to remove great pain is not going to work in the real world. This seems borrowed from the stage magician's handbook – the trance induction gimmick placed on the lady about to be sawed in half. This is dream logic at work. It is also worth comment that many people would express outrage that the examiner lied about the test not causing pain. Betty, instead, is grateful and loses all fear. I accept this is a plausible first reaction, yet it seems curious she does not come back to this violation of trust later. Specifically, what woman would ignore the chance to bring back the incident when the book is being taken back? The creeps thrust a damn needle in her belly and they can't give her a book at least in consolation for the suffering she had to endure? (Men, I'm sure, know what I'm getting at; regardless of what ladies may feign to overlook.) Instead, "I said that I was very happy about meeting him, and honored, and thanked him for being kind" (Fuller, 1966: 349).

There will be comments on other unreal things as we go along, but this will form our pretext for inquiring into terrestrial origins of the dream. The medical character of the dream is easy enough to understand when we recall events in the days leading up to the dreams. Betty had become concerned that she and her husband might have been exposed to radiation from the flying saucer. It was common knowledge that there was a possibility that nuclear engines powered saucers. Encounter sites were routinely gone over with Geiger counters in the 1950s on the basis of that suspicion.

Betty discussed her fear of contamination with her sister who, in turn, contacted someone described in the Fuller book as a physicist – probably not – who suggests an ordinary compass might detect radiation if it showed disturbance on contact with the car's surface.

Finding a compass, Betty rushed out into the rain and ran the compass along the wet side of the car. At first there was no effect, but then she saw some shiny circles on the car, each the size of a silver dollar. At that moment, she recalled that the beeping noise they heard the previous night came from the direction of the trunk. Placing the compass on one the spots, the needle wavered. "She almost panicked, but got control of herself" (Fuller, 1966: 39). She tried it again and the needle went out of control. She eventually gets Barney to do the test, but he didn't think anything abnormal was going on and suggests the compass was just reacting to the metal of the car. But the test convinced her. This left her haunted by the realization she and her husband had been contaminated (Fuller, 1966: 40).

The circles on the trunk echo a UFO case from the 1957 Sputnik UFO flap. Mildred Wetzel at that time was reported to have pockmarks on the car that were tested with a Geiger counter and showed radioactivity. (Michel, 1958: 254). This may be some sort of folkloric cousin to the sociologically notorious Seattle Windshield Pitting Epidemic when people started to connect windshield-pits to fallout from a nuclear test (Medalia, Nahum, Larsen, 1958). Commentators dismiss the notion that a compass could detect radioactivity. Barney probably had it right. Normal magnetism in the metal could probably explain a compass needle wavering off magnetic north. A needle out of control might signify other things, but this is of no consequence here. The important point is this. Regardless of the test's validity, Betty feared she had been exposed to radioactive contamination.

Memories, Dreams and Medicine

Let's consider the medical parts of Betty's dream. The examiner asks her name. They discuss what vegetables are. She tries to tell him about meat and milk, but their meaning elude him. "My hair was closely examined, and he removed a few strands and then cut a larger piece on the back left-hand side. I was not able to see what he used for cutting purposes." He looks down her throat. He looks in her ears and collects wax. He examines the hands and fingernails and takes a piece of the fingernail. Next, a look at the feet. "They showed much interest in my skin…" An apparatus gives them a magnified look at it. Then one scrapes a letter opener-like instrument along the arm.

A machine is pulled over with wires that each end in a needle. The needle is touched to points all over her body. It is a test of her nervous system. Sometimes it made a limb jerk or twitch. "Both men were highly interested in this test." Then comes the pregnancy test. A needle is inserted into her navel with a sudden thrust. There is great pain. The examiners are startled and the leader "waved his hand in front of my eyes. Immediately the pain was completely gone, and I relaxed." The test ends and they discuss things for awhile, but then the examiner returns to look at her teeth to see if they are removable. Barney wore dentures and they were amazed they were removable. Discussion resumes with stuff like the star map, but there are no more medical matters.

One can hardly deny the differences to typical doctor's exams are more striking than the few similarities. John Altschuler notes that skin scrapings are done to look for bacterial infections or fungus, but generally they are not done at all. Ditto for nail scrapings. He notes some speak of DNA sampling to determine genetic type, but he doubts it would be a rich source of DNA. John Miller concurs and adds, "I don't know what it means" (Pritchard, 1994: 196). Richard Hall correctly notes Betty Hill's was the first case of this procedure. Hair samples are somewhat atypical although it might tell one some things about the diet of the person over time. Where's the blood sample, the urine sample?

One should regard these things in the context of Betty's fear she had been contaminated by radiation from the UFO. In the 1950s, the medical consequences of nuclear fallout were given international prominence in the wake of a test called Project Bravo. On March 1, 1954 the U.S. detonated an atomic bomb on the Bikini atoll of the Marshall Islands. Fallout ash descended on a Japanese fishing boat called the *Lucky Dragon*. Most the crew of 23 fell ill with nausea, pain, and skin inflammation. Doctors in Tokyo examined the men, cross-checking data with the medical experiences gained from Hiroshima. They were confused however by the presence of residual radioactivity. "Even after hair cuts, nail-clippings, and a thorough scrubbing, the fishermen retained radioactivity on their skin" (Radnet, 1999).

Newsreels of Marshall Islanders being examined after Project Bravo contain one image demonstrating the nature of hair loss caused by the contamination. An examiner gently pulls a clump of several strands of hair from the head. No scissors or other implement is used. Only two fingers are used. Another image, said to be of skin lesions, shows patches of depigmentation on the arm of a native. The image allows an impression that layers of skin had been peeled or scraped off. (The relevant newsreel clips appear in the documentary *Race for the Superbomb* aired January 11, 1999, on PBS's *The American Experience*.) The procedures of hair sampling, nail cutting, skin inspection, and skin scraping evident in the medical encounters of Marshall Islanders with doctors studying radioactive fallout echo the procedures of Betty's examiners.

The needles run over Betty's body have their obvious analogue in the compass needle run over the car. The reactions of twitching are interpretable as nervous anxiety over the results of the compass needle test.

The pregnancy test has multiple interpretations. First, fallout was known to cause mutations and fetal deformities from the experience in Hiroshima. Pregnancy would be undesirable and of high concern. The navel could be metaphorically a match to the circular pockmark on the car truck and the pain of Betty and the startled examiner would reflect fear of death coupled with the disbelief she experienced from Barney.

Vegetables, meat, and especially milk were all things that possessed hazards of contamination from fallout. In the *Lucky Dragon* incident, tuna was warehoused while the officials pondered the issue of whether the contamination was bad enough to prevent selling it. Milk was widely feared because of tests that showed the presence of strontium-90. With vegetables, the question was whether washing them would be enough to remove the danger of fallout. The fact that the meaning of these foods eludes the understanding of the alien could be taken to indicate a crude form of denial or cover-up analogous to governmental behavior of downplaying radiation dangers is being played upon.

The earwax sample and the foot exam presumably derive from other material in Betty's experience. If anyone wishes to consider them evidence in favor of an alien procedure, it would be nice to know what purpose they serve. The mouth exam may be an intrusion of more normal medical procedures into the dream or perhaps is a set-up for the comic moment of the aliens amazed over Barney's dentures. This moment is another of those details that seems doubtful for aliens presumed to have been around for a decade studying humankind. There is a good possibility it points to a story that made the wire services in January 1950 – the Koehler retrieval yarn.

Among the features of interest are these details: "Medical reports, according to (Koehler), showed that these men were almost identical with earth-dwelling humans, except for a few minor differences. They were of uniform height of three feet, were uniformly blond, beardless and their teeth were completely free of fillings or cavities. They were dressed in uniform clothing made from blue material unknown on earth, the threads in the clothing seeming to be sort of wire. The jackets had six buttons, and the trousers were tight-fitting. The shoes were of a slip-on type. They did not wear undergarments, but had their bodies taped. [Koehler] said that it was a matter of speculation whether this was the customary garb of these people, or whether these were 'space suits' or flying suits" (Steinman, 1986: 104). The article also notes the ships seemed to be magnetically controlled and powered and seemed to invariably crash near radar stations, possibly because radar attracted them or interfered with their control systems. The cabin was stationary within a large and rapidly-rotating ring and "was constructed of a metal resembling aluminum." Koehler had acquired a clock or automatic calendar from one of the crafts. On the face of it was "an indentation, which, rotating around the disc, completed a cycle each 28 days, lunar month." He felt it had to have come from Venus; it having a similar atmosphere to ours and "magnetic properties that would make it the logical home base of these space ships" (Steinman, 1986: 104). When Keyhoe met face-to-face with Koehler after the tale began spreading, he observed he had none of the artifacts on hand – everything being analysed "somewhere else" – and Keyhoe sensed Koehler was hugely enjoying himself. Keyhoe felt it was a gag, and learned a while later from a Chicago paper that he confessed to Associated Press that it was a big joke (Keyhoe, 1950: 165-6).

Comparing the Stories

The similarities to Betty's dreams are several. "The men were all dressed alike, presumably in uniform, of a light navy blue color with a gray shade in it. They wore trousers and short jackets, that gave the appearance of zippered sports jackets, but I am not aware of zippers or buttons or closing. Shoes were a low, slip-on style, resembling a boot. I cannot remember any jewelry, or insignia. They were all wearing military caps, similar to the Air Force, but not so broad on top. They were very human in their appearance, not frightening" (Fuller, 1966: 344). The main differences are their size – 5 ft to 5 ft 4 in – rather than 3 ft, black hair instead of blond, and the buttons.

They are surprised and confused by Barney's dentures, a nice detail that you might expect from aliens with perfect teeth. The interior of the craft was of metal construction "like stainless steel or aluminum." In the regression, there is a segment where Betty tries to explain the concepts of age and confronts mystification. "What is a year?" She gets into the idea of days, hours, and minutes and shows him her watch, but "he did not understand" (Fuller, 1966: 210). This is possibly related to the different conceptions of measuring time inherent in the clock described by Koehler.

This detail was quickly paralleled in the March 28, 1950, Samuel Easton Thompson encounter with nudist Venusians. During a pair of interviews with Kenneth Arnold within a couple months of the event, Thompson revealed they have no sense of time; in fact the whole concept of time was foreign to them (Clark, 1981).

Betty also describes the craft as having a spinning rim (discussed elsewhere). The correspondence is not exact. Given both this is a dream and this source pre-dates it by over a decade, who should expect otherwise? I also concede that certain similarities like the aluminum construction, the spinning rim, and time-related confusion involve common ufolore that might be creating accidental matches here. Yet, there is enough here – the teeth issue, talk of blue jackets and trousers so unlike the preferred silvery skin-tight one-piece suits of later abductions (Bullard, 1987: 249), slip-on shoes, the uniform size – to worry that Koehler's gag claimed Betty as a victim.

It has been objected that this tale occurred far too long before the experience to be a credible influence. Yet later abductions borrow material in the same manner. Herbert Schirmer's 1967 abduction includes details even more unmistakably borrowed from the Koehler yarn, like "UFOs have been knocked out of the air by radar" and "bases on Venus" (Norman, 1973: 141-62).

Additional features of Betty's experience can be understood by the fact that she had read Donald Keyhoe's book *The Flying Saucer Conspiracy* after the UFO sighting but shortly before she began having the dreams. Keyhoe's book cites nearly a dozen occupant cases. Most of them are outright rejected. These include a zebra-striped spacemen – used by *Time* (1954) to ridicule the dream-like character of Martians in the 1954 French wave – an elephant-faced entity, a six-armed 13 foot tall creation with strange burning eyes, the Flatwoods space-monster, and contactee hoaxes (Keyhoe, 1955: 240, 184, 64, 147-8). Conversely, Keyhoe practically endorses a Pearl Harbor report of a flyer who frightfully proclaimed: "I actually saw him" referring to the pilot of a saucer (Keyhoe, 1955: 63-4, 246). Note the pronoun is him – not it. This should have impressed Betty as meaning Keyhoe might be open to Barney's somewhat similar experience.

Keyhoe also expresses a measure of acceptance of a series of UFO stories from Venezuela involving hairy dwarfs. One of these serves as a likely model for the events in the early part of the dream narrative. Two peasants first spot a bright light like a car on the nearby road. Hovering a few feet from the ground is a round machine with a brilliant glow coming from the underside. "Four little men" come out and try to drag Jesus Gomez toward the object. There is a struggle, and the evidence of that struggle gives it a special credibility in Keyhoe's eyes. Keyhoe next cites the experience of Jesus Paz who was found unconscious after being set upon by a hairy dwarf. He follows this with Jose Parra's sighting, next to a saucer, of six small hairy creatures who transfix him with a bright light (Keyhoe, 1955: 240-6). Betty avoids talk of hairy dwarfs. Barney did not mention the form for one thing. Keyhoe's book also has one character remark on the possible blasphemy of the idea of strange creatures since "man was made in God's image" (Keyhoe, 1955: 65). Climate forces some variations on the basic form, but intelligent life might be created in obeisance to this dictate.

In Betty Hill's nightmare she must fight for consciousness and she finds herself surrounded by four men 5 ft to 5 ft 4 in tall, about her size but shorter than Barney. Barney is unconscious and is being dragged along by another group of men. They numbered eight to eleven while standing in the middle of the road (Keyhoe, 1966: 343).

The behavior of the aliens is very professional and business-like. They are dressed in a somewhat military style. They are not frightening per se. This keeps to Keyhoe's predilections for aliens who are making a scientific study of the planet out of "neutral curiosity" or as a prelude to a mass landing (Keyhoe, 1955: 58, 65, 108, 182, 190, 208, 292). The presumption that the operation has a military character follows from an assumption of reciprocal interests – they are interested in our "atomic plants, dock yards, airfields, naval bases" (Keyhoe, 1955: 208). Keyhoe also argues with friends about possible extraterrestrial missiles fired at New Mexico for ranging purposes (Keyhoe, 1955: 133, 234, 281-2).

Going to the Movies

Keyhoe also felt Mars was inhabited and a probable source of the saucers (Keyhoe, 1955: 154, 173, 183). This might be one reason that several other elements of the story look like they came from the movie *Invaders from Mars* (1953). It is also a natural choice if one regards the medical theme as central. It was one of only a pair of 1950s' films with medical motifs in an alien abduction setting – the other was *Killers from Space* (1954).

Near the climax of this film a woman and a boy are abducted by mutants from Mars and taken to a room within a saucer. The woman is placed on a rectangular table that slides into the scene. She struggles briefly till a light shines on her face which causes her to relax and lose consciousness. A needle surrounded by a clear plastic sheath for part of its length is aimed at the back of her neck. A device at the end of the needle is going to be surgically implanted there.

In *The Interrupted Journey* we are confronted with a woman and a man abducted by aliens that are eventually described by Betty as "like Mongoloids" – itself a kind of mutant (Fuller, 1966: 309). In the original nightmare she compares the noses to the aliens to Jimmy Durante. This would be a rather apt description of the noses on the mutants in the film. Barney, curiously, did not see the Durante noses. They are not part of his drawings and he even states, "I didn't notice any proboscis, there just seemed to be two slits that represented the nostrils" (Fuller, 1966: 305). It is perhaps in deference to Barney's on-the-scene memories that this detail gets edited out in the hypnosis sessions. Talk of big noses may also have prompted jokes after the speeches she gave and her unconscious took the opportunity to remove this annoying detail. Desert people typically have larger noses due to the survival value of the humidifying of air the structure provides, so this coincidence may be less a matter of borrowing from the film than a common recognition that Mars is a desert planet.

There are some preliminary tests of a routine sort in the dream. Betty lies down on the examining table. Needles are placed on various parts of her body including the back of the neck. The fact that Betty is tranquilized by way of the eyes is vaguely similar to the woman being tranquilized by the use of light.

I am indebted to Al Lawson for calling my attention to the fact that the needle-in-the-navel motif owes its origin to imagery appearing during the operating scene. Shortly after the operation begins, the camera cuts to a high-angle view of the surgical theatre. At least that is what it is supposed to be. The image has an ambiguous character in terms of scale and content. You are supposed to interpret it as a view of the architecture of the interior of the saucer with the dominant structure being a tubular metal beam of conduit connecting ceiling to floor. It bears a stylistic similarity to the neck implanter in having a clear plastic sheath surrounding the upper half of its length. The ambiguity of the image, however, admits an alternative interpretation. Lighting of the floor suggests the curvature of an abdomen. The place where the floor and tube intersects is surrounded by a round indentation. It's the navel. In the brief snatch of time the image is seen, some people will miss the intended interpretation and see a huge hypodermic needle has been thrust into the woman's navel. For those who see a contradiction between offering this as a source when I have already claimed the source involved the compass needle test for radiation, the response is that dream material is often over-determined. Multiple causes are often present because of the associative nature of memory. The compass test calls up memories of needles from elsewhere in the past and feeds in the *Invaders from Mars* cluster of associations as a result.

There is no conference with the aliens in *Invaders to Mars* and you might not expect the star map scene to originate there as a consequence, but dreams have an odd penchant for distortion and condensation of details. Earlier in the movie, the boy and woman have a meeting with a scientist at an observatory. This character Dr. Kelston has a large star map on the wall behind him. He points at the map during this meeting and discusses the proximity of Mars to Earth. The most striking thing about this discussion to the alert movie-goer is that, while he points to the map as though these two planets are represented on it, in fact there is nothing there where the Earth should be. Kelston is faking it.

Any similarity between Kelston's star map and Betty Hill's is almost purely accidental. The paradox they share, however, is not. Betty's sketch has the two planets Kelston's lacks. (This might confuse people who recall Marjorie Fish's work on Betty's sketch of the map and the fact that Fish chose to regard everything on it as stars. Betty explicitly says the map shows "numerous sized stars and planets." The lines on it represent expeditions "from one planet to another" [Fuller, 1966: 348]. The two round objects I'm speaking of have curved longitude-like lines on them and seem far more likely to be planets than stars.) When the alien asks Betty where on the map the Earth is, she relives the moviegoer's puzzlement. She has no idea.

There was also a scene cut out in the theatrical release but restored when the film appeared on television that bears comment. (Warren, 1982: 120). Kelston presents a large scrapbook with newspaper columns about saucer activities to the boy before the star map discussion. In Betty's dream, the incident with the large book bearing symbols in vertical columns similarly occurs before the star map discussion (Fuller, 1966: 348).

Is a Cloud a Brick?

All this guesswork into the origins of Betty's experience indisputably has none of the rigour of mathematical theorem. Dreams and nightmares by their very nature forbid precision since veridical replay is avoided in favor of metaphorical expansiveness and exploration of creative play. There can be no methodology applied to make the exercise certain to the satisfaction of all. There will always be the argument that this is pure foolishness, for the human environment provides an infinite variety of stimuli to work with, and with enough time someone would find patterns in the randomness. Clouds occasionally look like faces, but they are not alive.

For me, the issue is not one of achieving certainty but plausibility and competitive penetration of insight. Believing Betty's dream to be memories of a materially real extraterrestrial visitation asks one to believe a cloud is a brick. The figures in it behave irrationally. It is an irrationality more suited to dreams than a people studying our planet. It is also an irrationality more suited to dreams than aliens who wish their actions to be forgotten. A more consistent paranoia would have us postulate that the only feature of Betty's dream that is real is their desire for her to forget her experience. The amnesia ray works perfectly and inserts a devilish impulse: Believe what you will shall be the whole of their command.

What of Barney? comes the rejoinder. He is a second witness. He confirms the dream was not a dream.

But does he really? We've already noted that his reaction to the eyes is radically different from Betty's. He missed the Jimmy Durante noses. Betty sees dark hair and military caps (Fuller, 1966: 344). Barney says: "I didn't notice any hair – or headgear for that matter" (Fuller, 1966: 305). These things seem worth worrying about and we note that that some ufologists have worried about them. Asked by APRO about certain incongruities, Betty theorized that "her dreams were rationalizations and that in them she tried to make them more humanlike than they really were." The Lorenzens said this was precisely the thought they had been entertaining (Lorenzen, 1967: 80). Dreams as rationalizations! Am I the only person who feels this is simply bizarre?

Saucers Make the Head Spin

Some people will stipulate that the dream and regression can be ignored and that we can't learn anything useful about the aliens from them. There remains however the impressive fact that Betty and Barney both consciously recall seeing a structured flying saucer. It was not just a light in the sky. The nature of the flying saucer in the Hill case however is vulnerable to a number of objections. There are of course the standard general problems. Number one is that it is explicitly felt by both of them is to be a flying saucer. When Barney sketches an overhead perspective of the vehicle, it is perfectly round just as one would expect of a flying saucer. In the letter to Keyhoe, Betty similarly affirms, "it appeared to be pancake in shape" (Fuller, 1966: 47). The sense they are seeing the standard model comes in her taunt to Barney after the encounter, "Do you believe in flying saucers, now?" (Fuller, 1966: 350). This is even more firmly supported in a different statement. "But there was this rim that went around the craft. And I don't know why, but I had the idea that this rim was movable, that it would spin around the perimeter, maybe. Like a huge gyroscope of some kind. I don't know for sure and this is just my impression" (Fuller, 1966: 309). A spinning rim would be most consistent with a circular structure than other geometric possibilities. The inherent problem is that flying saucers come from a journalistic error. By Kenneth Arnold's account, he described the motion of the mysterious objects he saw as "erratic, like a saucer if you skip it across water." He stated the objects were not round – this is confirmed by the drawing in his report to the Air Force, which more resembles a shoe heel – and that it arose from "a great deal of misunderstanding" on the part of reporter Bill Bequette. Nobody realized the error and it became the presumption thereafter that saucers were the shape of UFOs (Kottmeyer, 1993). The shape of the craft in the Hill case conforms to the myth of our era and that looks unfortunate.

Betty states that during the initial sighting, "it gave the appearance of spinning all the time" (Fuller, 1966: 176). In the letter to Keyhoe, "the object was spinning and appeared to be lighted on only one side which gave it a twinkling effect" (Fuller, 1966: 46). Spinning saucers were more common in the Fifties and Sixties than they are today and this raises additional concerns about cultural shaping of the experience. Barney's description of red lights on both sides, the fin, and the picture windows do not mention any spinning, but the rim detail, already cited, perhaps explains all this, and happily averts questions about whether a spinning saucer should be manned. In the regression, Betty denies the spinning was there when it came close and puts the twinkling effect down to the double set of windows on one side of the craft. One still has cause to wonder why the rim spins though (Kottmeyer, 2000).

And this leads to us to general problem three: what propels such a craft? We hear nothing of rocket flames, helicopter blades, jet engines. There are no propellers (Fuller, 1966: 103). The letter to Keyhoe remarks, "This flying object was at least as large as a four-motor plane, its flight was noiseless." The most common notion appearing in the UFO literature is that saucers are held aloft by a magnetic drive. Beyond the general physical implausibility of the notion, such drives are generally held by ufologists to have side effects like making engines stall. The car in the Hill case was running throughout the sighting (Fuller, 1966: 47).

The fourth general problem is that this UFO, like so many others, draws attention to itself. The letter again: "At first we noticed a bright light object in the sky which seemed to be moving rapidly." A few lines later they speak of "bright blue-white light" followed shortly by "two red lights appeared on each side." As Hilary Evans, among others, has observed, the lighting of UFOs is paradoxical, "...why are some of them are so keen to advertise their presence while others keep the lowest profile?" (Evans, 1983: 139-40). The paradox is heightened in the Hill case for we cannot ascribe the mixed message to different groups of aliens. The occupants of this brilliant craft themselves solidly indicate they want nobody to know of their activities. It looks blindingly strange.

Then there is the problem of the idiosyncratic look of the Hill saucer. "He saw wings protrude on each side and the red light were on the wing tips." And the front was "ringed with windows" (Fuller, 1966: 47). In Barney's drawing it looks like the complete wall is made of 18 squares of glass arranged in a 9 by 2 curved rectangle. They are huge, but prevented from being one solid window by a system of struts (Fuller, 1966: 115). "They're not like a commercial plane …My God, no! I've got to shake my head. I've got – I've got – this can't be true" (Fuller, 1966: 112). It allows full length viewing of the figures inside. These features are clearly unlike any other flying saucers for which detailed drawings exist. This is not to deny partially similar cases exist. Drawings in the Chiles-Whitted classic of July 24, 1948, are somewhat suggestive in that both pilots drew double rows of square windows. Whitted drew a 3 x 2 array; Capt. Chiles however drew an 8 x 2 array spanning nearly the full length of the craft that is provocatively similar, save for two major wrinkles in the comparison. Both pilots in the case describe the craft as cylindrical and rocket-like (Gross, 1982: 34-8, 60-5). And Whitted's sketch has a note emphasizing, "No Fins." The August 25, 1952, William Squyres close encounter of the third kind features several large windows in the mid-section with a man visible inside, but the windows are arrayed from top to rear, and the craft has an array of propellers spinning along the outside (Hynek, 1977: 200-3). You could perversely argue this is fully consistent with the recurrently observed inconsistency of saucer shapes (Evans, 1983: 137-9). Yet, what should one make of such a glass wall being on a saucer?

The analogy that springs to mind is glass-bottomed boats that allow humans to sightsee beneath bodies of water. It would be swell to adapt this for orbital appreciation of outer space and viewing the Earth. Yet the rest of the case doesn't seem to argue for this being an alien tour boat. The people aboard seem military in dress and behavior and the interaction with the Hills has a medical character. There's no bar, lounge seating, purser, family groups, or anything else pointing to this being a luxury liner. Generally you don't see anything like this on military aircraft presumably because you don't really need that much window to fly safely or do reconnaissance work. Still, the senior officer could have ordered it as a perk for his personal enjoyment. Or perhaps the Earth Reconnaissance Project commandeered a used tour bus during a budget cutback. Who knows? The proper question here might be whether the windows are more useful for allowing Barney to see inside than allowing the crew to look out.

The Trouble with Aliens

I shall leave to others the issue of explaining what the Hills actually were looking at. My point is that the extraterrestrial hypothesis has too many problems to take things at face value. The paradoxes of its concealment make belief a trap. Wouldn't aliens concerned with their existence being known be better at disguise than what we see here? Couldn't they do things with nanotechnology? Techno-bugs identical to insects could collect skin samples and other tissues in our sleep and none would suspect a thing. Couldn't they make perfectly human replicants and infiltrate medical centers right under our noses?

Inversely, if aliens truly have the ability to alter minds, how do we know anything about this experience is true? Every detail, even the command to not know this experience, could be wrong. It could all be an exercise in creating belief rather than undermining it, with best-seller status of the book a sign of extraordinary success rather than failure.

It can't be proved. In the nature of the situation, how could it ever? Disproof lies only in the paradoxes and ironies and a wary pragmatism. What use is it to believe this experience where one does not know what is worth believing? A half-century of extraterrestrial belief has brought us only errors and confusions like this. It is hopefully not an error to try to understand dreams even if it proves nothing more than a pleasant diversion.

The aliens ask us to disbelieve and by their concealment they prove their sincerity. We cannot know their motives with assurance. If benevolent, belief may be a source of injury. If malevolent, belief may be a source of danger (Kottmeyer 1997). Cynicism can be a virtue, but here it looks irrelevant. Betty chose to remember what they wanted her to forget. But what good came of so many believing her? Real abductees do not need therapy, according to Betty; thus bringing them to light has no psychological benefit. (Hill, 1995: 82). The few she considers real are extremely rare and mostly unknown to the media (Hill, 1995: 82, 85). There has been a tragic spread of abduction belief, which Betty, confessing guilt, fears often involves harmful belief in nightmarish fantasies (Hill, 1995: 78). Nobody of conscience can think this was a good thing. Real or not, the alien's warning should have been heeded. We should not have known of this experience.

Further Notes On Wraparound Eyes

Some readers are doubtless wondering what happened to the argument over wraparound eyes and "The Bellero Shield." This issue has received a degree of notoriety and controversy and I still hold my argument is valid, but the preceding section emerged as a meditation on the paradoxes of concealment and the inutility of ETH belief in interpreting dreams. The issue of the wraparound eyes, I feel, has little role in an assessment of the Hill case despite what some ufologists have written. The value is showing how a detail of probable falsity happened to spread to other abduction cases thus hinting at cultural aspects to abduction experiences or reports. A thorough discussion of it would have amounted to a huge detour from the course the argument needed to take. My thoughts on this side issue are offered in these further notes.

The Eyes that Spoke

In his final book, *Aliens From Space*, Donald Keyhoe briefly recounted his involvement in starting the investigation of Barney and Betty Hill that eventually led to John Fuller's publication of *The Interrupted Journey*, the first major work of the alien abduction mythos. Keyhoe was mystified more than anything else by the hideous faces of the aliens. The heads were oddly shaped with no ears and compressed noses and mouths. Worst of all were long slanting eyes that extended along the side of the head creating a sinister look. "What caused the subconscious minds of these two people to create these pictures from their imaginations has never been fully explained" (Keyhoe, 1973: 243-5).

Keyhoe could not accept the case 100 percent, he later admitted in a 1975 interview, but he did not reject it either. As mysteries go, Keyhoe's question seemed safely rhetorical. Who knows why anyone dreams of one monster and not another? How would anyone even begin to investigate such a problem?

What could not have been foreseen was how serendipity might step in to break this minor mystery. The local PBS station a few years ago decided to rerun the old TV series *The Outer Limits*. It was one of the most visually amazing programs of my youth, and I eagerly tuned in to experience once more such sights as the horrifying Zanti misfits, the bee girl, moonstone, Borderland's ionic gale, the down-shifting time machine of "Controlled Experiment" and David McCallum's evolution into a mega-brain.

It was during the showing of the episode "The Bellero Shield" that I felt the uncanny frisson of *déjà vu*. The eyes of the alien were unusually long and wrapped around the side of the face. It quickly hit me that these eyes were just like the wraparound eyes that were drawn in *The Interrupted Journey* – and the later more detailed drawing the Hills did in collaboration with the artist David Baker (*UFO Investigator*, April 1972). Though I couldn't articulate it at that instant, there were other similarities, which had contributed to the sense of a close relationship: no ears, no hair, no nose, and a cranium shaped like a bullet tilted backwards 45 degrees. I was excited by the possibility of a match because I was reasonably sure there were few or no other examples of aliens with wraparound eyes in science fiction cinema. Moments later, however, my excitement became subdued. It dawned on me that *The Outer Limits* was a series of the mid-Sixties and the Hill case dated to the early Sixties – 1961 or 1962. "The Bellero Shield" couldn't have been an influence. Still, the book came out in 1966. Could the lag be significant?

After the program ended, I dug into my library for a round of late-night research.

Behind the scenes

"The Bellero Shield" aired February 10, 1964. The Hills' UFO encounter happened in the morning of September 20, 1961. That probably should have killed the idea of any kind of influence, but the resemblance was just so compelling I couldn't shake the feeling there had to be a relationship. I reread *The Interrupted Journey*. To my delight I discovered there was no mention of wraparound eyes in the earliest account. Betty's dreams, written down a matter of days after the UFO sighting, mention men with Jimmy Durante noses, dark or black hair and eyes and a relaxed human appearance that she said was "not frightening." This is all quite different from the final product. The changes emerge in the hypnotic regression with Dr. Simon. The most salient issue was to know when the wraparound eyes were first described. That turned out to be during a hypnosis session involving Barney dated February 22, 1964. Not only did "The Bellero Shield" precede Barney's first mention of wraparound eyes, it did by only 12 days! I was immensely pleased.

I ordered the script of the show next. My thoughts were so distracted I realized I had missed the dialogue. This yielded additional evidence for the relationship. Judith, played by Sally Kellerman, is conversing with the Bifrost alien and asks it if it can read her mind. It answers, "No, I cannot read your mind. I cannot even understand your language. I analyse your eyes. In all the universes, in all the unities beyond all the universes, all who have eyes, have eyes that speak…" Judith, intrigued, asks how it speaks her language. It elaborates, "I learn each word just before I speak it. Your eyes teach me" (Script, scene 24).

In saying all eyes speak, the Bifrost alien is conveying a truth and simultaneously dodging the human/alien language barrier problem by a unique dab of poetic license.

In the same hypnosis session in which Barney drew the wraparound eyes, there is this exercise in confusion: "Yes. They won't talk to me. Only the eyes are talking to me. I-I-I-I don't understand that. Oh – the eyes don't have a body. They're just eyes…" (Fuller, 1966: 124). Barney's confusion about the talking eyes is one most viewers probably shared over the writer's gimmick employed by the episode's creators. The notion shared by both texts that eyes can talk defies dismissal via appeal to commonness or coincidence. By any measure, the case for influence here is not just satisfactory, it is exemplary. At least one abduction researcher has granted this point (Bullard, 1991: 40).

A spot of confabulation

The discovery of this pseudomemory will not shock hypnosis experts. They have long been aware of the danger of confabulation in regression work. There was no reason to expect *The Interrupted Journey*'s narrative to be immune from such contamination. Belatedly, Keyhoe's question thus finds itself answered with the mundane corollary that Barney had watched the science fiction/horror series *The Outer Limits* shortly before his subconscious was called upon to imagine what a scary alien ought to look like. Betty's dream aliens were too normal to justify the fear he displayed during the original UFO experience.

Barney's confabulation has other interesting repercussions. As Thomas E. Bullard (1987) has pointed out, "wraparound eyes is a term that has become common in the abduction literature." Case after case can be pointed to of people describing alien abductors with eyes that wrap, curl, or taper around the head. Some that UFO buffs may recognize include: Carol Wayne Watts, 1967 (Kimery, 1976: 33); "Canadian Rock Band Abducted," (Fenwick, Tokarz, & Muskat, 1971); David Delmundo's 1972 contact with the turban-sporting Ohneshto (Stevens, 1982: 148); the 1977 Langenargen abduction, a major German case (Schneider & von Ludwiger, 1993); the Andreasson Affair (Fowler, 1979: 25); Harrison Bailey (Rogo, 1980: 130); South Dakota Connection (Christensen, 1983); Paris Colorado (Stevens, 1989: 341); the Mirassol abductions (Buhler, Pereira, Pires, 1985: 298); "Jennifer" (Carpenter, 1991: 100); Tom Holloway, D.D.S (Boylan, 1994: 99). Others exist – one researcher in 1976 spoke of eight instances of wraparound eyes in 51 abductions but adds the owners differed in virtually every other physical respect (Hendry, 1979: 140). This group will suffice to indicate the influential nature of the Hill case on the history of the imagery of abduction experiences. Before the Hills, wraparound eyes seem largely, probably totally, absent in the UFO literature. Cinematic aliens sporting wraparound eyes are similarly largely absent. But not totally. I eventually discovered one other instance. It is an unnamed mutant in the film *Evil Brain from Outer Space*, a Japanese film imported in 1964. Interestingly, one of the heads of Projects Unlimited, which provided the monsters for *The Outer Limits*, was named Wah Ming Chang. He was a talented sculptor and designed most of the head sculpts for the series. This may hint at cultural roots in Eastern myth or *kabuki* theatre, but I'm not prepared to follow the trail the distance to prove it.

The motif of the speaking eyes did not share in the popularity of the wraparound eyes. There is one example in Edith Fiore's *Encounters*. The abductee named Victoria describes aliens communicating by simply looking at each other. It is tempting to speculate that the alien bonding practices involving staring described in Jacobs's *Secret Life* are descended from Barney's talking eyes, but there are many complicating factors such as strong hints of *Star Trek*'s Vulcan mind meld and a rich cluster of psychological symbolisms in staring eyes, such as love, intimacy, supervision, contempt, and predators, that seem more rewarding avenues of interpretation. The paucity of speaking eyes probably reflects the poor nature of verbal memory compared to visual memory. The confusing nature of the idea of talking eyes probably doesn't help. It may also be that hideous eyes have a defining role in creating an appropriately paranoia-inspiring iconography. As Keyhoe apparently sensed, they are more believably alien. The eyes say "Them."

To the psychosocial theorist, the eyes whisper "Us."

The Eyes Still Speak

Defenders of the reality of the alien abduction phenomenon have taken notice of my argument that Barney Hill was influenced by the *Outer Limits* episode "The Bellero Shield" which appeared in *The REALL News* (July 1994) and elsewhere. Evidently disturbed by its implications they have offered some counter-arguments that they hope refute or render uncertain this claim of influence. Those appearing in Jerome Clark's *The UFO Book: Encyclopedia of the Extraterrestrial* (Visible Ink Press, 1998: 15, 291-2) will be addressed in what follows.

Assertions versus evidence

Both Jerome Clark and Thomas E. Bullard offer our first argument in their independent entries on "Abduction Phenomenon" and "Hill Abduction Case." Simply put, they feel Barney probably did see wraparound eyes on the entity long before "The Bellero Shield" aired. His earlier, conscious recall of what happened on the date of initial sighting seems to suggest this interpretation to them. Bullard states Barney "remembered a being with compelling eyes looking down at him from a UFO. If he saw the *Outer Limits* episode, he might have borrowed the wraparound eyes as a metaphor, but his preoccupation with the staring entity and its eyes began years before this television image could have influenced him." Clark states "In his conscious memory, dating from that night in September 1961 (long before the airing of the show, in other words), Barney could recall seeing the beings only from a distance, from which perspective the precise shape of the eyes may not have been easily apparent. He did, however, remember vividly the intense stare and the apparent mental message that the beings were about to capture him. The sense of being caught in the stare, and of being the recipient of communication in that state, is consistent with his later testimony."

Observe that neither Bullard nor Clark offers quotations in support of their attempted refutations. Let's look at the actual record provided by John Fuller in *The Interrupted Journey*. In the first document on the case, Information Report 100-1-61, neither the figures on the craft or their eyes are mentioned. Fuller avers this was because of fear of ridicule. The next document is Betty Hill's letter to Donald Keyhoe. In it she states "one figure was observing us from the windows." Barney is described as hysterical and "laughing and repeating that they are going to capture us" (p. 47). Is this consistent with seeing a being with compelling eyes?

Next we come to Webb's report of October 26, 1961. In it the leader in the craft is described as peering out of the window at Barney. The being is not close enough to observe facial characteristics, but Barney could see a grin on one figure and an expressionless face. The eyes are not emphasized and no word of elongation or eyes that speak (p. 54).

When we come to the account of the Hohmann, Jackson, McDonald meeting of November 1961 the description runs as follows: "moving figures in the craft, the one that kept looking back at me with those eyes. He gave me the impression – and this was dim in my memory, but there just the same – that he was a capable person, and there can be no nonsense here. We have business to attend to." There is still no mention of wraparound eyes or eyes that speak and it seems odd that he can discern such impressions as the person being a no-nonsense capable person and yet overlook these traits if they were consciously present (p. 67).

Further along, (p. 76) Barney is wrestling with his emotions that are described as "The unexplained panic, that he knew to be foreign to his general reactions plagued him, in addition to the curtain of absolute blankness that descended at that moment." Basically, what he is preoccupied with is not "those eyes" but the missing time and his hysteria. This is also manifestly the issue in his presenting complaints to Dr. Simon.

This is the extent of the paper trail on these matters prior to the hypnosis sessions with Dr. Simon. However, there is one account I skipped. In Chapter One, Fuller describes Barney seeing the craft in these terms: "His memory at this point is blurred. For a reason he cannot explain, he was certain he was about to be captured. He tried to pull the glasses away from his eyes, to turn away, but he couldn't. As the focus became sharp, he remembered the eyes of the one crewmember who stared down at him. Barney had never seen eyes like that before" (p. 32). Bullard has admitted in correspondence that this was the source of his impression that Barney had seen compelling eyes, albeit it is clear that Barney feels the compulsion to watch before he had focused the glasses. The bigger problem is that Fuller does not give his sources for this construction of this account. Given what we see in the extant paper trail, it seems likely that Fuller is incorporating material post-dating the hypnosis sessions with Dr. Simon.

Clark's assertions that Barney was "caught in the stare" and that he received "communication in that state" or an "apparent mental message" have no support in the paper trail and it is a puzzle how he even got the impression such things happened. Barney's sense of imminent capture is more simply understood as his reading of the situation that he believes a craft is hovering out there and is interested in him for some reason. He didn't need a mental message to infer there might be reason to worry that something like capture is being considered. Clark's claim that the conscious memories are consistent with the hypnosis session has additional problems. The speaking eyes belong to a figure standing in the road, not the figure in the craft that purportedly generated the sense of imminent capture. The message of the speaking eyes in the hypnosis session was "Don't be afraid." Barney says in the hypnosis session that he isn't. Yet in the conscious recollections of both Barney and Betty, he panicked and became hysterical. Perhaps I'm quibbling, but that doesn't look consistent to me.

When Barney watched television

Our second argument appears in the writings of both Bullard and Clark though with different degrees of emphasis and detail. Writes Clark in *The UFO Book*: "Kottmeyer did not trouble to inquire of Betty Hill, who is still alive, if she and her husband were in the habit of watching *Outer Limits*. (When asked by another writer, Betty said: 'As for the *Outer Limits* – never heard of it. Barney worked nights. If he was not working, we were never home because of our community activities. If we had been home, I am sure this title would not interest us.')" In a summer 1996 review of Sagan's book *The Demon-Haunted World*, Clark frets that Sagan "recycles Martin Kottmeyer's specious theory, by now an all-but-unkillable canard, that Barney Hill got the idea for wraparound eyes from a 1964 episode of *Outer Limits*. To start with the Hills never watched the show; Betty had never even heard of it until I asked her about it last year." Despite the word "start" there, this is the only argument he uses in the Sagan review to show him and me wrong. Bullard simply says Betty says Barney did not see *The Outer Limits* episode, without offering quotes or reference. The context suggests he puts less weight on this argument and offers it more in an informational way than a way of killing a canard.

True, I didn't inquire. Wraparound eyes and speaking eyes are so exotic and the congruence in time so impressive, anything that Betty might say would be irrelevant. If she had said Barney had seen it, I would not have used it because it would be a weak argument guaranteed to be picked apart, dismissed, and form a target of innuendo. Historians, indeed most people, know that second-hand decades-old memories are unreliable. The fact that Clark happened to be the first to inquire Betty on the point in 1995 despite my "canard" being around since 1990 shows how unusual Clark's action was.

Betty says she never heard of *The Outer Limits*. The issue is whether or not Barney saw it. Betty says Barney worked nights. The implication here would seem to be that Barney could not see the show because he was working when the show was airing. Peter Brookesmith has established (by enquiring of Betty Hill) that Barney was working from midnight to 8:00 a.m. *The Outer Limits* aired from 7:30 to 8:30 p.m. on Monday evenings. Betty's statement thus seems largely irrelevant or invalid.

I might be inclined to take the comment about community activities more seriously if it meant as a corollary that the Hills did not even own a TV or that nobody in their community owned TV sets. As Peter Brookesmith has suggested in his book *Alien Abductions* (1998), this may decrease the chances Barney saw the show, but it increases the odds he may have run into someone who saw the show and told Barney about it. The statement that such a title would not interest them means little since they could have been flipping through the channels and watched the relevant parts not even knowing what show it was. Brookesmith mentions that when he talked with Betty Hill in April 1997, she elaborated on this point by indicating their interests were rather more intellectual than one might guess. The problem here is that *The Outer Limits* was a show by intellectuals, promoted as a show dealing in ideas, and that the specific episode "The Bellero Shield" was conspicuously Shakespearean in tone to the point of having obvious adaptations from *Macbeth*. Clearly, she is not helping her case with such an upside-down argument.

Clark's faith that he has proven the claim of influence specious and nothing more than a canard is a poor gamble ultimately. Random chance arranging the congruence of speaking, wraparound eyes with the ancillary details appearing so close in time in both *The Outer Limits* and Barney's regression is too huge an improbability. The safe bet is Betty is wrong or overlooking something. Clark could have spared Betty and himself some embarrassment if he had simply exercised a little common sense.

In your face

The next argument is uniquely Clark's. He points out that Barney said the talking eyes at one point came so close to him that they pressed against him. "And I felt like the eyes had pushed into my eyes," seems to be the line he is not quoting (p. 154). He points out that recent abduction accounts bear this detail even though it had been overlooked in subsequent rehashes of the Hill case. He quotes a passage from the sessions of one of David Jacobs's subjects named Karen Morgan, which, presumably, Clark thinks illustrates the point. Oddly, it does not. Morgan describes the eyes overwhelming her, going inside of her, and making her gone. Not only does Morgan not say the eyes pressed against hers, but Barney never said the eyes went inside him, overwhelmed him, or made him gone. Adding to the inconsistency is the fact that Morgan describes eyes that are all black and Barney drew eyes showing iris, pupil, and white.

Clark's point would have been more correctly illustrated with three other cases in Jacobs that do actually describe alien faces pressed against the faces of abductees. And, indeed, he does better his point by recalling a similar account gathered by Karla Turner in a different work. Clark asserts, "Even Kottmeyer refrains from contending such accounts can be traced to a few overlooked sentences among the many Barney spoke during hours of hypnotic testimony. Having exhausted his argument he retreats into 'psychological symbolisms,' which he finds meaningful and others may see as evidence of Kottmeyer's reluctance to entertain more heretical and disturbing possibilities."

I stated in my *REALL News* article that it would be tempting to speculate that the alien bonding practices described in the Jacobs book are descended from Barney's talking eyes. I refrained because I saw there were differences that also needed to be taken into account and, while it was something clearly interesting enough to mention in passing, I didn't want to clutter up a nice piece with a lengthy digression. Fuller's book remains in print and is far from obscure or inaccessible. It is possible that an abductee read it and passed along the eye-to-eye closeness detail in conversation. The complicating factor is that when Spock of *Star Trek* mind-melded with humans, his face is almost eyeball-to-eyeball close as well. Given the iconic status of *Trek* in our culture, who can deny that this might be a more plausible source of influence, especially in the absence of further details being borrowed from Fuller's book?

The Lynn Miller account in the Jacobs book, to expand on this, speaks of the alien touching her head and of there being a situation of vulnerability, which is redolent of Spock's reservations about performing mind-melding because of the terrible intimacy of the process, an intimacy suggestive of sexual union. Thinking of *Trek* when thinking about these differences is only natural. Bringing Barney into the argument demands we ask why he did not speak of vulnerability or pleasurable feelings with a sexual component as Miller did.

There is additionally a complication apparent to anyone familiar with the historical legacy of exaggerated eye imagery in the world's storehouse of art, myth, and psychology. Eyes are rich in associations repeatedly exploited by the imagination. Miller and *Trek* may both be tapping into this cluster of common symbols, rendering the need for Miller to know *Trek* or Fuller's book moot. What Clark sees as restraint, exhausting the argument, and a retreat, I felt was only being up-front about alternative interpretations. There's just no pleasing some people.

And just what does Clark want us to entertain that is so heretical and disturbing? Aliens are able to overwhelm you, make you gone just by looking into your eyes. Such lyrical horror seems to me the province of people like Stephen King and Whitley Strieber, whose rhetoric of magical powers and ethereal mind are more suited to the easy speculations of fiction than the rigor of logic.

One small measure of the ease with which this idea comes can be seen in Camille Flammarion's 1890 work of fiction *Urania*. Flammarion was one of the first writers of scientific romance to imagine worlds populated by non-humans. On one such distant world he describes aliens with glowing eyes that had a special quality. "More than that, the power of their glance is such that they exert an electric and magnetic influence of variable intensity, and which under conditions has the effect of lightning, causing the victim upon whom the force and energy of their will is fixed to fall down dead" (p. 37). This could be considered an exact match to being made gone and overwhelmed, but before we start calling Flammarion an early abductee let's not overlook the fact that the alien eyes aren't black.

What Clark promotes is a return to the ancient beliefs of the evil eye and possession, magical doctrines discarded by educated men for many, many years. That is truly disturbing and I do not apologize for being reluctant to join Clark in his courageous appetite for worm-eaten concepts.

The limits of explanation

Clark further makes a number of accusations that I suppose form a type of argument. He says my claim of influence tells us nothing about the Hill experience. I took a small detail out of a much larger context of a complex experience. And I asked you to think of it as the only issue of consequence and to dismiss similar testimony about this detail as irrelevant to considerations about its reality status. What is missing is "a coherent hypothesis though it is hard to imagine what that hypothesis might be." He felt my claims were an effort to "explain away the Hill encounter." My inclination is to ask the reader to dig up my earlier paper and see how hallucinatory this sounds. My interest was to tell people about my discovery of the compelling coincidence of speaking and wraparound eyes appearing in a fictional alien encounter on *The Outer Limits* mere days before it appeared in Barney Hill's hypnosis testimony and the implications of people repeating this description in later accounts. I said nothing about this being an explanation for the whole of the Hill case, nor asked anyone to think it is the only thing of interest in the case. I trust most readers and editors appreciated the succinct character of my argument and regard Clark's demands for a lengthy exegesis of a complex experience as sophistry – to say nothing about impractical outside of a book.

My claim was simple and coherent. It should be evident by now that it is Clark's own comments that are largely incoherent and what is missing from his own account is an honest attempt to come to terms with that coincidence. Clark evidently believes Barney never saw "The Bellero Shield," but why then did that show happen to have wraparound and speaking eyes in it? I've viewed hundreds of SF films and state with no fear of contradiction that such traits are too exotic and scarce to seriously believe that random chance could arrange the coincidence.

As a final note, I am pleased to report that Clark has admitted in correspondence he erred about the argument in point 1, grants point 2 was open to obvious reservations, and agrees random chance is hard to swallow. He has other ruminations on this affair, which I cherish, but I won't force his hand. In *The UFO Book* he regarded the counter-arguments to Barney being influenced as "the triumph of uncertainty" and proof of how the inspection of skeptical arguments shows them to be ramshackle structures. Inspection of the inspection has negated this triumph. The claim for influence still stands.

...and Speak

There have been others offering comments besides Clark and Bullard, and not just those in the ETH camp. Paul Devereux (1995) has written: "But the eye is so fundamental to human psychology that the dominance of such a feature in the image of the alien probably hints at deeper sources than mere cultural precedent." He notes the phenomenon of eye idols in ancient art and how the eye often makes up a larger fraction of face – "huge globular eyes hypnotically staring out of the unrecorded past of 5000 years ago with defiant authority" (Devereux & Brookesmith, 1997: 103). I had noted this same historical material in a 1991 *Magonia* article and with a similar conclusion (Kottmeyer 1991b). The muddle is Devereux's use of "but," which implies a dichotomy where none exists. Large eyes are indeed panhuman and reflect archetypal processes. The attribution of magical effects to eyes is also widespread and, for most purposes, can also be regarded as an archetypal phenomenon. Eye idols and their parallels are large in size. However they are not wraparound in shape. I recommend a book by Albert M. Potts called *The World's Eye* (University Press of Kentucky, 1982) for its coverage of eye imagery across a number of cultures. An instance or two of wraparound eyes are present – a New Zealand *tiki* mask looks acceptably close to the upswept eyes in Barney's drawing for the Fuller book (Potts, 1982: 47). They are not however widespread. The post-Hill run of wraparound eyes is indeed mere culture.

Not so damn silly

Elsewhere, Greg Sandow (1998/9) has stated I reach an "all-time high" in silliness in my observation that Barney Hill's alien and "The Bellero Shield" share talk of eyes that speak. So, too, he states, do eyes in "a thousand poems, not to mention romance novels. Kottmeyer should read some books that aren't science fiction." Sandow should watch some films that are. Barney wasn't looking at a beautiful woman that he felt romantic longings towards. He was looking at a no-nonsense Nazi-like saucer pilot who was filling him with fear. For those who share Sandow's amusement, I recommend the more relevant and sobering exercise of finding, say, a thousand examples of stories, in any cultural realm, of aliens or saucer pilots or even – why be picky? – Nazis in combination with the idea of speaking eyes.

Another owl story

Also, this gem recently came my way. Rattvik Martansberg sent a letter to the Swedish Air Force in 1952 about an experience he had a few years earlier of a pair of big cigar-shaped objects that had a narrow pin like a car radio antenna up front. There were a lot of holes along the side of each. Behind one large window was a strange face that looked like an owl face with large eyes and a mouth instead of a bill. "In fact I had nightmares a couple of nights afterwards due to the remarkable large owl-head, behind the large windowpane. I thought it was some kind of mask, of course, but the gaze was very sharp and piercing, in some way" (Aldrich, 1997: 134-7).

First thoughts might tempt an ufologist to consider this a provocative parallel to Barney's talk of being looked at by "those eyes" and it is doubly impressive since it is certain they occurred independently. Barney could not possibly have known of this item buried in Swedish AF files. Second thoughts would soon intrude however when we learn that a defense official did some background checking and the percipient was regarded by locals as a chatterbox and fantasy-prone. Police said he was "always lying." He went bankrupt the prior year and had been involved in shady businesses. He had also crash-landed his plane a few years earlier. It all points to psychological origins in this Swedish case. The official saved it to show to everyone in defense intelligence. As the diagnosis seems probable, the issue of the Swedish case's similarity would inevitably rebound with questions about Barney's talk of being looked at as having a psychological basis. Probably it does. Barney was in a state of agitation before the sighting as evidenced by his complaint, when they stopped at a restaurant, that everybody in the street was looking at them. This complaint – "all eyes are upon us" – was evidently a delusion of observation, for he himself realized subsequently that everybody was actually behaving in a pleasant manner and that he had better get a hold of himself. (Fuller, 1966: 98-9). Theory would suggest both the sense of being watched in the restaurant and by the saucer leader were manifestations of a reactive paranoia probably caused by some episode of shame preceding the events of that evening (Kottmeyer, 1991a). We shouldn't guess what that might be, but possibilities easily spring to mind to those familiar with the wartiness of humans.

References to "No One Should Know of This Experience"

Bullard, Thomas E. 1987. *Ufo Abductions: The Measure of a Mystery*. Fund for UFO Studies.
Clark, Jerome. 1981. "The Coming of the Venusians," *Fate*. January, pp. 49-55.
Craig, Roy. 1995. *UFOs: An Insider's View of the Official Quest for Evidence*. University of North Texas Press.
Evans, Hilary. 1983. *The Evidence for UFOs*. Aquarian.
Freud, Sigmund. 1965. *The Interpretation of Dreams*. Avon.
Fuller, John. 1966. *The Interrupted Journey*. Dell.
Gillmor, Daniel S., ed. 1969. *Scientific Study of Unidentified Flying Objects*. Bantam.
Gross, Loren 1982. *UFOs: A History, volume 1: July 1947-December 1948*. Arcturus Book Service.
Hans Holzer. 1976. T*he Ufonauts* Fawcett Gold Medal, 1976.
Hill, Betty. 1995. *A Common Sense Approach to UFOs* Greenland, NH.
Hynek, J. Allen. 1997. *The Hynek UFO Report* Dell.
Jacobs, David M. 1998. *The Threat* Simon & Schuster.
Jordan, Debbie & Mitchell, Kathy. 1994. *Abducted!* Dell, 1994, pp. 300-1.
Keyhoe, Donald. 1950. *The Flying Saucers are Real*. Fawcett Gold Medal.
Keyhoe, Donald. 1955. *The Flying Saucer Conspiracy*. Fieldcrest.
Keyhoe, Donald. 1973. *Aliens from Space* Doubleday,
Kottmeyer, Martin. 1993 "The Saucer Error" *The REALL News*, Vol.1, No. 4, May, pp. 1, 6.
Kottmeyer, Martin. 1994. "Alienating Fancies: The Influencing Machine Fantasy in Ufology and the Extraterrestrial Mythos." *Magonia*, No. 49 June, pp. 3-10.
Kottmeyer, Martin. 1997. "ETHics: The Ethics of UFO Belief" *The Excluded Middle*, No. 7, pp. 10-11.
Kottmeyer, Martin. 1998. "Still Waiting: A List of Predictions from the UFO Culture," *The Anomalist* website, http://www.anomalist.com/features/waiting.html posted December.
Kottmeyer, Martin. 2000. "Should Saucers Spin?" *Magonia Monthly Supplement* No. 23 January, pp. 1-4.
Lorenzen, Jim & Coral. *Abducted!* 1977. Berkley Medallion.
Lorenzen, Jim & Coral. 1967. *Flying Saucer Occupants*. Signet
Lorenzen, Jim & Coral. 1968. *UFOs Over the Americas*. Signet
McCampbell, James M. 1976. *Ufology*. Celestial Arts.
Medalia, Nahum Z. and Larsen, Otto N. 1958. "Diffusion and Belief in a Collective Delusion: The Seattle Windshield Pitting Epidemic" *American Sociological Review*, Vol. 23, pp. 180-6.
Michel, Aime. 1958. *Flying Saucers and the Straight-Line Mystery*. Criterion.
Norman, Eric. 1973. *Gods and Devils from Outer Space*. Lancer, pp. 141-62. Condon report, case 42
Pritchard, Andrea, ed. 1994. *Alien Discussions*. North Cambridge Press.

Radnet website, 1999 accessed. "Information about source points of anthropogenic radioactivity: item 3A Marshall Islands – Lucky Dragon Incident."
Regan, Dennis & Allen William. 1997. "Investigation and Analysis of Sound Pulses Recorded During a Period of UFO Activity in Bragg Creek, Alberta, Canada" 1997 *MUFON UFO Symposium Proceedings*, pp. 177-93.
Siegel, Ronald K. 1989. *Intoxication*. E.P. Dutton.
Steinman, William S. 1986. *UFO Crash at Aztec*. America West.
Time. 1954. "Martians Over France" *Time*, October 25, p. 71.
Vallée, Jacques. 1969. *Passport to Magonia*. Henry Regnery Co.

References to Further Notes on Wraparound Eyes

Aldrich, Jan. 1997. *Project 1947: A Preliminary Report on the 1947 UFO Sighting Wave*. UFO Research Coalition.
Boylan, Richard J. & Lee K. 1994. *Close Extraterrestrial Encounters*. Wildflower.
Brookesmith, Peter. *Alien Abductions*. 1998. Barnes & Noble.
Buhler, Walter K., & Pereira, Guilherme & Pires, Ney Matiel. 1985. *UFO Abduction at Mirassol*. UFO Photo Archives.
Bullard, Thomas E. 1991. "Folkloric Dimensions of the UFO Phenomenon," *Journal of UFO Studies* No. 3, pp. 1-58.
Bullard, Thomas E. 1987. *UFO Abductions: The Measure of a Mystery*. FFUFOR.
Carpenter, John S. 1991. "Double Abduction Case: Correlation of Hypnosis Data," *Journal of UFO Studies* No. 3, pp. 91-114.
Christensen, Marge. 1983. "The South Dakota Connection" *MUFON UFO Journal* No. 181, March, pp. 3-5.
Devereux, Paul and Brookesmith, Peter. 1997. *UFOs and Ufology: The First 50 Years*. Facts on File, p. 103 and letter by Devereux, 1995. *The Skeptic* (U.K.), Vol. 9, No. 3, p. 27.
Fenwick, Lawrence J. & Tokarz, Harry & Muskat, Joseph "Canadian Rock Band Abducted," *Flying Saucer Review*, Vol. 29, No. 3, pp. 2-9.
Flammonde, Camille. 1890. *Urania*. Estes & Lauriat.
Fowler, Raymond. 1979. *The Andreasson Affair*. Prentice-Hall.
Fuller, John. 1966. *The Interrupted Journey*. Dell.
Hendry, Allan. 1979. *The UFO Handbook*. Doubleday.
Keyhoe, Donald. 1973. *Aliens from Space*. Doubleday.
Kimery, Tony L. 1976. "Carroll Wayne Watts – Contactee, Hoaxer, or Innocent Bystander," *Official UFO*, Vol. 1, No. 11, October, pp. 32-7, 64-6.
Kottmeyer, Martin. 1991a. "Eye in the Sky" *Magonia*, No. 40, pp. 3-8.
Kottmeyer, Martin. 1991b. "Eye-yi-yi" *Magonia*, No. 41, pp. 5-9.
Rogo, D. Scott, ed. 1980. *UFO Abductions*. Signet New American Library, p. 130.
Sandow, Greg. 1998/99. "The Abduction Conundrum" *The Anomalist*, No. 7, Winter. p. 51.
Schneider, Adolf & Illobrand von Ludwiger. 1993. "Brilliantly Shining Objects and Strange figures in Langenargen" in *Interdisciplinary UFO Research*, MUFON-CES Report #11, p. 142.
Stevens, Wendelle. 1982. *UFO Contact from Undersea*. Wendelle Stevens.
Stevens, Wendelle C. 1989. *UFO Contact from the Reticulum Update*, Wendelle C. Stevens.
Warren, Bill. 1982. *Keep Watching the Skies!* MacFarland.

Martin S. Kottmeyer says his interest in ufology is "mainly in the nature of a mental hobby akin to solving crossword puzzles." A prolific student of the historical, cultural and psychological facets of UFO culture, his bibliography runs to around 150 items – mostly articles for magazines, which include *The Anomalist*, *Archaeus*, *Magonia*, the MUFON *UFO Journal*, *The* REALL *News* (newsletter of the Rational Examination Association of Lincoln Land), *UFO* magazine, and *The Wild Places*. Ronald Story's *Encycopedia of Extraterrestrial Encounters* collects a number of his longer studies, and the Fundacion Anomalia published his prize-winning essay "Trance Mutations" as half of a 2001 Spanish-language book. He considers that, collectively, his articles on the Hill abduction account present conclusions about the case that are instructive about the history and nature of the alien abduction experience as a whole. He works a farm near Carlyle, Illinois.

Index

Abortions, 159-160
Adamski, George, 91
Aliens From Space (movie), 293
Andreasson, Betty, 95, 98, 102, 106, 295
Angelucci, Orfeo, 93
APRO (Aerial Phenomena Research Organization), 71, 200-1, 214, 263, 289
Atterberg, Charles W., 197-9, 234

Beeping sounds, 32, 36-7, 41, 53, 57 179, 189, 210, 214-7, 242-244, 254-257, 274-281
"Bellero Shield, The" (TV show), 20, 49, 68, 110, 122, 167, 226-8, 293-7, 300, 302. See also *Outer Limits, The*
Bifrost, 20, 49, 226-7, 294-5
Blandine, 133-5, 141
Boas, Antonio Villas, 92, 103, 105, 121, 158, 201, 264-5
Boston Traveler (newspaper), 19, 63, 71, 214, 249
Brookesmith, Peter, 9, 10, 14, 17, 24, 152-185, 246, 262, 299-300
Bullard, Eddie, 9, 10, 12, 24, 25, 26, 91-126, 159, 165, 260, 265, 266-267, 295, 297-299, 303

Cannon Mountain, 24, 29-30, 52
Car, spots on trunk of, 34, 42, 206, 216-7, 243-4, 281
Carr, Scott, 15
Child welfare, 28, 37, 217, 246
CIA, 73, 238
Civil rights, 172, 213, 217-8, 246-7
Clark, Jerome, 68, 72, 78, 80 86, 88, 297-303

Close Encounters of the Third Kind (movie), 94, 96, 102
Common Sense Approach to UFOs, A, 65-68, 141, 203
Compass, reaction of, 34, 42, 243, 281, 283, 287
Communion, 96, 102-4, 136, 204
Conspiracy theories, 155, 164, 206
Coulombe, Don and Michelle, 12
CSICOP (Committee for Scientific Investigation of Claims of the Paranormal), 10, 90, 208
CTA-102, 197

Danjo, Yari, 198-9
Da Silva, Rivalino Mafra, 92
Delsey, 14, 29-33, 40, 50, 57, 274
Dennis, Christi, 140-1
Devereux, Paul, 158-9, 164, 303

Evans, Hilary, 10, 16, 24, 26, 79, 82, 127-151, 175, 290

Fish, Marjorie, 17, 23, 82, 169, 194-8, 230-6, 263, 270, 282, 288
Fitch, C.W., 214-5
Flying Saucer Conspiracy, The, 35-7, 240, 261-2, 285,
Flying Saucer Gazette (journal), 15
Flying Saucers and the People Who See Them (BBC-tv show), 45, 61, 68
Firmage, Joe, 11, 12, 25
Freud, Sigmund, 113, 117, 129, 137, 173, 279-280
Friedman, Stanton, 84, 195, 209, 211
Fuller, John, 14, 19, 32, 24, 36, 42-3, 46-7, 51, 58, 62-68, 71,

79-81, 88, 95, 103, 106, 106, 127-9, 145, 147, 178, 181, 192, 197, 200, 201, 211-228, 239, 241, 243, 246, 251, 256, 260-1, 264-5, 274, 293, 297-8, 301, 303

Gliese Catalogue, 235
Gill, Reverend William, 91, 156
Glenda, 132-5, 141
Godfrey, Alan, 136
Grays, The, (Greys), 25, 97, 147, 158-160, 165-6, 204, 261, 265
Hall, Richard, 41, 215, 240-3, 282
Hallucination, 44-5, 50, 87, 121, 135, 137, 143, 146, 269
Hartmann, Ernest, 114-5, 124, 174
Henderson, Major Paul W., 35, 71
Hickson, Charles, and Calvin Parker, 72, 95
Hohmann, Robert E., 42-3, 65, 71, 80-1, 130, 240-1, 245-6, 255, 297
Hopkins, Budd, 12, 59, 67, 72, 78, 88.96, 103, 104, 105, 137, 159, 161, 166, 203-205
Human Papillomary Virus (HPV), 176-7, 185
Hybrids, human–alien, 100, 103-4, 121, 159-161, 266
Hypnosis, 23, 25, 36, 43-67, 78-82, 88-9, 96, 103, 105, 109-112, 114, 117-131, 135-6, 141-2, 145, 149-150, 167-8, 172, 174, 177, 181, 188, 190-2, 200-7, 214, 221-228, 233, 237, 245-6, 248, 250, 252, 255-261, 265-6, 268, 270, 275, 287, 294-5, 298, 302

IBM, 42-3, 240
Incident at Exeter, 64, 213
Indian Head Symposium, 9-17, 24-6
Interrupted Journey, The, 19, 36, 46-7, 51, 58, 64-5, 68, 71, 104,
190, 192, 197, 201, 213, 230, 233, 261, 273, 287, 293-5, 297
Invaders From Mars (movie), 288
Irwin, Pvt. Gerry, 92-3

Jackson, C.D., 42-3, 65, 71, 130, 240-1, 245, 255, 297
Jacobs, David, 67, 71-2, 86, 101, 104, 106, 203, 276, 300
Jupiter, 22, 187-9, 198, 220-2, 253-4

Keyhoe, Major Donald E., 35, 37 42, 47, 52, 68, 80, 93, 148, 156, 167-170, 213, 240-1, 245, 261-2, 274, 284-6, 289-290, 293-7
Kirk, Allan, 138-9
Klass, Philip, 22, 80, 87, 188, 192-3, 204, 220-2, 225-6, 253-4
Koch, Joachim, 198
Koehler, George, 283-5
Kottmeyer, Martin, 9,10, 49, 87, 167, 172, 226-227, 272-307
Kyborg, Hans-Juergen, 198

Larson, Sandra, 96, 202, 265, 279
Lawson, Al, 148, 287
Lewis, James, 75, 162, 174
Lindner, Robert, 138-9
Look (magazine), 64, 71, 95
Lorenzen, Coral and James, 201-2, 275, 289
Luttrell, John H., 19, 63, 65-6, 212, 214, 249

Mack, Dr. John E., 67, 72, 75, 98, 158, 166, 203, 205
Marden, Kathy, 11, 12, 26, 68, 120, 174
Martinek, Mary 11, 17
Matheson, Terry, 79, 81, 163-165
McDonald, Major James, 42-3

INDEX 309

Mill Brook Road, 13, 19, 228-9, 251-2
Miller, Janet, 33, 80
Miller, Lynn, 301
Missing time, 14, 48, 59, 67, 72, 74, 82, 93, 96, 99, 101, 130, 177, 179, 182, 200-1, 228-9, 246, 254-8, 276, 298
Missing Time, 67, 102, 203, 228, 254
Mitchell, Walter, 233-4,
Mizrach, Steve, 161
Moody, Sgt. Charles, 95, 102, 202, 265
Moon, 29, 37, 50-2, 70, 120, 169, 186-190, 219-221, 243-6, 253-5
Moseley, Jim, 11, 71, 200, 238
MUFON (Mutual UFO Network), 69, 126, 238, 307

NICAP (National Investigations Committee on Aerial Phenomena), 35, 41-44, 51, 62, 71, 93, 103-4, 201, 215, 227, 240-4, 249, 257, 267
Nightmares, 37, 41, 45, 55, 62, 96-7, 107, 111-6, 119, 128, 167, 173, 259, 261, 286-8, 304

O'Brien, Barbara, 135, 138, 140-1
Owls, 277-8, 304
Oswald, John P., 200, 264
Outer Limits, The (TV series) 20, 49, 68, 110, 167, 226-7, 293-6, 299-302. See also "Bellero Shield, The"

Peabody, Gail, 43, 251
Pease Air Force Base, 34-35, 44, 193-4, 216, 229, 254
Peebles, Custis, 162
Pegasus, 197
Persinger, Michael, 87, 107
Piegeay, Blandine, 133-5, 141
Pink residue, 32, 216, 255
Pflock, Karl, 9, 10, 14, 17-8, 24, 79, 103, 146, 148, 177,
189, 191, 238, 246, 253
Project Blue Book, 35
Psychopathology, 106-7, 152
Puddy, Maureen, 144-5

Quintero, Anibal, 143-4
Quirke, Dr. Patrick 43-4

Radioactivity, 34, 281-2
Reagan, Fred, 92
Rogo, D. Scott, 134, 141
Rodeghier, Mark, 80

Sagan, Carl, 74, 82, 197-8, 232, 299
Sandow, Greg, 10, 12, 24, 303-304
Saturn, 22, 187, 198, 220, 253-4
Saunders, David, 195, 234
Schirmer, Herbert, 95, 102, 277, 285
Schmidt, Reinhold, 93
Schnabel, Jim, 80
Schwartz, Dr. Berthold E., 79, 200
Science fiction, 70-1, 93-4, 102, 110, 140, 147, 167, 170, 226-7, 286, 295, 304
Sheaffer, Robert, 10, 12, 15, 22, 24, 76, 186-208, 209, 214-215, 219-222, 225, 235, 253-254
Simon, Dr. Benjamin, 45-68, 78, 822, 109, 117, 119-120, 127, 145-8, 173-5, 188, 190-2, 198, 200, 212-9, 224-7, 250-1, 255, 258-9, 262-7, 274-5, 294, 298,
Sleep paralysis, 93, 99-101, 110, 269
Sprinkle, Leo, 140, 158, 204
Soter, Steven, 82, 87, 197
Stacy, Dennis, 10, 12, 24, 28-69, 159-160, 239, 241, 256
Star map, 23, 68, 72, 78, 101, 194, 197-8 206, 210, 230-6, 263, 282, 288
Stephens, Dr. Duncan, 44-5
Strieber, Whitley, 94, 96, 102-

4, 136-7, 204, 301
Swett, Capitan Ben, 44

Truzzi, Marcello, 10, 12, 16, 24, 70-90
Twilight Zone, The (TV series), 52, 70

UFO Incident, The (TV movie), 65,
   71, 95, 103, 192, 201-2, 230, 265
U.S. Post Office, 63, 171-2, 217

Vallée, Jacques, 65, 68, 80, 82, 156
Virgin Mary, visions of, 131-3, 143

Walton, Travis, 72, 95, 202, 265
Warts, genital, 44, 51, 119-120,
   176-7, 185, 206, 216-7
WBZ radio, 44, 212, 248
Webb, Walter, 10, 14, 21, 41-44, 46,
   50, 51, 59, 62, 68, 71, 74, 103-105,
   130, 170, 172, 177, 191, 212-217,
   220, 227, 230, 239-271, 297

Zeti Reticuli, 12, 16, 82, 196-
   7, 231, 234-6, 263
Zetetic Scholar (journal), 10, 90

Printed in the USA
CPSIA information can be obtained
at www.ICGtesting.com
LVHW012248141123
763925LV00003B/116